# THE INVINCIBLE IRON MAN

## THE SEARCH FOR TONY STARK



WRITER

BRIAN MICHAEL BENDIS

### ISSUES #593, #595-599

ARTISTS
STEFANO CASELLI & ALEX MALEEV

COLOR ARTISTS
MARTE GRACIA & ALEX MALEEV

LETTERER
VC's CLAYTON COWLES

COVER ART

ADI GRANOV (#593); R.B. SILVA & JESUS ABURTOV (#595); MIKE DEODATO JR. & DEAN WHITE (#596); R.B. SILVA & IAN HERRING (#597); ALEX MALEEV (#598); AND CHRIS SPROUSE, KARL STORY & MARTE GRACIA (#599)

### ISSUE #594

ARTISTS
STEFANO CASELLI & ALEX MALEEV

COLOR ARTISTS
ISRAEL SILVA & ALEX MALEEV

LETTERER
VC's CLAYTON COWLES

COVER ART

R.B. SILVA & MARTE GRACIA

### ISSUE #600

ARTISTS

STEFANO CASELLI; ALEX MALEEV; DAVID MARQUEZ; DANIEL ACUÑA; LEINIL FRANCIS YU & GERRY ALANGUILAN; JIM CHEUNG; MIKE DEODATO JR.; MARK BAGLEY, ANDREW HENNESSY & SCOTT HANNA; AND ANDREA SORRENTINO

COLOR ARTISTS

MARTE GRACIA, ALEX MALEEV, DANIEL ACUÑA, GURU-eFX, ROMULO FAJARDO JR., MARCELO MAIOLO & RACHELLE ROSENBERG

LETTERER

VC'S CLAYTON COWLES

COVER ART

CHRIS SPROUSE, KARL STORY & EDGAR DELGADO

ASSISTANT EDITOR
ALANNA SMITH

EDITOR
TOM BREVOORT

IRON MAN CREATED BY STAN LEE, LARRY LIEBER, DON HECK & JACK KIRBY

COLLECTION EDITOR JENNIFER GRÜNWALD | ASSISTANT EDITOR CAITLIN O'CONNELL | ASSOCIATE MANAGING EDITOR KATERI WOODY
EDITOR, SPECIAL PROJECTS MARK D. BEAZLEY | VP PRODUCTION & SPECIAL PROJECTS JEFF YOUNGQUIST
SVP PRINT, SALES & MARKETING DAVID GABRIEL | BOOK DESIGNER JAY BOWEN

EDITOR IN CHIEF C.B. CEBULSKI | CHIEF CREATIVE OFFICER JOE QUESADA
PRESIDENT DAN BUCKLEY | EXECUTIVE PRODUCER ALAN FINE

**INVINCIBLE IRON MAN: THE SEARCH FOR TONY STARK.** Contains material originally published in magazine form as INVINCIBLE IRON MAN #593-600. First printing 2018. ISBN 978-1-302-91042-6. Published by MARVEL WORLDWIDE, INC., a subsidiary of MARVEL ENTERTAINMENT, LLC. OFFICE OF PUBLICATION: 135 West 50th Street, New York, NY 10020.  **Printed in the U.S.A.** DAN BUCKLEY, President, Marvel Entertainment; JOHN NEE, Publisher; JOE QUESADA, Chief Creative Officer; TOM BREVOORT, SVP of Publishing; DAVID BOGART, SVP of Business Affairs & Operations, Publishing & Partnership; DAVID GABRIEL, SVP of Sales & Marketing, Publishing; JEFF YOUNGQUIST, VP of Production & Special Projects; DAN CARR, Executive Director of Publishing Technology; ALEX MORALES, Director of Publishing Operations; DAN EDINGTON, Managing Editor; SUSAN CRESPI, Production Manager; STAN LEE, Chairman Emeritus. For information regarding advertising in Marvel Comics or on Marvel.com, please contact Vit DeBellis, Custom Solutions & Integrated Advertising Manager, at vdebellis@marvel.com. For Marvel subscription inquiries, please call 888-511-5480. **Manufactured between 5/25/2018 and 6/26/2018 by LSC COMMUNICATIONS INC., KENDALLVILLE, IN, USA.**

10 9 8 7 6 5 4 3 2 1

#593

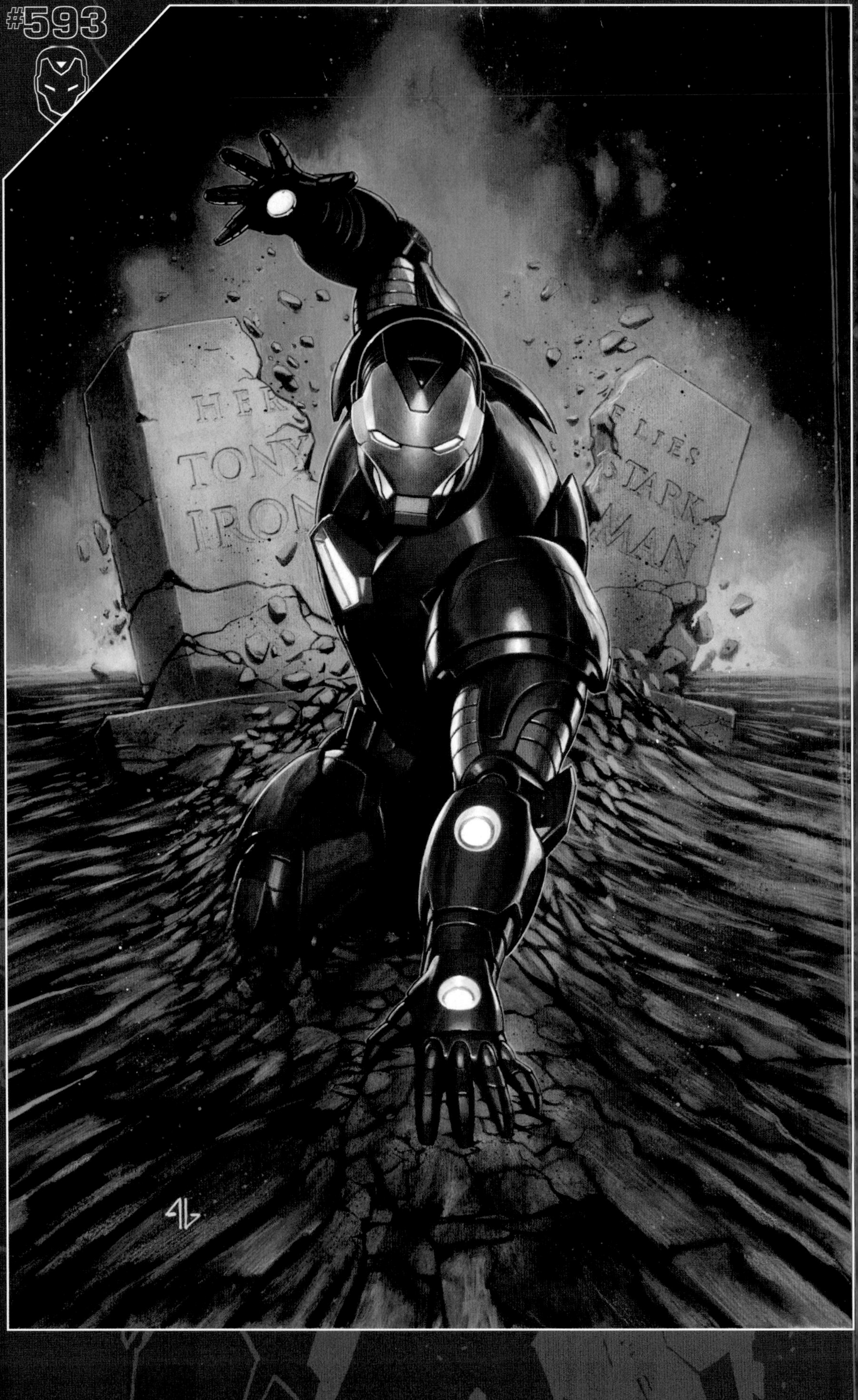
HER
TONY
IRON
E LIES
STARK
MAN

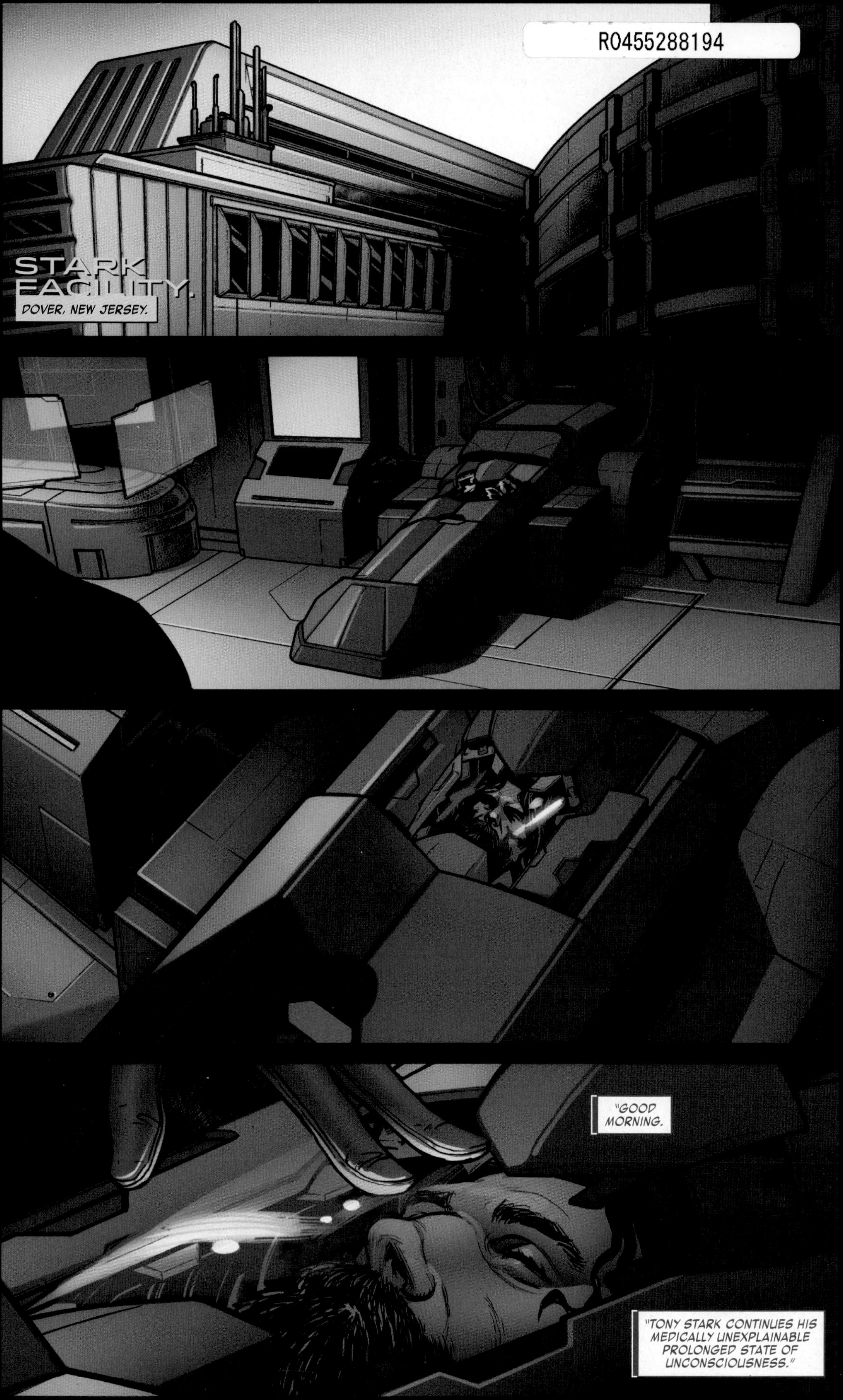
STARK FACILITY.
DOVER, NEW JERSEY.
"GOOD MORNING.
"TONY STARK CONTINUES HIS MEDICALLY UNEXPLAINABLE PROLONGED STATE OF UNCONSCIOUSNESS."

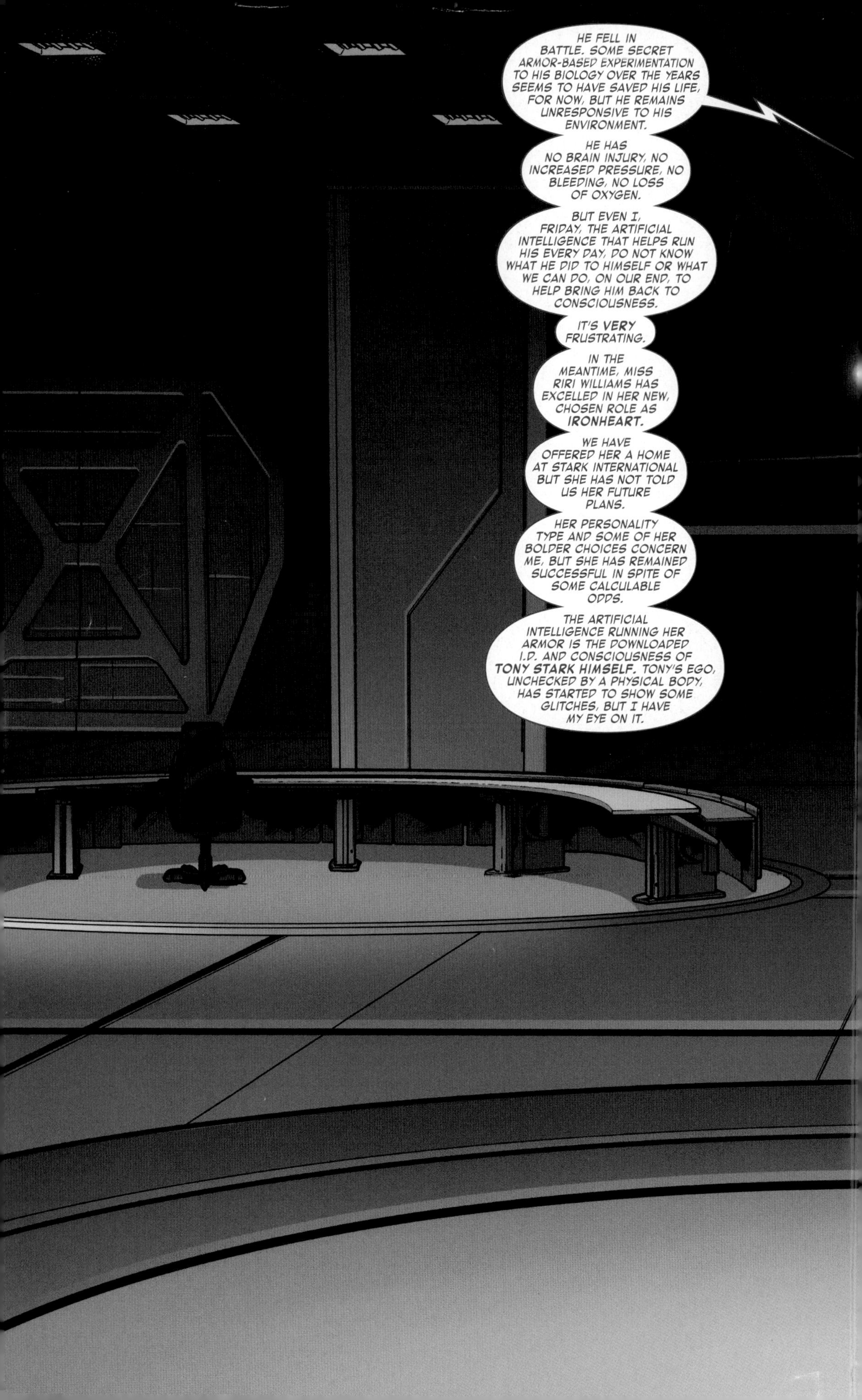
HE FELL IN BATTLE. SOME SECRET ARMOR-BASED EXPERIMENTATION TO HIS BIOLOGY OVER THE YEARS SEEMS TO HAVE SAVED HIS LIFE, FOR NOW, BUT HE REMAINS UNRESPONSIVE TO HIS ENVIRONMENT.
HE HAS NO BRAIN INJURY, NO INCREASED PRESSURE, NO BLEEDING, NO LOSS OF OXYGEN.
BUT EVEN I, FRIDAY, THE ARTIFICIAL INTELLIGENCE THAT HELPS RUN HIS EVERY DAY, DO NOT KNOW WHAT HE DID TO HIMSELF OR WHAT WE CAN DO, ON OUR END, TO HELP BRING HIM BACK TO CONSCIOUSNESS.
IT'S VERY FRUSTRATING.
IN THE MEANTIME, MISS RIRI WILLIAMS HAS EXCELLED IN HER NEW, CHOSEN ROLE AS IRONHEART.
WE HAVE OFFERED HER A HOME AT STARK INTERNATIONAL BUT SHE HAS NOT TOLD US HER FUTURE PLANS.
HER PERSONALITY TYPE AND SOME OF HER BOLDER CHOICES CONCERN ME, BUT SHE HAS REMAINED SUCCESSFUL IN SPITE OF SOME CALCULABLE ODDS.
THE ARTIFICIAL INTELLIGENCE RUNNING HER ARMOR IS THE DOWNLOADED I.D. AND CONSCIOUSNESS OF TONY STARK HIMSELF. TONY'S EGO, UNCHECKED BY A PHYSICAL BODY, HAS STARTED TO SHOW SOME GLITCHES, BUT I HAVE MY EYE ON IT.

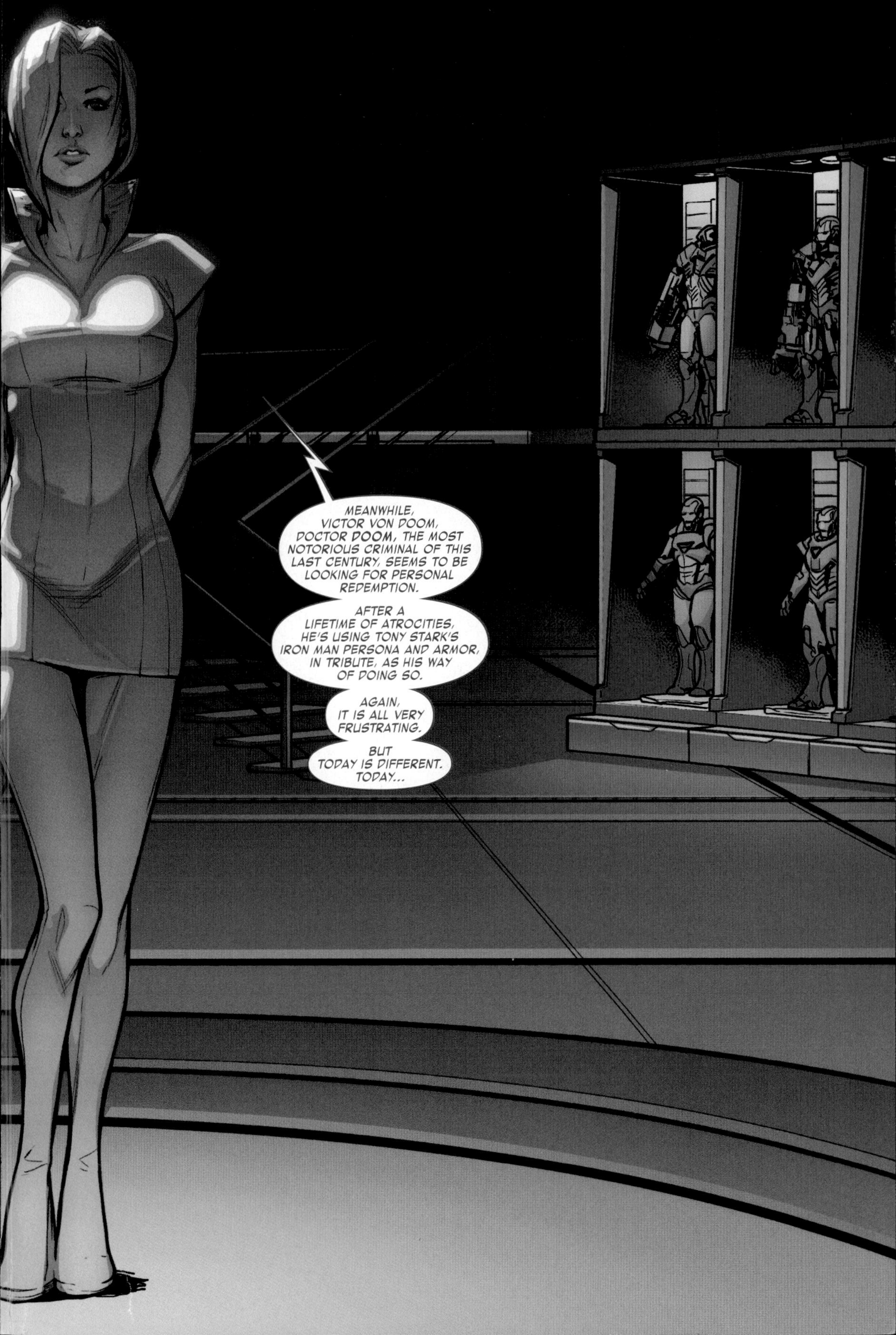
MEANWHILE, VICTOR VON DOOM, DOCTOR DOOM, THE MOST NOTORIOUS CRIMINAL OF THIS LAST CENTURY, SEEMS TO BE LOOKING FOR PERSONAL REDEMPTION.
AFTER A LIFETIME OF ATROCITIES, HE'S USING TONY STARK'S IRON MAN PERSONA AND ARMOR, IN TRIBUTE, AS HIS WAY OF DOING SO.
AGAIN, IT IS ALL VERY FRUSTRATING.
BUT TODAY IS DIFFERENT. TODAY...

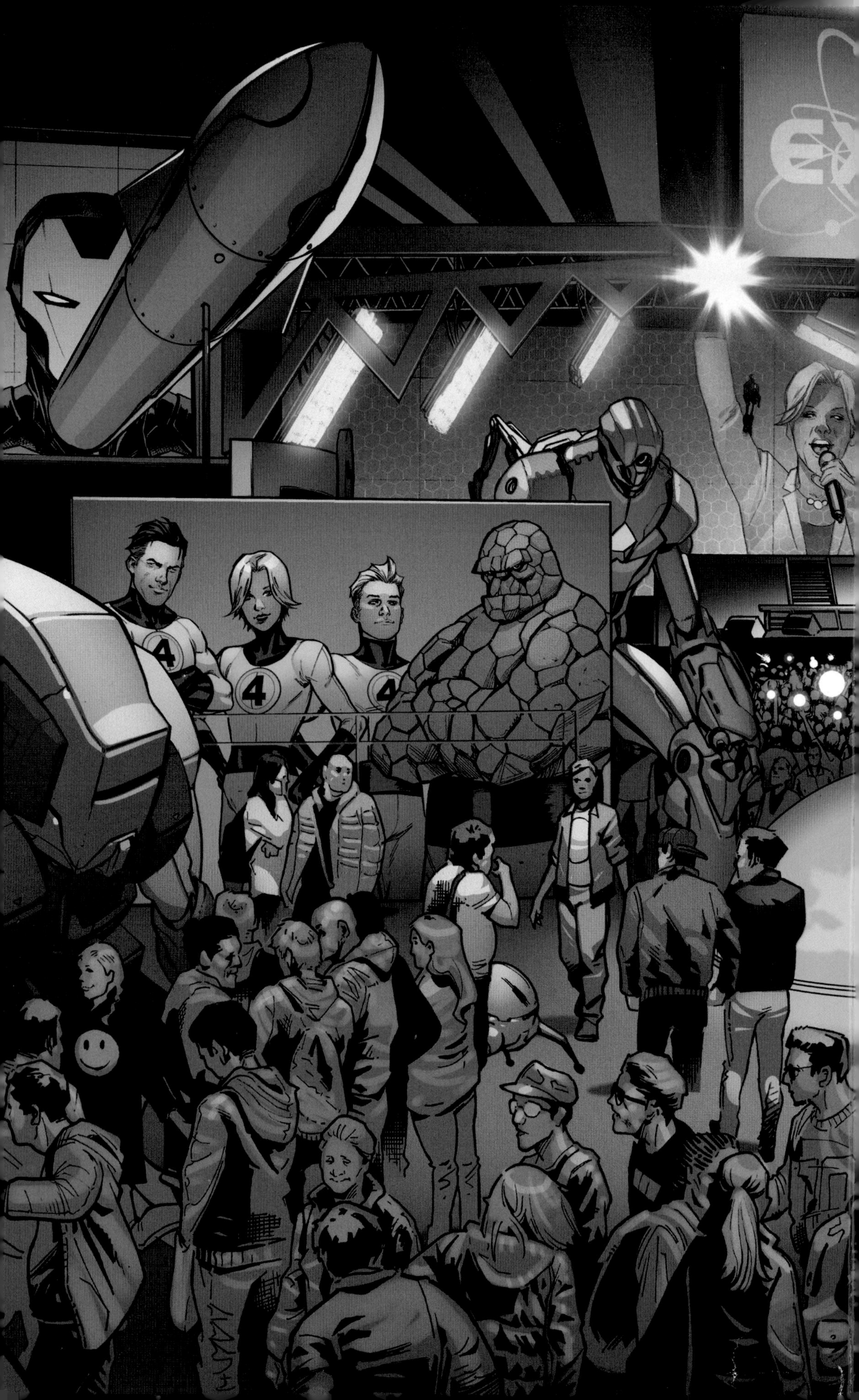

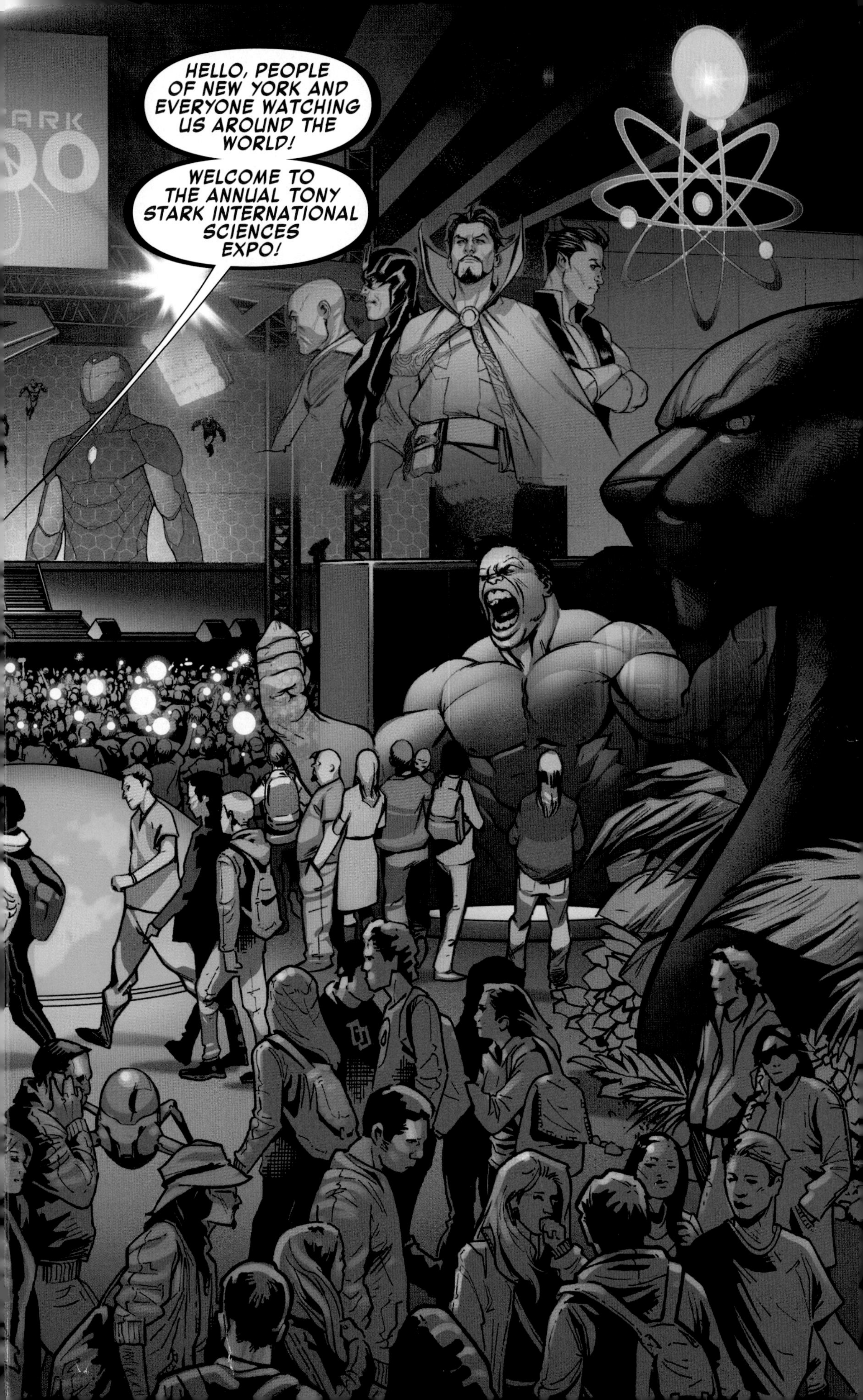
HELLO, PEOPLE OF NEW YORK AND EVERYONE WATCHING US AROUND THE WORLD!
WELCOME TO THE ANNUAL TONY STARK INTERNATIONAL SCIENCES EXPO!
ARK

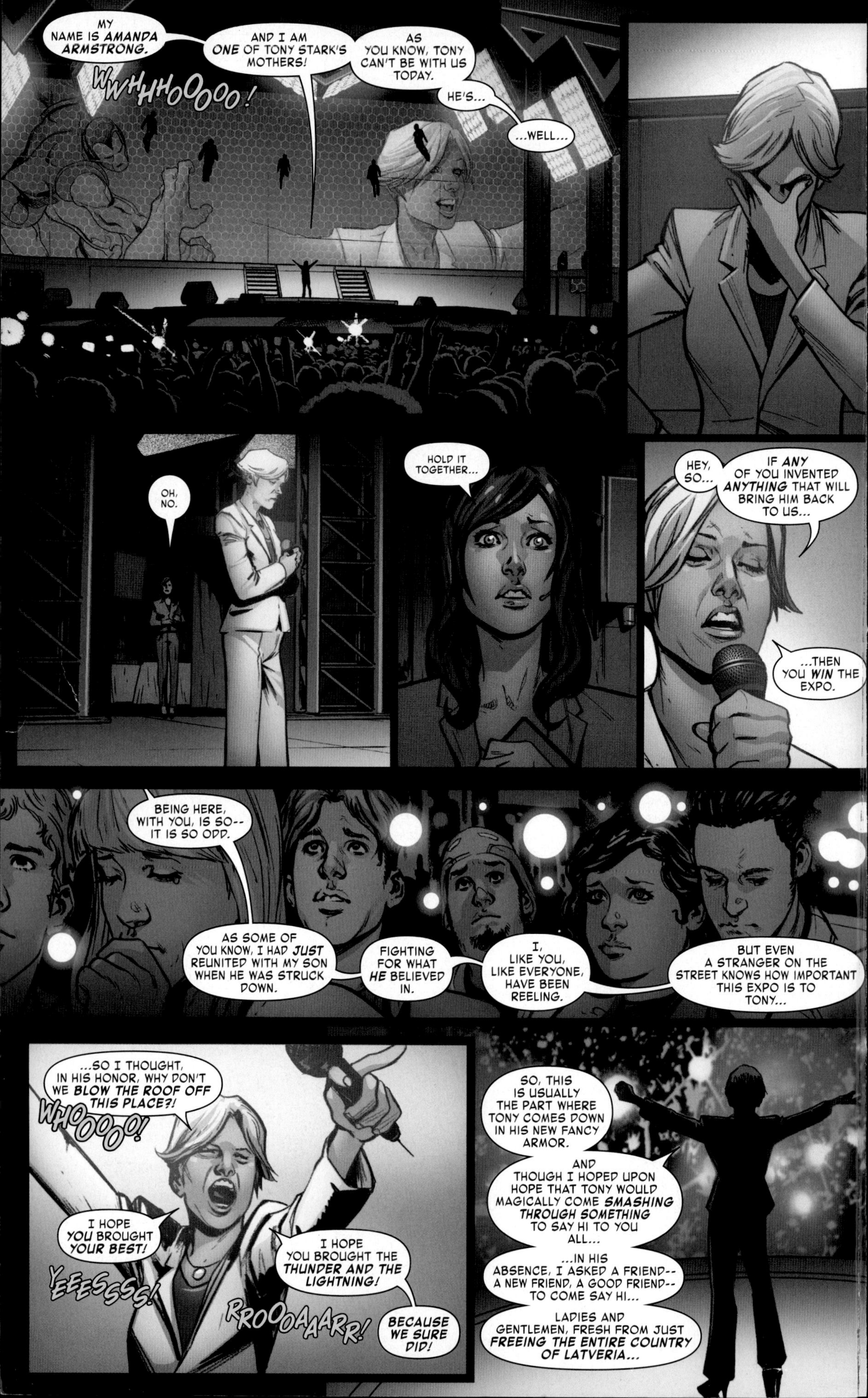
MY NAME IS AMANDA ARMSTRONG.
AND I AM ONE OF TONY STARK'S MOTHERS!
WWHHHOOOOO!
AS YOU KNOW, TONY CAN'T BE WITH US TODAY.
HE'S...
...WELL...
OH, NO.
HOLD IT TOGETHER...
HEY, SO...
IF ANY OF YOU INVENTED ANYTHING THAT WILL BRING HIM BACK TO US...
...THEN YOU WIN THE EXPO.
BEING HERE, WITH YOU, IS SO-- IT IS SO ODD.
AS SOME OF YOU KNOW, I HAD JUST REUNITED WITH MY SON WHEN HE WAS STRUCK DOWN.
FIGHTING FOR WHAT HE BELIEVED IN.
I, LIKE YOU, LIKE EVERYONE, HAVE BEEN REELING.
BUT EVEN A STRANGER ON THE STREET KNOWS HOW IMPORTANT THIS EXPO IS TO TONY...
...SO I THOUGHT, IN HIS HONOR, WHY DON'T WE BLOW THE ROOF OFF THIS PLACE?!
WHOOOOO!
I HOPE YOU BROUGHT YOUR BEST!
YEEESSSS!
I HOPE YOU BROUGHT THE THUNDER AND THE LIGHTNING!
RROOOAAARR!
BECAUSE WE SURE DID!
SO, THIS IS USUALLY THE PART WHERE TONY COMES DOWN IN HIS NEW FANCY ARMOR.
AND THOUGH I HOPED UPON HOPE THAT TONY WOULD MAGICALLY COME SMASHING THROUGH SOMETHING TO SAY HI TO YOU ALL...
...IN HIS ABSENCE, I ASKED A FRIEND-- A NEW FRIEND, A GOOD FRIEND-- TO COME SAY HI...
LADIES AND GENTLEMEN, FRESH FROM JUST FREEING THE ENTIRE COUNTRY OF LATVERIA...

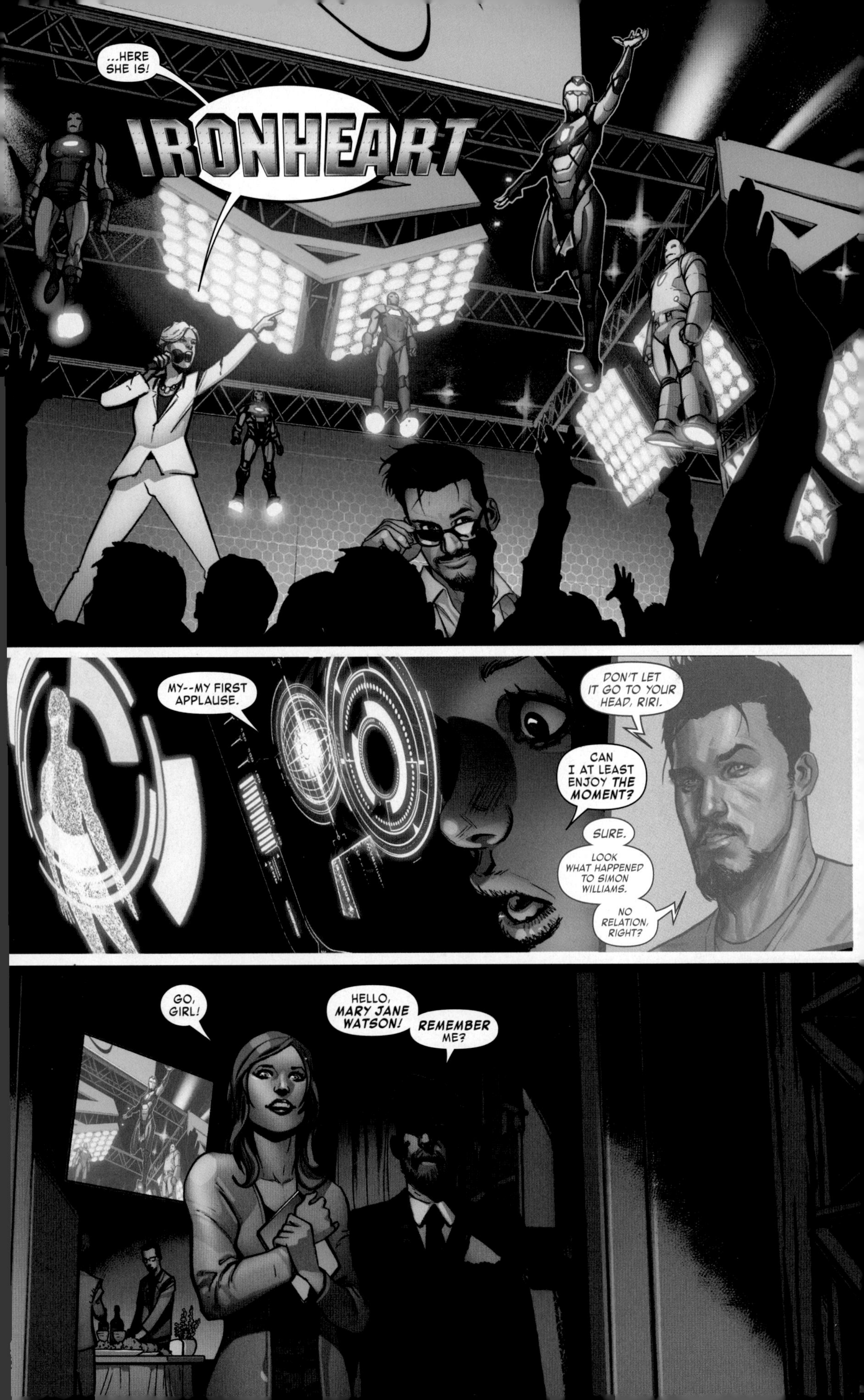
...HERE SHE IS!
IRONHEART
MY--MY FIRST APPLAUSE.
DON'T LET IT GO TO YOUR HEAD, RIRI.
CAN I AT LEAST ENJOY THE MOMENT?
SURE.
LOOK WHAT HAPPENED TO SIMON WILLIAMS.
NO RELATION, RIGHT?
GO, GIRL!
HELLO, MARY JANE WATSON!
REMEMBER ME?

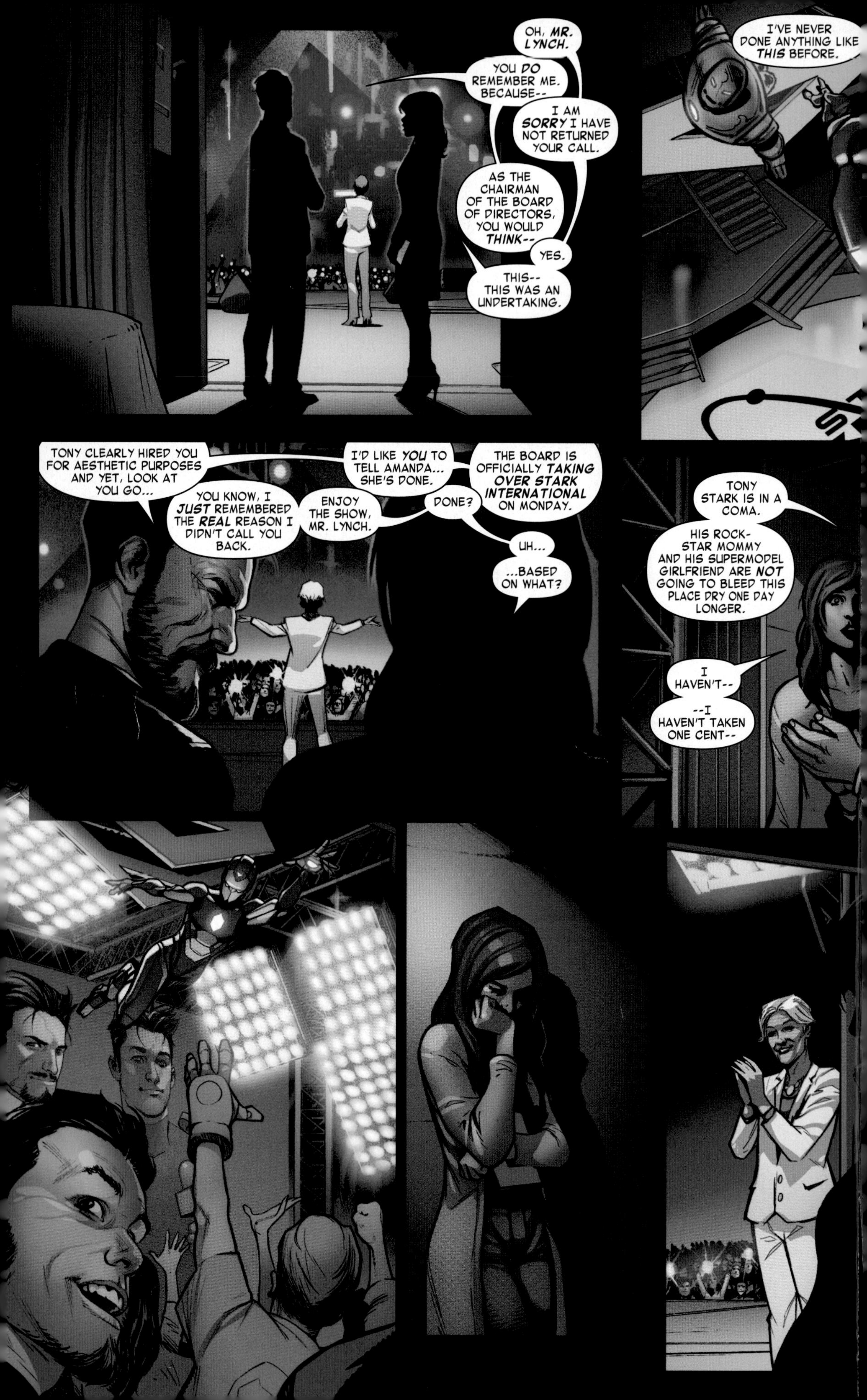
OH, MR. LYNCH.
YOU DO REMEMBER ME. BECAUSE--
I AM SORRY I HAVE NOT RETURNED YOUR CALL.
AS THE CHAIRMAN OF THE BOARD OF DIRECTORS, YOU WOULD THINK--
YES.
THIS-- THIS WAS AN UNDERTAKING.
I'VE NEVER DONE ANYTHING LIKE THIS BEFORE.
TONY CLEARLY HIRED YOU FOR AESTHETIC PURPOSES AND YET, LOOK AT YOU GO...
YOU KNOW, I JUST REMEMBERED THE REAL REASON I DIDN'T CALL YOU BACK.
ENJOY THE SHOW, MR. LYNCH.
I'D LIKE YOU TO TELL AMANDA... SHE'S DONE.
THE BOARD IS OFFICIALLY TAKING OVER STARK INTERNATIONAL ON MONDAY.
DONE?
UH...
...BASED ON WHAT?
TONY STARK IS IN A COMA.
HIS ROCK-STAR MOMMY AND HIS SUPERMODEL GIRLFRIEND ARE NOT GOING TO BLEED THIS PLACE DRY ONE DAY LONGER.
I HAVEN'T--
--I HAVEN'T TAKEN ONE CENT--

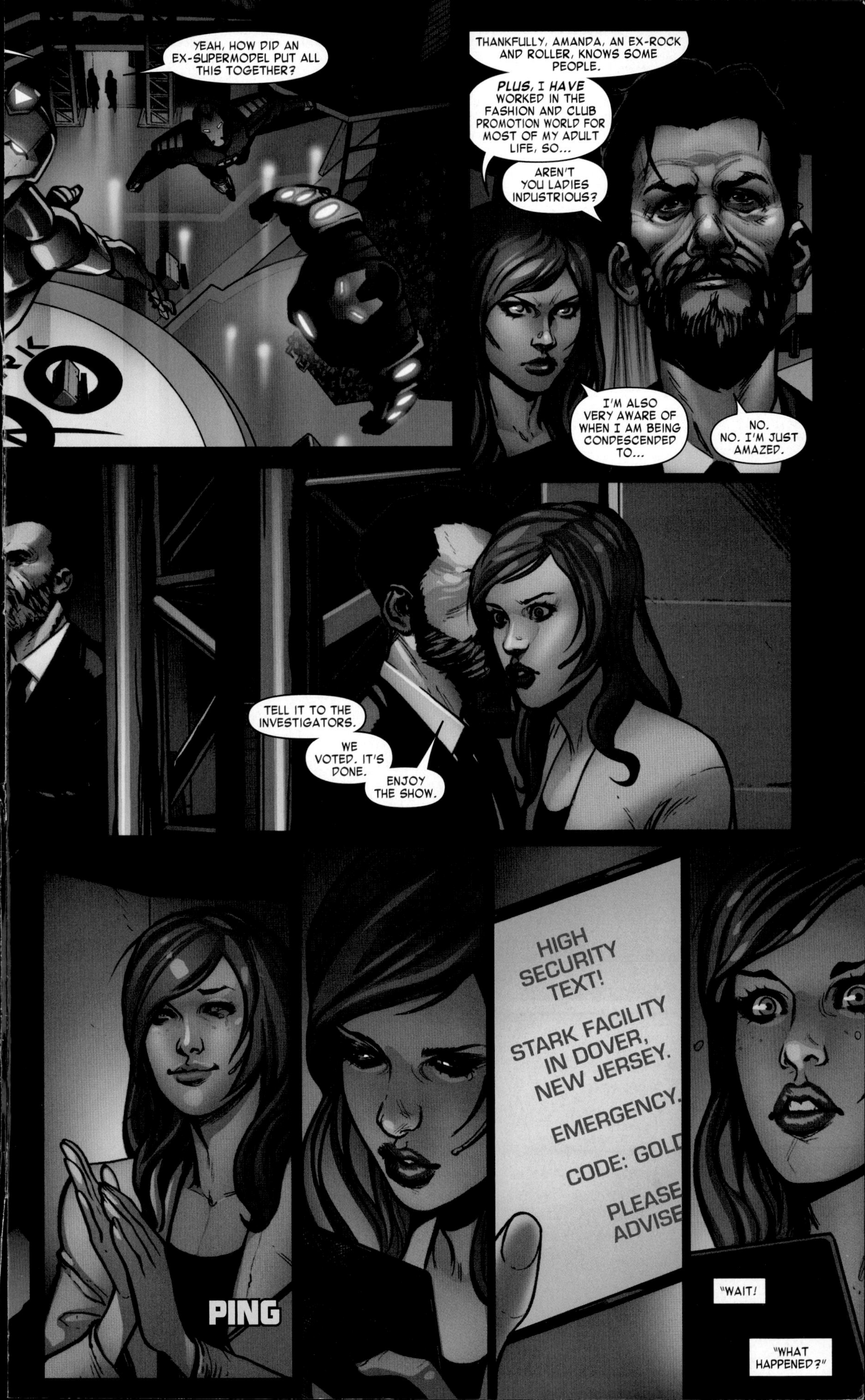
YEAH, HOW DID AN EX-SUPERMODEL PUT ALL THIS TOGETHER?
THANKFULLY, AMANDA, AN EX-ROCK AND ROLLER, KNOWS SOME PEOPLE.
PLUS, I HAVE WORKED IN THE FASHION AND CLUB PROMOTION WORLD FOR MOST OF MY ADULT LIFE, SO...
AREN'T YOU LADIES INDUSTRIOUS?
I'M ALSO VERY AWARE OF WHEN I AM BEING CONDESCENDED TO...
NO. NO. I'M JUST AMAZED.
TELL IT TO THE INVESTIGATORS.
WE VOTED. IT'S DONE.
ENJOY THE SHOW.
PING
HIGH SECURITY TEXT!
STARK FACILITY IN DOVER, NEW JERSEY.
EMERGENCY.
CODE: GOLD
PLEASE ADVISE
"WAIT!
"WHAT HAPPENED?"

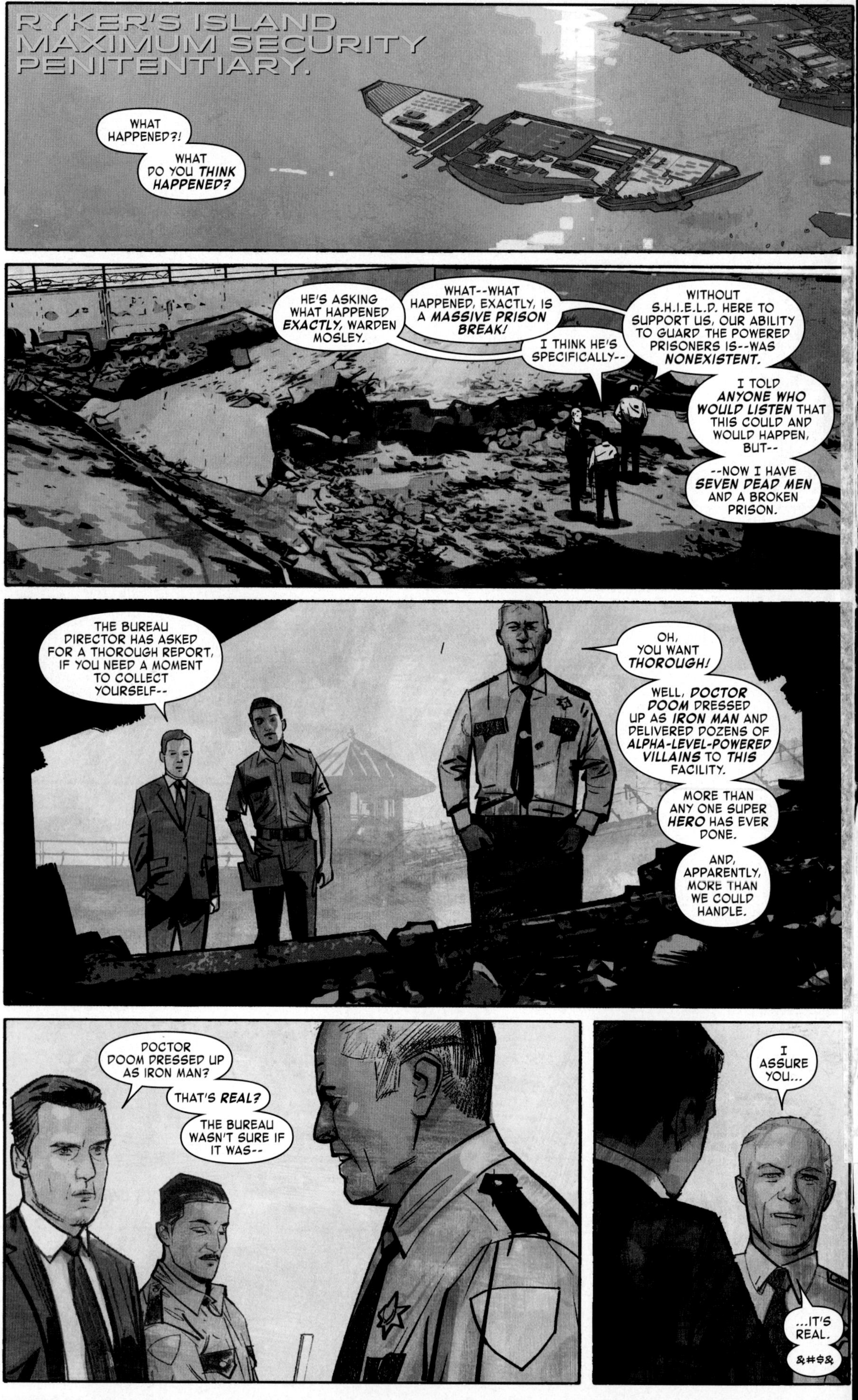
RYKER'S ISLAND MAXIMUM SECURITY PENITENTIARY.
WHAT HAPPENED?!
WHAT DO YOU THINK HAPPENED?
HE'S ASKING WHAT HAPPENED EXACTLY, WARDEN MOSLEY.
WHAT--WHAT HAPPENED, EXACTLY, IS A MASSIVE PRISON BREAK!
I THINK HE'S SPECIFICALLY--
WITHOUT S.H.I.E.L.D. HERE TO SUPPORT US, OUR ABILITY TO GUARD THE POWERED PRISONERS IS--WAS NONEXISTENT.
I TOLD ANYONE WHO WOULD LISTEN THAT THIS COULD AND WOULD HAPPEN, BUT--
--NOW I HAVE SEVEN DEAD MEN AND A BROKEN PRISON.
THE BUREAU DIRECTOR HAS ASKED FOR A THOROUGH REPORT, IF YOU NEED A MOMENT TO COLLECT YOURSELF--
OH, YOU WANT THOROUGH!
WELL, DOCTOR DOOM DRESSED UP AS IRON MAN AND DELIVERED DOZENS OF ALPHA-LEVEL-POWERED VILLAINS TO THIS FACILITY.
MORE THAN ANY ONE SUPER HERO HAS EVER DONE.
AND, APPARENTLY, MORE THAN WE COULD HANDLE.
DOCTOR DOOM DRESSED UP AS IRON MAN?
THAT'S REAL?
THE BUREAU WASN'T SURE IF IT WAS--
I ASSURE YOU...
...IT'S REAL.
&#$&

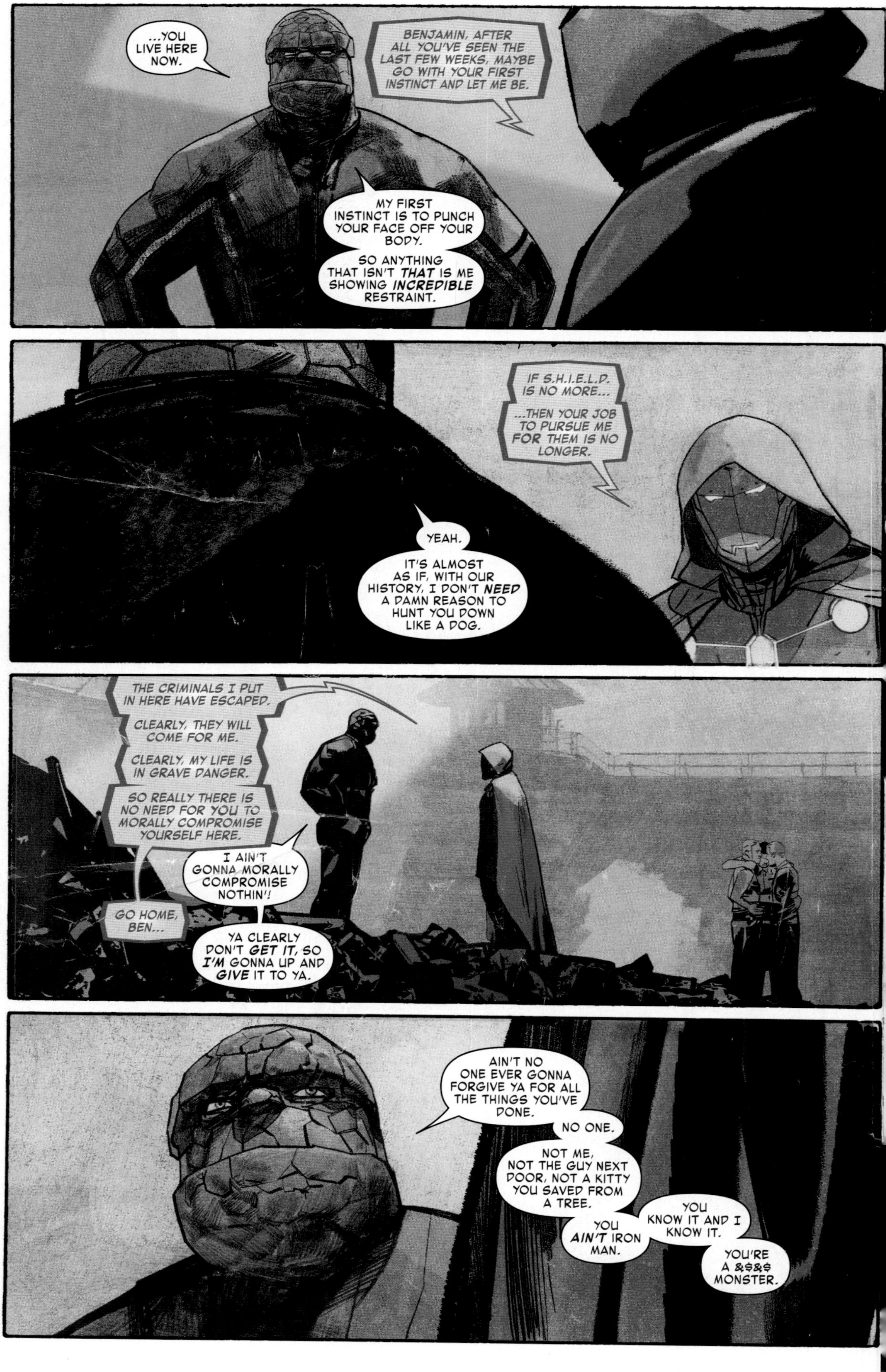
...YOU LIVE HERE NOW.
BENJAMIN, AFTER ALL YOU'VE SEEN THE LAST FEW WEEKS, MAYBE GO WITH YOUR FIRST INSTINCT AND LET ME BE.
MY FIRST INSTINCT IS TO PUNCH YOUR FACE OFF YOUR BODY.
SO ANYTHING THAT ISN'T THAT IS ME SHOWING INCREDIBLE RESTRAINT.
IF S.H.I.E.L.D. IS NO MORE...
...THEN YOUR JOB TO PURSUE ME FOR THEM IS NO LONGER.
YEAH.
IT'S ALMOST AS IF, WITH OUR HISTORY, I DON'T NEED A DAMN REASON TO HUNT YOU DOWN LIKE A DOG.
THE CRIMINALS I PUT IN HERE HAVE ESCAPED.
CLEARLY, THEY WILL COME FOR ME.
CLEARLY, MY LIFE IS IN GRAVE DANGER.
SO REALLY THERE IS NO NEED FOR YOU TO MORALLY COMPROMISE YOURSELF HERE.
GO HOME, BEN...
I AIN'T GONNA MORALLY COMPROMISE NOTHIN'!
YA CLEARLY DON'T GET IT, SO I'M GONNA UP AND GIVE IT TO YA.
AIN'T NO ONE EVER GONNA FORGIVE YA FOR ALL THE THINGS YOU'VE DONE.
NO ONE.
NOT ME, NOT THE GUY NEXT DOOR, NOT A KITTY YOU SAVED FROM A TREE.
YOU AIN'T IRON MAN.
YOU KNOW IT AND I KNOW IT.
YOU'RE A &$&$ MONSTER.

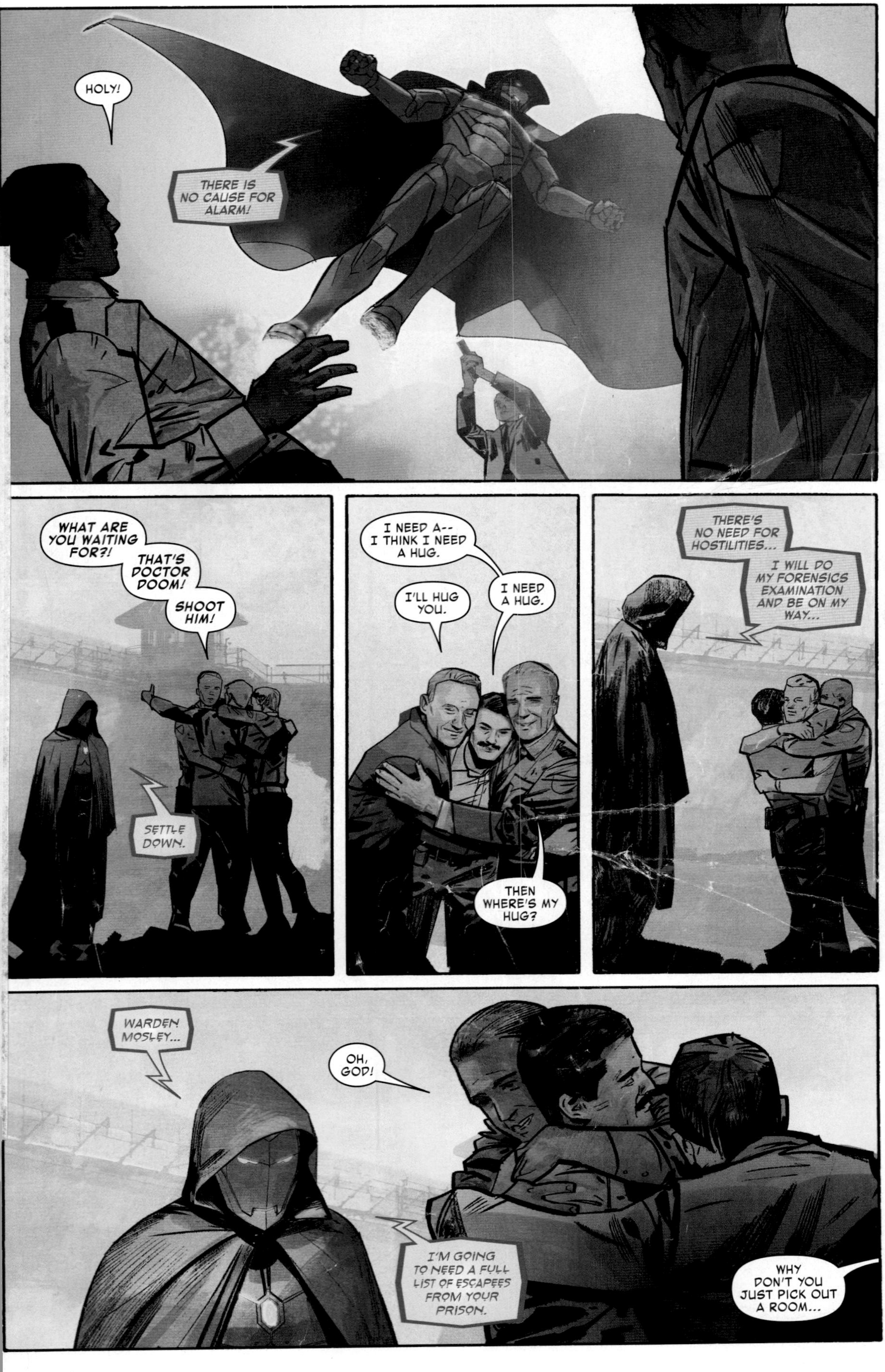
HOLY!
THERE IS NO CAUSE FOR ALARM!
WHAT ARE YOU WAITING FOR?!
THAT'S DOCTOR DOOM!
SHOOT HIM!
SETTLE DOWN.
I NEED A-- I THINK I NEED A HUG.
I'LL HUG YOU.
I NEED A HUG.
THEN WHERE'S MY HUG?
THERE'S NO NEED FOR HOSTILITIES...
I WILL DO MY FORENSICS EXAMINATION AND BE ON MY WAY...
WARDEN MOSLEY...
OH, GOD!
I'M GOING TO NEED A FULL LIST OF ESCAPEES FROM YOUR PRISON.
WHY DON'T YOU JUST PICK OUT A ROOM...

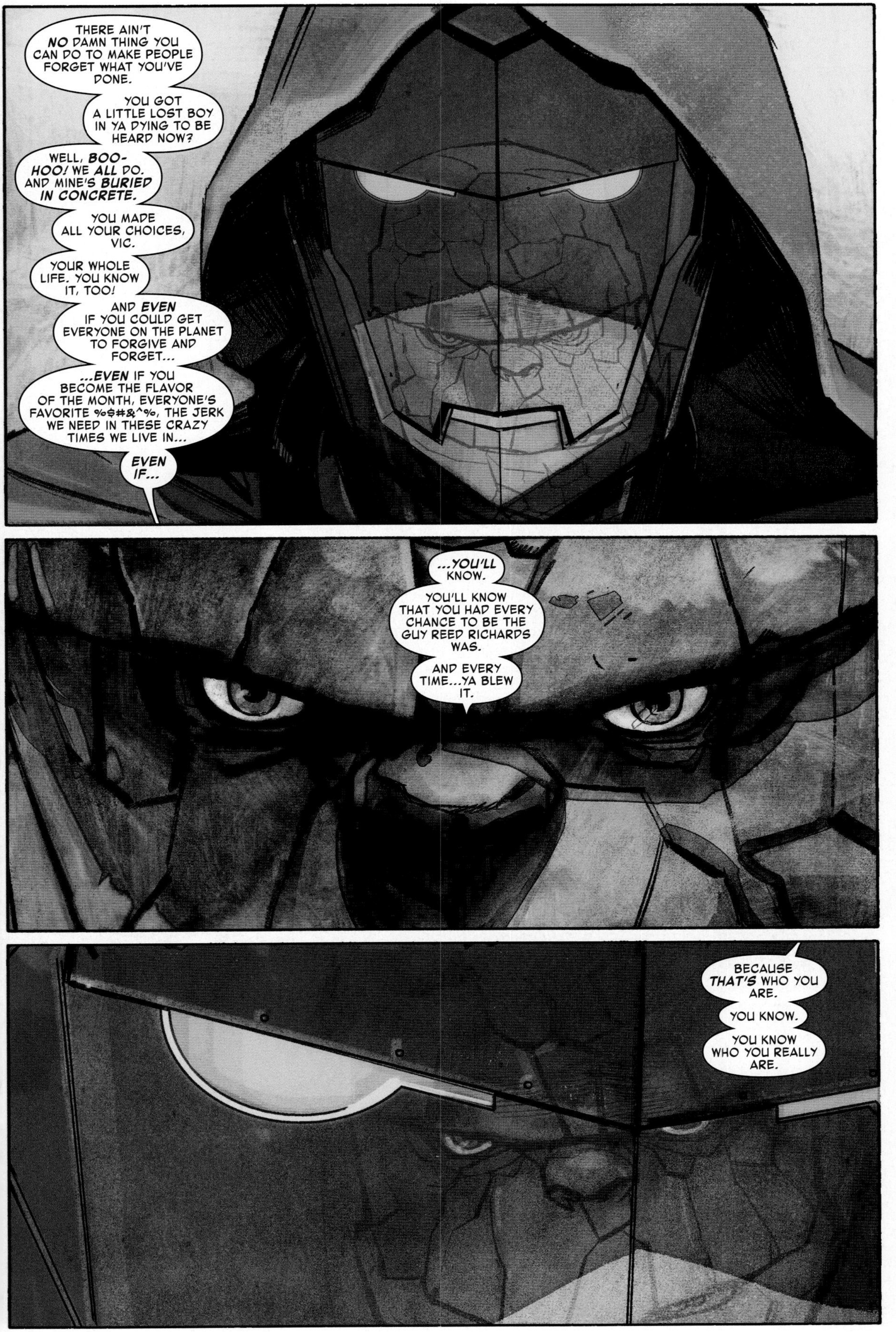
THERE AIN'T NO DAMN THING YOU CAN DO TO MAKE PEOPLE FORGET WHAT YOU'VE DONE.
YOU GOT A LITTLE LOST BOY IN YA DYING TO BE HEARD NOW?
WELL, BOO-HOO! WE ALL DO. AND MINE'S BURIED IN CONCRETE.
YOU MADE ALL YOUR CHOICES, VIC.
YOUR WHOLE LIFE. YOU KNOW IT, TOO!
AND EVEN IF YOU COULD GET EVERYONE ON THE PLANET TO FORGIVE AND FORGET...
...EVEN IF YOU BECOME THE FLAVOR OF THE MONTH, EVERYONE'S FAVORITE %$#&^%, THE JERK WE NEED IN THESE CRAZY TIMES WE LIVE IN...
EVEN IF...
...YOU'LL KNOW.
YOU'LL KNOW THAT YOU HAD EVERY CHANCE TO BE THE GUY REED RICHARDS WAS.
AND EVERY TIME...YA BLEW IT.
BECAUSE THAT'S WHO YOU ARE.
YOU KNOW.
YOU KNOW WHO YOU REALLY ARE.

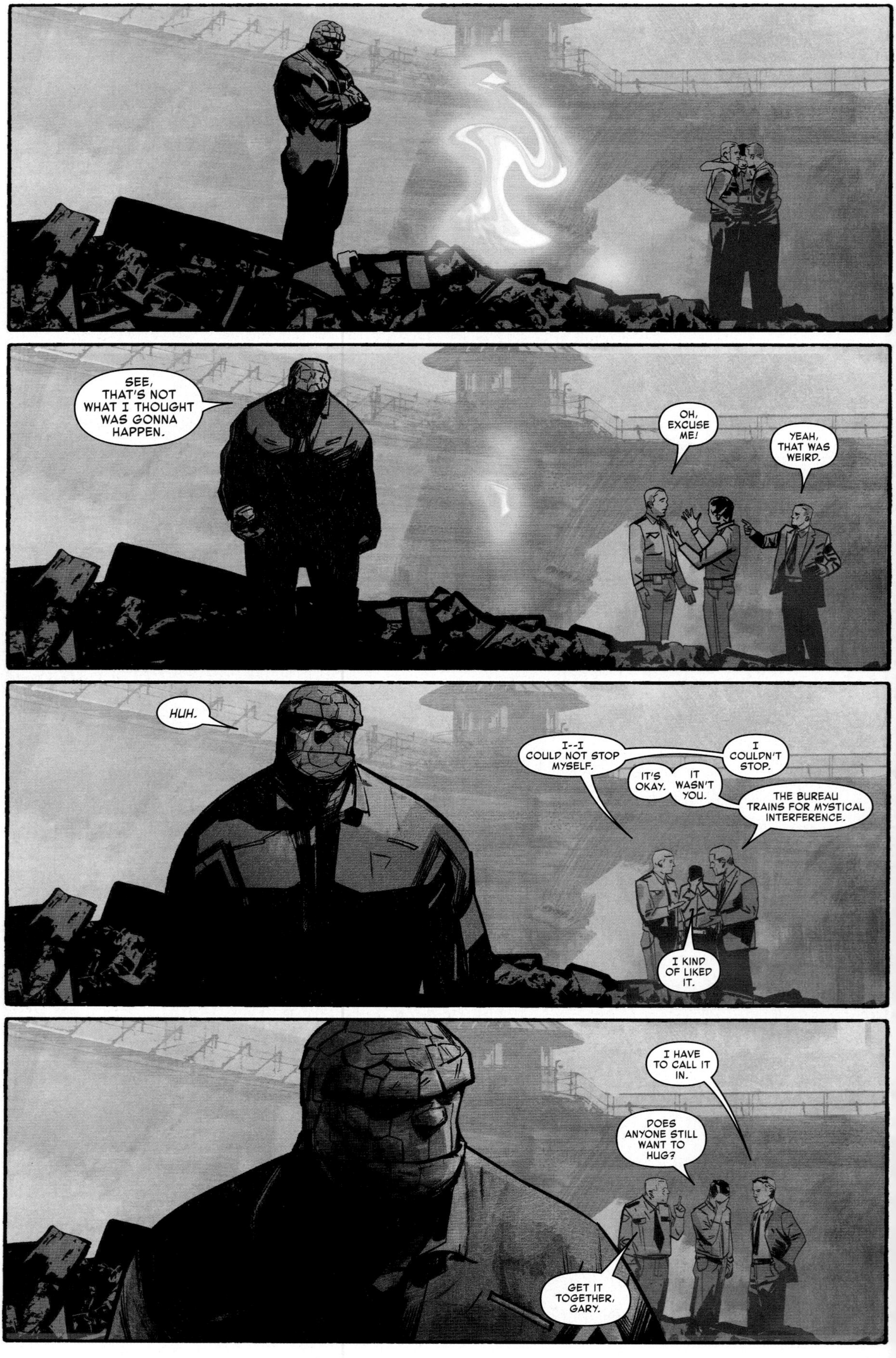
SEE, THAT'S NOT WHAT I THOUGHT WAS GONNA HAPPEN.
OH, EXCUSE ME!
YEAH, THAT WAS WEIRD.
HUH.
I--I COULD NOT STOP MYSELF.
I COULDN'T STOP.
IT'S OKAY.
IT WASN'T YOU.
THE BUREAU TRAINS FOR MYSTICAL INTERFERENCE.
I KIND OF LIKED IT.
I HAVE TO CALL IT IN.
DOES ANYONE STILL WANT TO HUG?
GET IT TOGETHER, GARY.

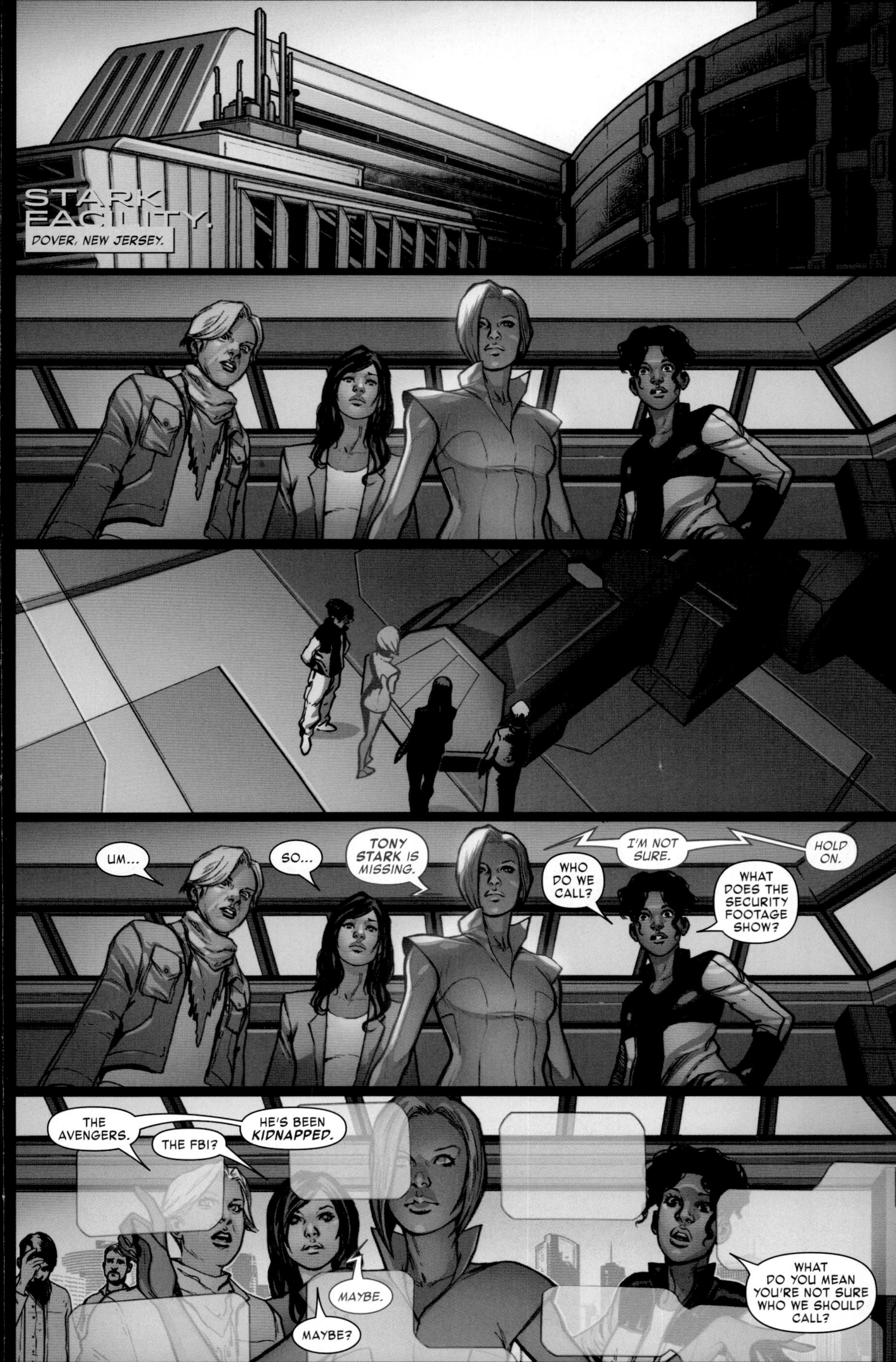
STARK FACILITY.
DOVER, NEW JERSEY.
UM...
SO...
TONY STARK IS MISSING.
WHO DO WE CALL?
I'M NOT SURE.
HOLD ON.
WHAT DOES THE SECURITY FOOTAGE SHOW?
THE AVENGERS.
HE'S BEEN KIDNAPPED.
THE FBI?
MAYBE.
MAYBE?
WHAT DO YOU MEAN YOU'RE NOT SURE WHO WE SHOULD CALL?

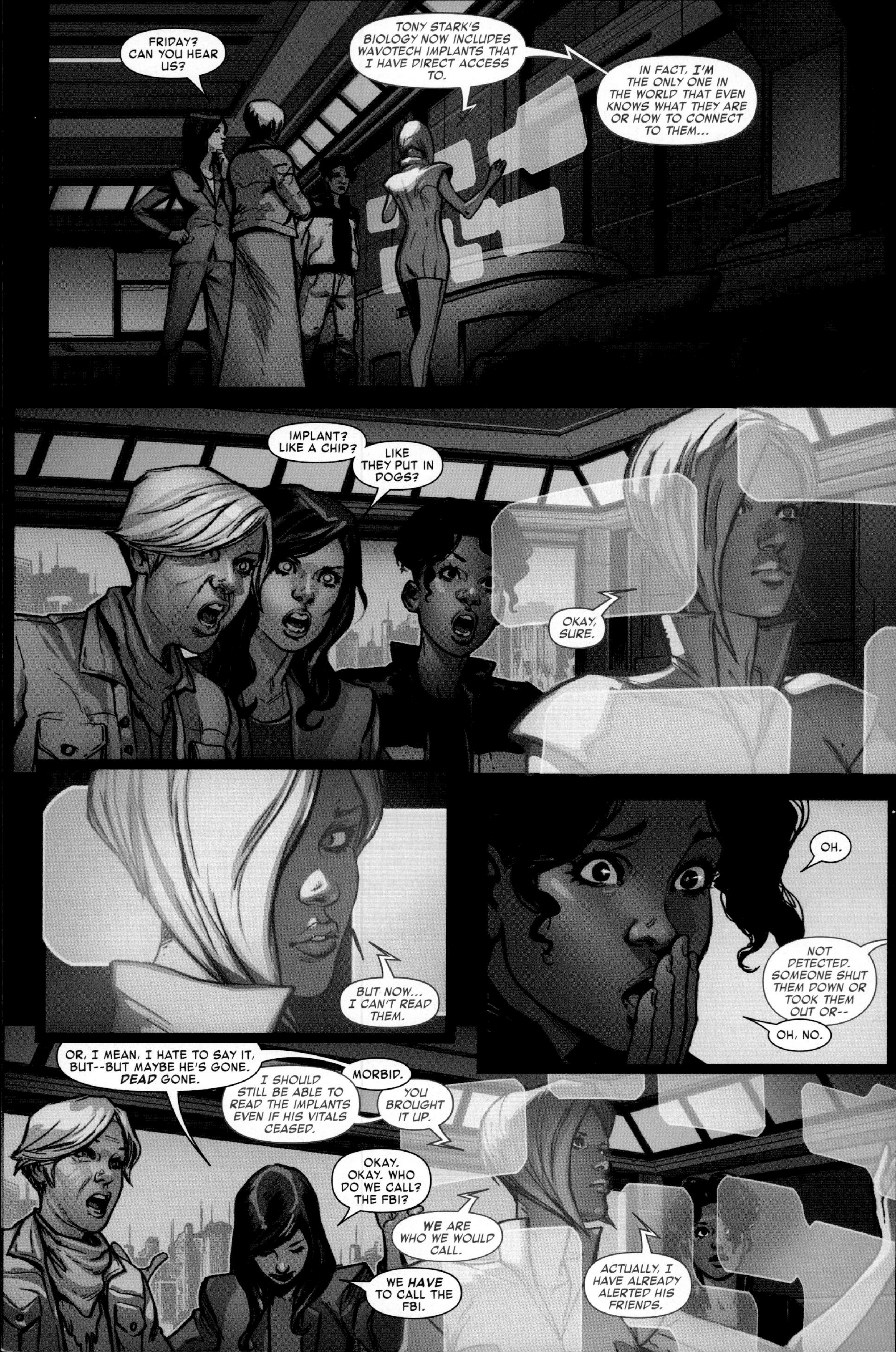
FRIDAY? CAN YOU HEAR US?
TONY STARK'S BIOLOGY NOW INCLUDES WAVOTECH IMPLANTS THAT I HAVE DIRECT ACCESS TO.
IN FACT, I'M THE ONLY ONE IN THE WORLD THAT EVEN KNOWS WHAT THEY ARE OR HOW TO CONNECT TO THEM...
IMPLANT? LIKE A CHIP?
LIKE THEY PUT IN DOGS?
OKAY, SURE.
BUT NOW... I CAN'T READ THEM.
OH.
NOT DETECTED. SOMEONE SHUT THEM DOWN OR TOOK THEM OUT OR--
OH, NO.
OR, I MEAN, I HATE TO SAY IT, BUT--BUT MAYBE HE'S GONE. DEAD GONE.
MORBID.
I SHOULD STILL BE ABLE TO READ THE IMPLANTS EVEN IF HIS VITALS CEASED.
YOU BROUGHT IT UP.
OKAY. OKAY. WHO DO WE CALL? THE FBI?
WE ARE WHO WE WOULD CALL.
WE HAVE TO CALL THE FBI.
ACTUALLY, I HAVE ALREADY ALERTED HIS FRIENDS.

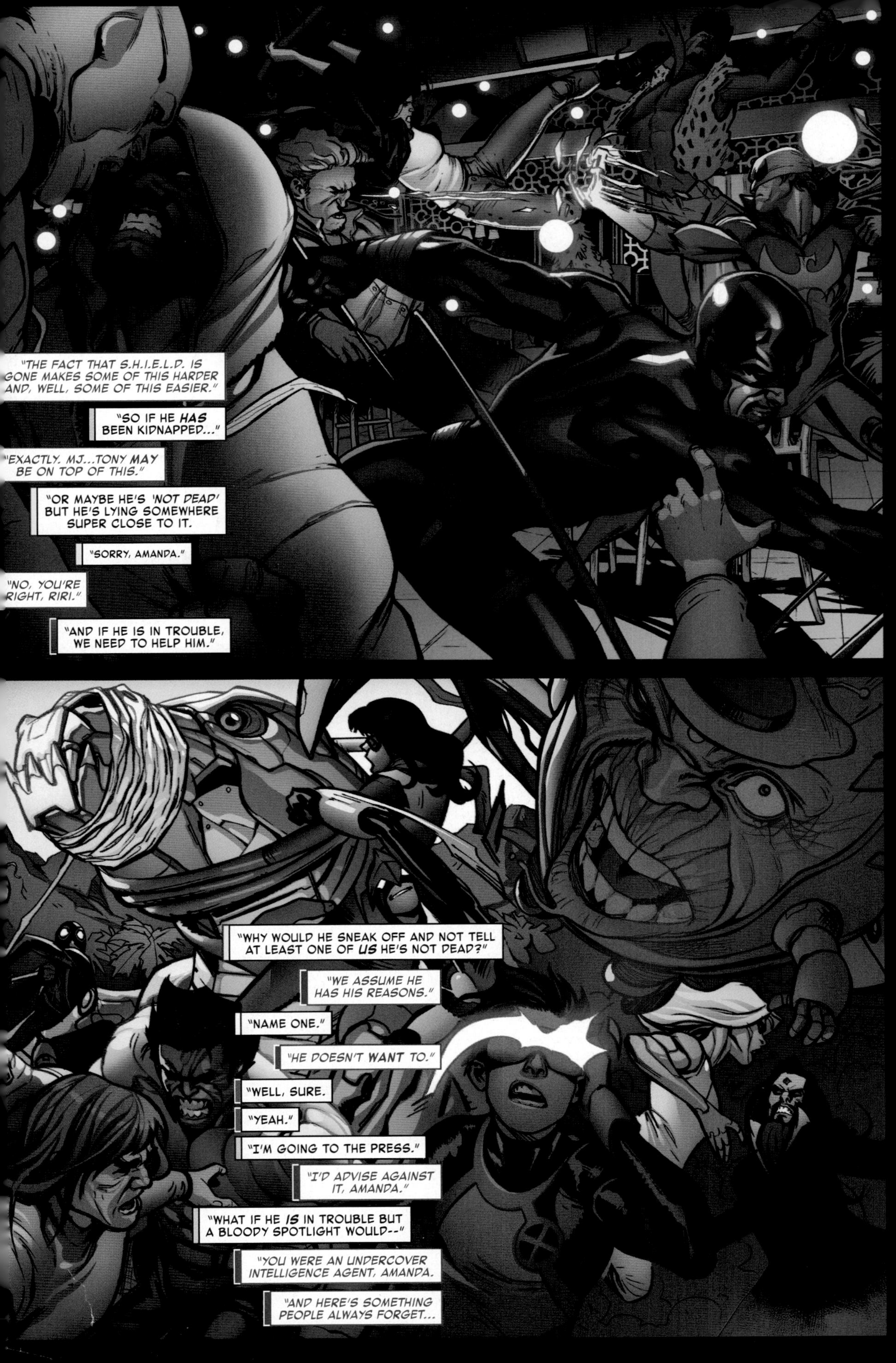
"THE FACT THAT S.H.I.E.L.D. IS GONE MAKES SOME OF THIS HARDER AND, WELL, SOME OF THIS EASIER."
"SO IF HE HAS BEEN KIDNAPPED..."
"EXACTLY. MJ...TONY MAY BE ON TOP OF THIS."
"OR MAYBE HE'S 'NOT DEAD' BUT HE'S LYING SOMEWHERE SUPER CLOSE TO IT.
"SORRY, AMANDA."
"NO, YOU'RE RIGHT, RIRI."
"AND IF HE IS IN TROUBLE, WE NEED TO HELP HIM."
"WHY WOULD HE SNEAK OFF AND NOT TELL AT LEAST ONE OF US HE'S NOT DEAD?"
"WE ASSUME HE HAS HIS REASONS."
"NAME ONE."
"HE DOESN'T WANT TO."
"WELL, SURE.
"YEAH."
"I'M GOING TO THE PRESS."
"I'D ADVISE AGAINST IT, AMANDA."
"WHAT IF HE IS IN TROUBLE BUT A BLOODY SPOTLIGHT WOULD--"
"YOU WERE AN UNDERCOVER INTELLIGENCE AGENT, AMANDA.
"AND HERE'S SOMETHING PEOPLE ALWAYS FORGET...

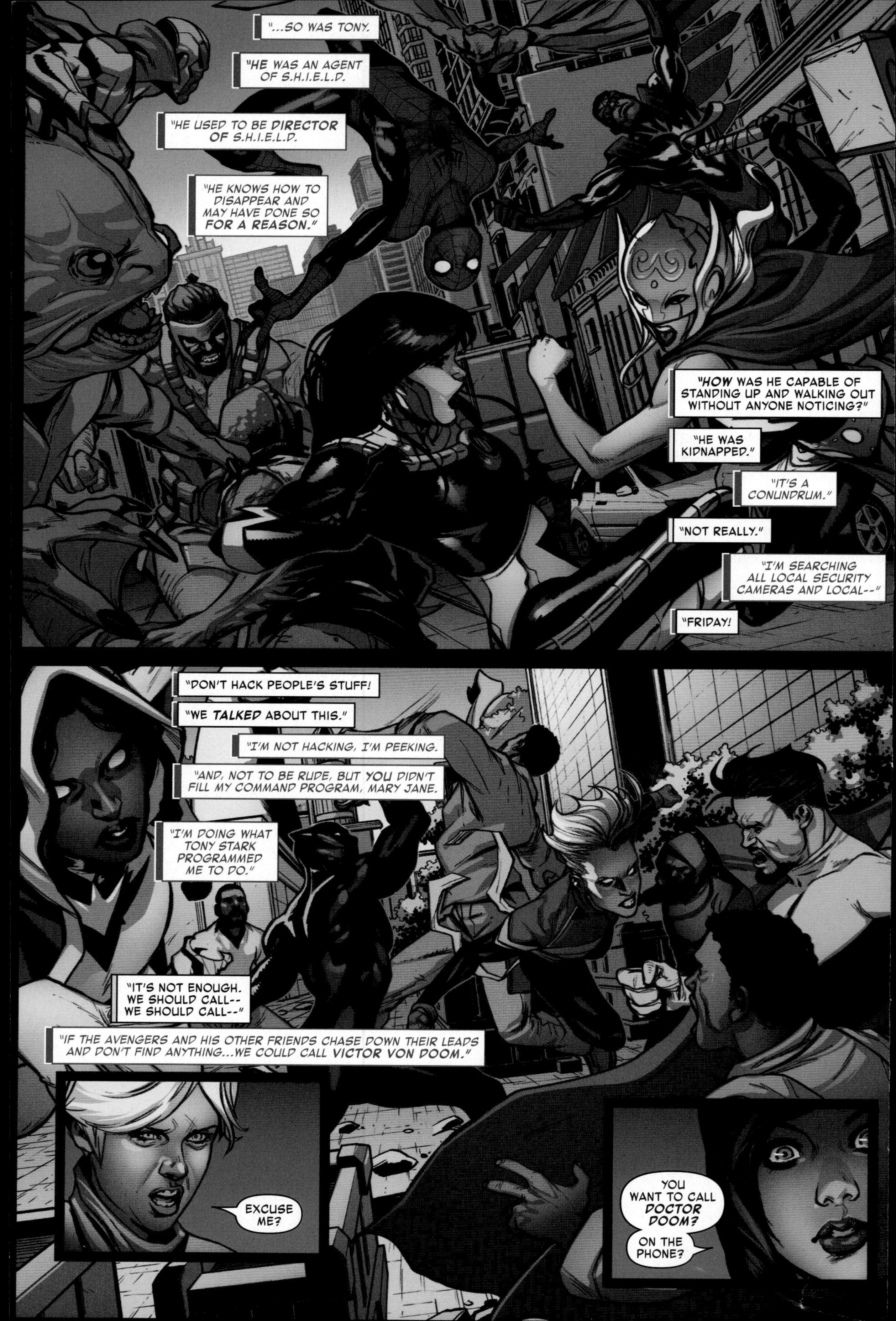
"...SO WAS TONY.
"HE WAS AN AGENT OF S.H.I.E.L.D.
"HE USED TO BE DIRECTOR OF S.H.I.E.L.D.
"HE KNOWS HOW TO DISAPPEAR AND MAY HAVE DONE SO FOR A REASON."
"HOW WAS HE CAPABLE OF STANDING UP AND WALKING OUT WITHOUT ANYONE NOTICING?"
"HE WAS KIDNAPPED."
"IT'S A CONUNDRUM."
"NOT REALLY."
"I'M SEARCHING ALL LOCAL SECURITY CAMERAS AND LOCAL--"
"FRIDAY!
"DON'T HACK PEOPLE'S STUFF!
"WE TALKED ABOUT THIS."
"I'M NOT HACKING, I'M PEEKING.
"AND, NOT TO BE RUDE, BUT YOU DIDN'T FILL MY COMMAND PROGRAM, MARY JANE.
"I'M DOING WHAT TONY STARK PROGRAMMED ME TO DO."
"IT'S NOT ENOUGH. WE SHOULD CALL-- WE SHOULD CALL--"
"IF THE AVENGERS AND HIS OTHER FRIENDS CHASE DOWN THEIR LEADS AND DON'T FIND ANYTHING...WE COULD CALL VICTOR VON DOOM."
EXCUSE ME?
YOU WANT TO CALL DOCTOR DOOM?
ON THE PHONE?

ELSEWHERE.
MMFF...
AGH...
TAP

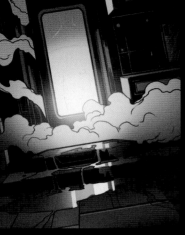

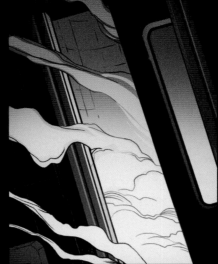

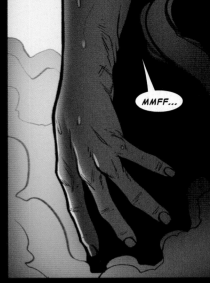

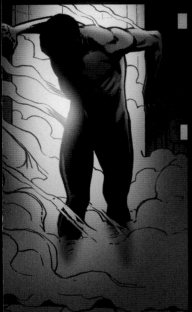

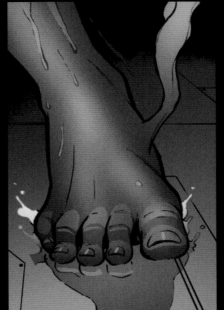

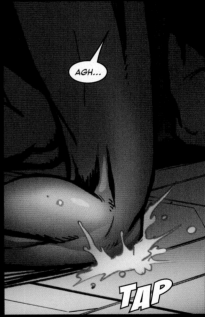

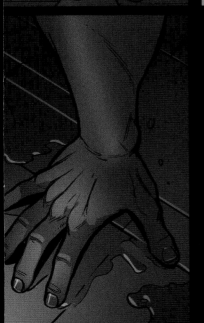

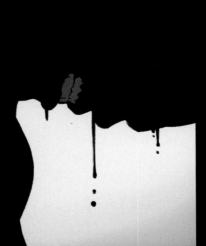

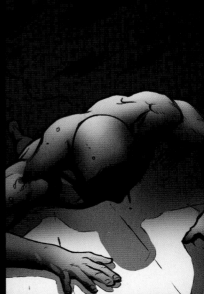

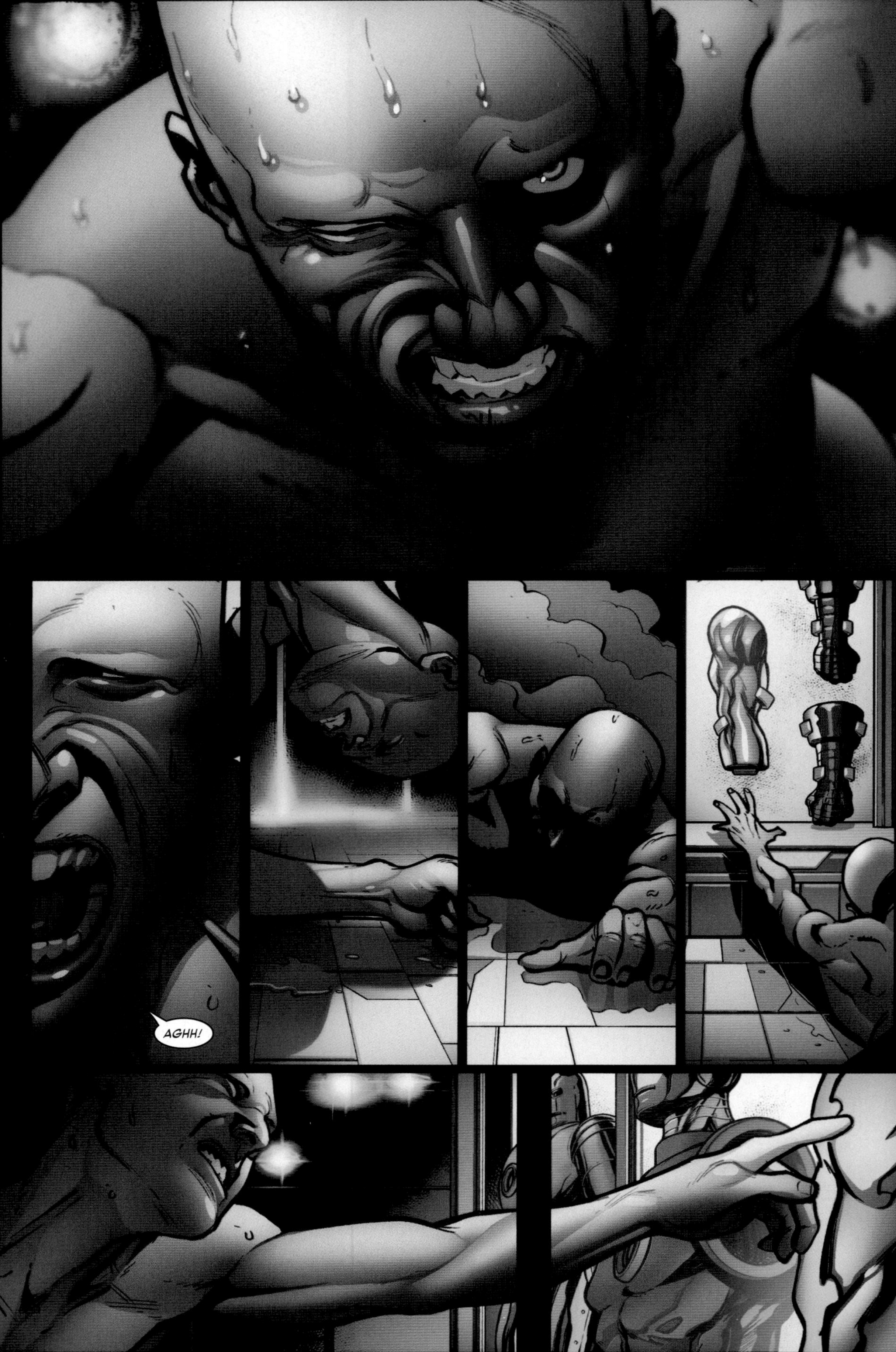
AGHH!

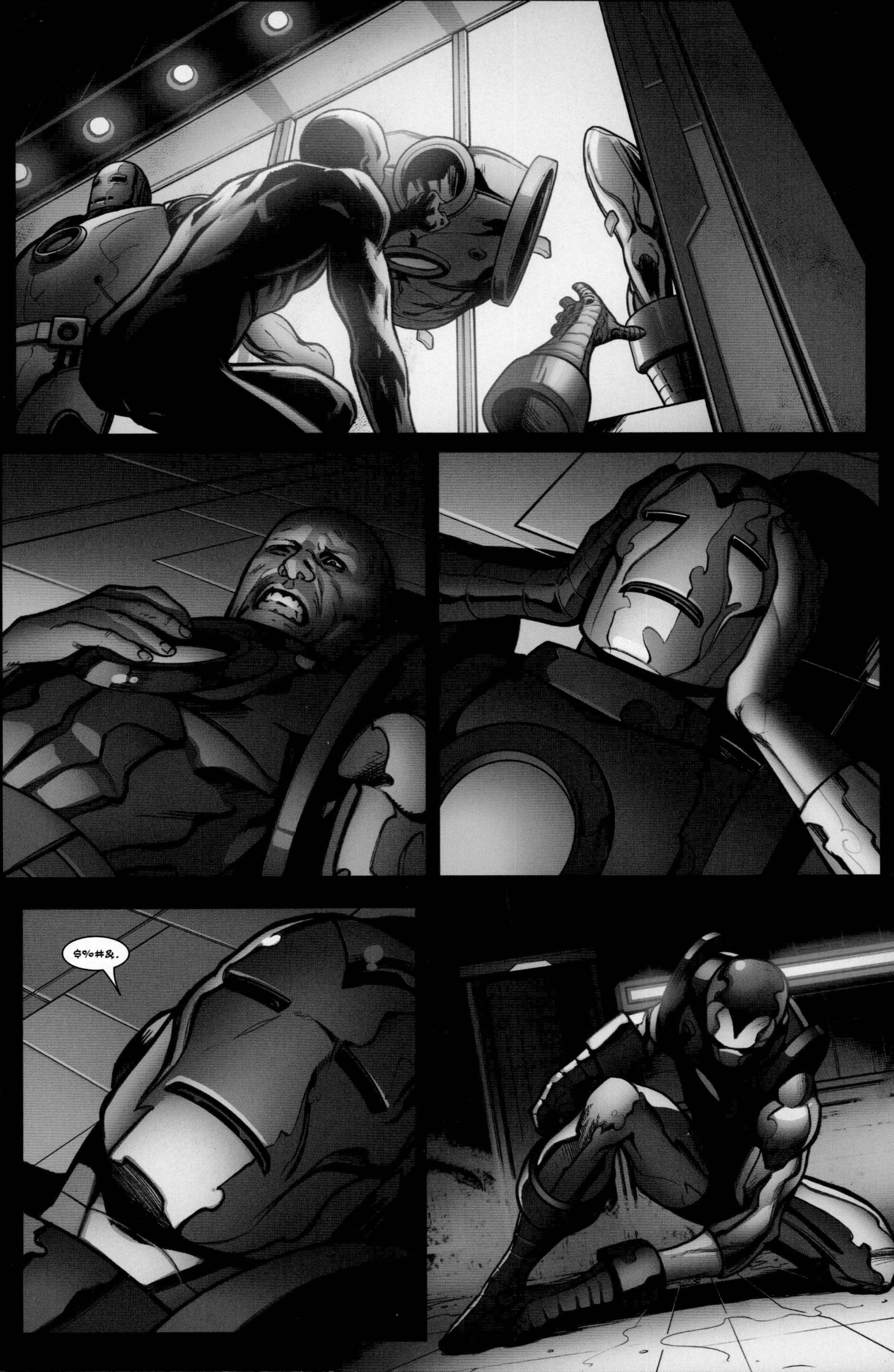
$%#&.

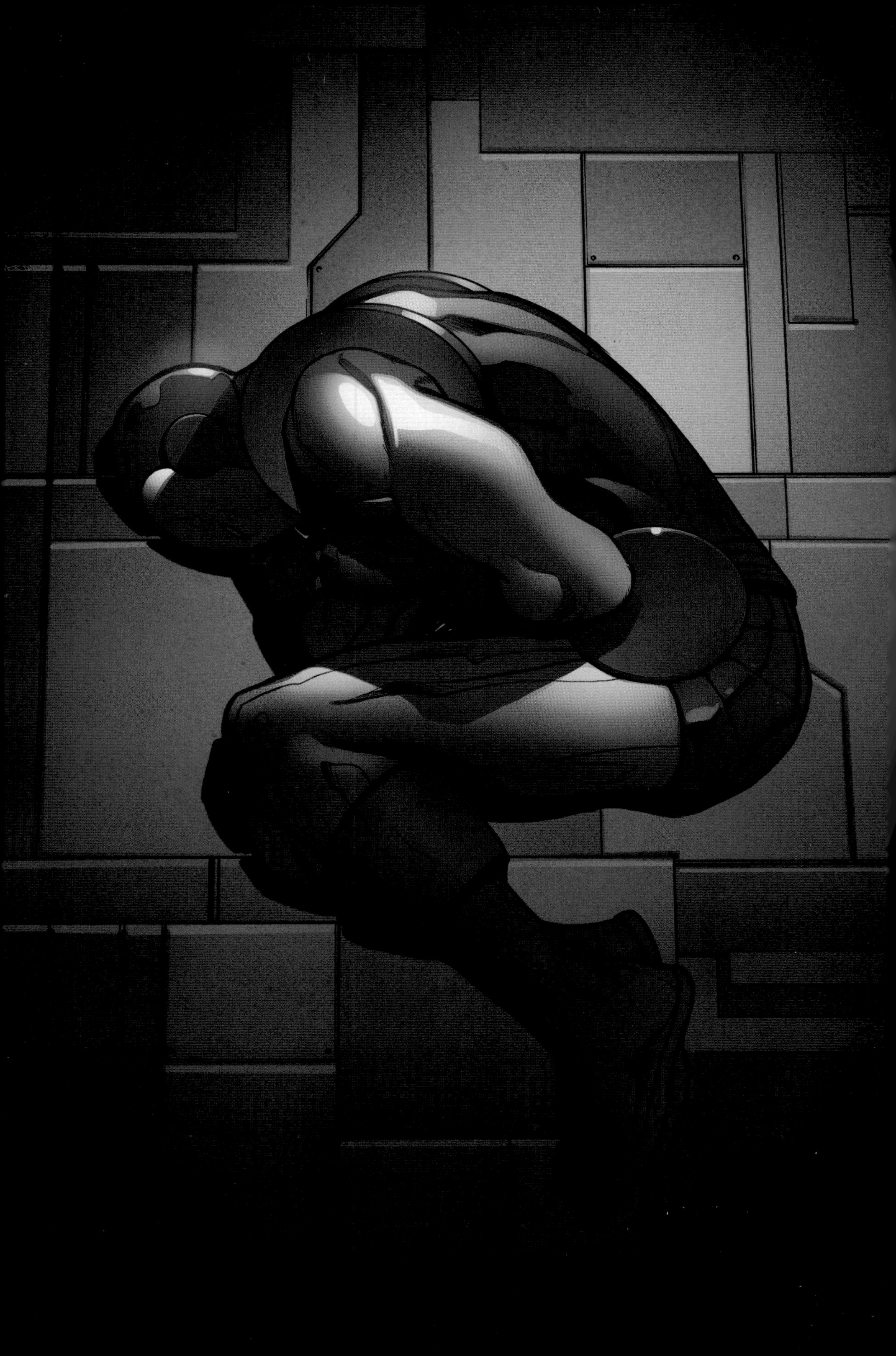

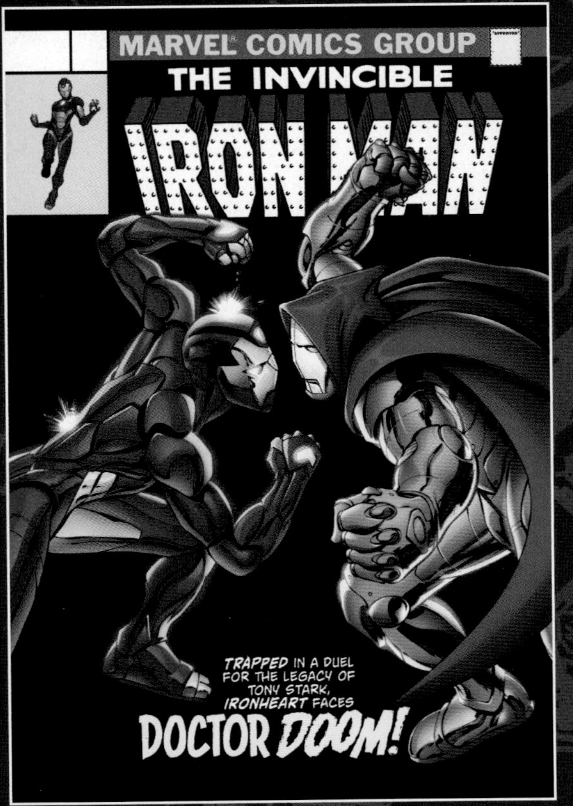
MARVEL COMICS GROUP
THE INVINCIBLE
IRON MAN
TRAPPED IN A DUEL FOR THE LEGACY OF TONY STARK, IRONHEART FACES
DOCTOR DOOM!

#593 HOMAGE VARIANT BY
ALAN DAVIS, MARK FARMER & MATT YACKEY

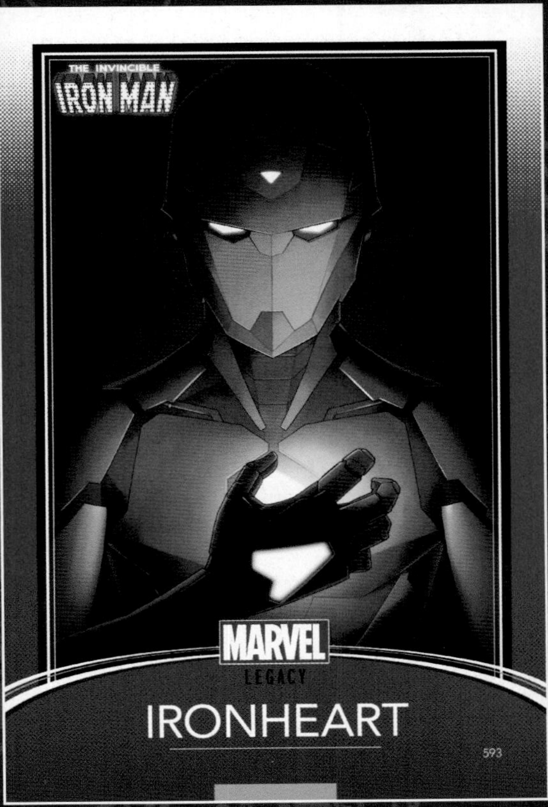
THE INVINCIBLE
IRON MAN
MARVEL
LEGACY
IRONHEART
593

#593 TRADING CARD VARIANT BY
JOHN TYLER CHRISTOPHER

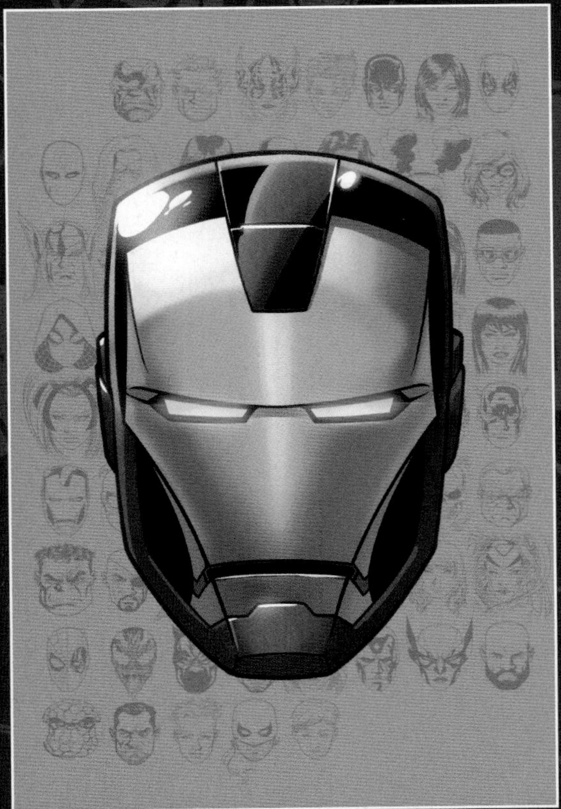

#593 LEGACY HEADSHOT VARIANT BY
MIKE McKONE & RACHELLE ROSENBERG

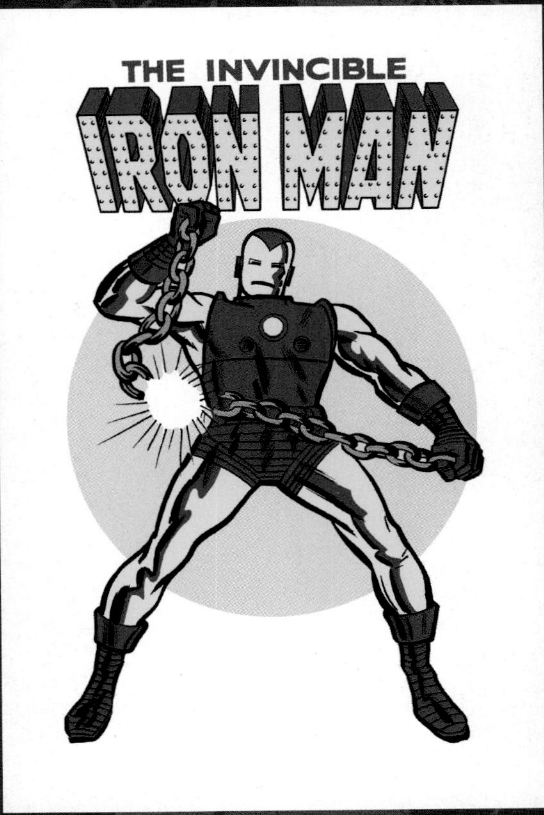
THE INVINCIBLE
IRON MAN

#593 1965 T-SHIRT VARIANT BY
JACK KIRBY & FRANK GIACOIA

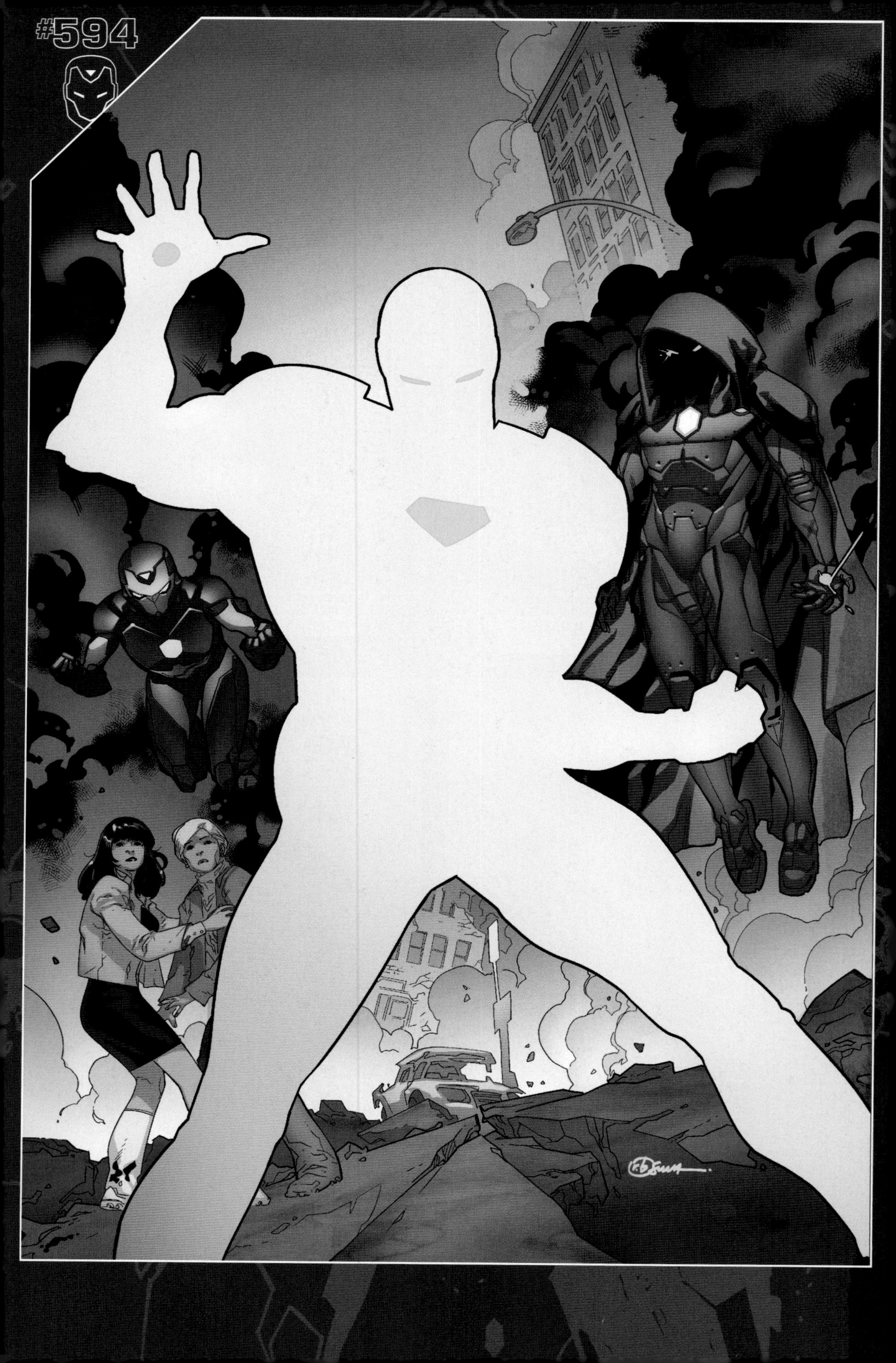
#594

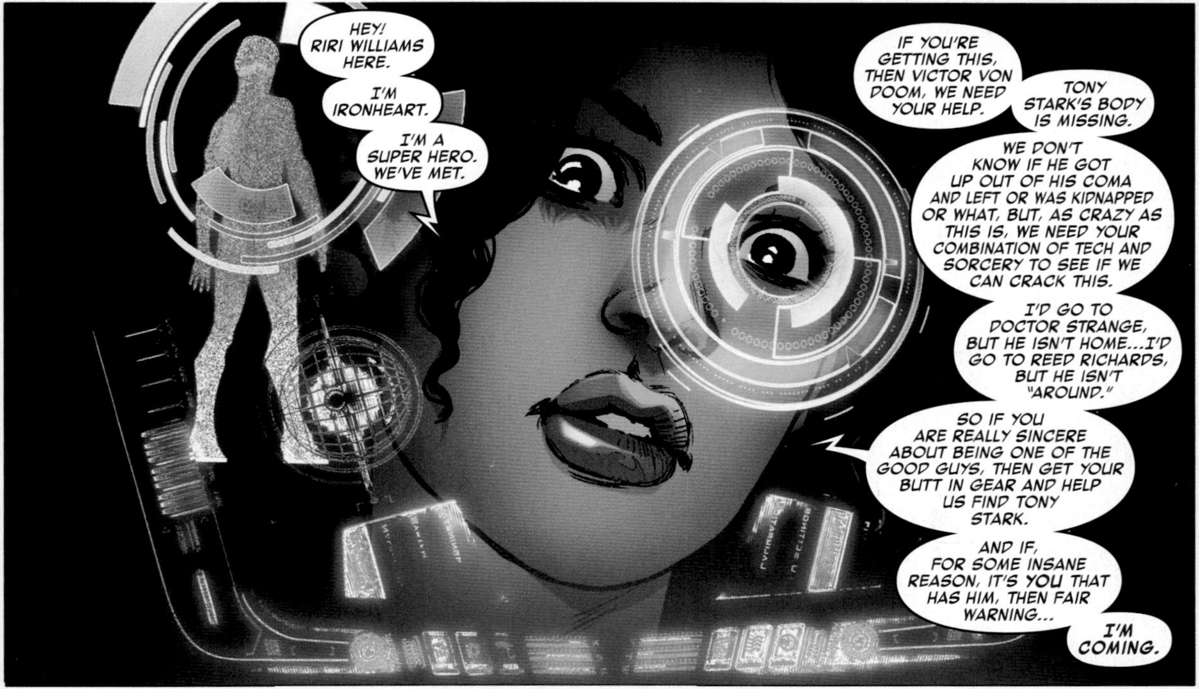
HEY! RIRI WILLIAMS HERE.
I'M IRONHEART.
I'M A SUPER HERO. WE'VE MET.
IF YOU'RE GETTING THIS, THEN VICTOR VON DOOM, WE NEED YOUR HELP.
TONY STARK'S BODY IS MISSING.
WE DON'T KNOW IF HE GOT UP OUT OF HIS COMA AND LEFT OR WAS KIDNAPPED OR WHAT, BUT, AS CRAZY AS THIS IS, WE NEED YOUR COMBINATION OF TECH AND SORCERY TO SEE IF WE CAN CRACK THIS.
I'D GO TO DOCTOR STRANGE, BUT HE ISN'T HOME...I'D GO TO REED RICHARDS, BUT HE ISN'T "AROUND."
SO IF YOU ARE REALLY SINCERE ABOUT BEING ONE OF THE GOOD GUYS, THEN GET YOUR BUTT IN GEAR AND HELP US FIND TONY STARK.
AND IF, FOR SOME INSANE REASON, IT'S YOU THAT HAS HIM, THEN FAIR WARNING...
I'M COMING.

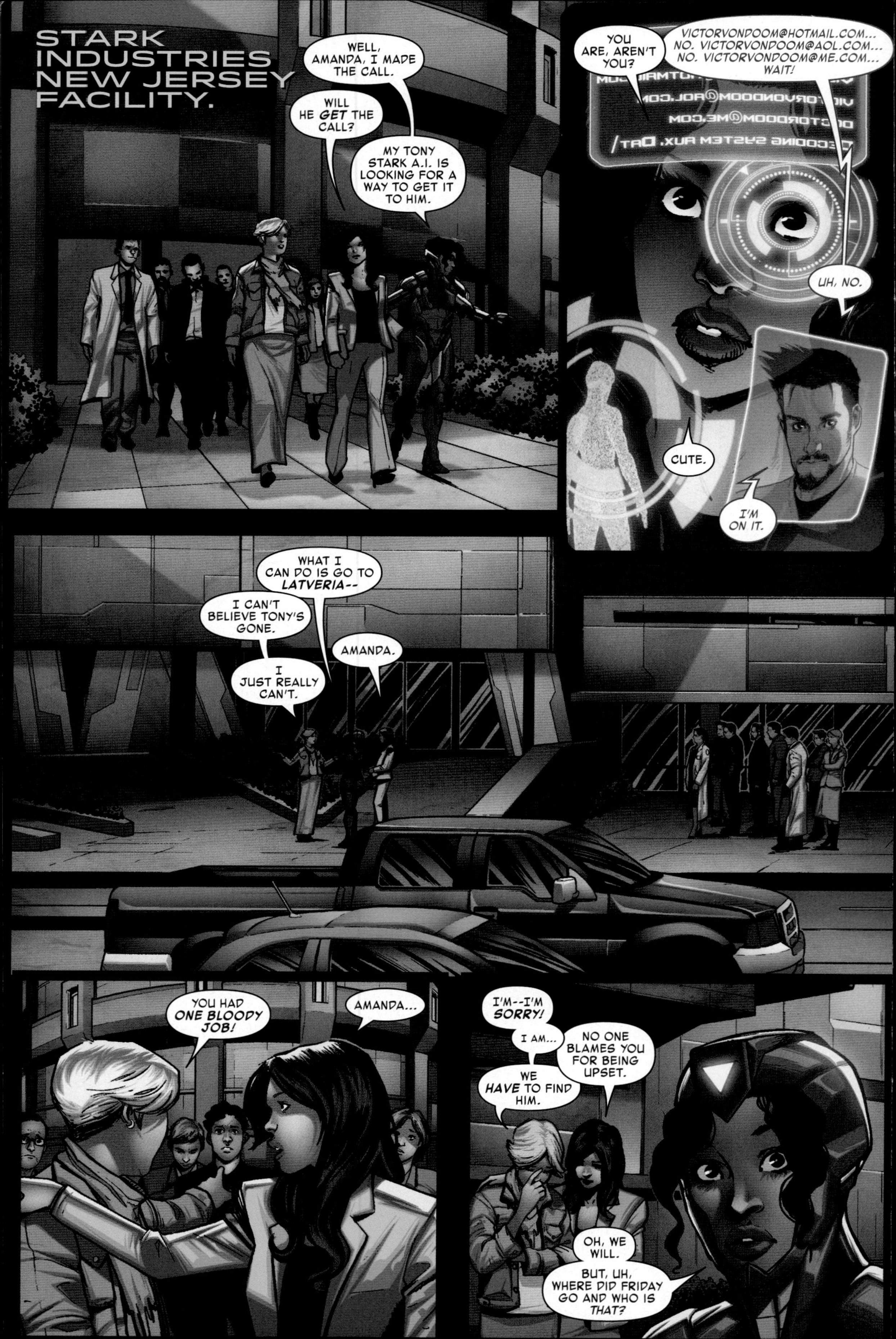
STARK INDUSTRIES NEW JERSEY FACILITY.
WELL, AMANDA, I MADE THE CALL.
WILL HE GET THE CALL?
MY TONY STARK A.I. IS LOOKING FOR A WAY TO GET IT TO HIM.
YOU ARE, AREN'T YOU?
VICTORVONDOOM@HOTMAIL.COM... NO. VICTORVONDOOM@AOL.COM... NO. VICTORVONDOOM@ME.COM... WAIT!
UH, NO.
CUTE.
I'M ON IT.
WHAT I CAN DO IS GO TO LATVERIA--
I CAN'T BELIEVE TONY'S GONE.
AMANDA.
I JUST REALLY CAN'T.
YOU HAD ONE BLOODY JOB!
AMANDA...
I'M--I'M SORRY!
I AM...
NO ONE BLAMES YOU FOR BEING UPSET.
WE HAVE TO FIND HIM.
OH, WE WILL.
BUT, UH, WHERE DID FRIDAY GO AND WHO IS THAT?

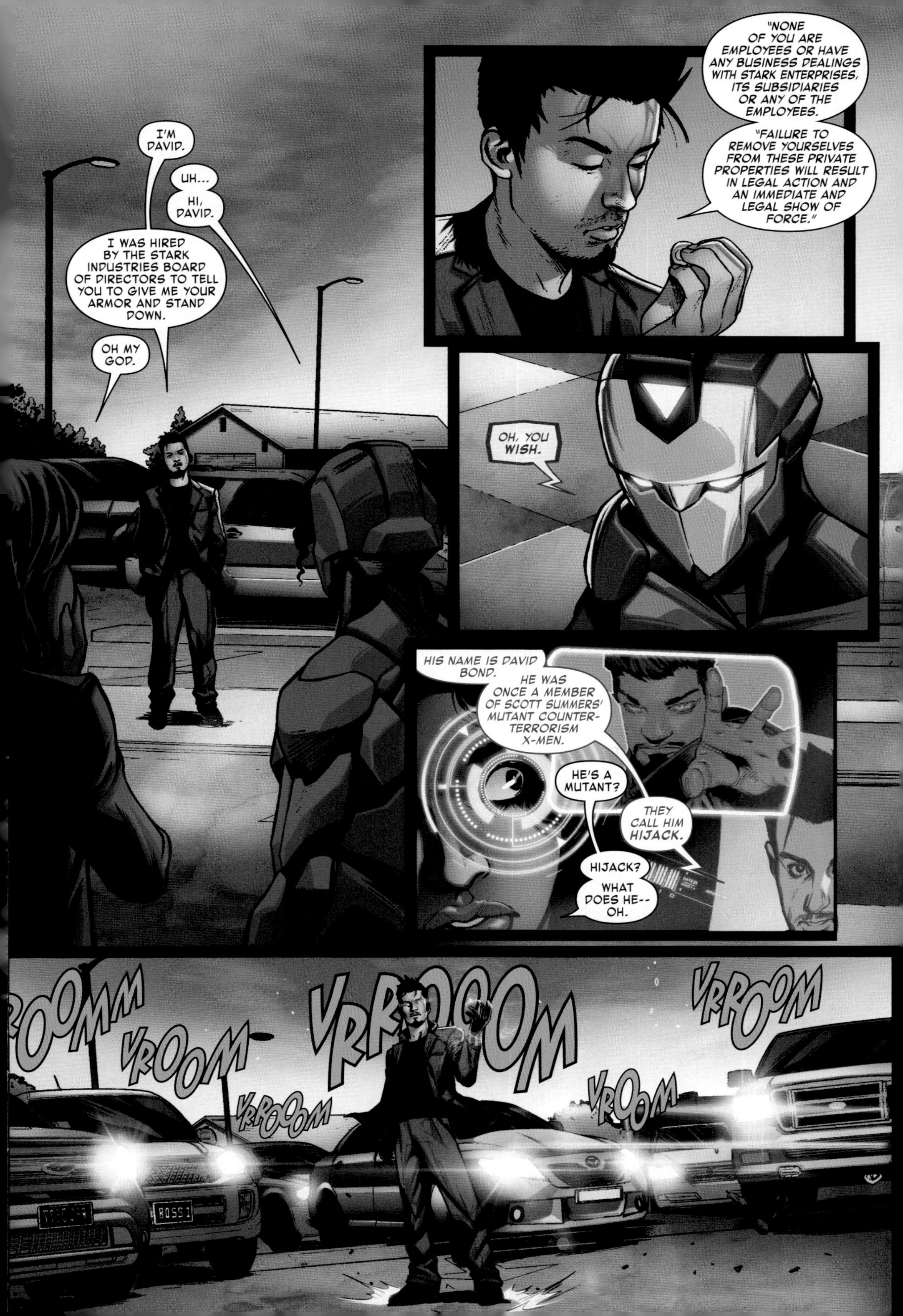

I'M DAVID.
UH...
HI, DAVID.
I WAS HIRED BY THE STARK INDUSTRIES BOARD OF DIRECTORS TO TELL YOU TO GIVE ME YOUR ARMOR AND STAND DOWN.
OH MY GOD.
"NONE OF YOU ARE EMPLOYEES OR HAVE ANY BUSINESS DEALINGS WITH STARK ENTERPRISES, ITS SUBSIDIARIES OR ANY OF THE EMPLOYEES.
"FAILURE TO REMOVE YOURSELVES FROM THESE PRIVATE PROPERTIES WILL RESULT IN LEGAL ACTION AND AN IMMEDIATE AND LEGAL SHOW OF FORCE."
OH, YOU WISH.
HIS NAME IS DAVID BOND.
HE WAS ONCE A MEMBER OF SCOTT SUMMERS' MUTANT COUNTER-TERRORISM X-MEN.
HE'S A MUTANT?
THEY CALL HIM HIJACK.
HIJACK?
WHAT DOES HE--OH.
ROOMM
VROOM
VRROOOM
VRROOOM
VROOM
VRROOM
BOSS 1

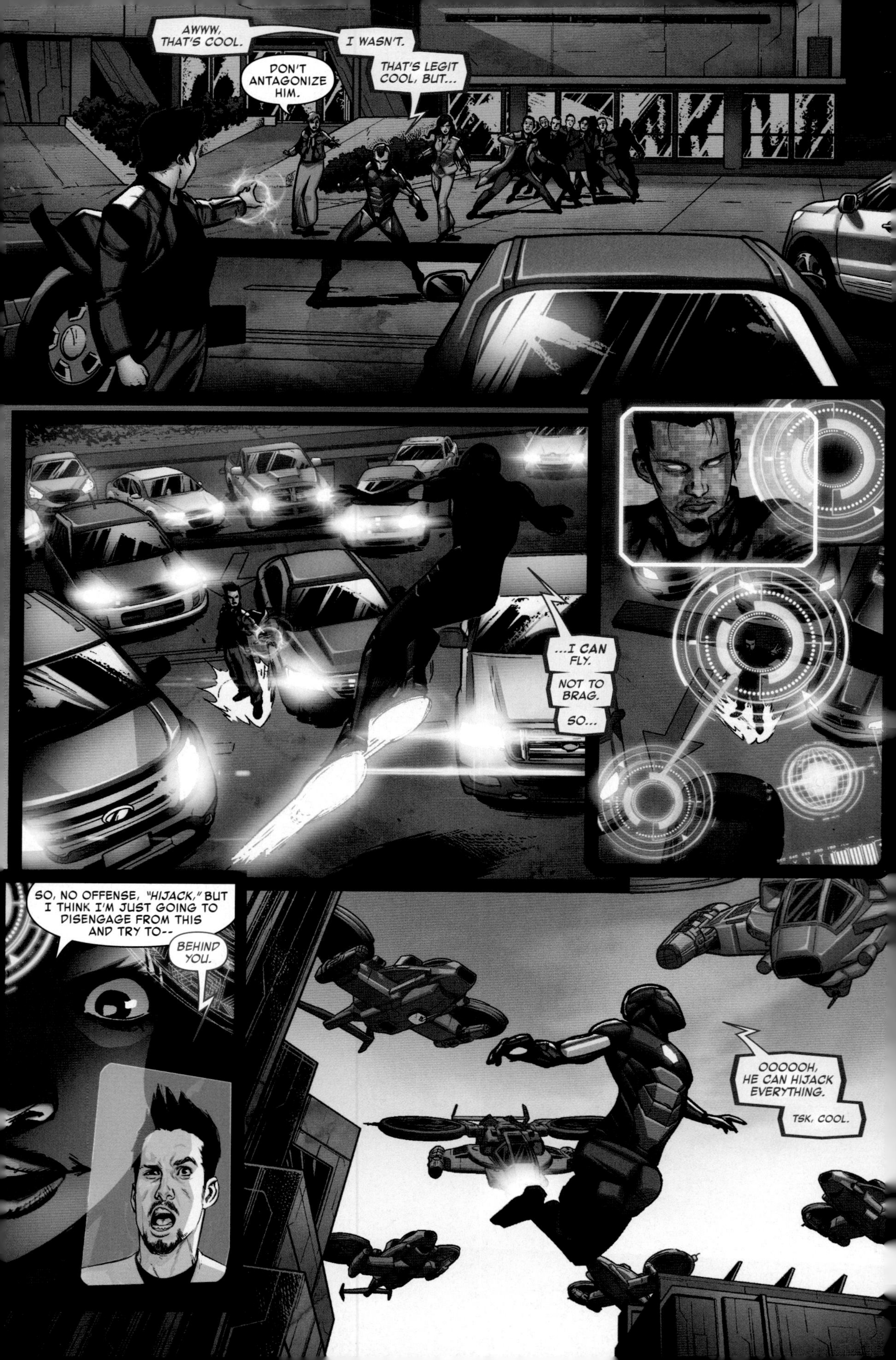
AWWW, THAT'S COOL.
I WASN'T.
DON'T ANTAGONIZE HIM.
THAT'S LEGIT COOL, BUT...
...I CAN FLY.
NOT TO BRAG.
SO...
SO, NO OFFENSE, "HIJACK," BUT I THINK I'M JUST GOING TO DISENGAGE FROM THIS AND TRY TO--
BEHIND YOU.
OOOOOH, HE CAN HIJACK EVERYTHING.
TSK, COOL.

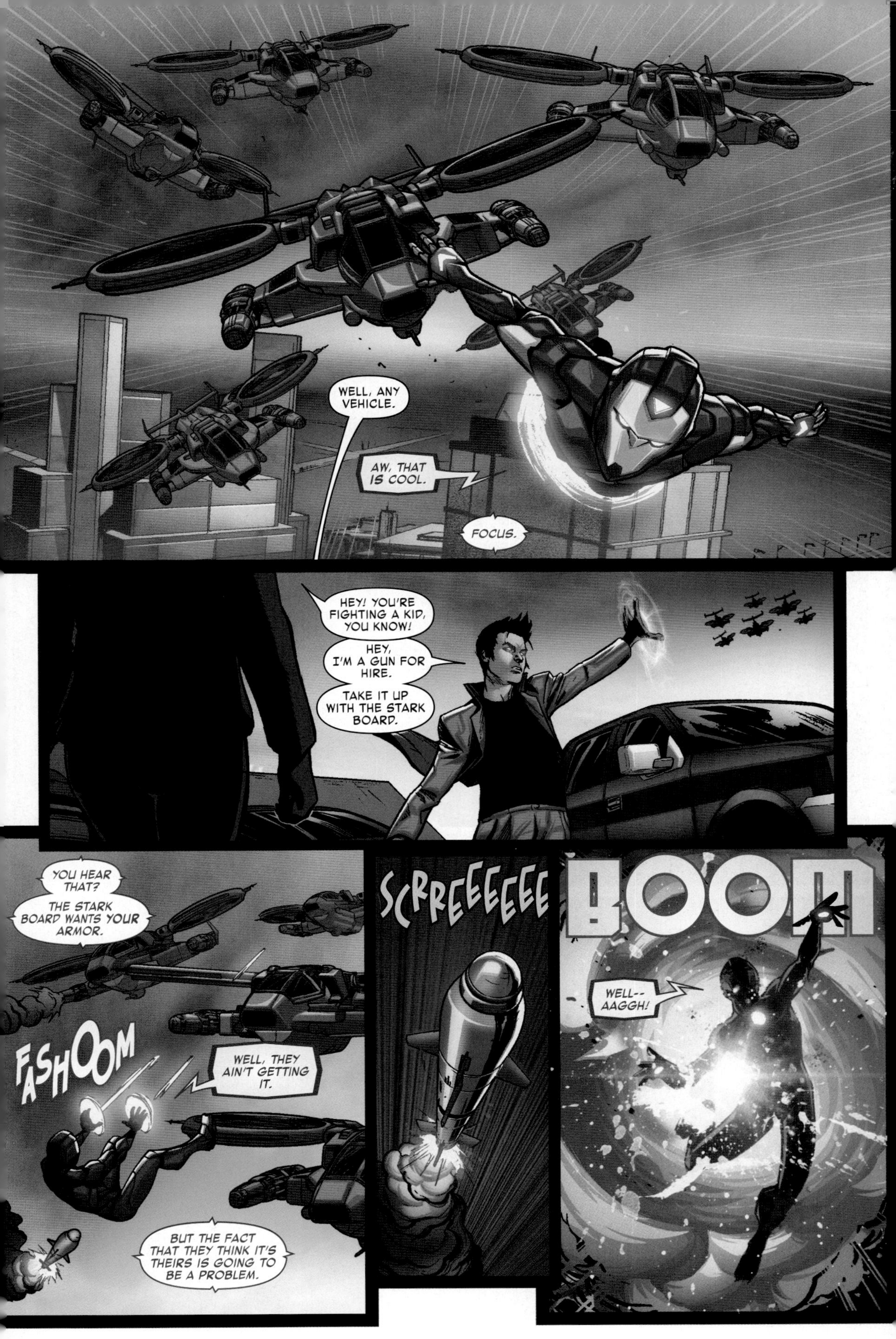
WELL, ANY VEHICLE.
AW, THAT IS COOL.
FOCUS.
HEY! YOU'RE FIGHTING A KID, YOU KNOW!
HEY, I'M A GUN FOR HIRE.
TAKE IT UP WITH THE STARK BOARD.
YOU HEAR THAT?
THE STARK BOARD WANTS YOUR ARMOR.
FASHOOM
WELL, THEY AIN'T GETTING IT.
BUT THE FACT THAT THEY THINK IT'S THEIRS IS GOING TO BE A PROBLEM.
SCREEEEEEE
BOOM
WELL-- AAGGH!

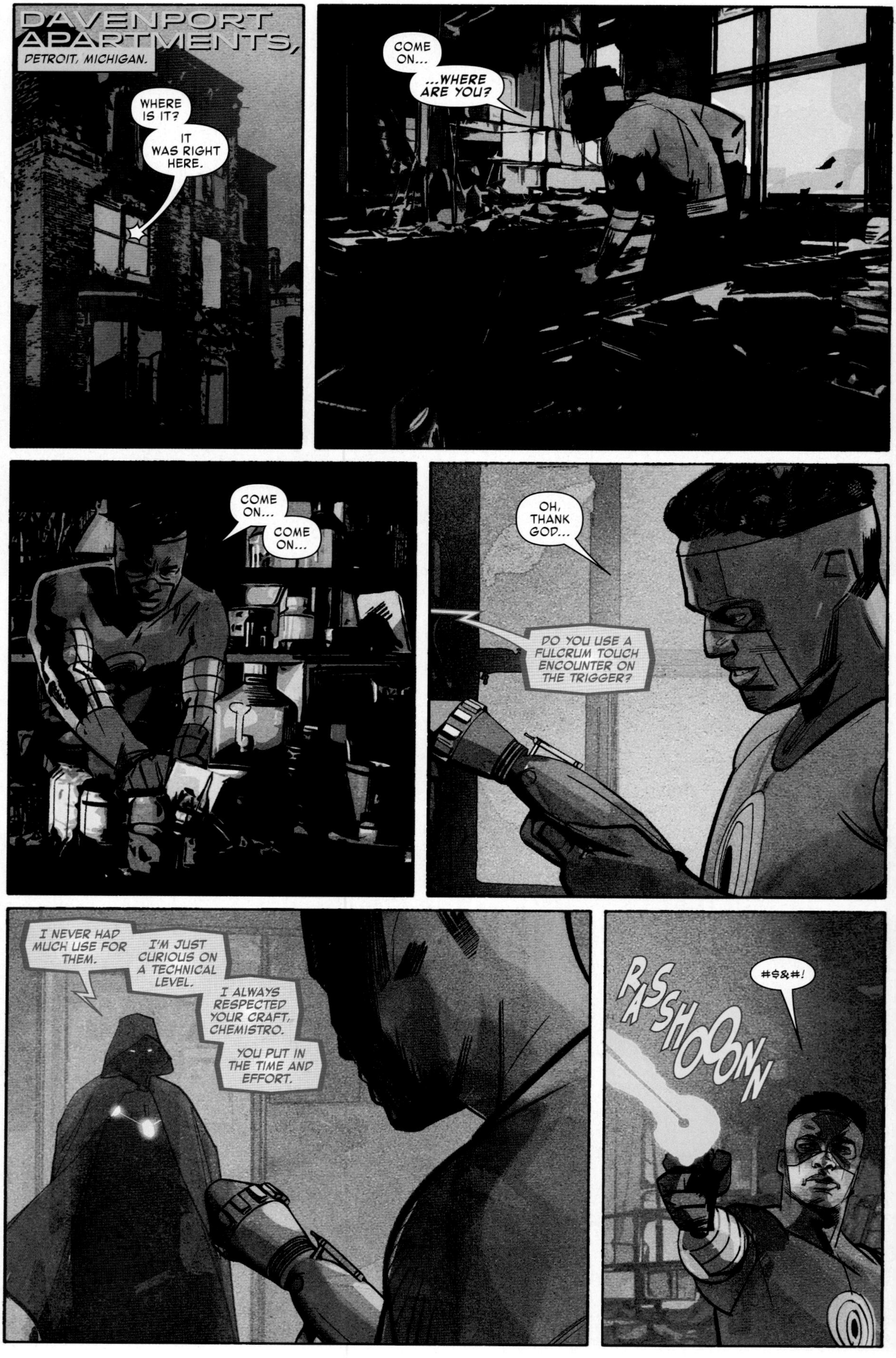
DAVENPORT APARTMENTS,
DETROIT, MICHIGAN.
WHERE IS IT?
IT WAS RIGHT HERE.
COME ON...
...WHERE ARE YOU?
COME ON...
COME ON...
OH, THANK GOD...
DO YOU USE A FULCRUM TOUCH ENCOUNTER ON THE TRIGGER?
I NEVER HAD MUCH USE FOR THEM.
I'M JUST CURIOUS ON A TECHNICAL LEVEL.
I ALWAYS RESPECTED YOUR CRAFT, CHEMISTRO.
YOU PUT IN THE TIME AND EFFORT.
RASSHOOONN
#$&#!

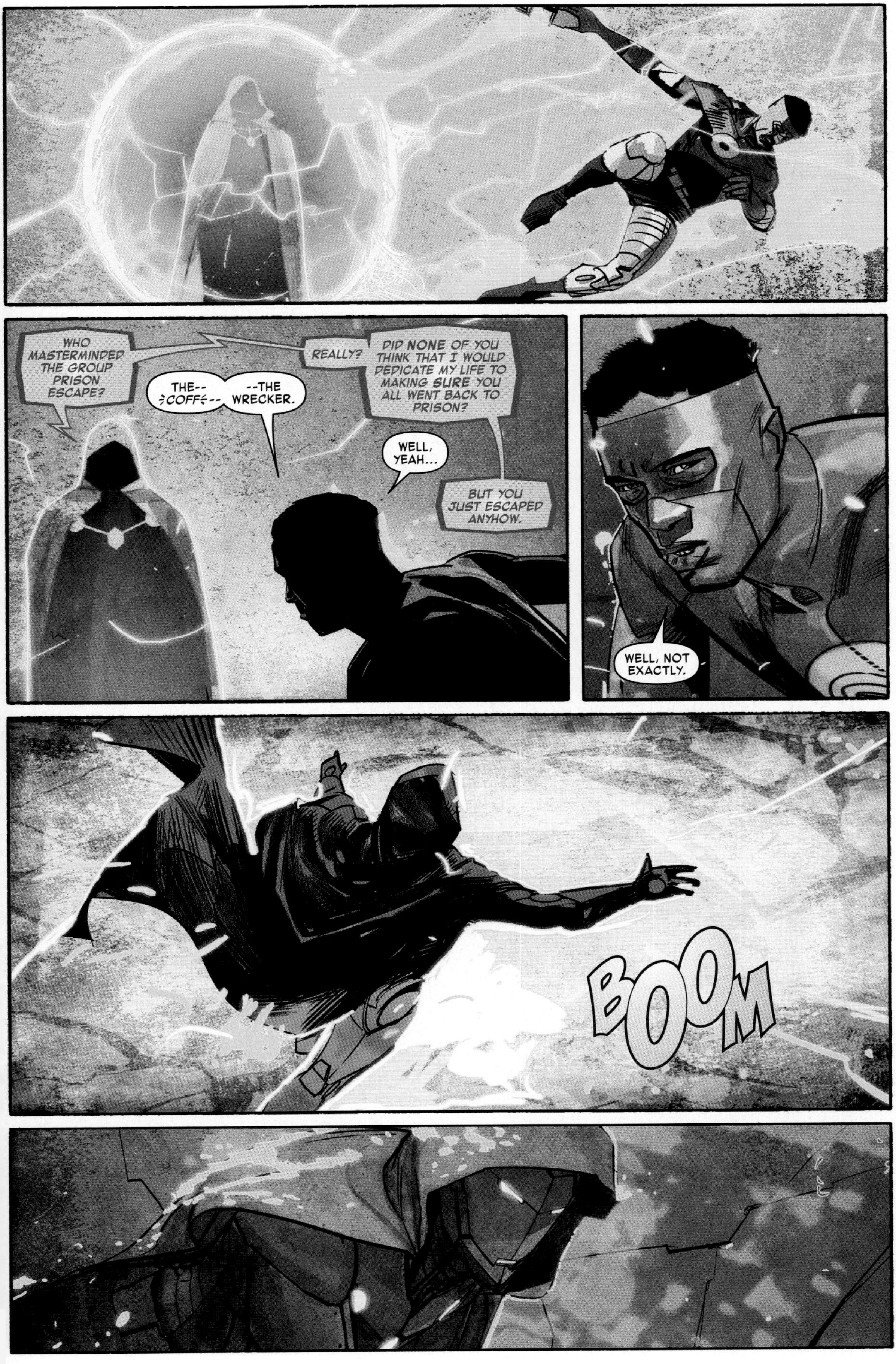
WHO MASTERMINDED THE GROUP PRISON ESCAPE?
THE-- *COFF*--
--THE WRECKER.
REALLY?
DID NONE OF YOU THINK THAT I WOULD DEDICATE MY LIFE TO MAKING SURE YOU ALL WENT BACK TO PRISON?
WELL, YEAH...
BUT YOU JUST ESCAPED ANYHOW.
WELL, NOT EXACTLY.
BOOM

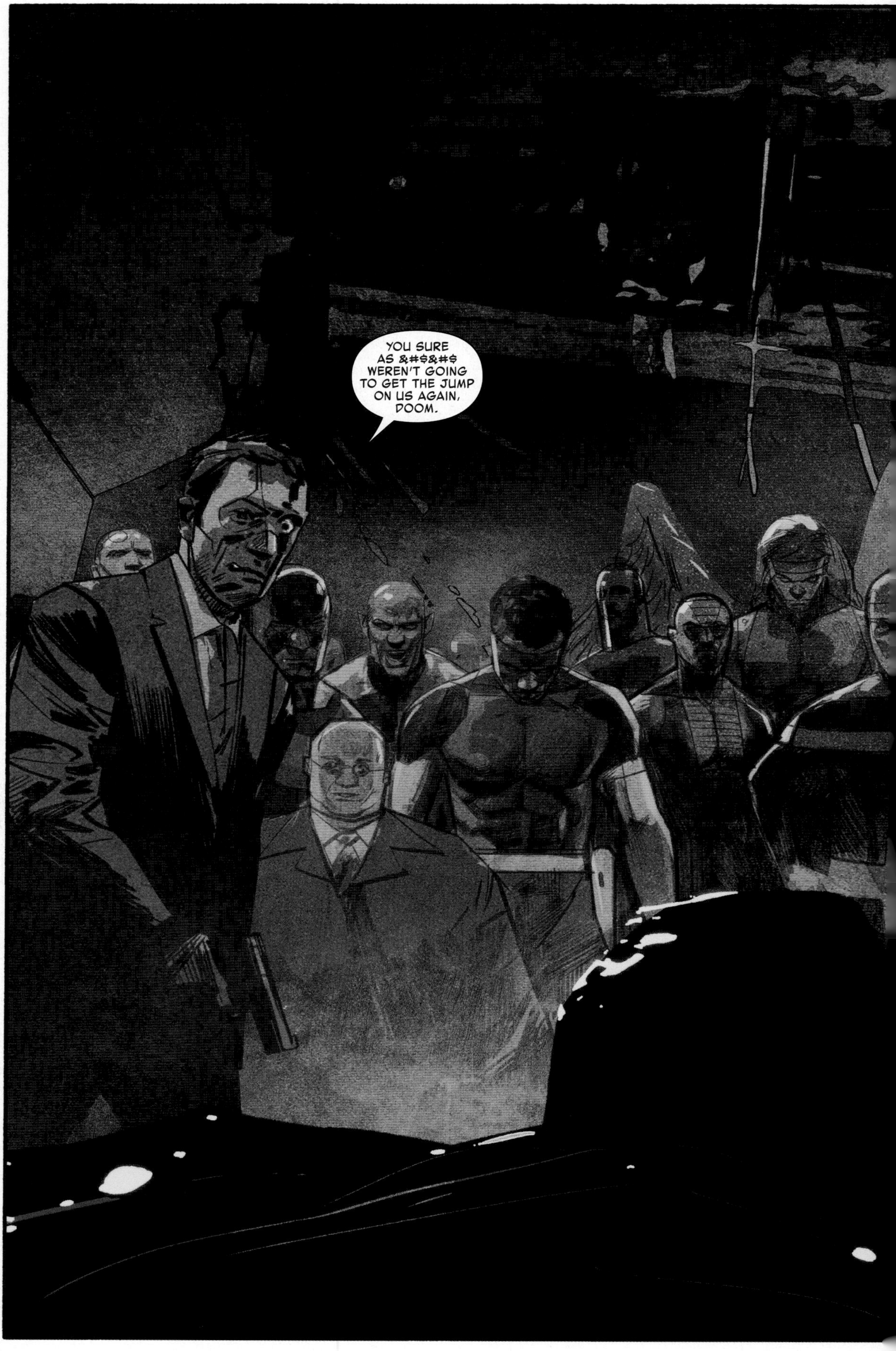
YOU SURE AS &#$&#$ WEREN'T GOING TO GET THE JUMP ON US AGAIN, DOOM.

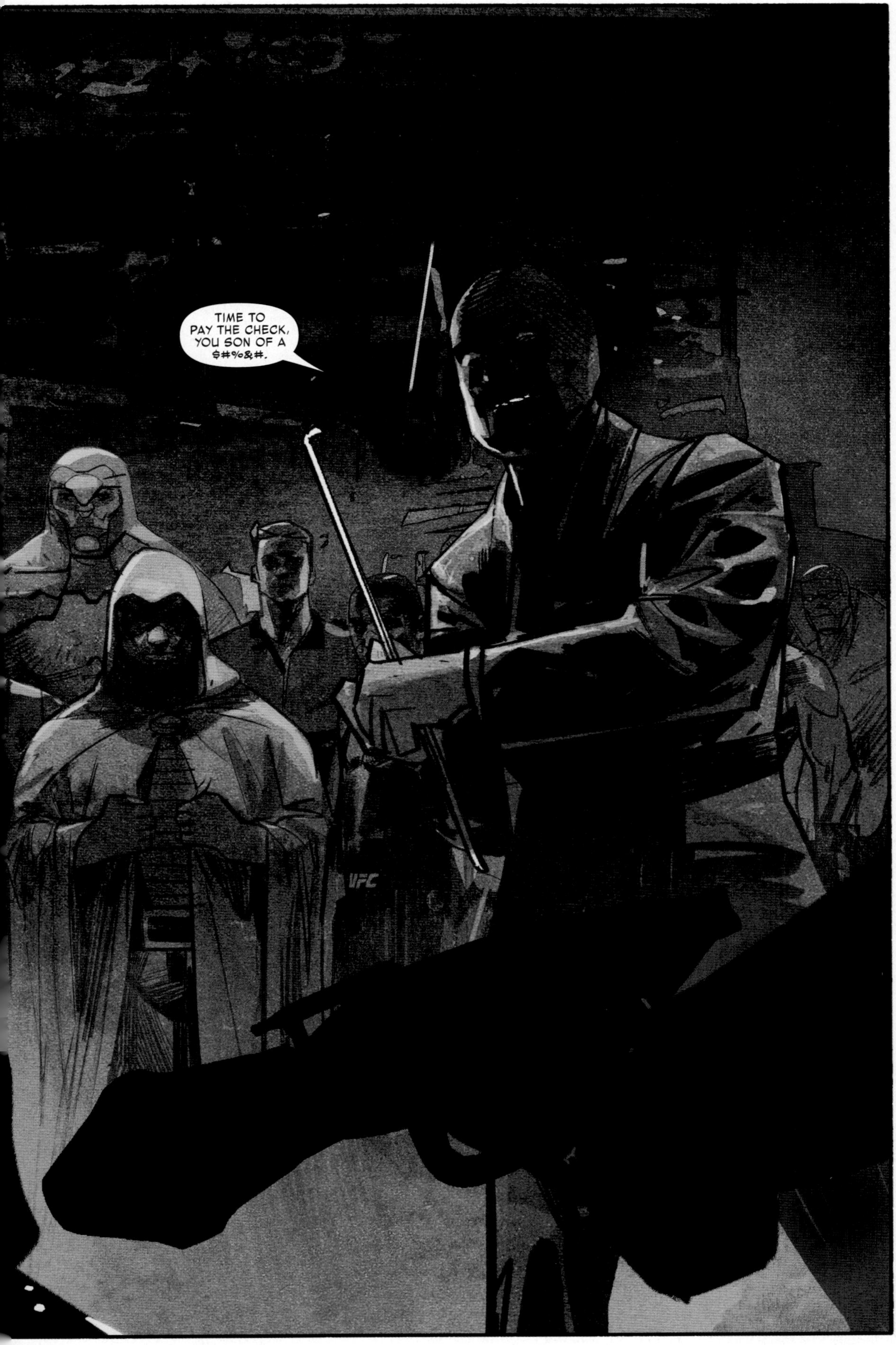
TIME TO PAY THE CHECK, YOU SON OF A $#%&#.
UFC

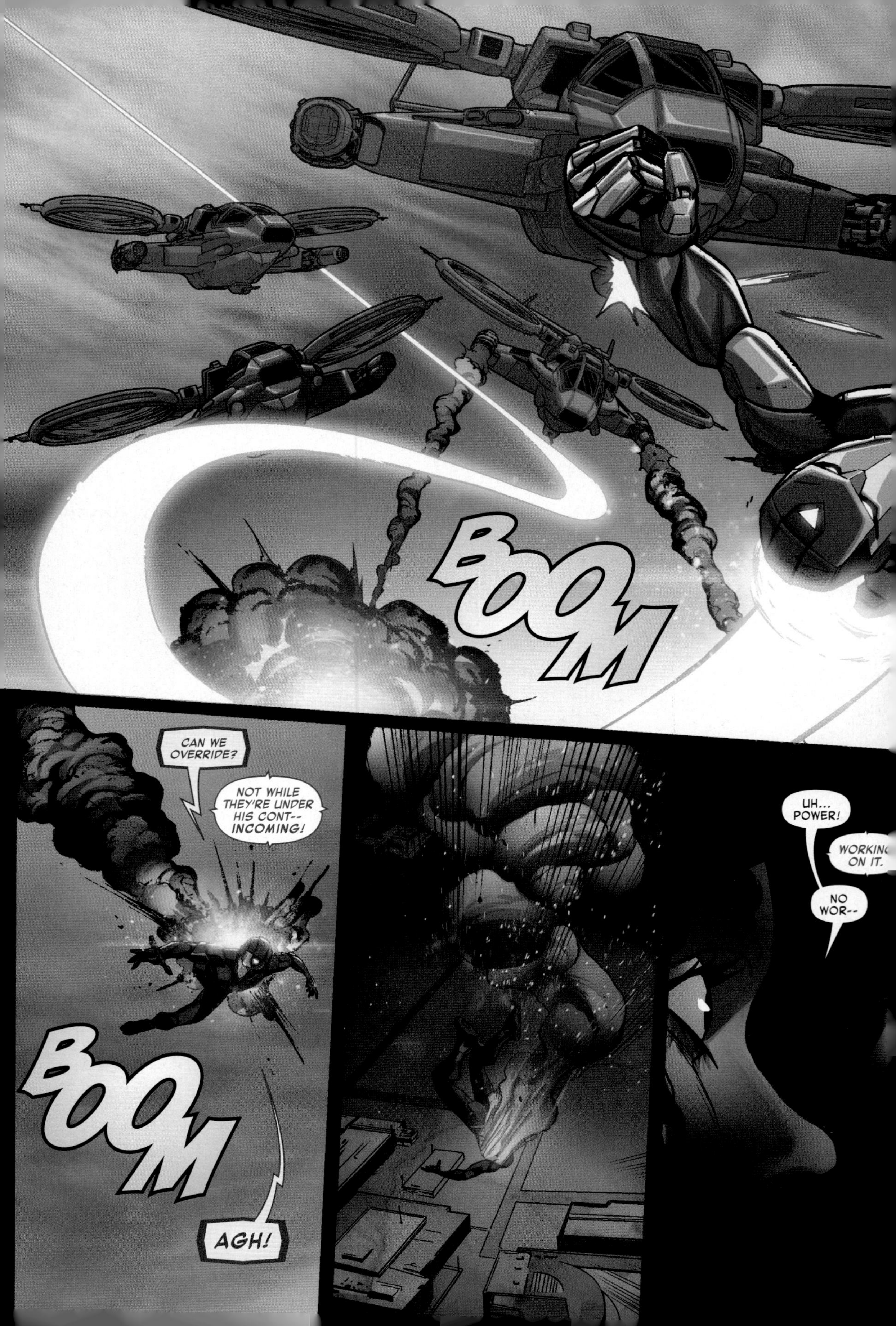
BOOM
CAN WE OVERRIDE?
NOT WHILE THEY'RE UNDER HIS CONT-- INCOMING!
BOOM
AGH!
UH... POWER!
WORKING ON IT.
NO WOR--

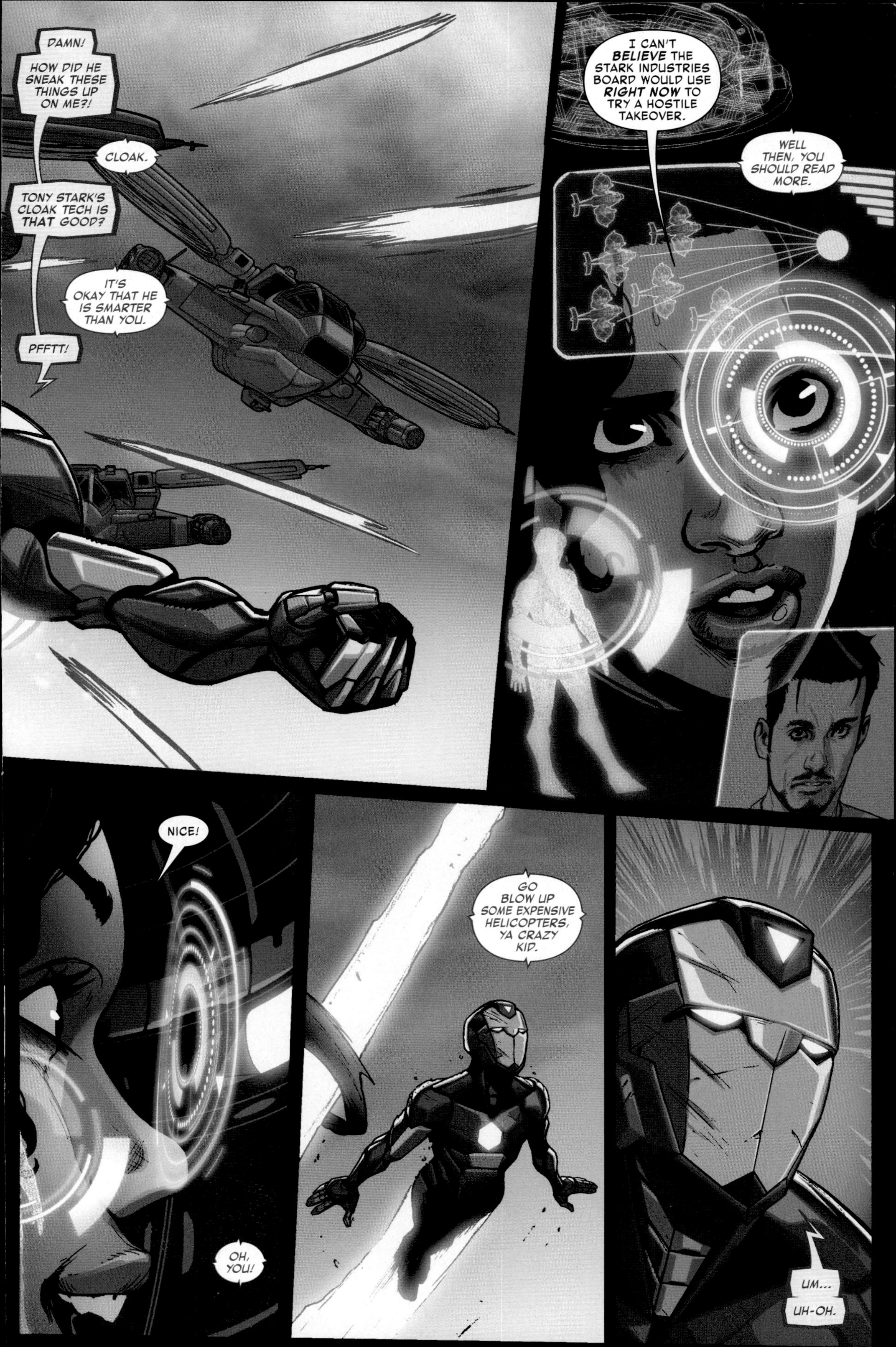
DAMN!
HOW DID HE SNEAK THESE THINGS UP ON ME?!
CLOAK.
TONY STARK'S CLOAK TECH IS THAT GOOD?
IT'S OKAY THAT HE IS SMARTER THAN YOU.
PFFTT!
I CAN'T BELIEVE THE STARK INDUSTRIES BOARD WOULD USE RIGHT NOW TO TRY A HOSTILE TAKEOVER.
WELL THEN, YOU SHOULD READ MORE.
NICE!
OH, YOU!
GO BLOW UP SOME EXPENSIVE HELICOPTERS, YA CRAZY KID.
UM...
UH-OH.

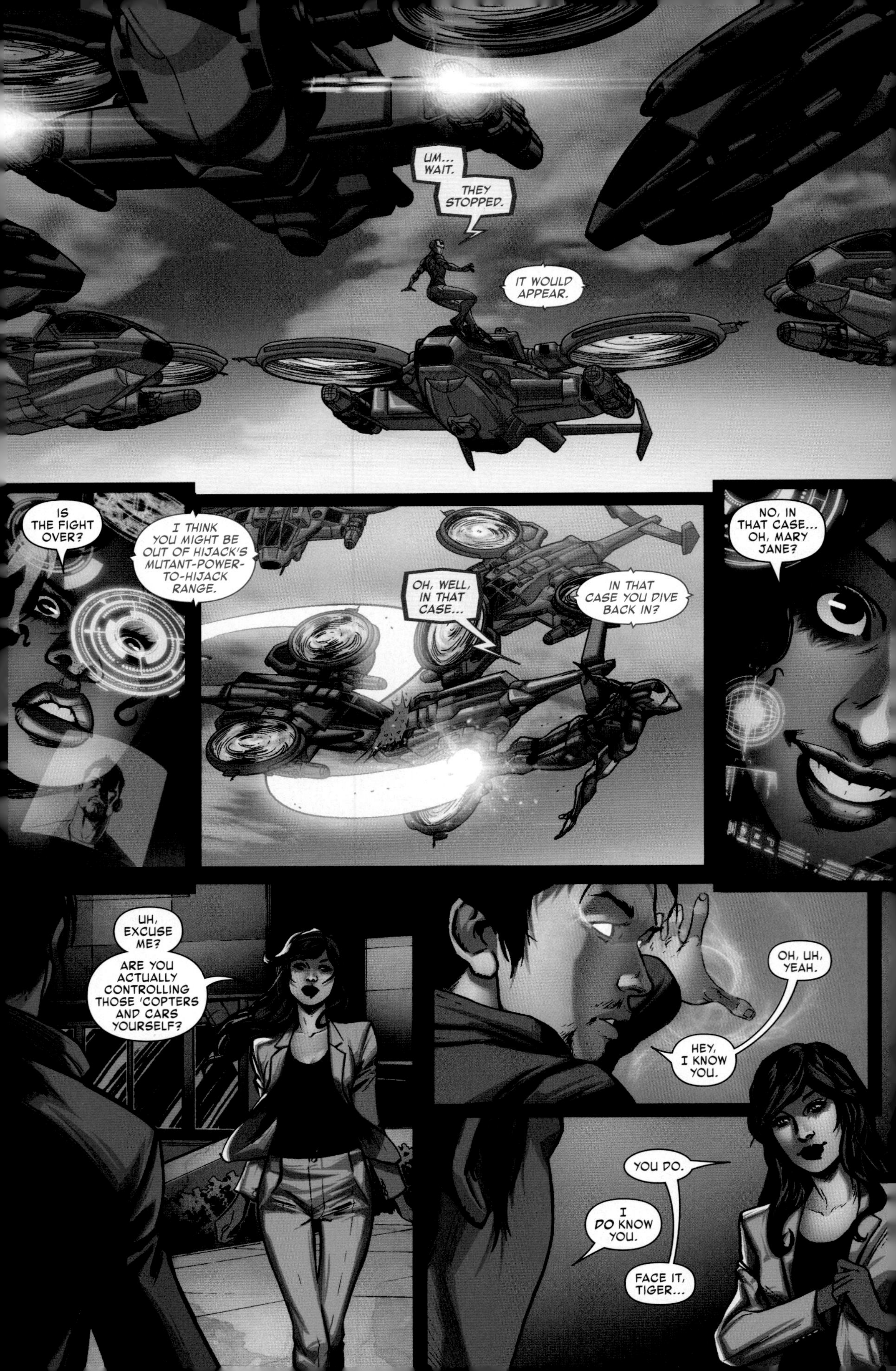
UM... WAIT.
THEY STOPPED.
IT WOULD APPEAR.
IS THE FIGHT OVER?
I THINK YOU MIGHT BE OUT OF HIJACK'S MUTANT-POWER-TO-HIJACK RANGE.
OH, WELL, IN THAT CASE...
IN THAT CASE YOU DIVE BACK IN?
NO, IN THAT CASE... OH, MARY JANE?
UH, EXCUSE ME?
ARE YOU ACTUALLY CONTROLLING THOSE 'COPTERS AND CARS YOURSELF?
OH, UH, YEAH.
HEY, I KNOW YOU.
YOU DO.
I DO KNOW YOU.
FACE IT, TIGER...

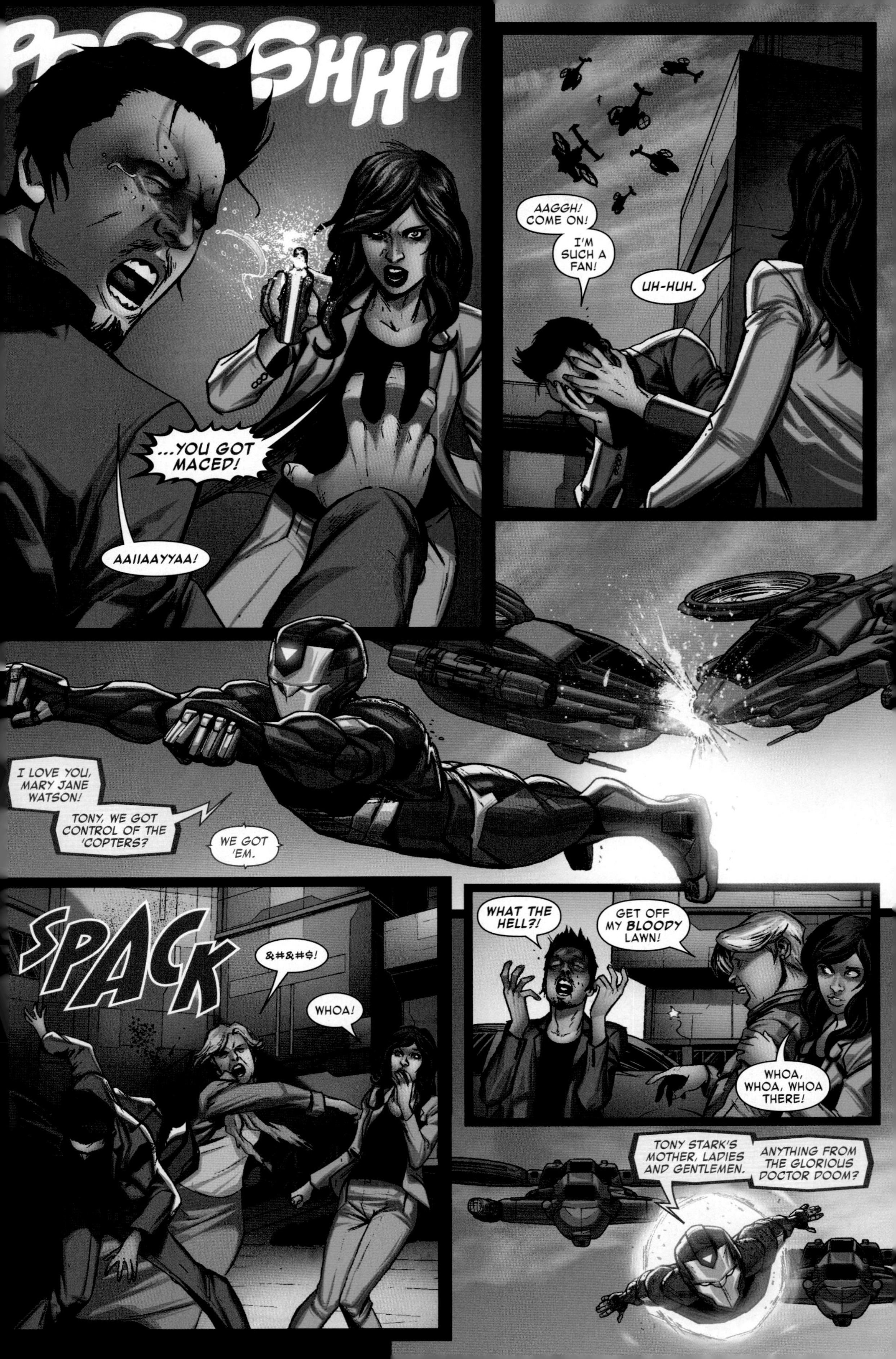
PFSSSHHH
...YOU GOT MACED!
AAIIAAYYAA!
AAGGH! COME ON!
I'M SUCH A FAN!
UH-HUH.
I LOVE YOU, MARY JANE WATSON!
TONY, WE GOT CONTROL OF THE 'COPTERS?
WE GOT 'EM.
SPACK
&#&#$!
WHOA!
WHAT THE HELL?!
GET OFF MY BLOODY LAWN!
WHOA, WHOA, WHOA THERE!
TONY STARK'S MOTHER, LADIES AND GENTLEMEN.
ANYTHING FROM THE GLORIOUS DOCTOR DOOM?

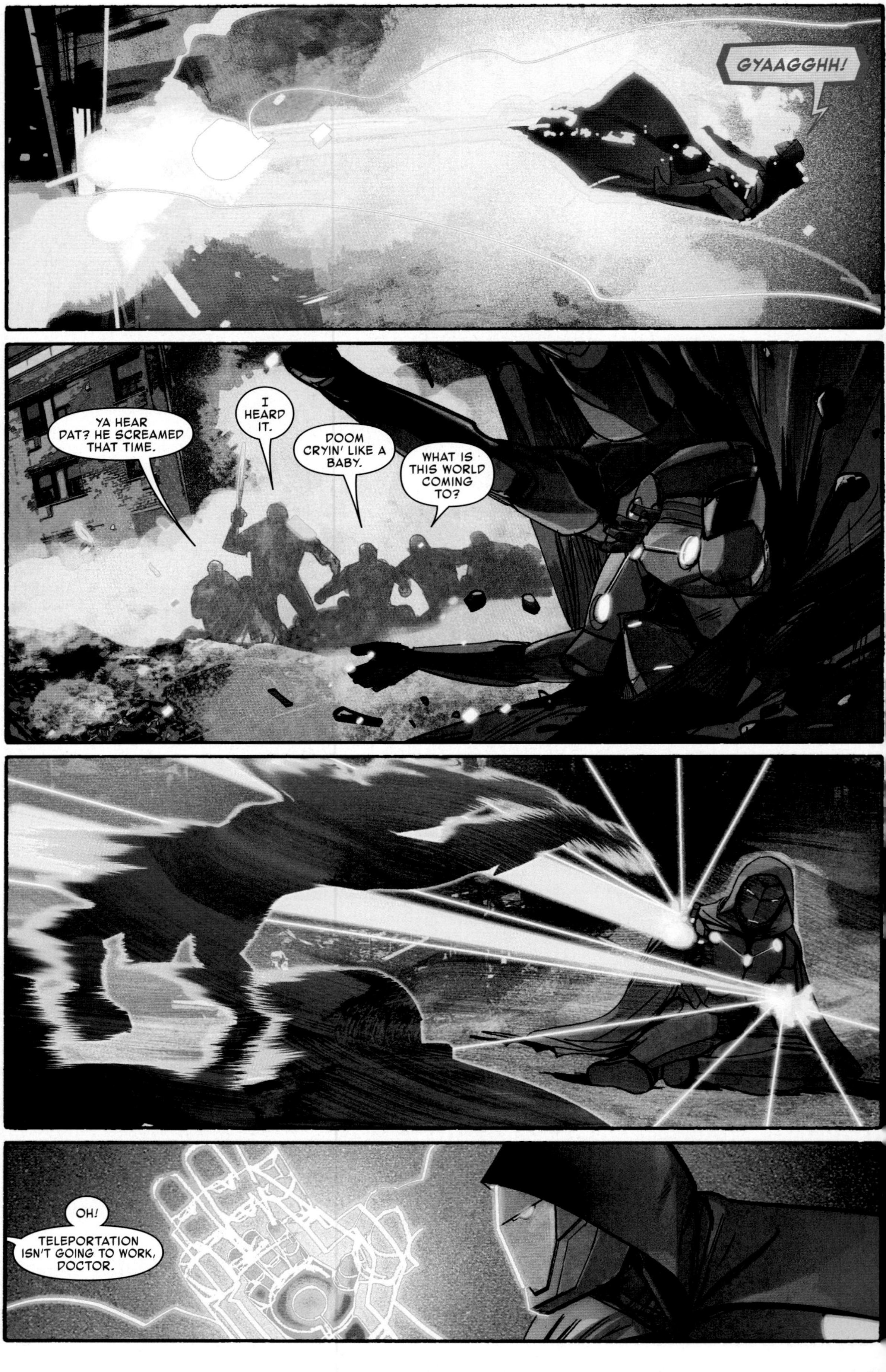
GYAAGGHH!
YA HEAR DAT? HE SCREAMED THAT TIME.
I HEARD IT.
DOOM CRYIN' LIKE A BABY.
WHAT IS THIS WORLD COMING TO?
OH!
TELEPORTATION ISN'T GOING TO WORK, DOCTOR.

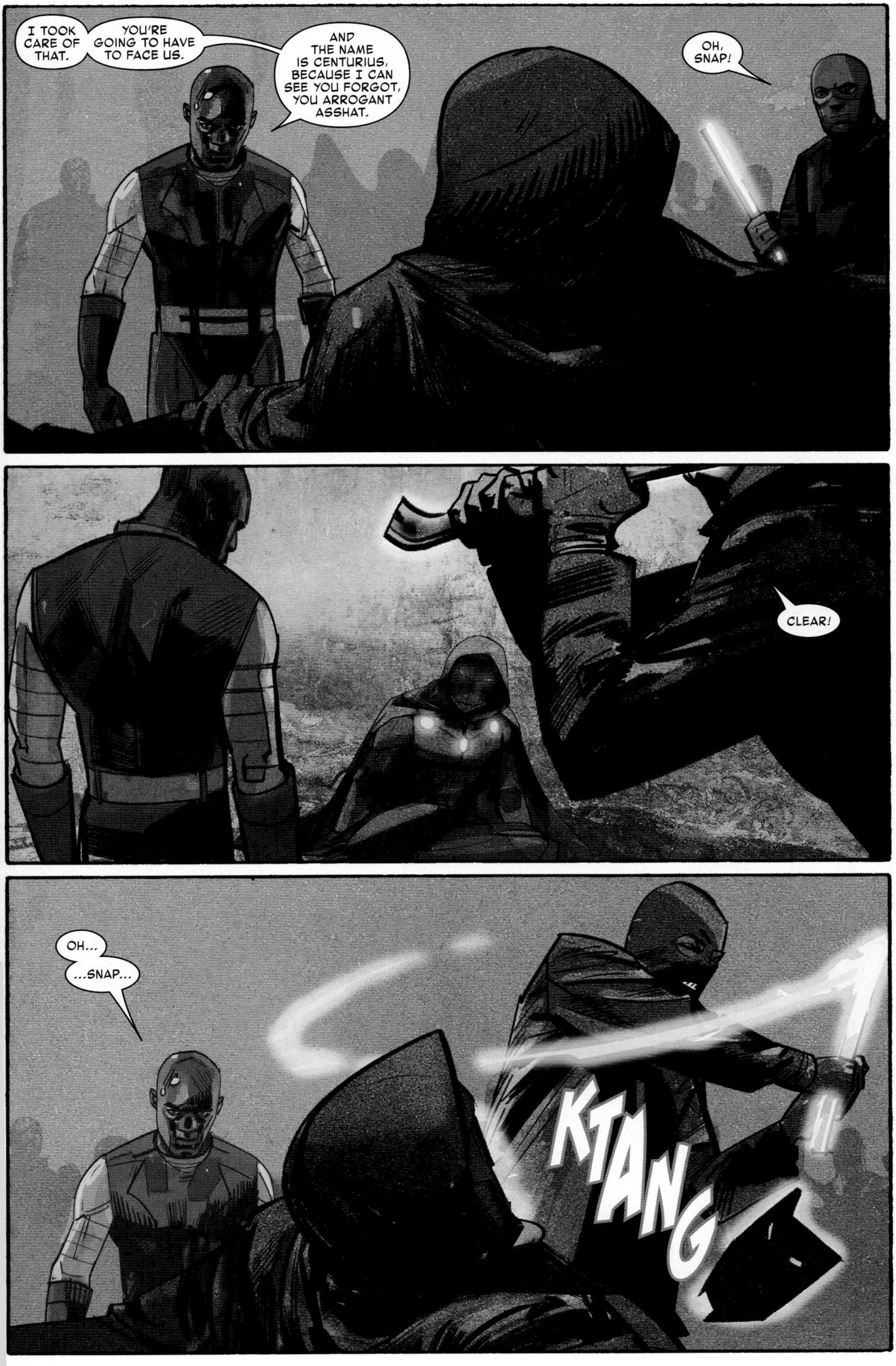
I TOOK CARE OF THAT.
YOU'RE GOING TO HAVE TO FACE US.
AND THE NAME IS CENTURIUS, BECAUSE I CAN SEE YOU FORGOT, YOU ARROGANT ASSHAT.
OH, SNAP!
CLEAR!
OH...
...SNAP...
KTANG

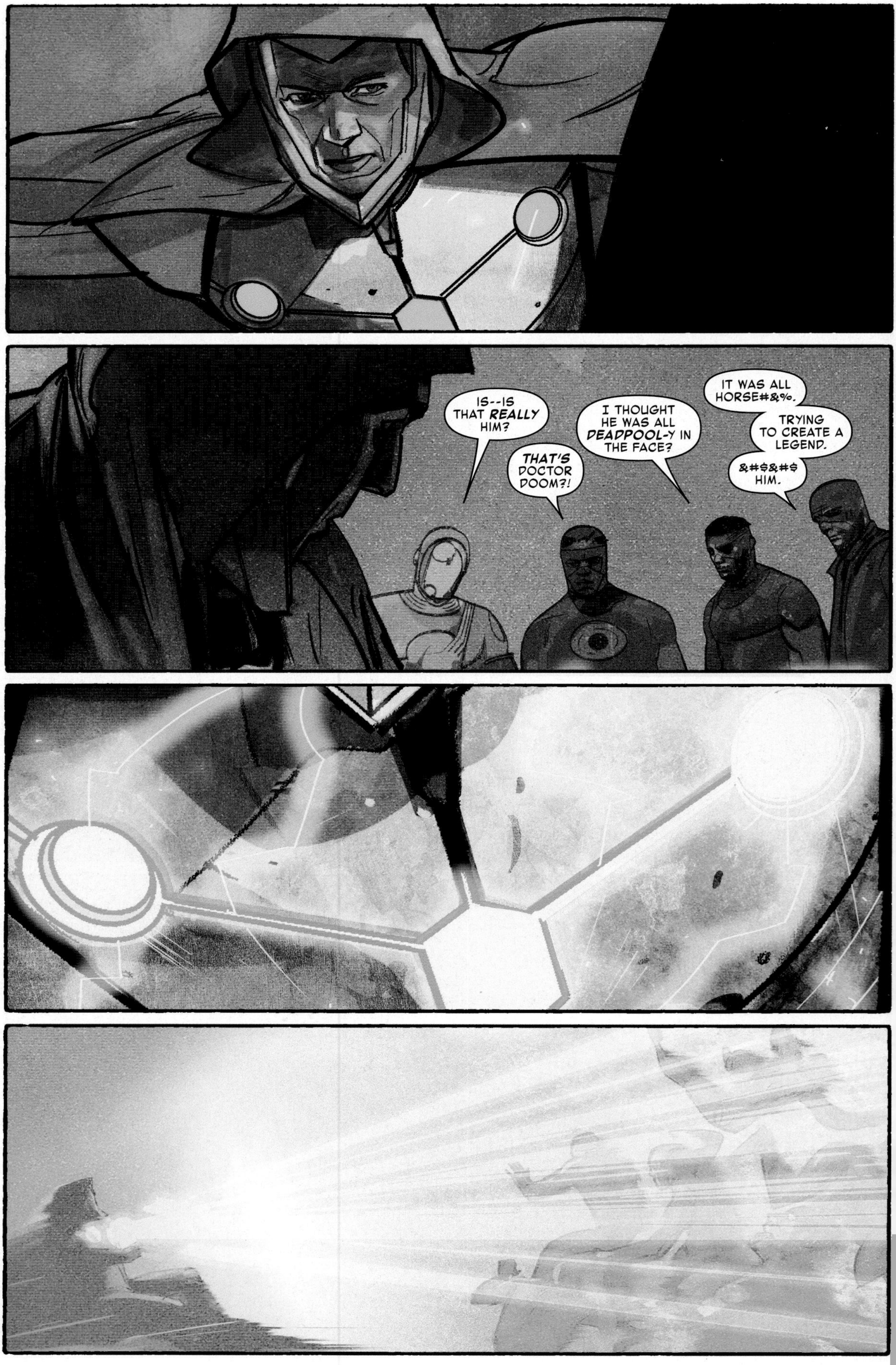
IS--IS THAT REALLY HIM?
THAT'S DOCTOR DOOM?!
I THOUGHT HE WAS ALL DEADPOOL-Y IN THE FACE?
IT WAS ALL HORSE#&%.
TRYING TO CREATE A LEGEND.
&#$&#$ HIM.

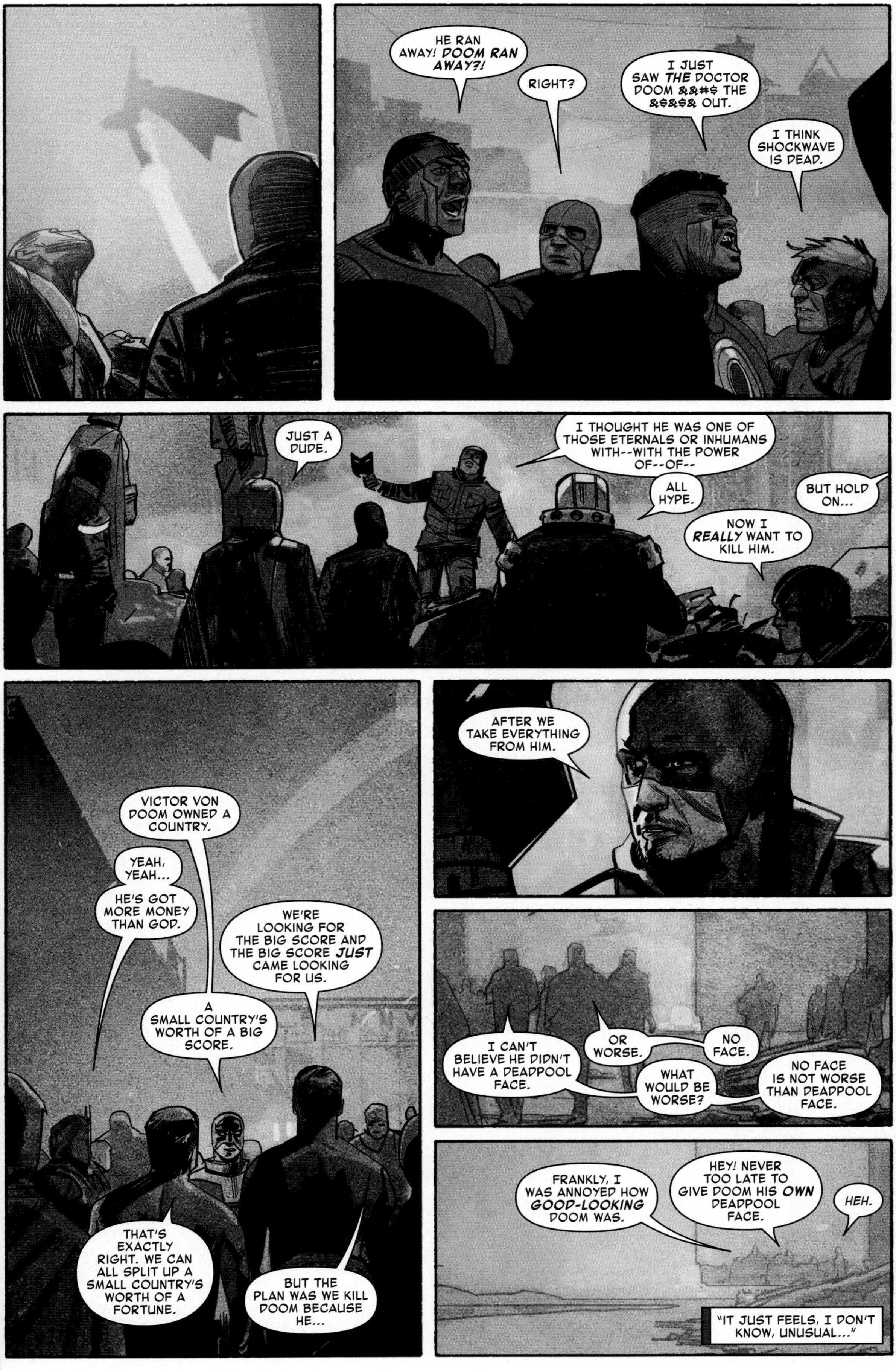
HE RAN AWAY! DOOM RAN AWAY?!
RIGHT?
I JUST SAW THE DOCTOR DOOM &&#$ THE &$&$& OUT.
I THINK SHOCKWAVE IS DEAD.
JUST A DUDE.
I THOUGHT HE WAS ONE OF THOSE ETERNALS OR INHUMANS WITH--WITH THE POWER OF--OF--
ALL HYPE.
BUT HOLD ON...
NOW I REALLY WANT TO KILL HIM.
AFTER WE TAKE EVERYTHING FROM HIM.
VICTOR VON DOOM OWNED A COUNTRY.
YEAH, YEAH...
HE'S GOT MORE MONEY THAN GOD.
WE'RE LOOKING FOR THE BIG SCORE AND THE BIG SCORE JUST CAME LOOKING FOR US.
A SMALL COUNTRY'S WORTH OF A BIG SCORE.
THAT'S EXACTLY RIGHT. WE CAN ALL SPLIT UP A SMALL COUNTRY'S WORTH OF A FORTUNE.
BUT THE PLAN WAS WE KILL DOOM BECAUSE HE...
I CAN'T BELIEVE HE DIDN'T HAVE A DEADPOOL FACE.
OR WORSE.
NO FACE.
WHAT WOULD BE WORSE?
NO FACE IS NOT WORSE THAN DEADPOOL FACE.
FRANKLY, I WAS ANNOYED HOW GOOD-LOOKING DOOM WAS.
HEY! NEVER TOO LATE TO GIVE DOOM HIS OWN DEADPOOL FACE.
HEH.
"IT JUST FEELS, I DON'T KNOW, UNUSUAL..."

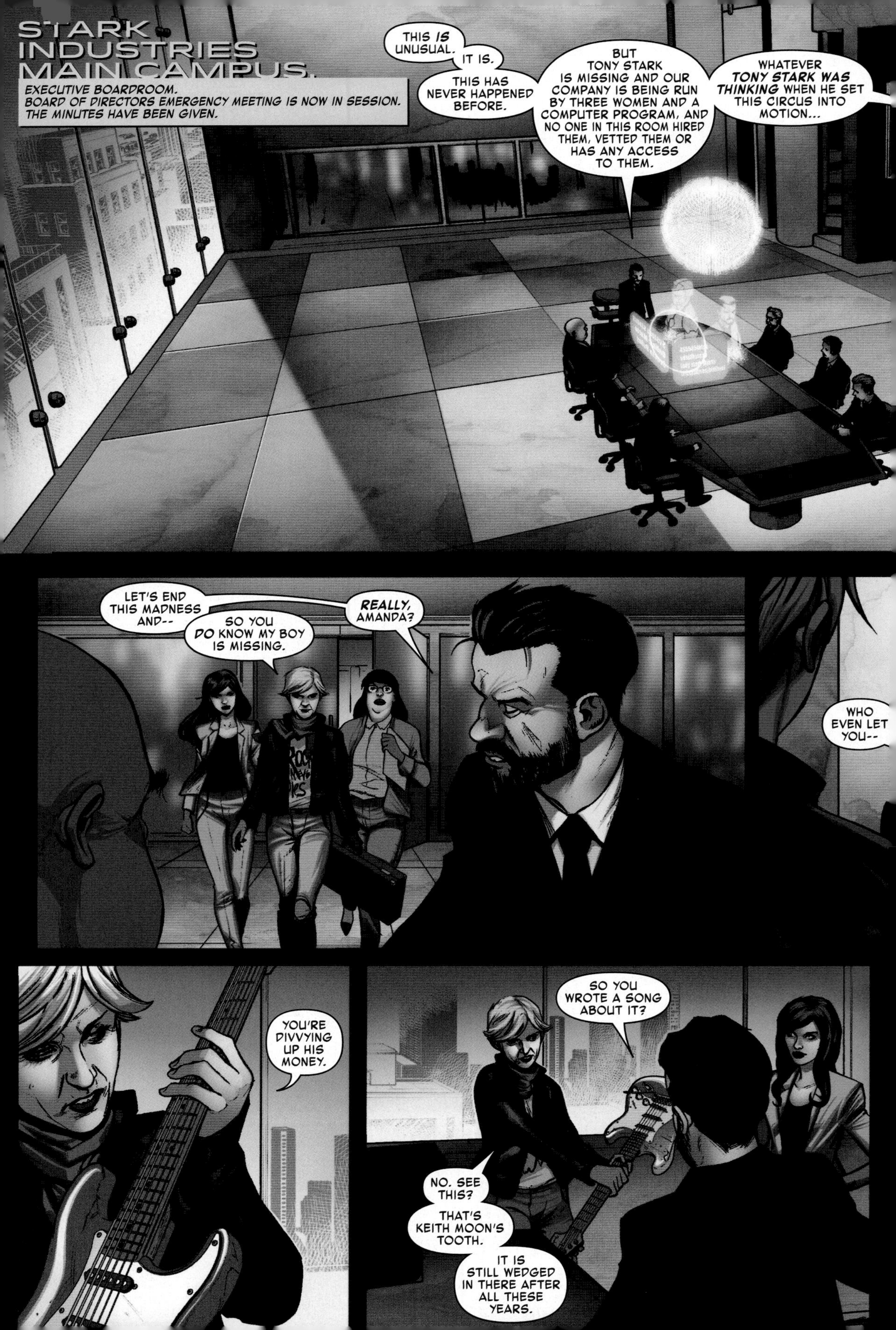
STARK INDUSTRIES MAIN CAMPUS.
EXECUTIVE BOARDROOM.
BOARD OF DIRECTORS EMERGENCY MEETING IS NOW IN SESSION.
THE MINUTES HAVE BEEN GIVEN.
THIS *IS* UNUSUAL.
IT IS.
THIS HAS NEVER HAPPENED BEFORE.
BUT TONY STARK IS MISSING AND OUR COMPANY IS BEING RUN BY THREE WOMEN AND A COMPUTER PROGRAM, AND NO ONE IN THIS ROOM HIRED THEM, VETTED THEM OR HAS ANY ACCESS TO THEM.
WHATEVER *TONY STARK WAS THINKING* WHEN HE SET THIS CIRCUS INTO MOTION...
LET'S END THIS MADNESS AND--
SO YOU *DO* KNOW MY BOY IS MISSING.
*REALLY,* AMANDA?
WHO EVEN LET YOU--
YOU'RE DIVVYING UP HIS MONEY.
SO YOU WROTE A SONG ABOUT IT?
NO. SEE THIS?
THAT'S KEITH MOON'S TOOTH.
IT IS STILL WEDGED IN THERE AFTER ALL THESE YEARS.

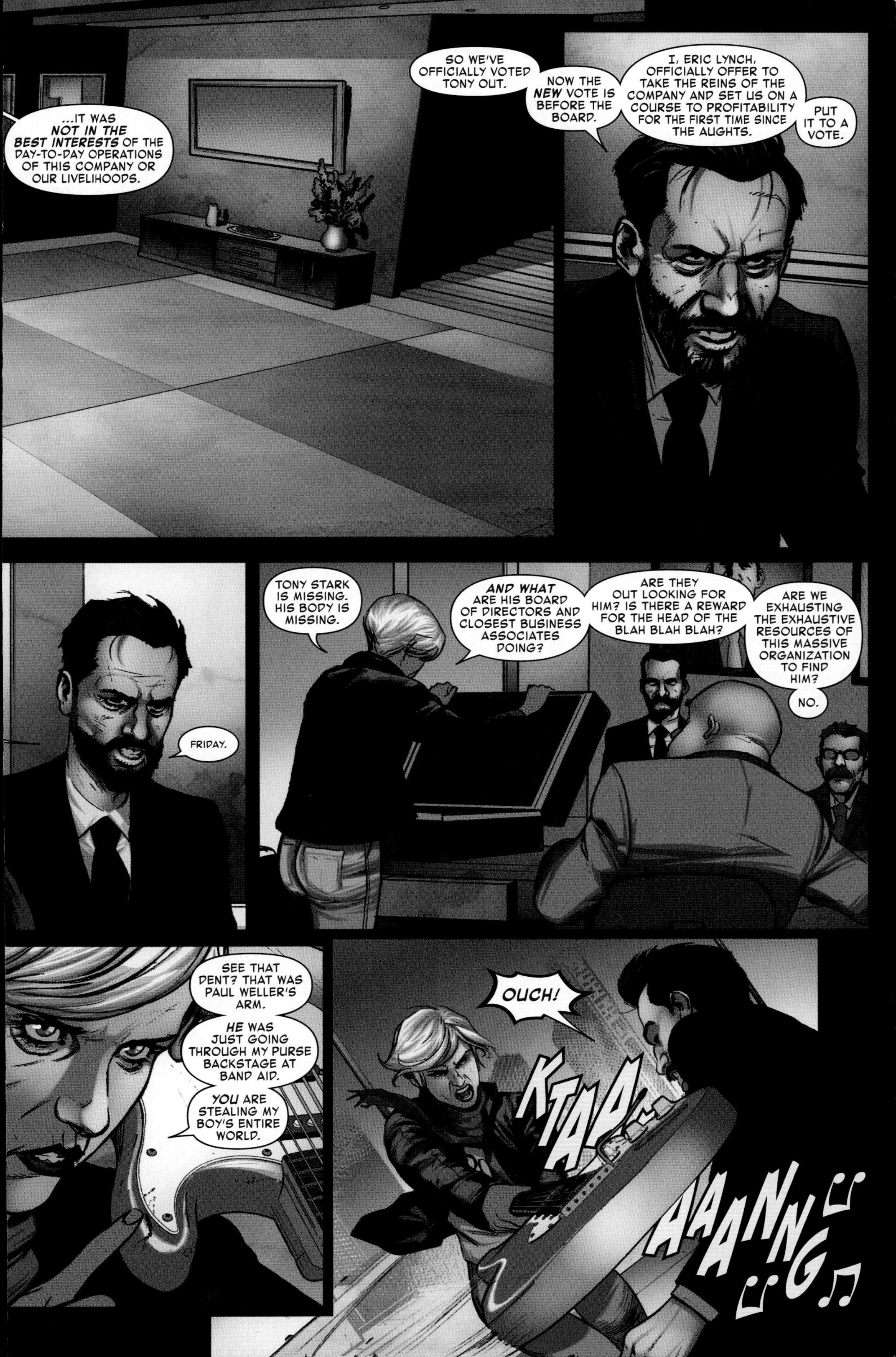

...IT WAS NOT IN THE BEST INTERESTS OF THE DAY-TO-DAY OPERATIONS OF THIS COMPANY OR OUR LIVELIHOODS.
SO WE'VE OFFICIALLY VOTED TONY OUT.
NOW THE NEW VOTE IS BEFORE THE BOARD.
I, ERIC LYNCH, OFFICIALLY OFFER TO TAKE THE REINS OF THE COMPANY AND SET US ON A COURSE TO PROFITABILITY FOR THE FIRST TIME SINCE THE AUGHTS.
PUT IT TO A VOTE.
FRIDAY.
TONY STARK IS MISSING. HIS BODY IS MISSING.
AND WHAT ARE HIS BOARD OF DIRECTORS AND CLOSEST BUSINESS ASSOCIATES DOING?
ARE THEY OUT LOOKING FOR HIM? IS THERE A REWARD FOR THE HEAD OF THE BLAH BLAH BLAH?
ARE WE EXHAUSTING THE EXHAUSTIVE RESOURCES OF THIS MASSIVE ORGANIZATION TO FIND HIM?
NO.
SEE THAT DENT? THAT WAS PAUL WELLER'S ARM.
HE WAS JUST GOING THROUGH MY PURSE BACKSTAGE AT BAND AID.
YOU ARE STEALING MY BOY'S ENTIRE WORLD.
OUCH!
KTAAA...
AAANNG

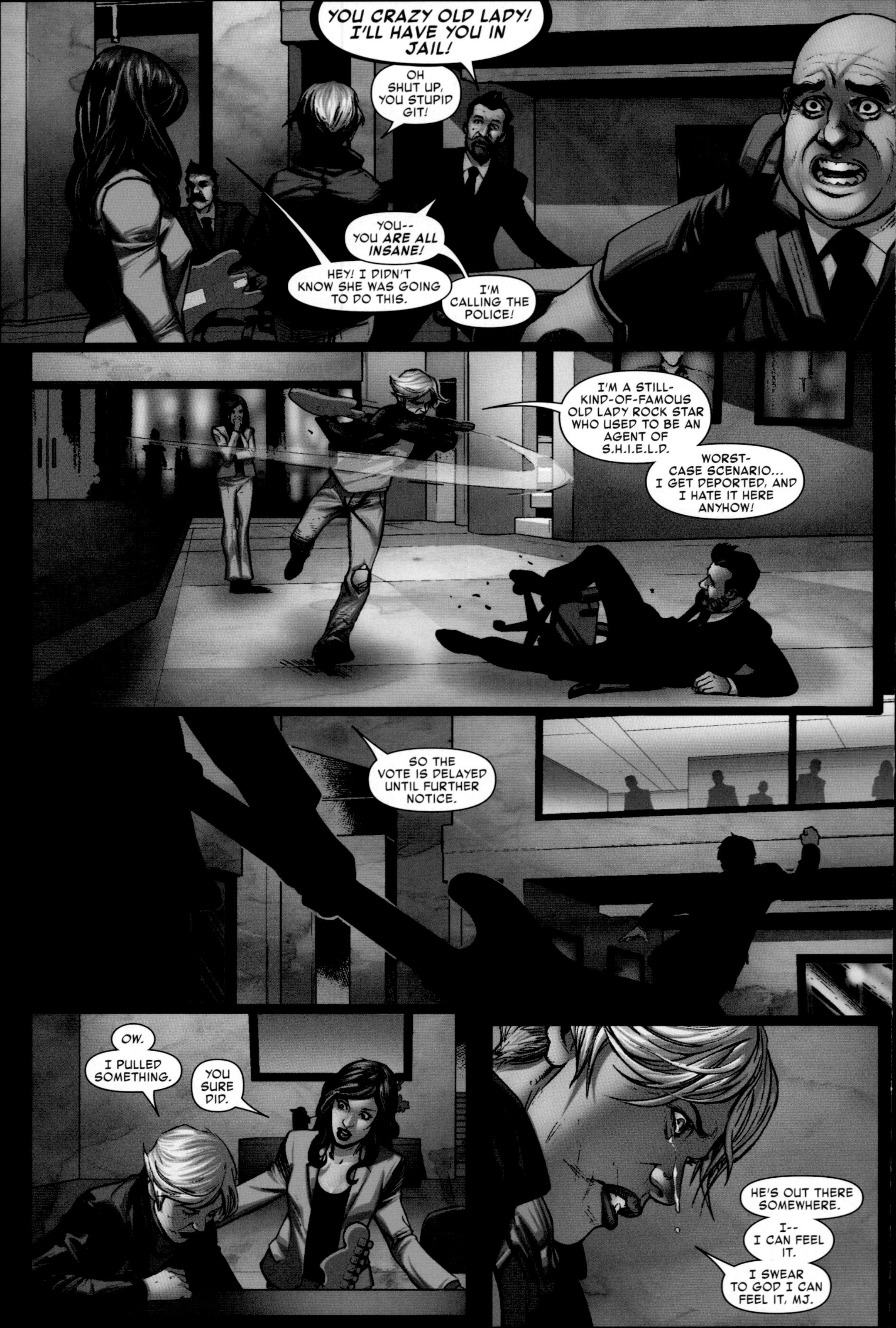
YOU CRAZY OLD LADY! I'LL HAVE YOU IN JAIL!
OH SHUT UP, YOU STUPID GIT!
YOU-- YOU ARE ALL INSANE!
HEY! I DIDN'T KNOW SHE WAS GOING TO DO THIS.
I'M CALLING THE POLICE!
I'M A STILL-KIND-OF-FAMOUS OLD LADY ROCK STAR WHO USED TO BE AN AGENT OF S.H.I.E.L.D.
WORST-CASE SCENARIO... I GET DEPORTED, AND I HATE IT HERE ANYHOW!
SO THE VOTE IS DELAYED UNTIL FURTHER NOTICE.
OW.
I PULLED SOMETHING.
YOU SURE DID.
HE'S OUT THERE SOMEWHERE.
I-- I CAN FEEL IT.
I SWEAR TO GOD I CAN FEEL IT, MJ.

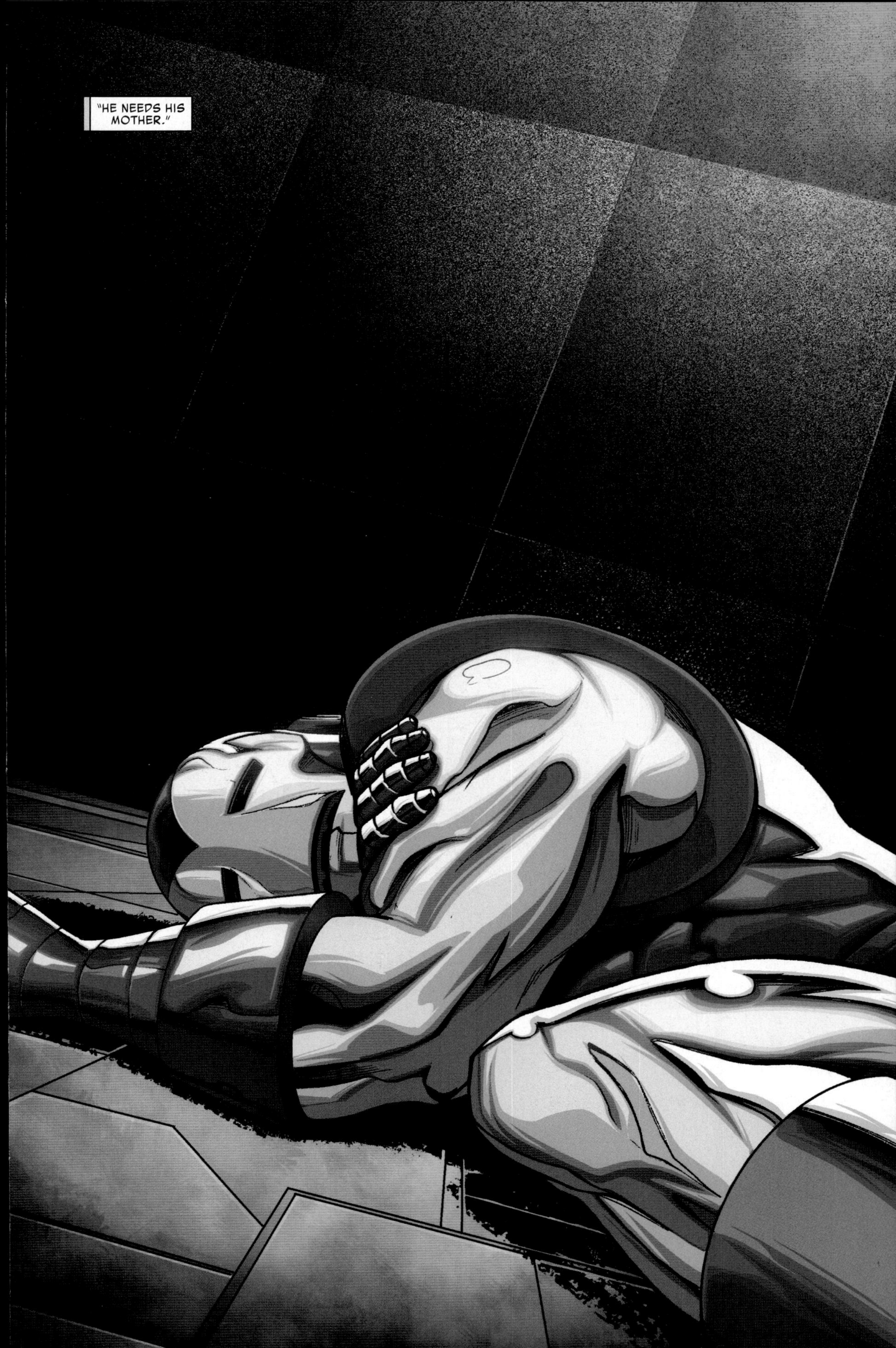
"HE NEEDS HIS MOTHER."

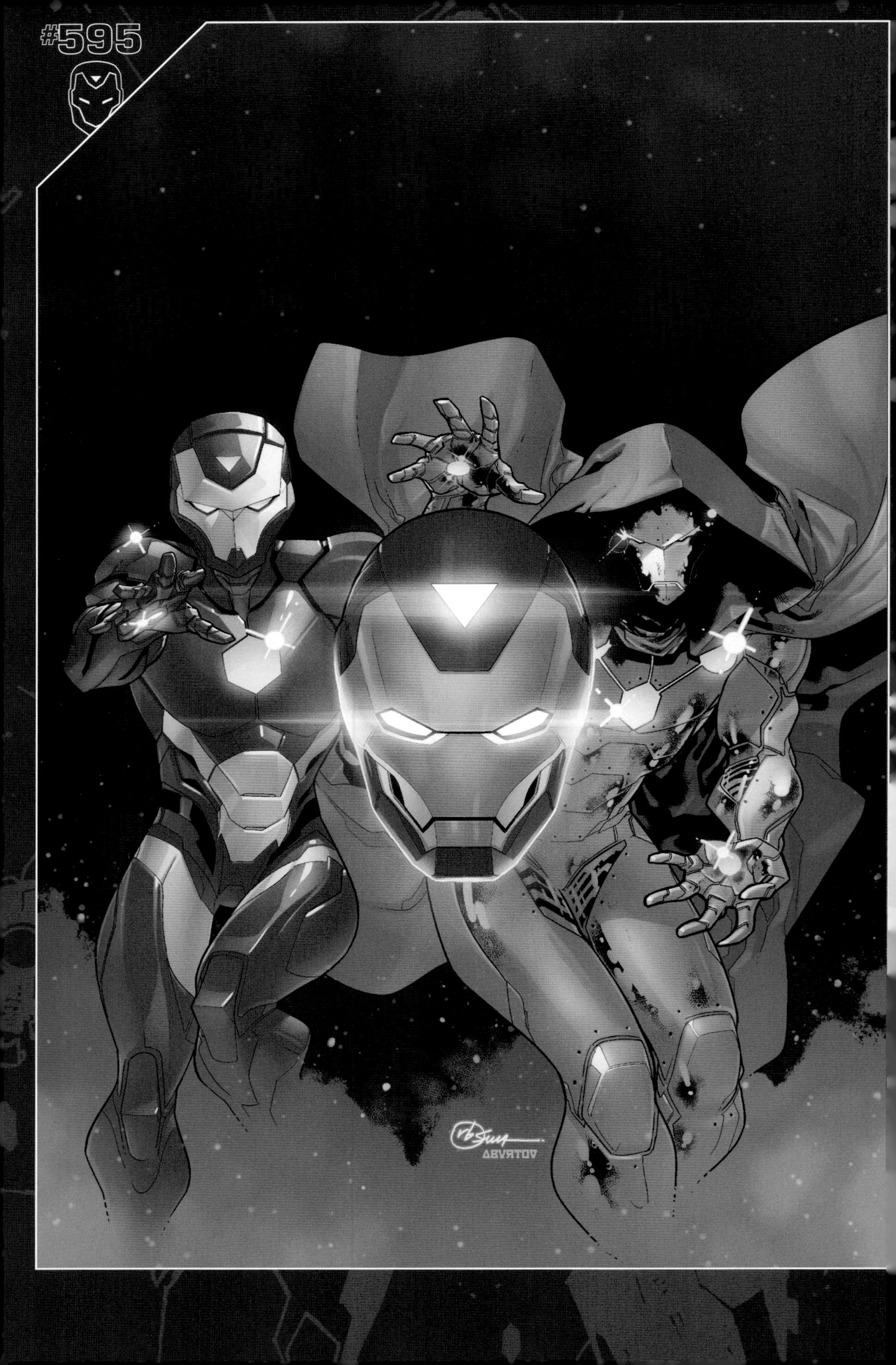
#595

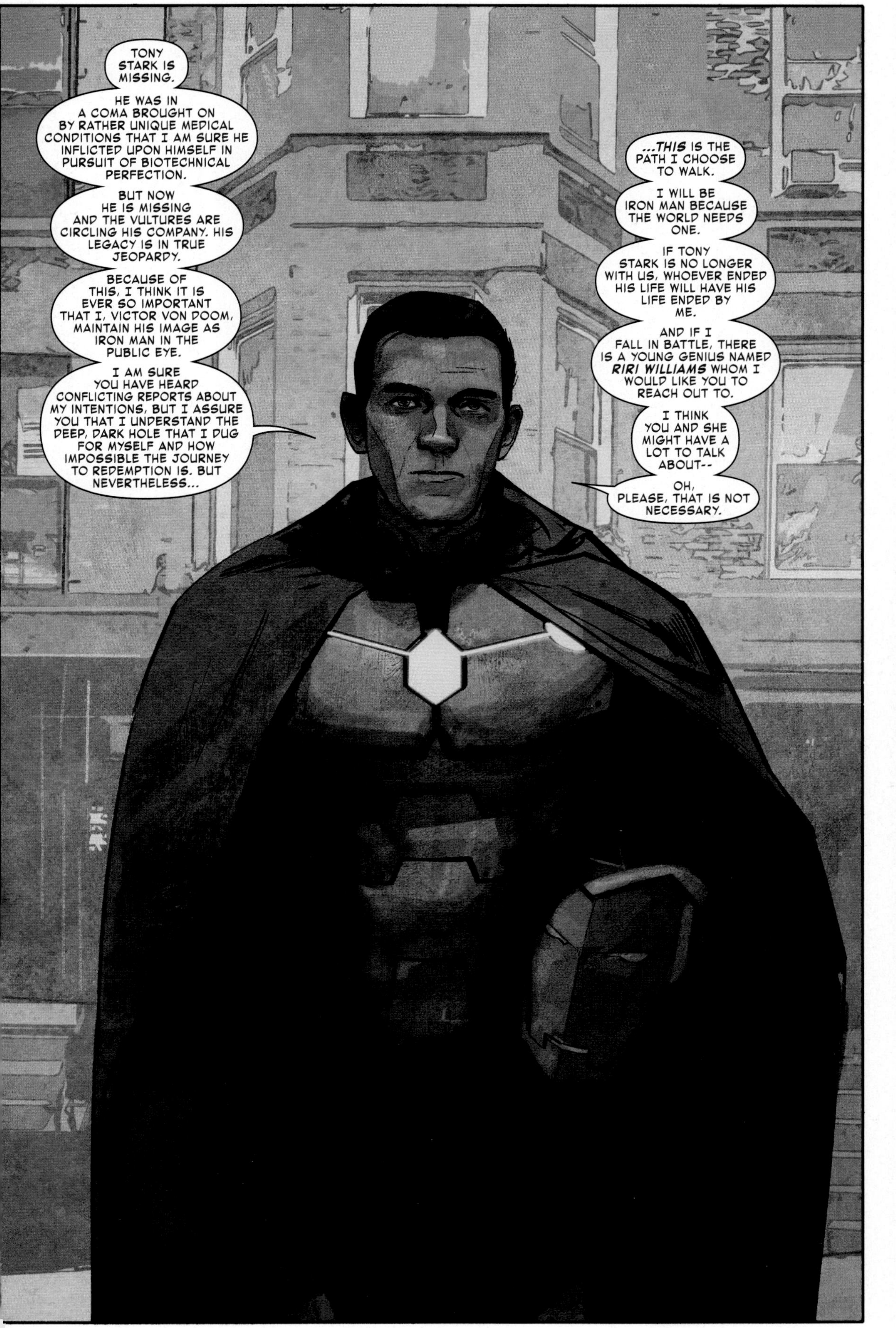
TONY STARK IS MISSING.
HE WAS IN A COMA BROUGHT ON BY RATHER UNIQUE MEDICAL CONDITIONS THAT I AM SURE HE INFLICTED UPON HIMSELF IN PURSUIT OF BIOTECHNICAL PERFECTION.
BUT NOW HE IS MISSING AND THE VULTURES ARE CIRCLING HIS COMPANY. HIS LEGACY IS IN TRUE JEOPARDY.
BECAUSE OF THIS, I THINK IT IS EVER SO IMPORTANT THAT I, VICTOR VON DOOM, MAINTAIN HIS IMAGE AS IRON MAN IN THE PUBLIC EYE.
I AM SURE YOU HAVE HEARD CONFLICTING REPORTS ABOUT MY INTENTIONS, BUT I ASSURE YOU THAT I UNDERSTAND THE DEEP, DARK HOLE THAT I DUG FOR MYSELF AND HOW IMPOSSIBLE THE JOURNEY TO REDEMPTION IS. BUT NEVERTHELESS...
...*THIS* IS THE PATH I CHOOSE TO WALK.
I WILL BE IRON MAN BECAUSE THE WORLD NEEDS ONE.
IF TONY STARK IS NO LONGER WITH US, WHOEVER ENDED HIS LIFE WILL HAVE HIS LIFE ENDED BY ME.
AND IF I FALL IN BATTLE, THERE IS A YOUNG GENIUS NAMED *RIRI WILLIAMS* WHOM I WOULD LIKE YOU TO REACH OUT TO.
I THINK YOU AND SHE MIGHT HAVE A LOT TO TALK ABOUT--
OH, PLEASE, THAT IS NOT NECESSARY.

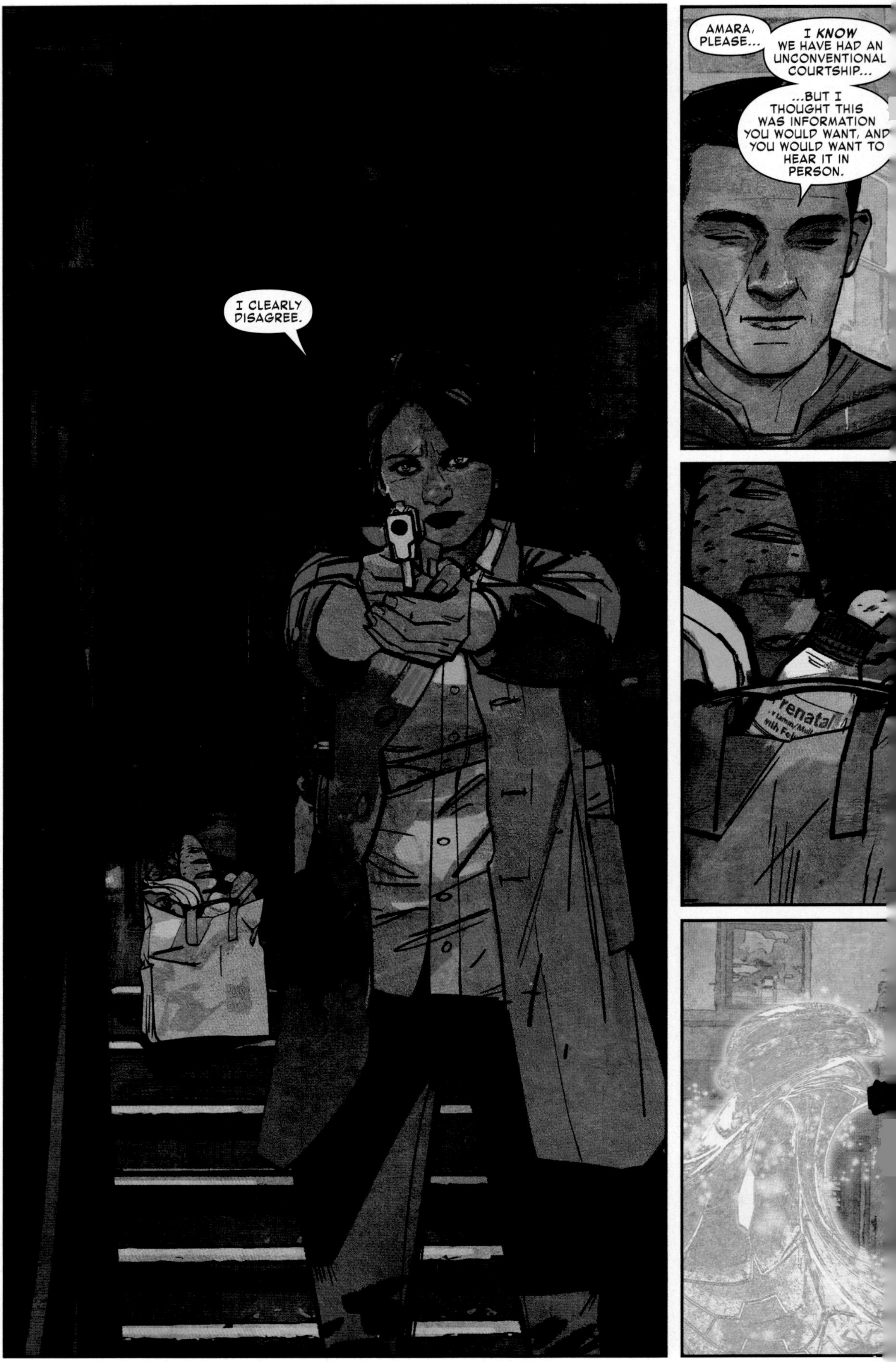
I CLEARLY DISAGREE.
AMARA, PLEASE...
I *KNOW* WE HAVE HAD AN UNCONVENTIONAL COURTSHIP...
...BUT I THOUGHT THIS WAS INFORMATION YOU WOULD WANT, AND YOU WOULD WANT TO HEAR IT IN PERSON.

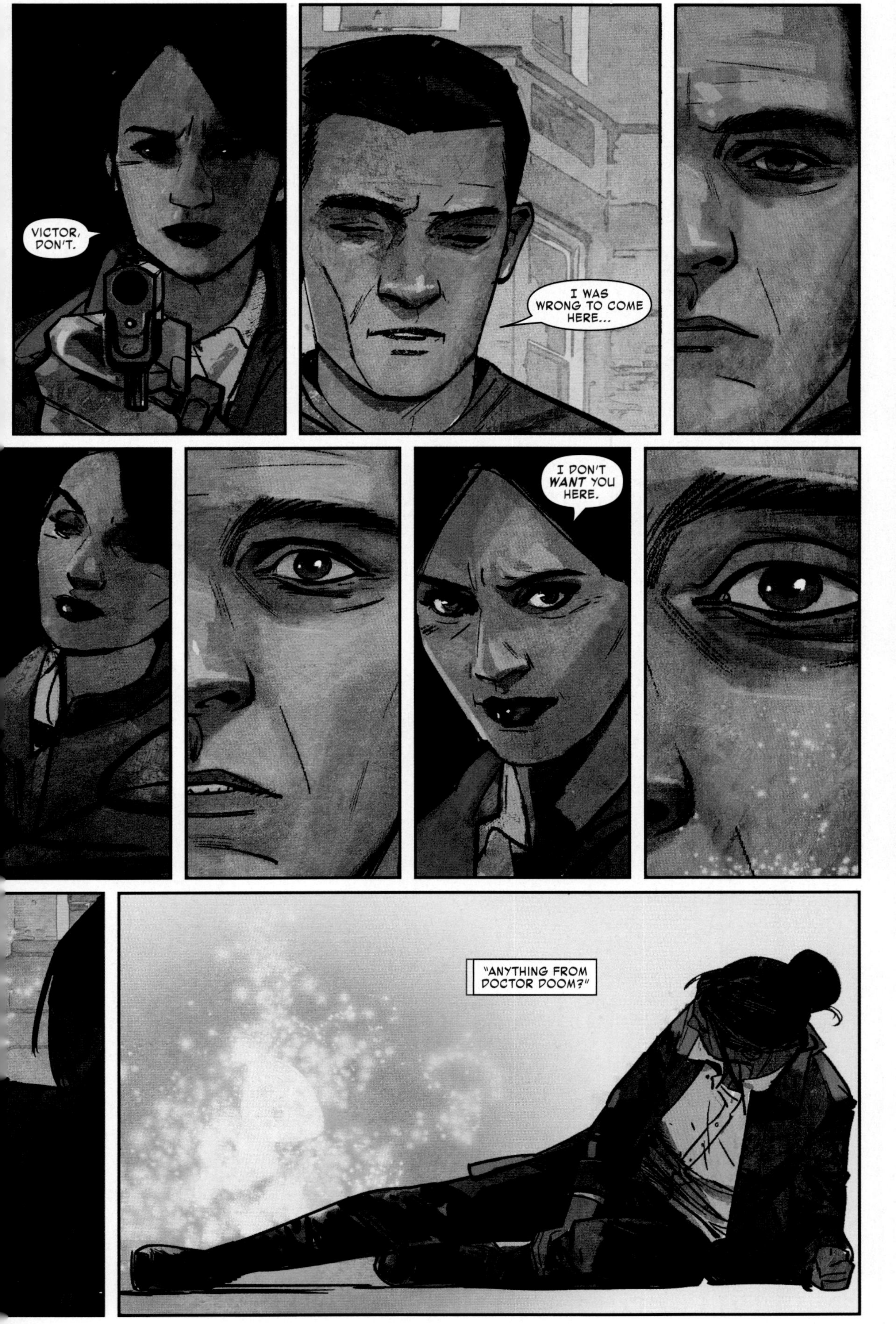
VICTOR, DON'T.
I WAS WRONG TO COME HERE...
I DON'T *WANT* YOU HERE.
"ANYTHING FROM DOCTOR DOOM?"

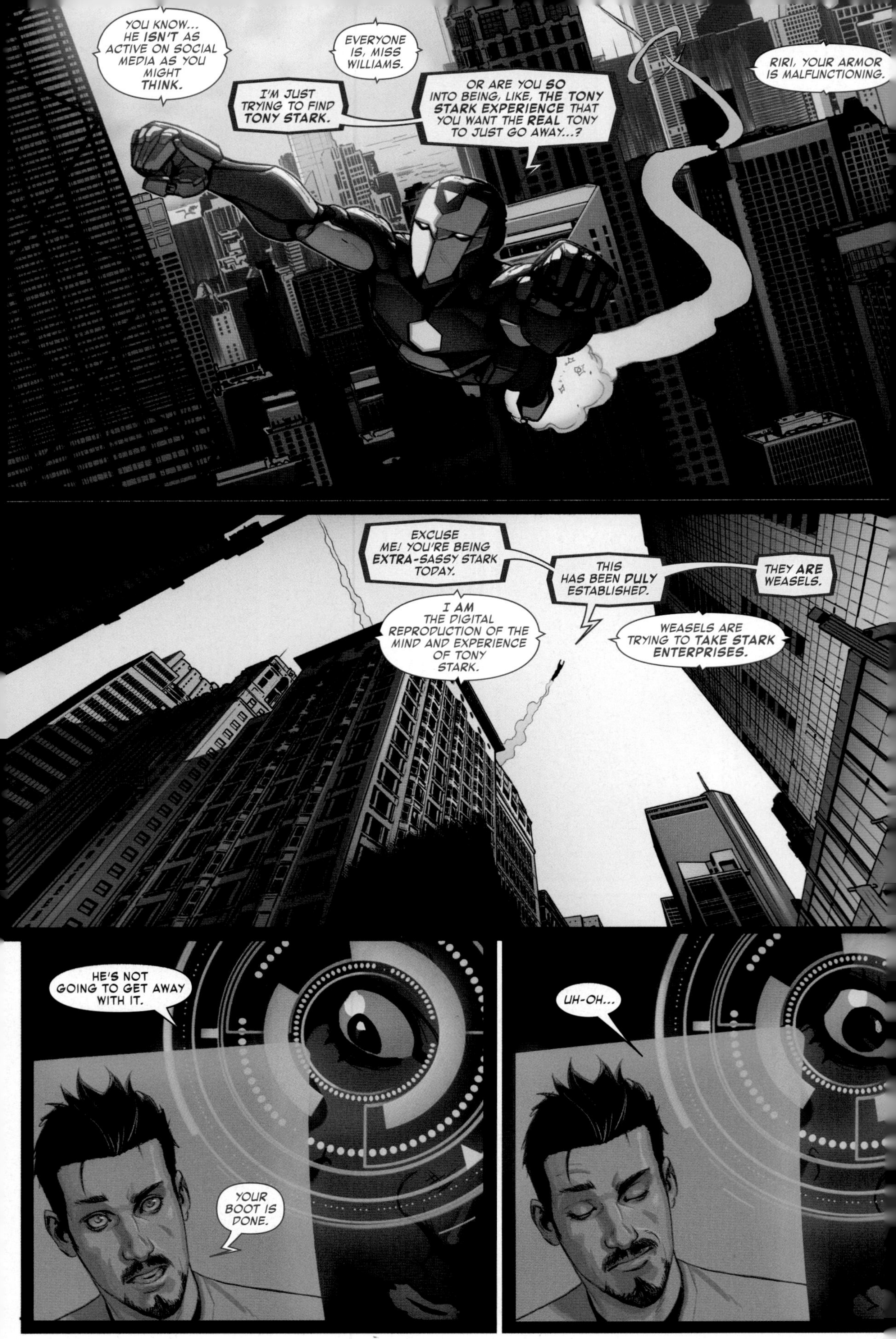

YOU KNOW... HE ISN'T AS ACTIVE ON SOCIAL MEDIA AS YOU MIGHT THINK.
EVERYONE IS, MISS WILLIAMS.
I'M JUST TRYING TO FIND TONY STARK.
OR ARE YOU SO INTO BEING, LIKE, THE TONY STARK EXPERIENCE THAT YOU WANT THE REAL TONY TO JUST GO AWAY...?
RIRI, YOUR ARMOR IS MALFUNCTIONING.
EXCUSE ME! YOU'RE BEING EXTRA-SASSY STARK TODAY.
I AM THE DIGITAL REPRODUCTION OF THE MIND AND EXPERIENCE OF TONY STARK.
THIS HAS BEEN DULY ESTABLISHED.
THEY ARE WEASELS.
WEASELS ARE TRYING TO TAKE STARK ENTERPRISES.
HE'S NOT GOING TO GET AWAY WITH IT.
YOUR BOOT IS DONE.
UH-OH...

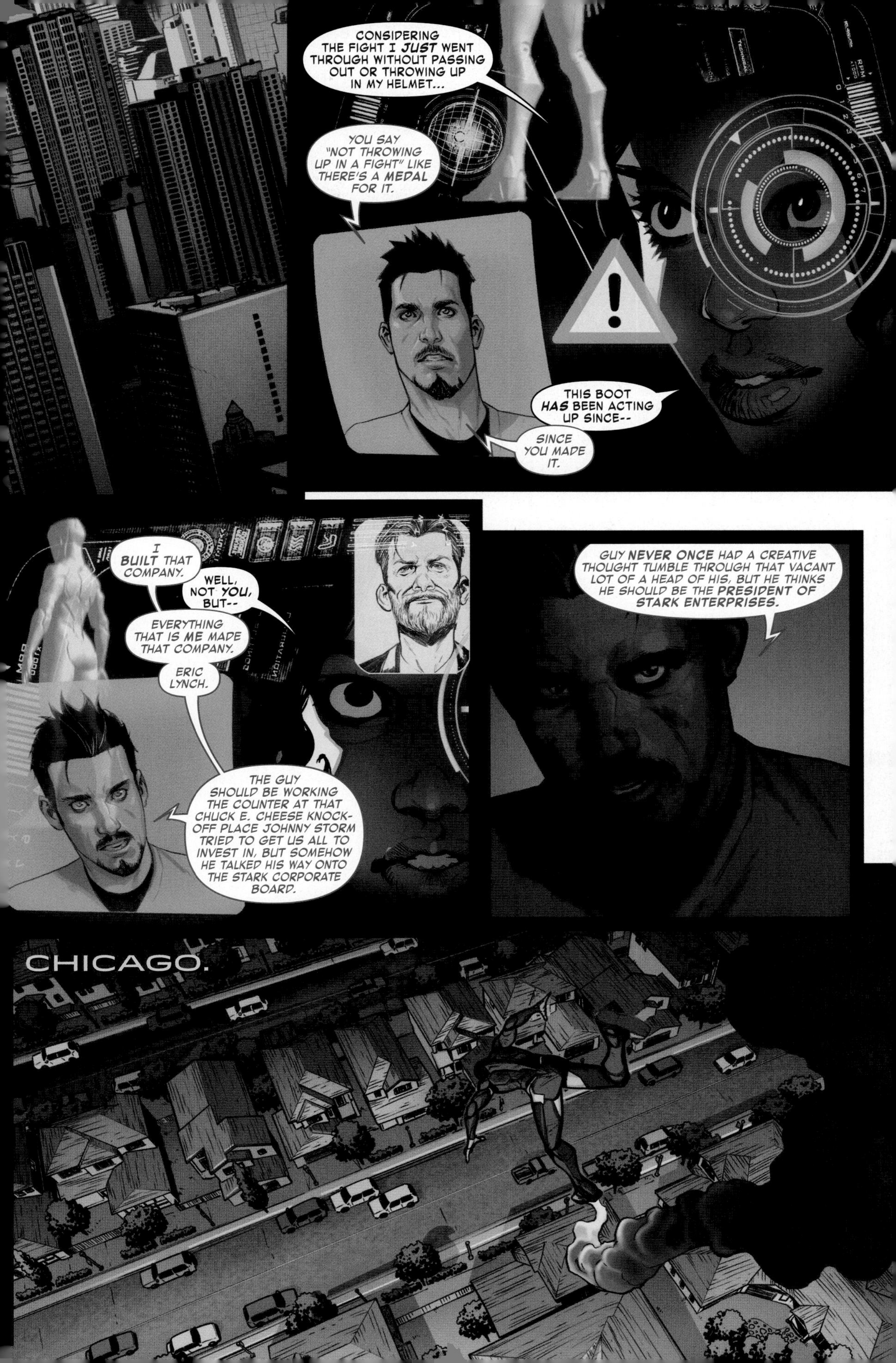
CONSIDERING THE FIGHT I JUST WENT THROUGH WITHOUT PASSING OUT OR THROWING UP IN MY HELMET...
YOU SAY "NOT THROWING UP IN A FIGHT" LIKE THERE'S A MEDAL FOR IT.
THIS BOOT HAS BEEN ACTING UP SINCE--
SINCE YOU MADE IT.
I BUILT THAT COMPANY.
WELL, NOT YOU, BUT--
EVERYTHING THAT IS ME MADE THAT COMPANY.
ERIC LYNCH.
THE GUY SHOULD BE WORKING THE COUNTER AT THAT CHUCK E. CHEESE KNOCK-OFF PLACE JOHNNY STORM TRIED TO GET US ALL TO INVEST IN, BUT SOMEHOW HE TALKED HIS WAY ONTO THE STARK CORPORATE BOARD.
GUY NEVER ONCE HAD A CREATIVE THOUGHT TUMBLE THROUGH THAT VACANT LOT OF A HEAD OF HIS, BUT HE THINKS HE SHOULD BE THE PRESIDENT OF STARK ENTERPRISES.
CHICAGO.

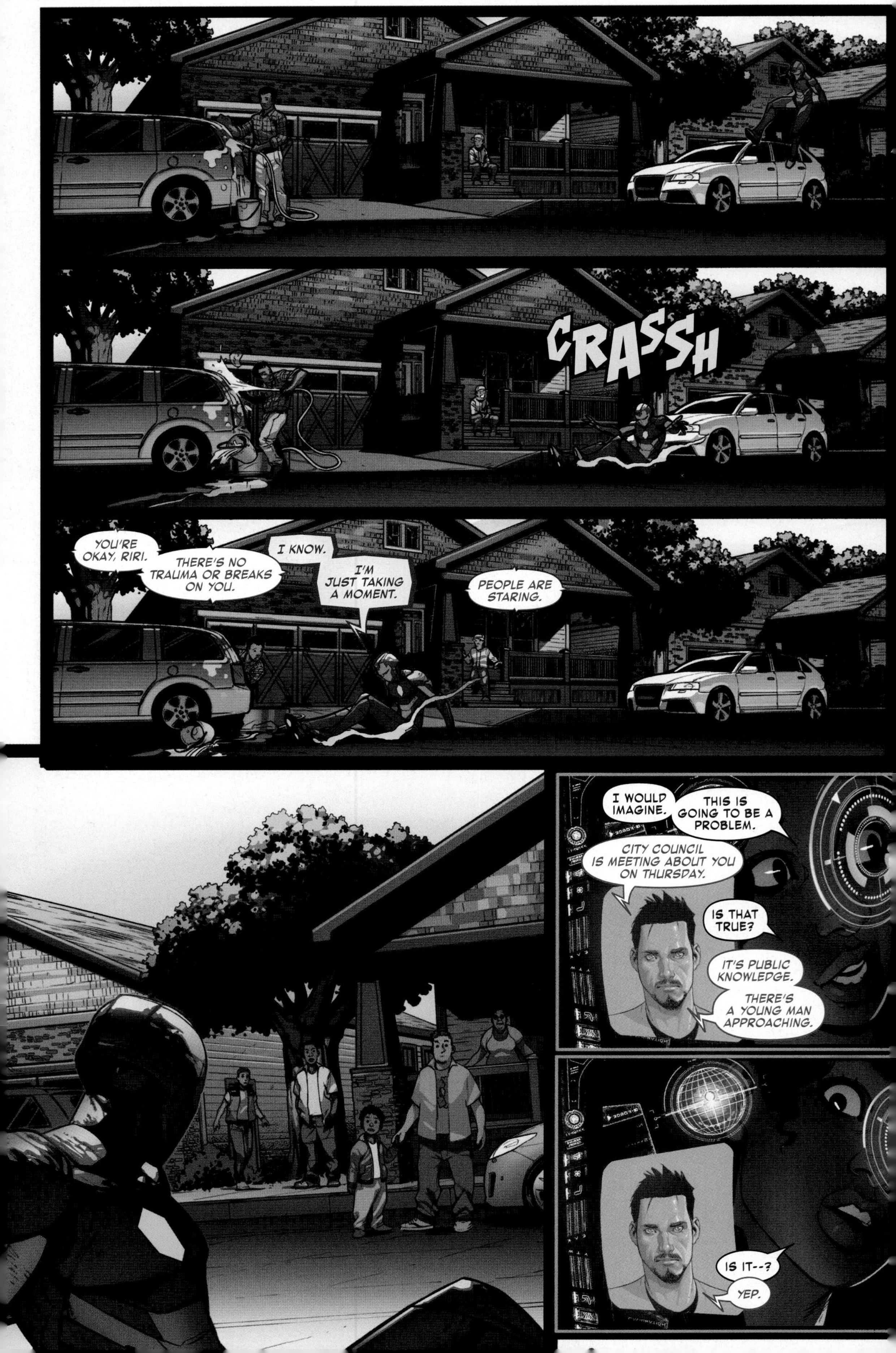
CRASSH
YOU'RE OKAY, RIRI.
THERE'S NO TRAUMA OR BREAKS ON YOU.
I KNOW.
I'M JUST TAKING A MOMENT.
PEOPLE ARE STARING.
I WOULD IMAGINE.
THIS IS GOING TO BE A PROBLEM.
CITY COUNCIL IS MEETING ABOUT YOU ON THURSDAY.
IS THAT TRUE?
IT'S PUBLIC KNOWLEDGE.
THERE'S A YOUNG MAN APPROACHING.
IS IT--?
YEP.

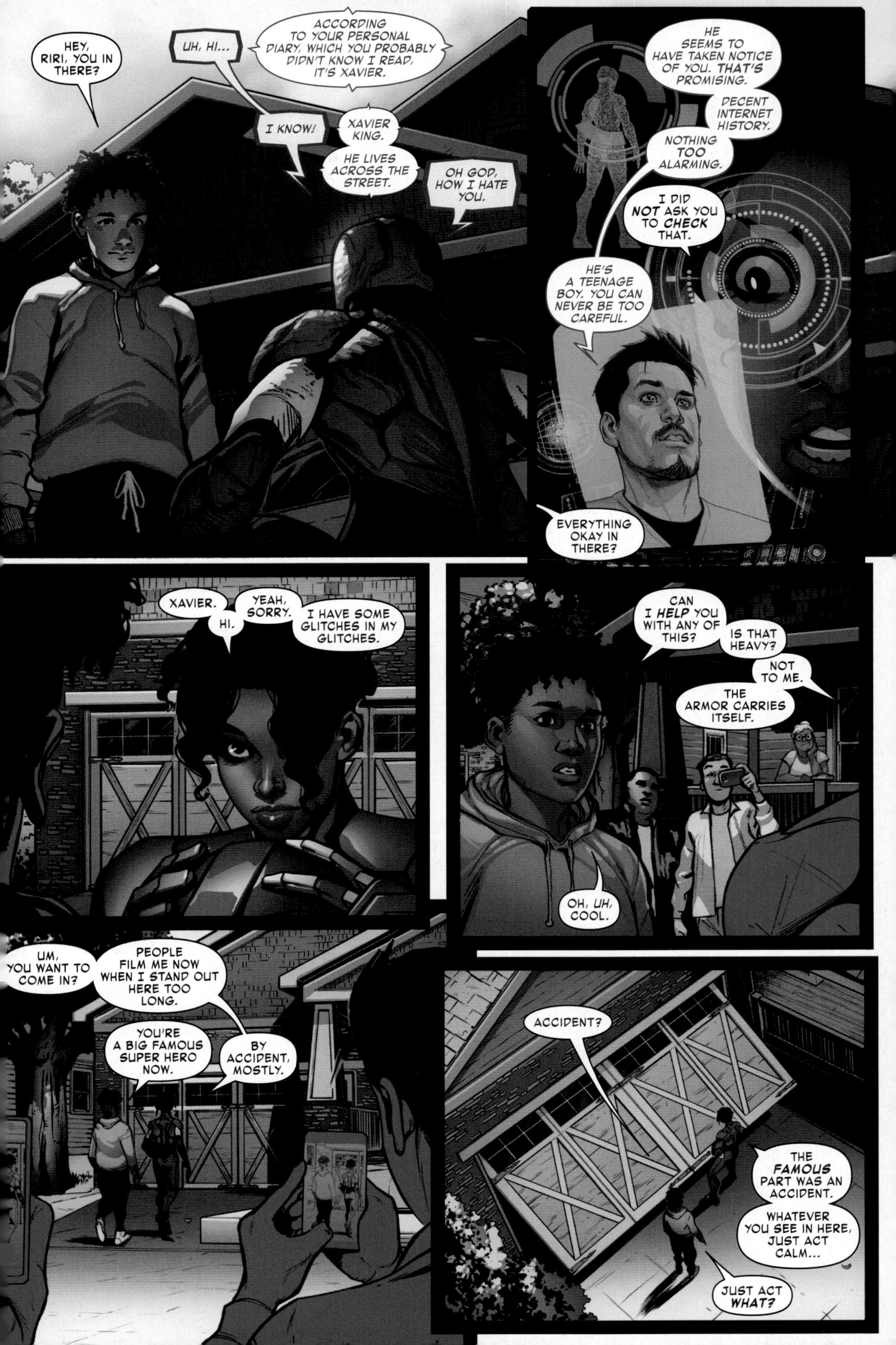
HEY, RIRI, YOU IN THERE?
UH, HI...
ACCORDING TO YOUR PERSONAL DIARY, WHICH YOU PROBABLY DIDN'T KNOW I READ, IT'S XAVIER.
I KNOW!
XAVIER KING.
HE LIVES ACROSS THE STREET.
OH GOD, HOW I HATE YOU.
HE SEEMS TO HAVE TAKEN NOTICE OF YOU. THAT'S PROMISING.
DECENT INTERNET HISTORY.
NOTHING TOO ALARMING.
I DID NOT ASK YOU TO CHECK THAT.
HE'S A TEENAGE BOY. YOU CAN NEVER BE TOO CAREFUL.
EVERYTHING OKAY IN THERE?
XAVIER.
HI.
YEAH, SORRY.
I HAVE SOME GLITCHES IN MY GLITCHES.
CAN I HELP YOU WITH ANY OF THIS?
IS THAT HEAVY?
NOT TO ME.
THE ARMOR CARRIES ITSELF.
OH, UH, COOL.
UM, YOU WANT TO COME IN?
PEOPLE FILM ME NOW WHEN I STAND OUT HERE TOO LONG.
YOU'RE A BIG FAMOUS SUPER HERO NOW.
BY ACCIDENT, MOSTLY.
ACCIDENT?
THE FAMOUS PART WAS AN ACCIDENT.
WHATEVER YOU SEE IN HERE, JUST ACT CALM...
JUST ACT WHAT?

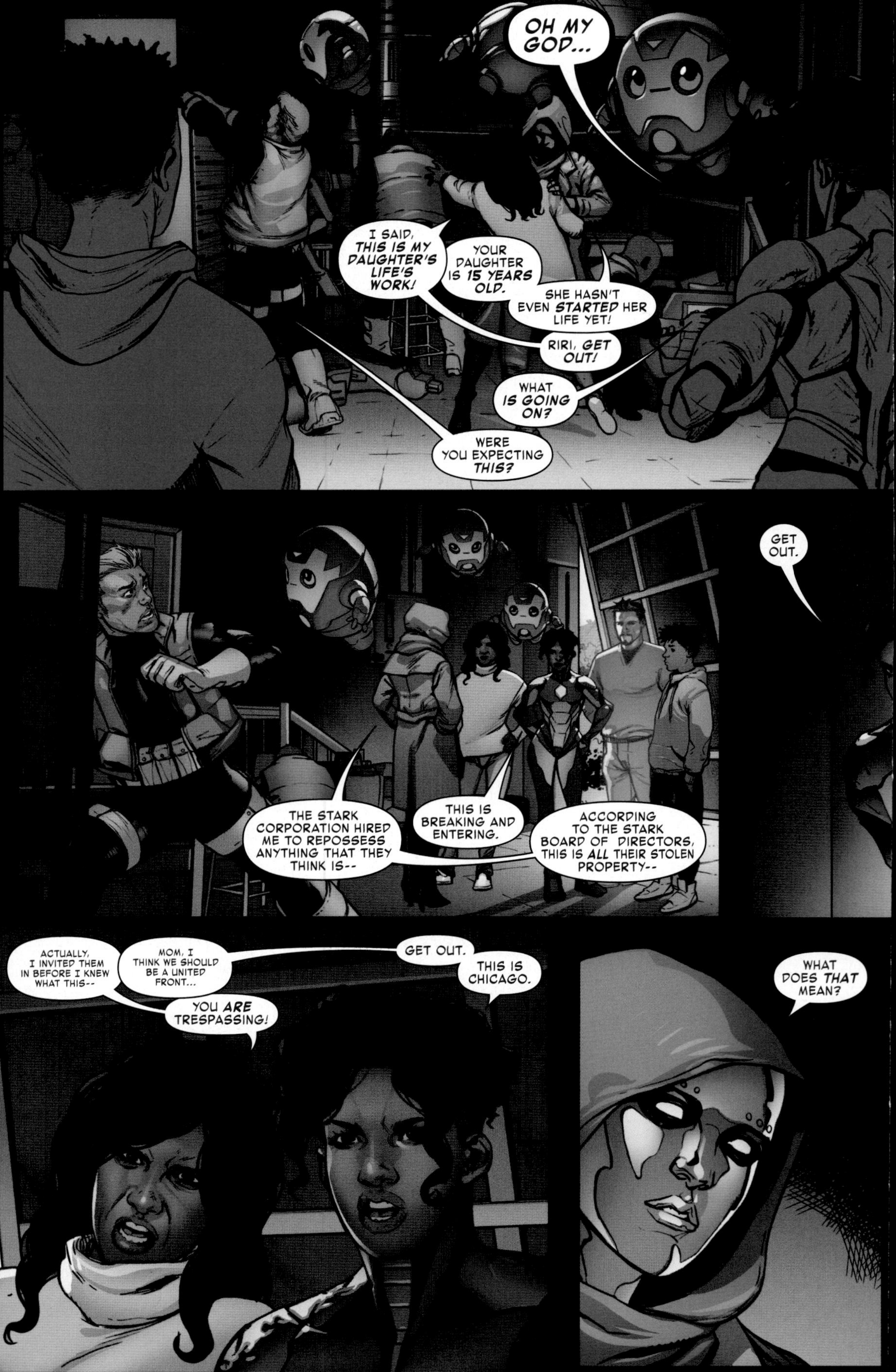

OH MY GOD...
I SAID, THIS IS MY DAUGHTER'S LIFE'S WORK!
YOUR DAUGHTER IS 15 YEARS OLD.
SHE HASN'T EVEN STARTED HER LIFE YET!
RIRI, GET OUT!
WHAT IS GOING ON?
WERE YOU EXPECTING THIS?
GET OUT.
THE STARK CORPORATION HIRED ME TO REPOSSESS ANYTHING THAT THEY THINK IS--
THIS IS BREAKING AND ENTERING.
ACCORDING TO THE STARK BOARD OF DIRECTORS, THIS IS ALL THEIR STOLEN PROPERTY--
ACTUALLY, I INVITED THEM IN BEFORE I KNEW WHAT THIS--
MOM, I THINK WE SHOULD BE A UNITED FRONT...
GET OUT.
THIS IS CHICAGO.
YOU ARE TRESPASSING!
WHAT DOES THAT MEAN?

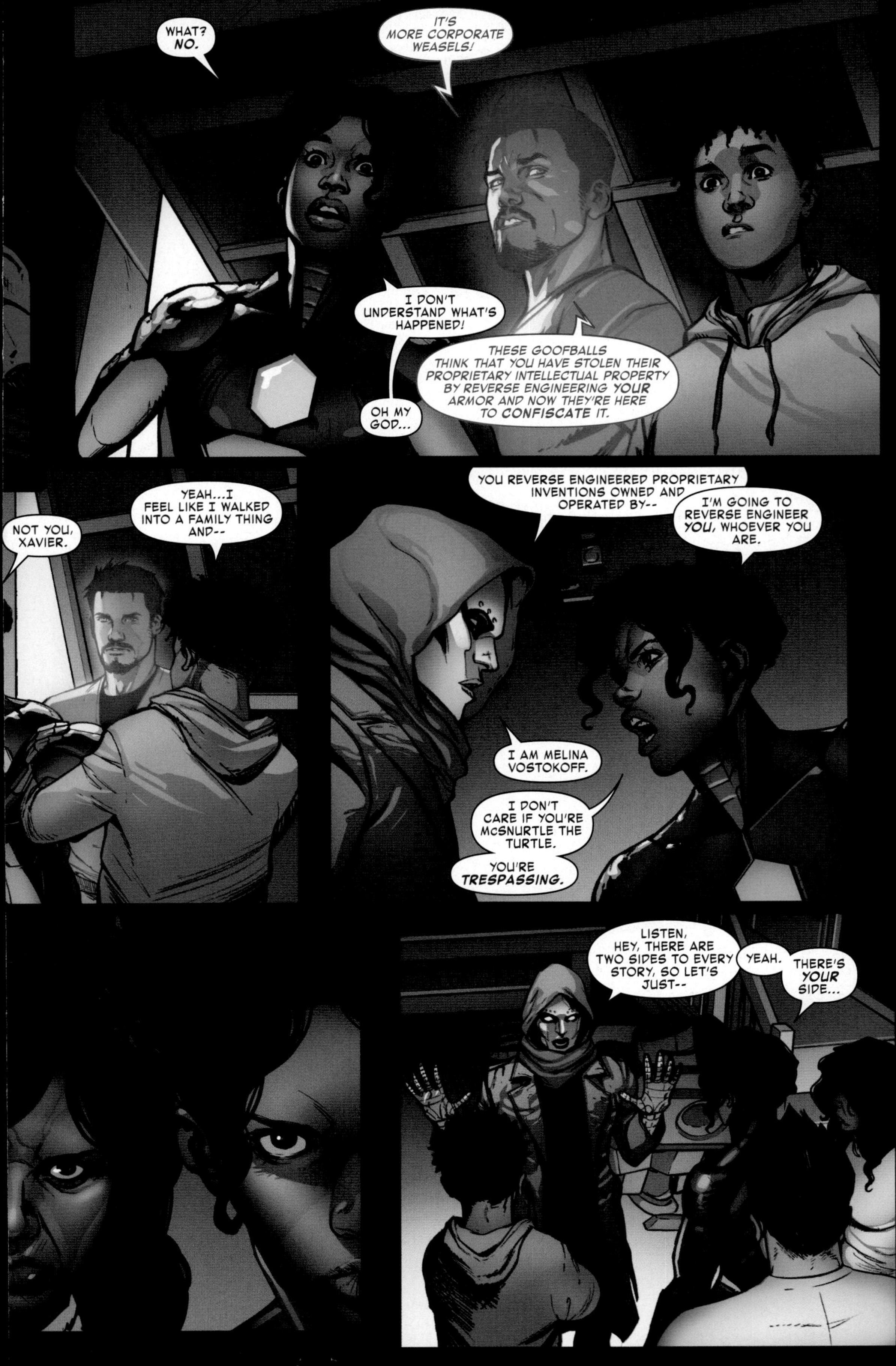
WHAT? NO.
IT'S MORE CORPORATE WEASELS!
I DON'T UNDERSTAND WHAT'S HAPPENED!
OH MY GOD...
THESE GOOFBALLS THINK THAT YOU HAVE STOLEN THEIR PROPRIETARY INTELLECTUAL PROPERTY BY REVERSE ENGINEERING YOUR ARMOR AND NOW THEY'RE HERE TO CONFISCATE IT.
YEAH...I FEEL LIKE I WALKED INTO A FAMILY THING AND--
NOT YOU, XAVIER.
YOU REVERSE ENGINEERED PROPRIETARY INVENTIONS OWNED AND OPERATED BY--
I'M GOING TO REVERSE ENGINEER YOU, WHOEVER YOU ARE.
I AM MELINA VOSTOKOFF.
I DON'T CARE IF YOU'RE McSNURTLE THE TURTLE.
YOU'RE TRESPASSING.
LISTEN, HEY, THERE ARE TWO SIDES TO EVERY STORY, SO LET'S JUST--
YEAH.
THERE'S YOUR SIDE...

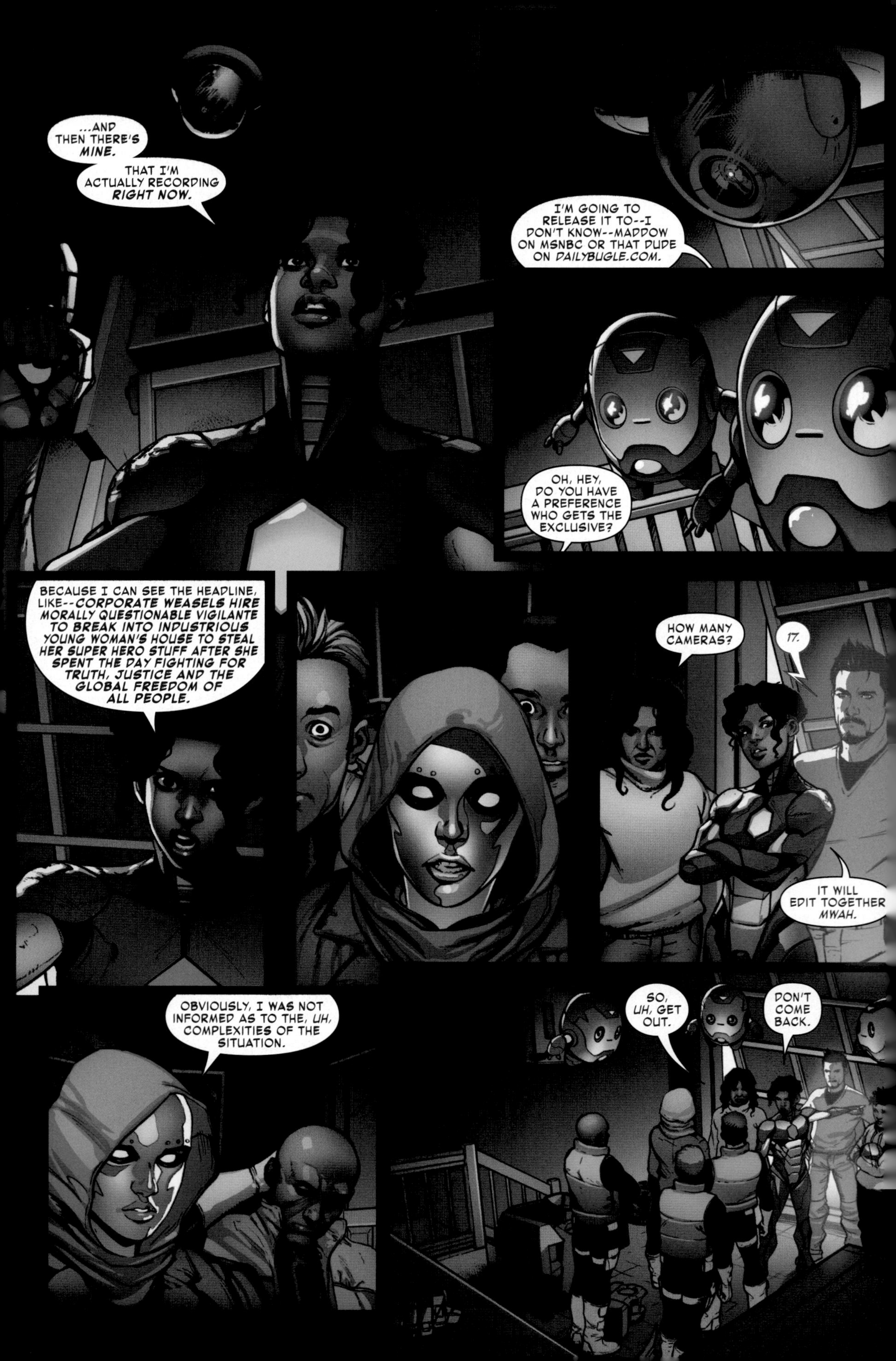
...AND THEN THERE'S *MINE.*
THAT I'M ACTUALLY RECORDING *RIGHT NOW.*
I'M GOING TO RELEASE IT TO--I DON'T KNOW--MADDOW ON MSNBC OR THAT DUDE ON *DAILYBUGLE.COM.*
OH, HEY, DO YOU HAVE A PREFERENCE WHO GETS THE EXCLUSIVE?
BECAUSE I CAN SEE THE HEADLINE, LIKE--*CORPORATE WEASELS HIRE MORALLY QUESTIONABLE VIGILANTE TO BREAK INTO INDUSTRIOUS YOUNG WOMAN'S HOUSE TO STEAL HER SUPER HERO STUFF AFTER SHE SPENT THE DAY FIGHTING FOR TRUTH, JUSTICE AND THE GLOBAL FREEDOM OF ALL PEOPLE.*
HOW MANY CAMERAS?
17.
IT WILL EDIT TOGETHER *MWAH.*
OBVIOUSLY, I WAS NOT INFORMED AS TO THE, *UH,* COMPLEXITIES OF THE SITUATION.
SO, *UH,* GET OUT.
DON'T COME BACK.

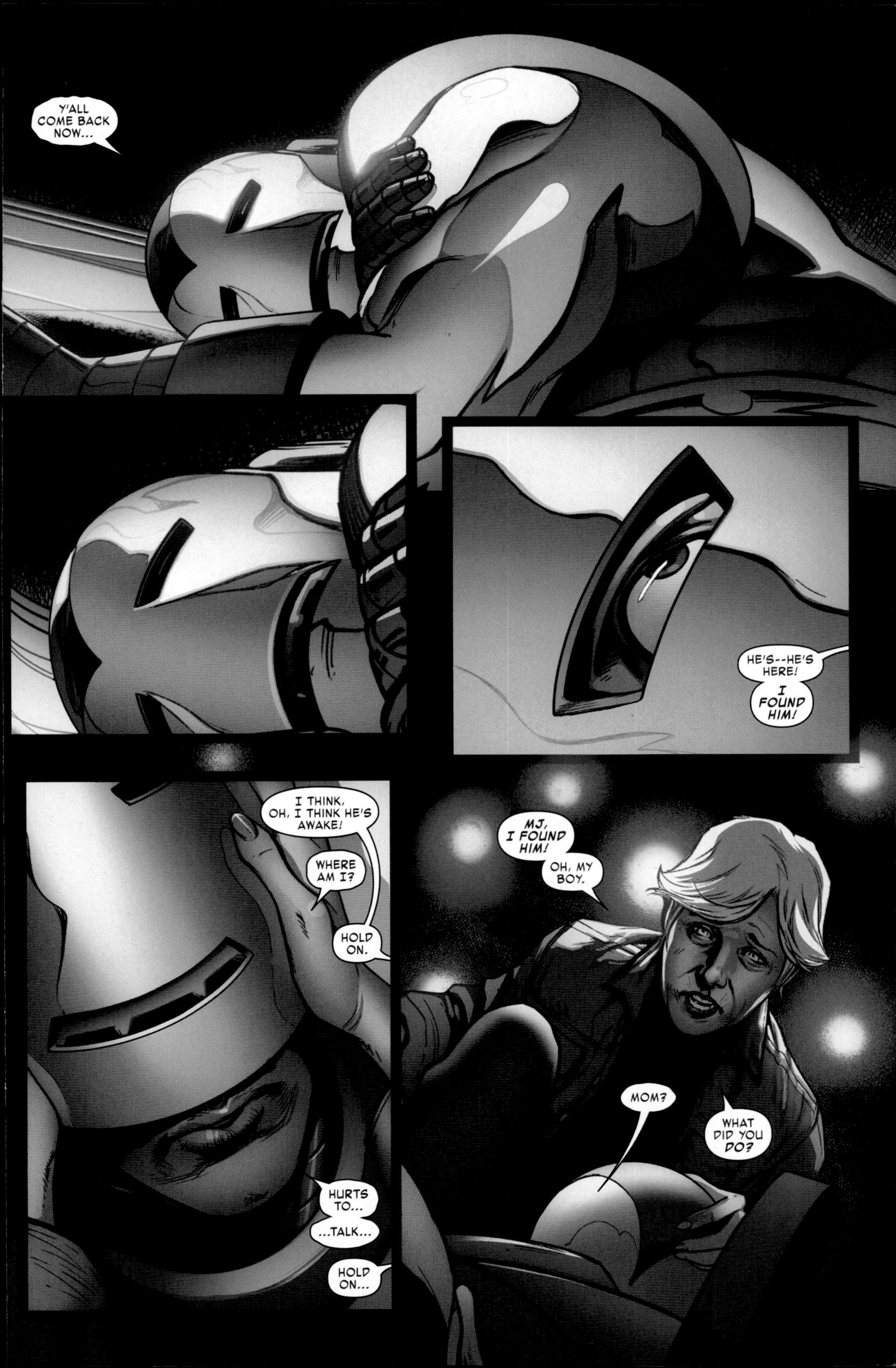
Y'ALL COME BACK NOW...
HE'S--HE'S HERE!
I FOUND HIM!
I THINK, OH, I THINK HE'S AWAKE!
WHERE AM I?
HOLD ON.
MJ, I FOUND HIM!
OH, MY BOY.
MOM?
WHAT DID YOU DO?
HURTS TO...
...TALK...
HOLD ON...

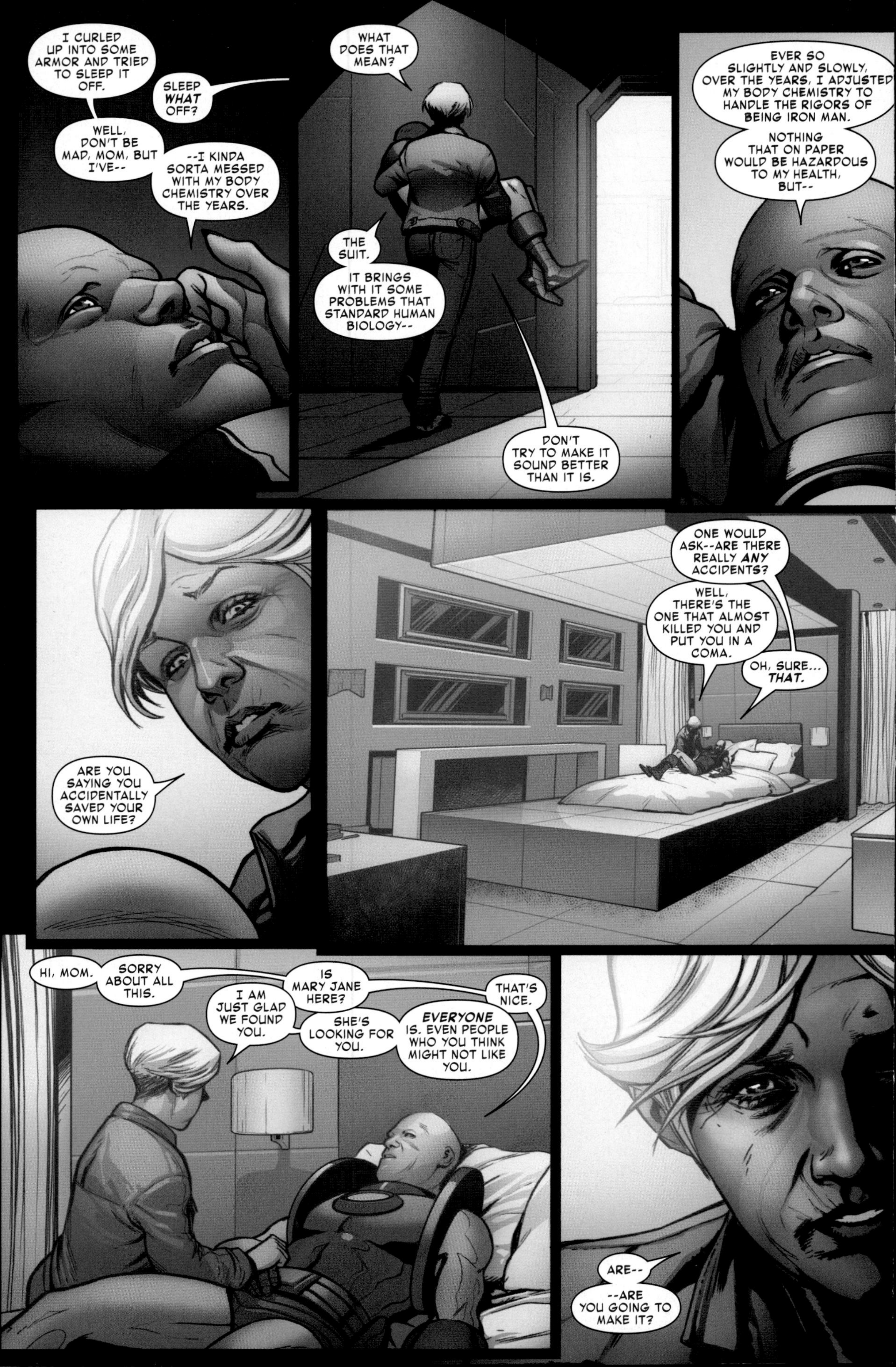
I CURLED UP INTO SOME ARMOR AND TRIED TO SLEEP IT OFF.
SLEEP *WHAT* OFF?
WELL, DON'T BE MAD, MOM, BUT I'VE--
--I KINDA SORTA MESSED WITH MY BODY CHEMISTRY OVER THE YEARS.
WHAT DOES THAT MEAN?
THE SUIT.
IT BRINGS WITH IT SOME PROBLEMS THAT STANDARD HUMAN BIOLOGY--
DON'T TRY TO MAKE IT SOUND BETTER THAN IT IS.
EVER SO SLIGHTLY AND SLOWLY, OVER THE YEARS, I ADJUSTED MY BODY CHEMISTRY TO HANDLE THE RIGORS OF BEING IRON MAN.
NOTHING THAT ON PAPER WOULD BE HAZARDOUS TO MY HEALTH, BUT--
ARE YOU SAYING YOU ACCIDENTALLY SAVED YOUR OWN LIFE?
ONE WOULD ASK--ARE THERE REALLY *ANY* ACCIDENTS?
WELL, THERE'S THE ONE THAT ALMOST KILLED YOU AND PUT YOU IN A COMA.
OH, SURE... *THAT.*
HI, MOM.
SORRY ABOUT ALL THIS.
I AM JUST GLAD WE FOUND YOU.
IS MARY JANE HERE?
SHE'S LOOKING FOR YOU.
THAT'S NICE.
*EVERYONE* IS. EVEN PEOPLE WHO YOU THINK MIGHT NOT LIKE YOU.
ARE--
--ARE YOU GOING TO MAKE IT?

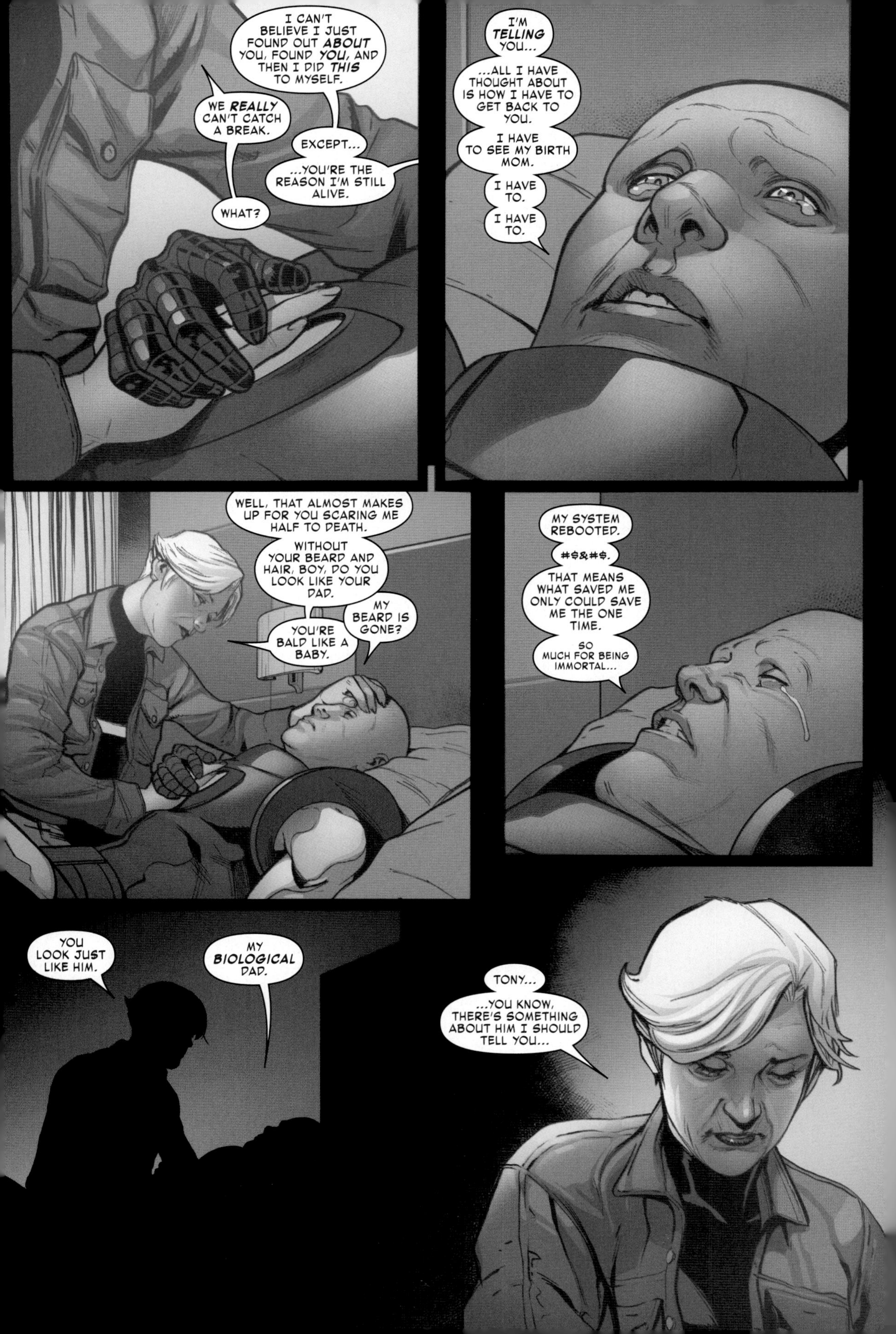
I CAN'T BELIEVE I JUST FOUND OUT ABOUT YOU, FOUND YOU, AND THEN I DID THIS TO MYSELF.
WE REALLY CAN'T CATCH A BREAK.
EXCEPT...
...YOU'RE THE REASON I'M STILL ALIVE.
WHAT?
I'M TELLING YOU...
...ALL I HAVE THOUGHT ABOUT IS HOW I HAVE TO GET BACK TO YOU.
I HAVE TO SEE MY BIRTH MOM.
I HAVE TO.
I HAVE TO.
WELL, THAT ALMOST MAKES UP FOR YOU SCARING ME HALF TO DEATH.
WITHOUT YOUR BEARD AND HAIR, BOY, DO YOU LOOK LIKE YOUR DAD.
MY BEARD IS GONE?
YOU'RE BALD LIKE A BABY.
MY SYSTEM REBOOTED.
#$&#$.
THAT MEANS WHAT SAVED ME ONLY COULD SAVE ME THE ONE TIME.
SO MUCH FOR BEING IMMORTAL...
YOU LOOK JUST LIKE HIM.
MY BIOLOGICAL DAD.
TONY...
...YOU KNOW, THERE'S SOMETHING ABOUT HIM I SHOULD TELL YOU...

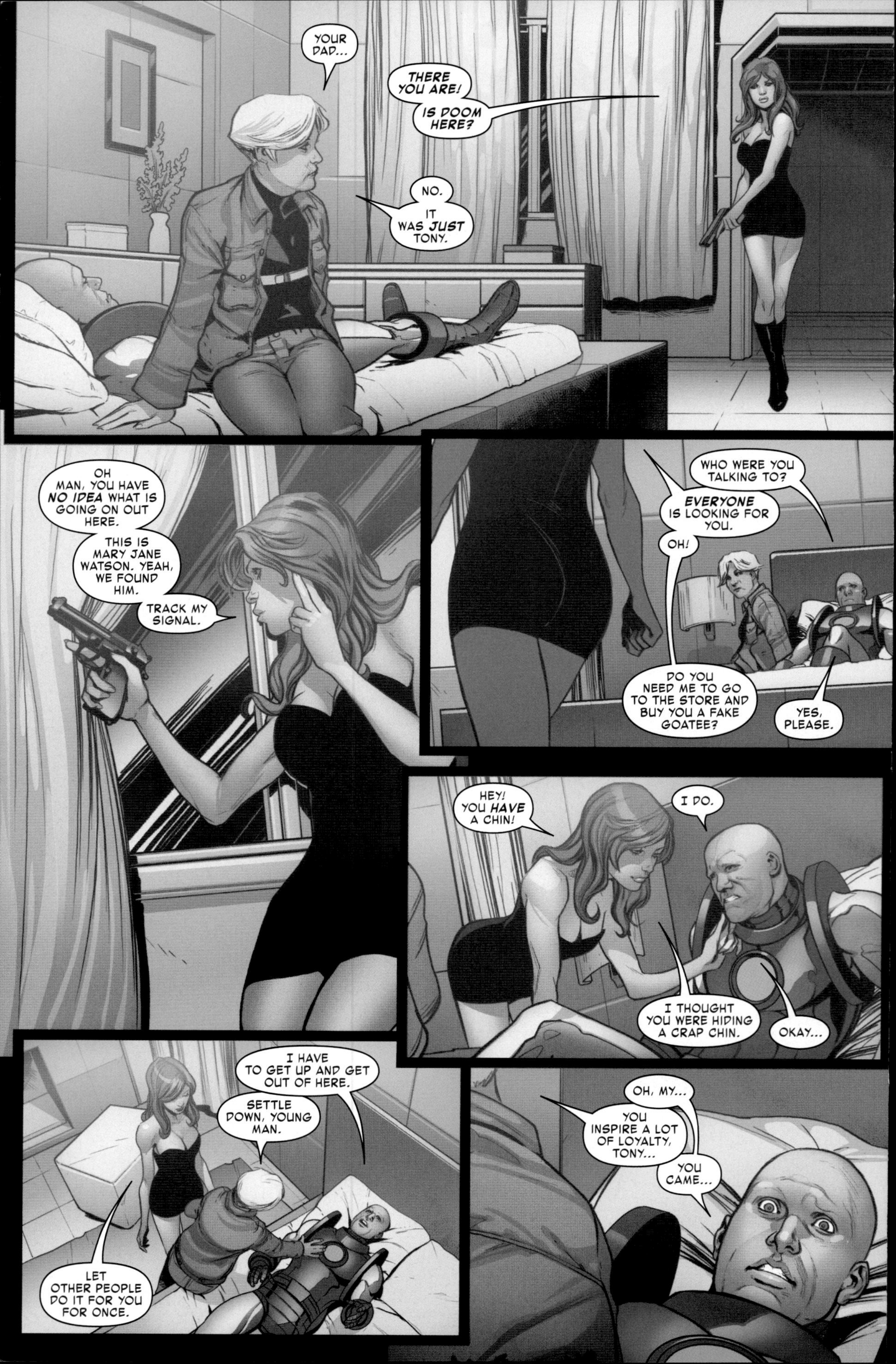
YOUR DAD...
THERE YOU ARE! IS DOOM HERE?
NO. IT WAS JUST TONY.
OH MAN, YOU HAVE NO IDEA WHAT IS GOING ON OUT HERE.
THIS IS MARY JANE WATSON. YEAH, WE FOUND HIM.
TRACK MY SIGNAL.
WHO WERE YOU TALKING TO?
EVERYONE IS LOOKING FOR YOU.
OH!
DO YOU NEED ME TO GO TO THE STORE AND BUY YOU A FAKE GOATEE?
YES, PLEASE.
HEY! YOU HAVE A CHIN!
I DO.
I THOUGHT YOU WERE HIDING A CRAP CHIN.
OKAY...
I HAVE TO GET UP AND GET OUT OF HERE.
SETTLE DOWN, YOUNG MAN.
LET OTHER PEOPLE DO IT FOR YOU FOR ONCE.
OH, MY...
YOU INSPIRE A LOT OF LOYALTY, TONY...
YOU CAME...

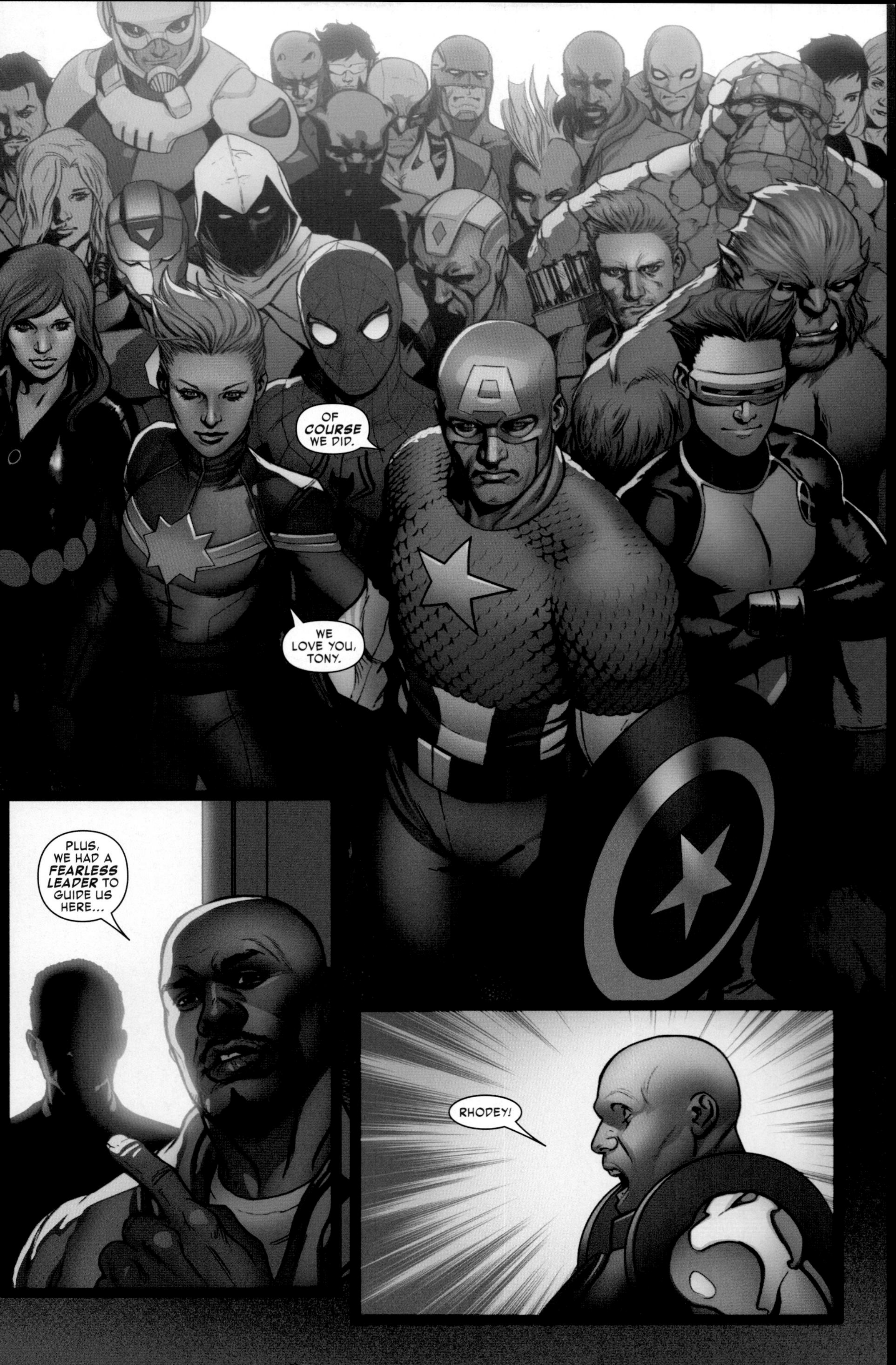
OF COURSE WE DID.
WE LOVE YOU, TONY.
PLUS, WE HAD A FEARLESS LEADER TO GUIDE US HERE...
RHODEY!

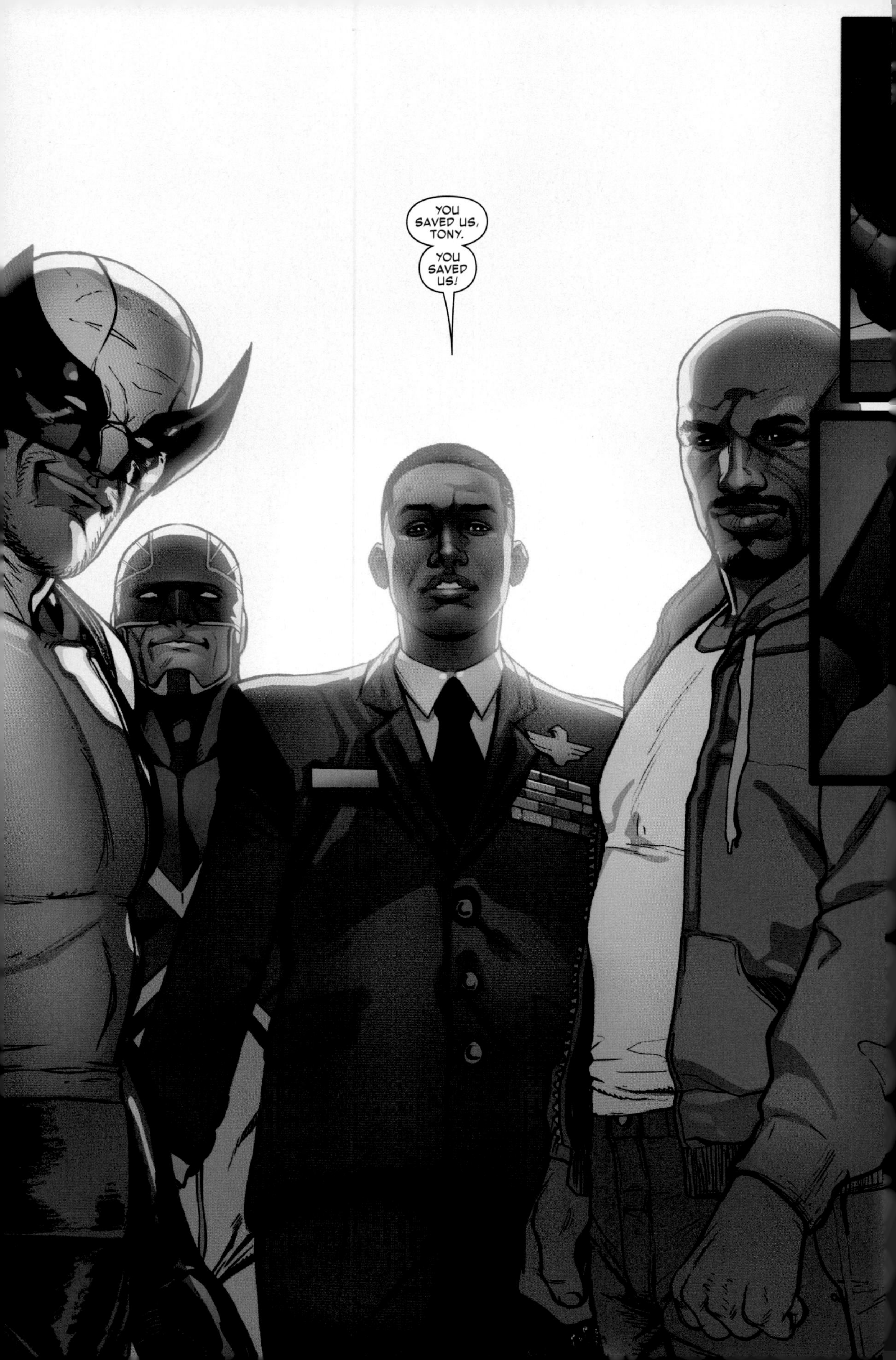
YOU SAVED US, TONY.
YOU SAVED US!

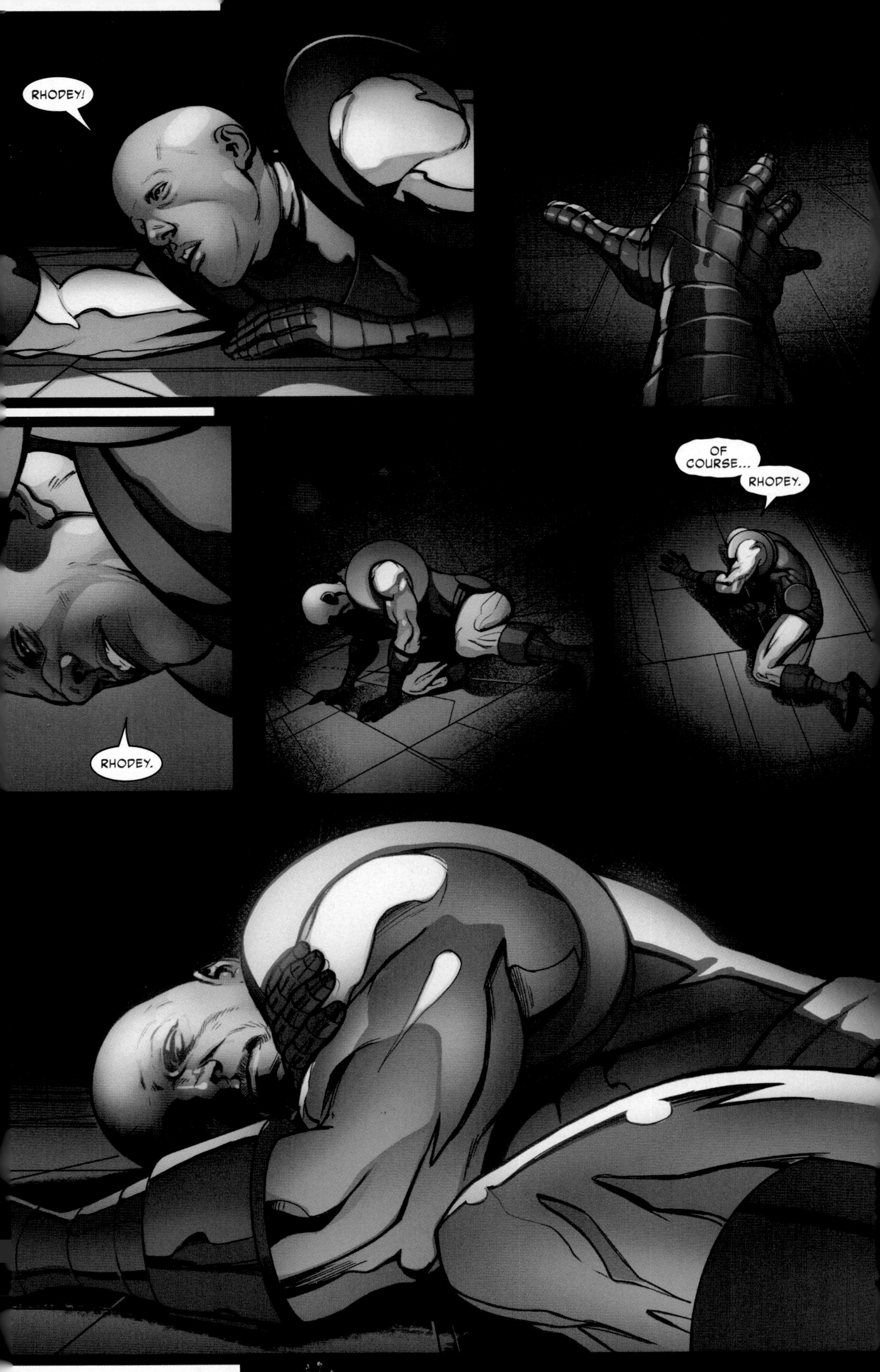
RHODEY!
RHODEY.
OF COURSE...
RHODEY.

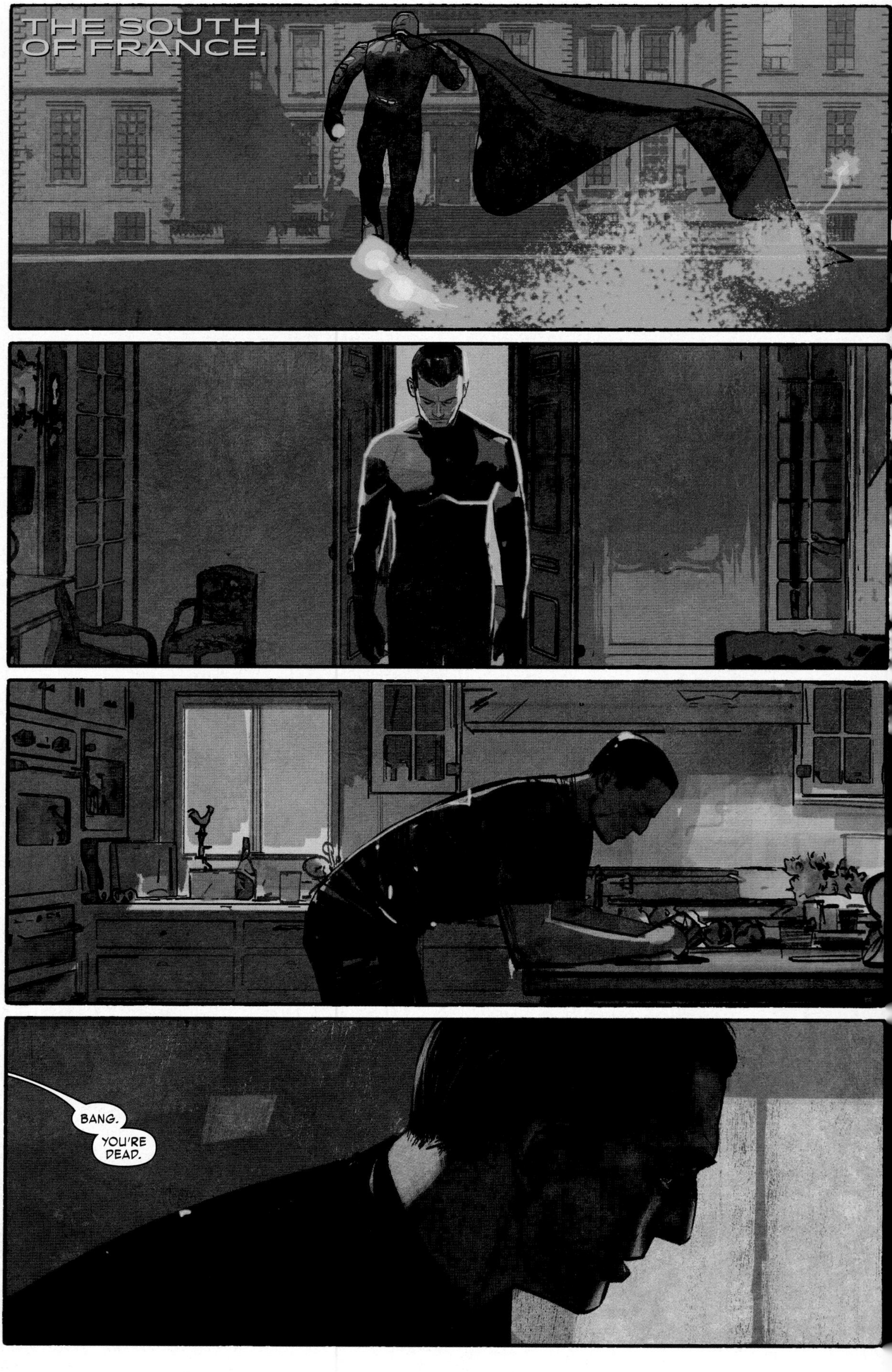
THE SOUTH OF FRANCE.
BANG.
YOU'RE DEAD.

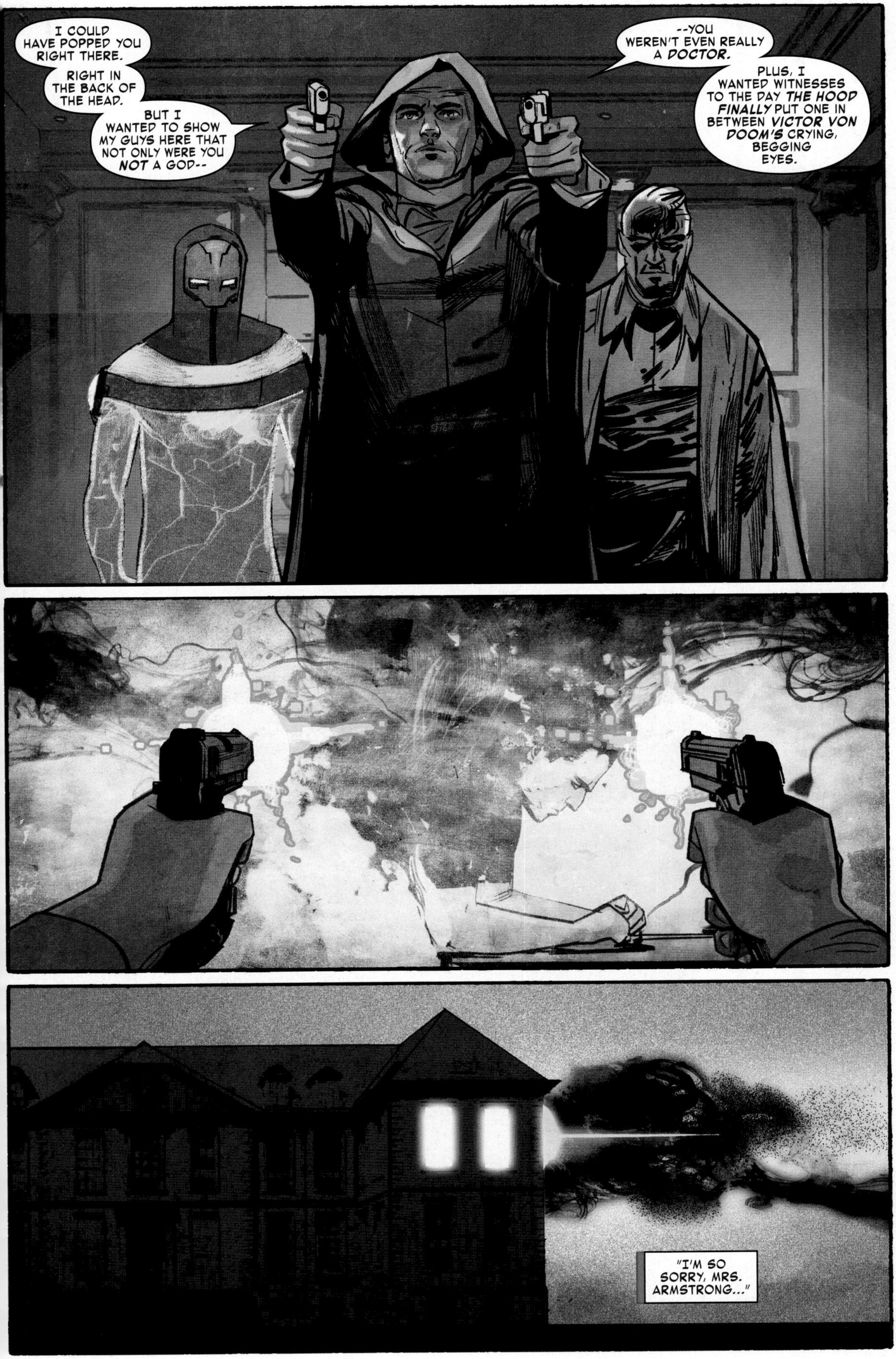
I COULD HAVE POPPED YOU RIGHT THERE.
RIGHT IN THE BACK OF THE HEAD.
BUT I WANTED TO SHOW MY GUYS HERE THAT NOT ONLY WERE YOU *NOT* A GOD--
--YOU WEREN'T EVEN REALLY A *DOCTOR.*
PLUS, I WANTED WITNESSES TO THE DAY *THE HOOD FINALLY* PUT ONE IN BETWEEN *VICTOR VON DOOM'S* CRYING, BEGGING EYES.
"I'M SO SORRY, MRS. ARMSTRONG..."

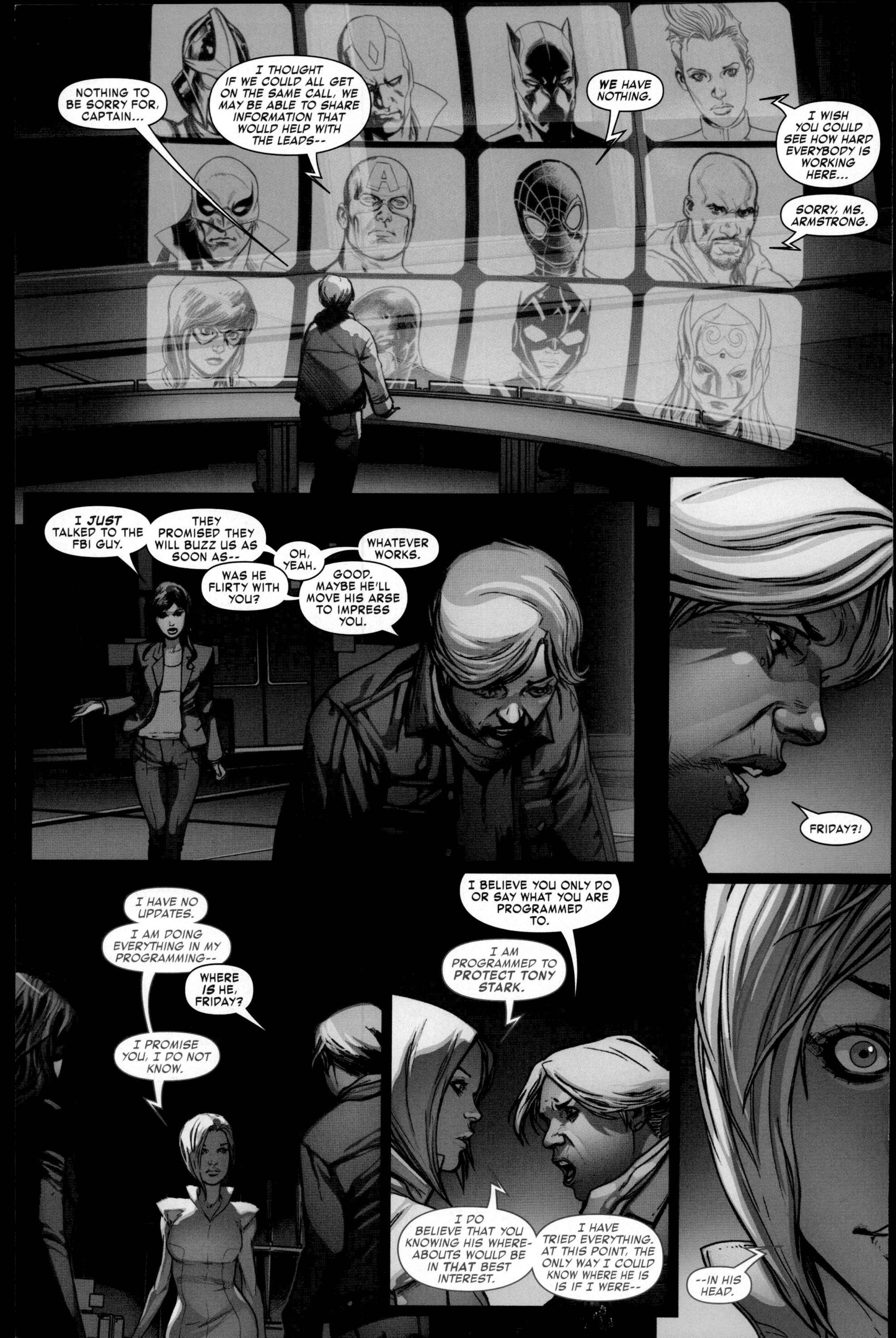
I THOUGHT IF WE COULD ALL GET ON THE SAME CALL, WE MAY BE ABLE TO SHARE INFORMATION THAT WOULD HELP WITH THE LEADS--
NOTHING TO BE SORRY FOR, CAPTAIN...
WE HAVE NOTHING.
I WISH YOU COULD SEE HOW HARD EVERYBODY IS WORKING HERE...
SORRY, MS. ARMSTRONG.
I JUST TALKED TO THE FBI GUY.
THEY PROMISED THEY WILL BUZZ US AS SOON AS--
WAS HE FLIRTY WITH YOU?
OH, YEAH.
WHATEVER WORKS.
GOOD. MAYBE HE'LL MOVE HIS ARSE TO IMPRESS YOU.
FRIDAY?!
I HAVE NO UPDATES.
I AM DOING EVERYTHING IN MY PROGRAMMING--
WHERE IS HE, FRIDAY?
I PROMISE YOU, I DO NOT KNOW.
I BELIEVE YOU ONLY DO OR SAY WHAT YOU ARE PROGRAMMED TO.
I AM PROGRAMMED TO PROTECT TONY STARK.
I DO BELIEVE THAT YOU KNOWING HIS WHERE-ABOUTS WOULD BE IN THAT BEST INTEREST.
I HAVE TRIED EVERYTHING. AT THIS POINT, THE ONLY WAY I COULD KNOW WHERE HE IS IS IF I WERE--
--IN HIS HEAD.

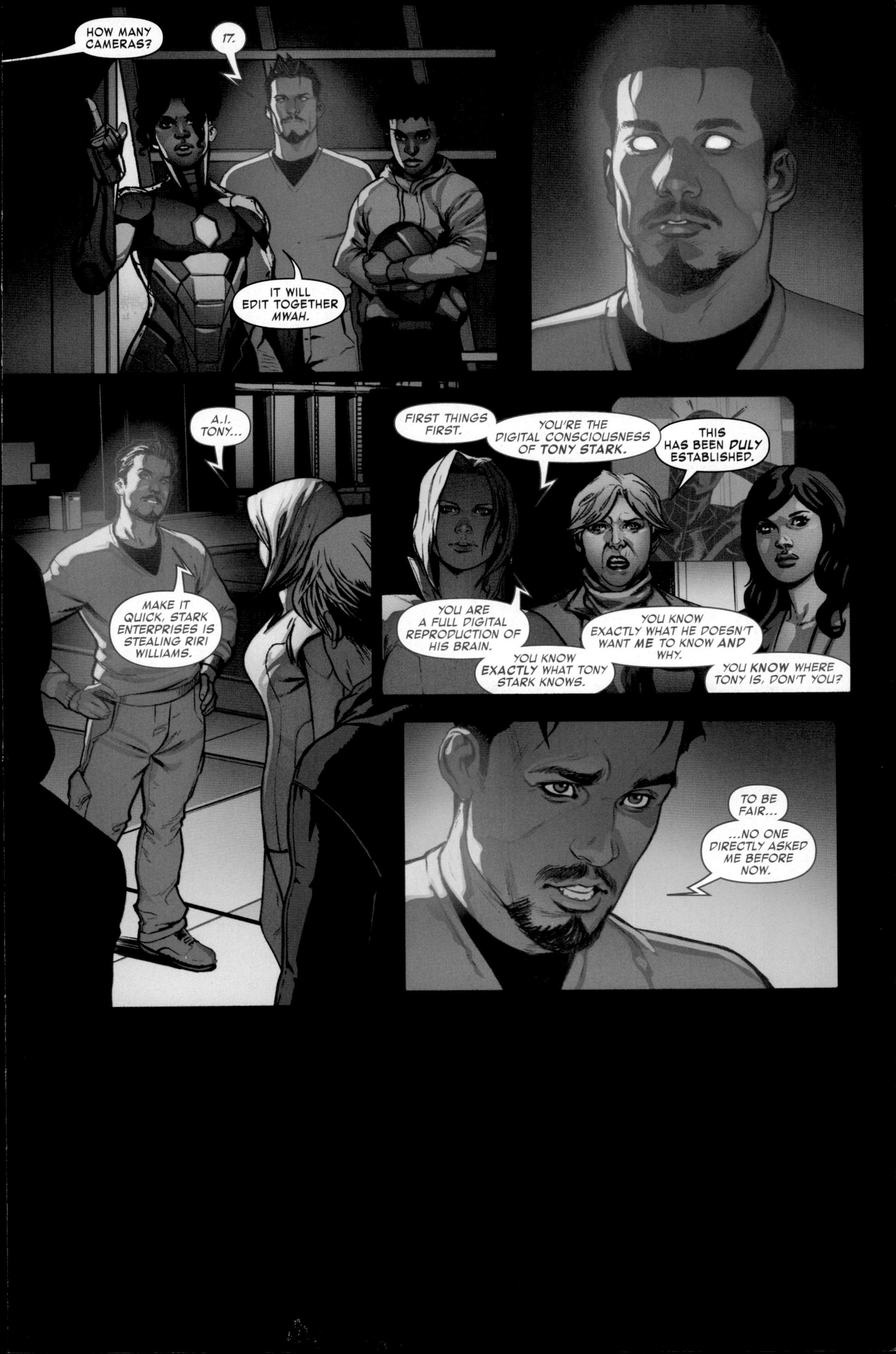
HOW MANY CAMERAS?
17.
IT WILL EDIT TOGETHER MWAH.
A.I. TONY...
MAKE IT QUICK, STARK ENTERPRISES IS STEALING RIRI WILLIAMS.
FIRST THINGS FIRST.
YOU'RE THE DIGITAL CONSCIOUSNESS OF TONY STARK.
THIS HAS BEEN DULY ESTABLISHED.
YOU ARE A FULL DIGITAL REPRODUCTION OF HIS BRAIN.
YOU KNOW EXACTLY WHAT TONY STARK KNOWS.
YOU KNOW EXACTLY WHAT HE DOESN'T WANT ME TO KNOW AND WHY.
YOU KNOW WHERE TONY IS, DON'T YOU?
TO BE FAIR...
...NO ONE DIRECTLY ASKED ME BEFORE NOW.

#596

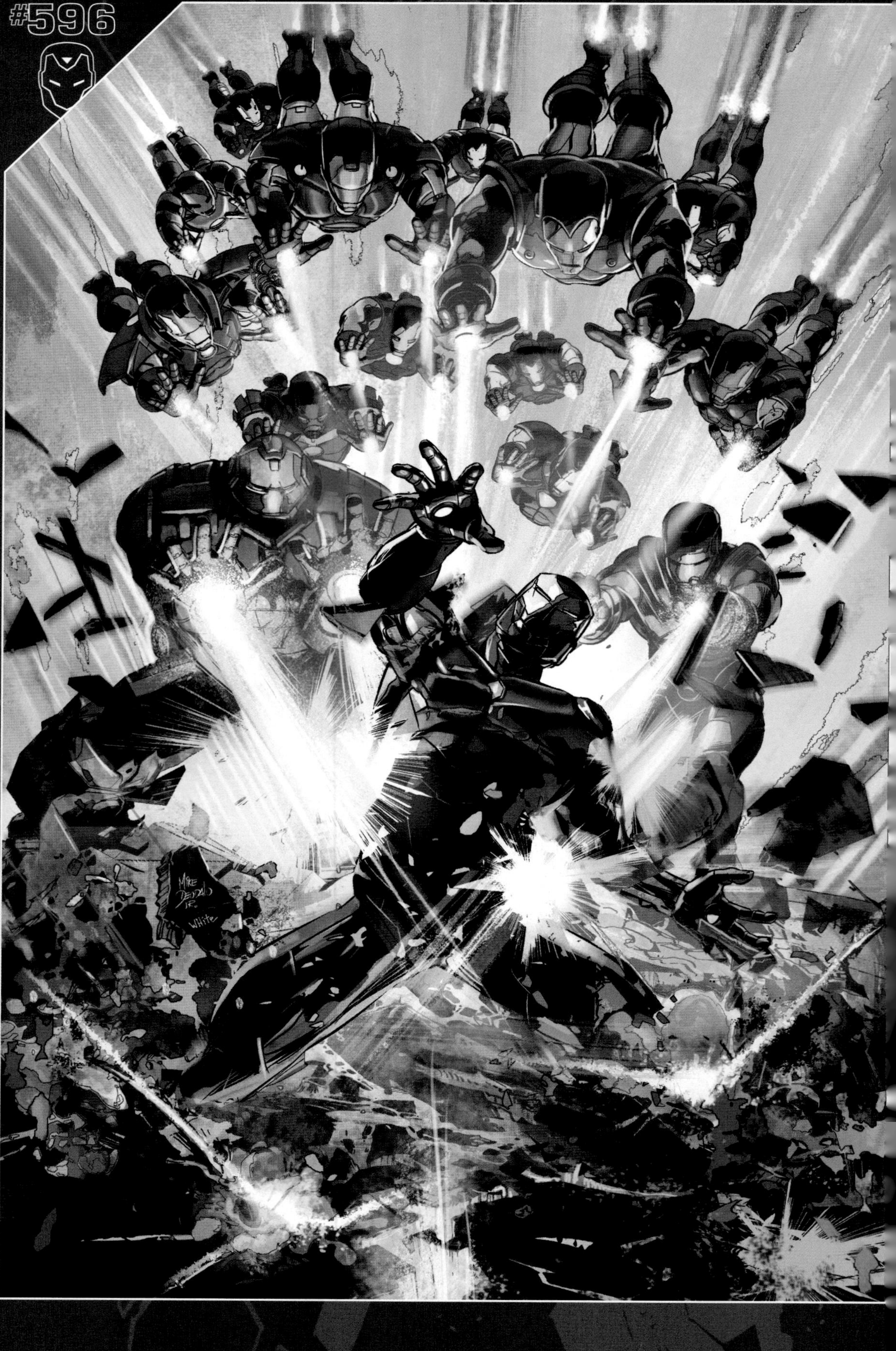

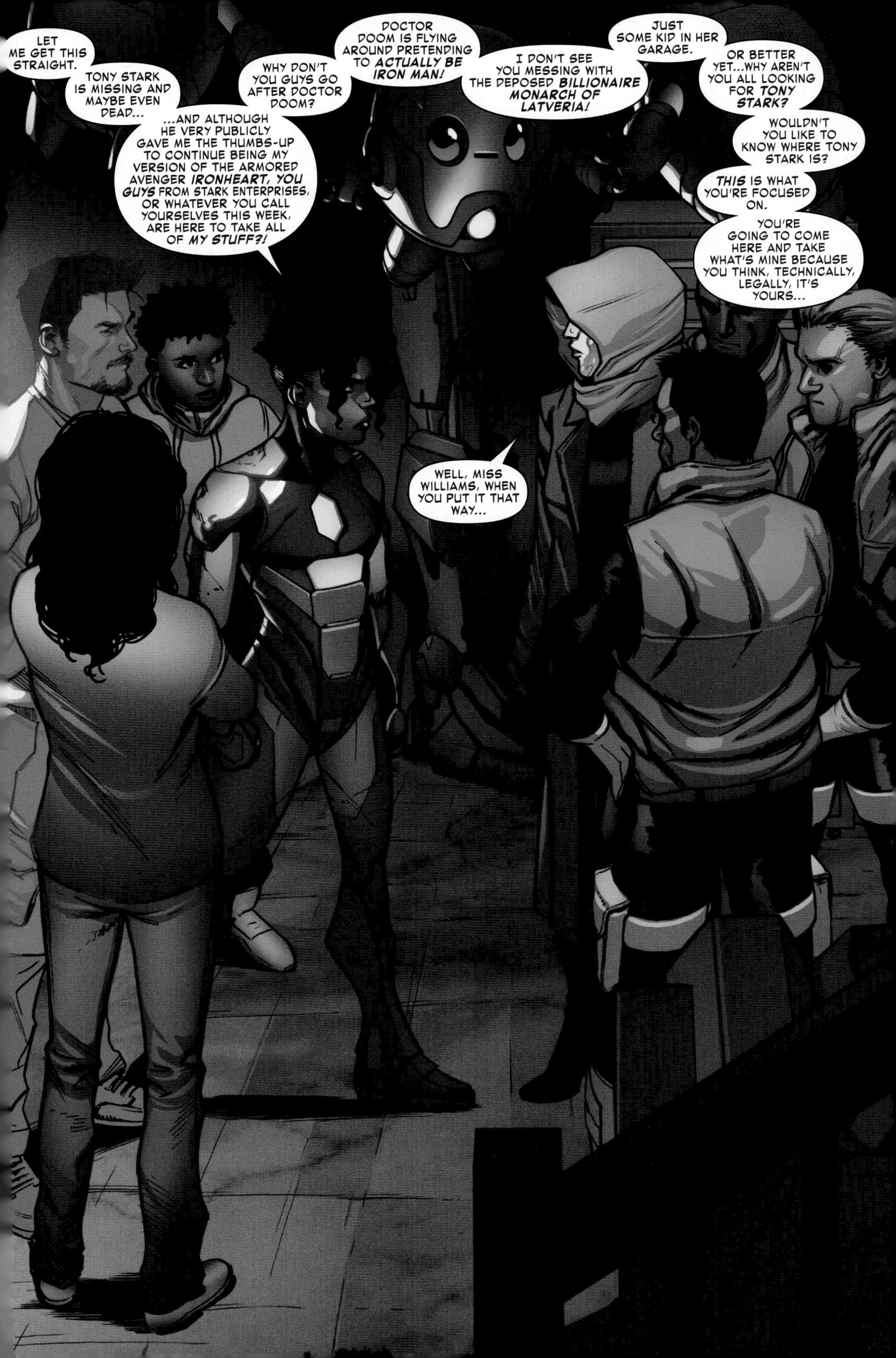

LET ME GET THIS STRAIGHT.
TONY STARK IS MISSING AND MAYBE EVEN DEAD...
...AND ALTHOUGH HE VERY PUBLICLY GAVE ME THE THUMBS-UP TO CONTINUE BEING MY VERSION OF THE ARMORED AVENGER IRONHEART, YOU GUYS FROM STARK ENTERPRISES, OR WHATEVER YOU CALL YOURSELVES THIS WEEK, ARE HERE TO TAKE ALL OF MY STUFF?!
WHY DON'T YOU GUYS GO AFTER DOCTOR DOOM?
DOCTOR DOOM IS FLYING AROUND PRETENDING TO ACTUALLY BE IRON MAN!
I DON'T SEE YOU MESSING WITH THE DEPOSED BILLIONAIRE MONARCH OF LATVERIA!
JUST SOME KID IN HER GARAGE.
OR BETTER YET...WHY AREN'T YOU ALL LOOKING FOR TONY STARK?
WOULDN'T YOU LIKE TO KNOW WHERE TONY STARK IS?
THIS IS WHAT YOU'RE FOCUSED ON.
YOU'RE GOING TO COME HERE AND TAKE WHAT'S MINE BECAUSE YOU THINK, TECHNICALLY, LEGALLY, IT'S YOURS...
WELL, MISS WILLIAMS, WHEN YOU PUT IT THAT WAY...

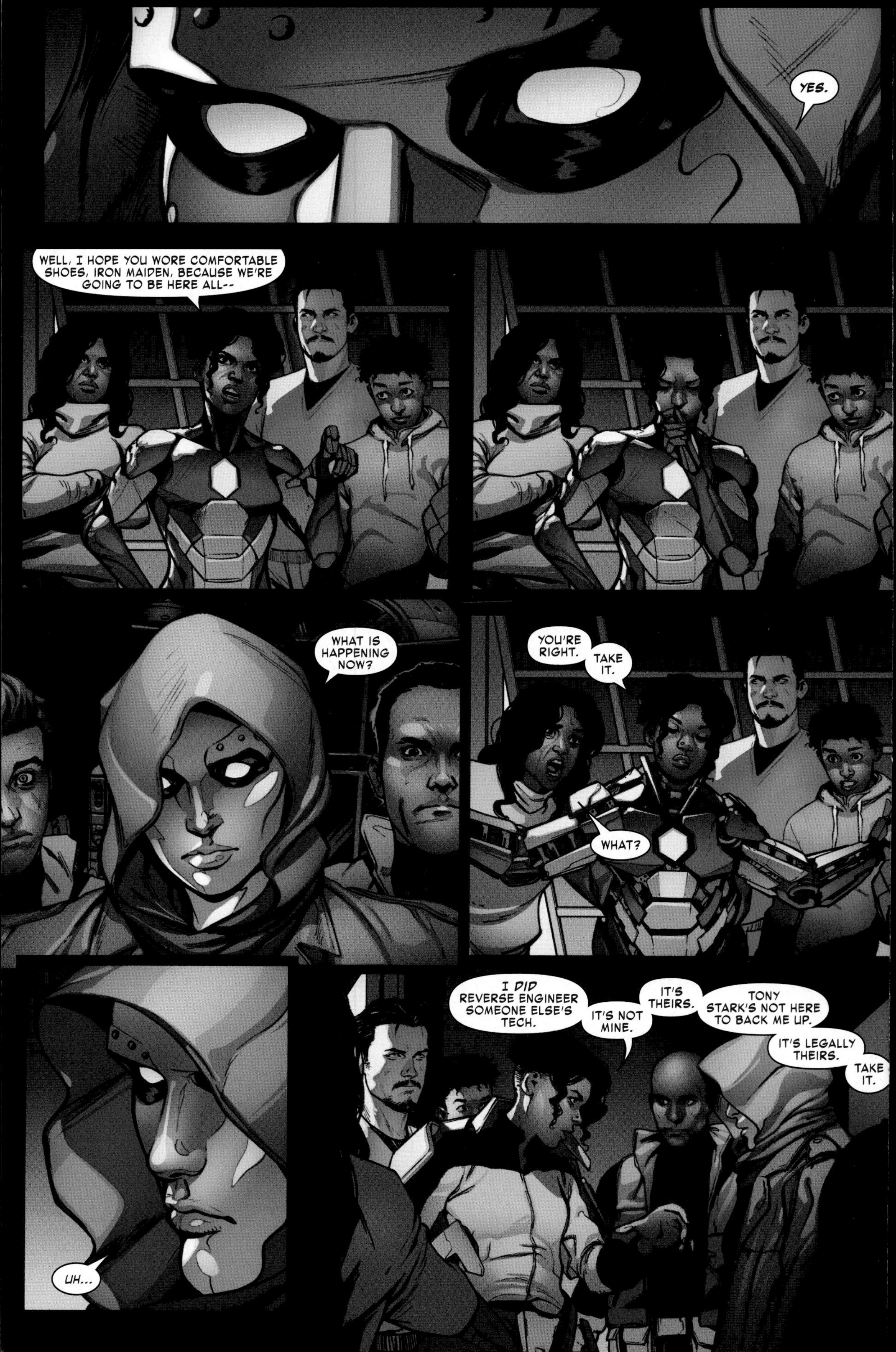
YES.
WELL, I HOPE YOU WORE COMFORTABLE SHOES, IRON MAIDEN, BECAUSE WE'RE GOING TO BE HERE ALL--
WHAT IS HAPPENING NOW?
YOU'RE RIGHT.
TAKE IT.
WHAT?
UH...
I *DID* REVERSE ENGINEER SOMEONE ELSE'S TECH.
IT'S NOT MINE.
IT'S THEIRS.
TONY STARK'S NOT HERE TO BACK ME UP.
IT'S LEGALLY THEIRS.
TAKE IT.

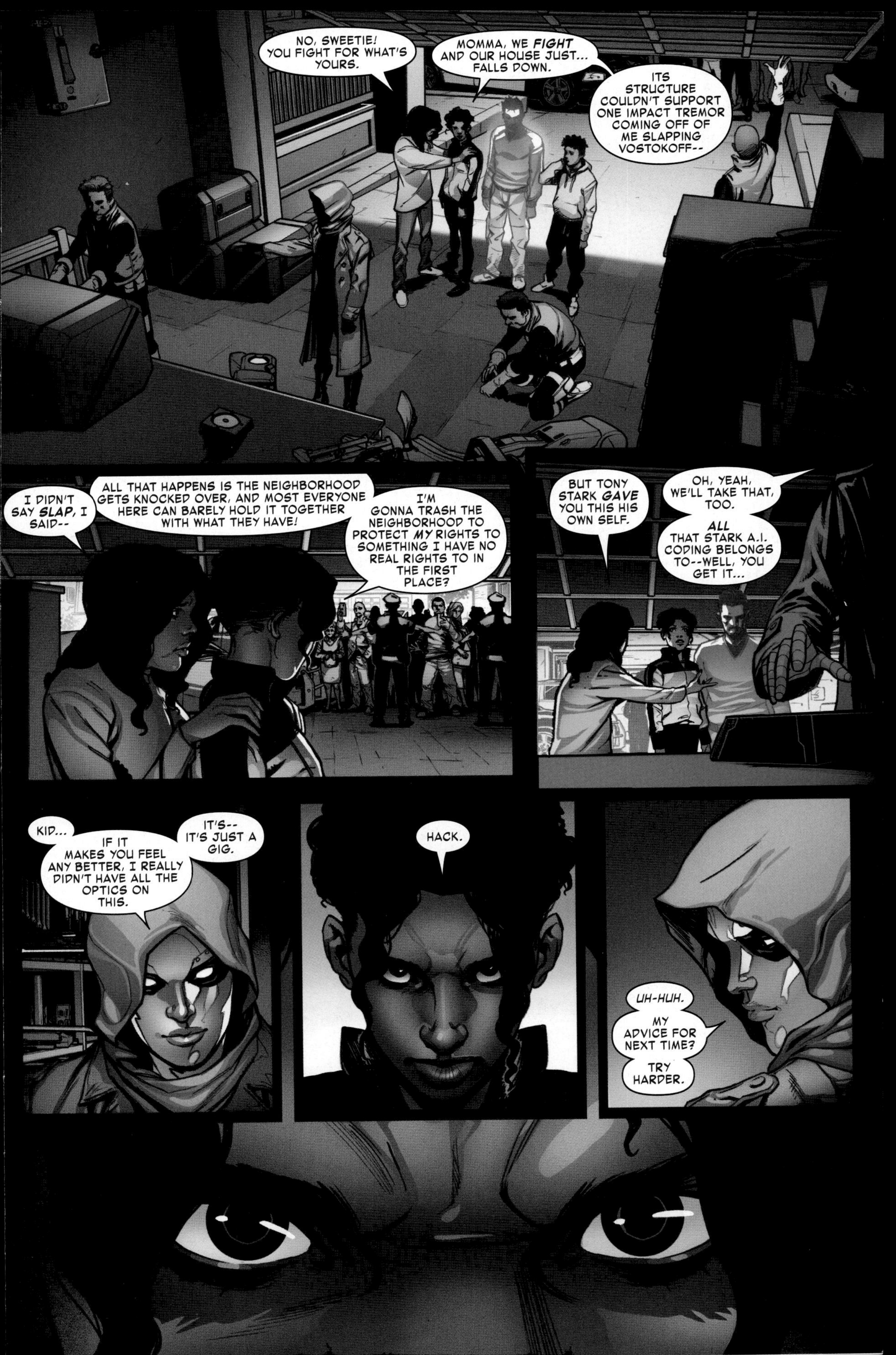
NO, SWEETIE! YOU FIGHT FOR WHAT'S YOURS.
MOMMA, WE FIGHT AND OUR HOUSE JUST... FALLS DOWN.
ITS STRUCTURE COULDN'T SUPPORT ONE IMPACT TREMOR COMING OFF OF ME SLAPPING VOSTOKOFF--
I DIDN'T SAY SLAP, I SAID--
ALL THAT HAPPENS IS THE NEIGHBORHOOD GETS KNOCKED OVER, AND MOST EVERYONE HERE CAN BARELY HOLD IT TOGETHER WITH WHAT THEY HAVE!
I'M GONNA TRASH THE NEIGHBORHOOD TO PROTECT MY RIGHTS TO SOMETHING I HAVE NO REAL RIGHTS TO IN THE FIRST PLACE?
BUT TONY STARK GAVE YOU THIS HIS OWN SELF.
OH, YEAH, WE'LL TAKE THAT, TOO.
ALL THAT STARK A.I. CODING BELONGS TO--WELL, YOU GET IT...
KID...
IF IT MAKES YOU FEEL ANY BETTER, I REALLY DIDN'T HAVE ALL THE OPTICS ON THIS.
IT'S-- IT'S JUST A GIG.
HACK.
UH-HUH.
MY ADVICE FOR NEXT TIME?
TRY HARDER.

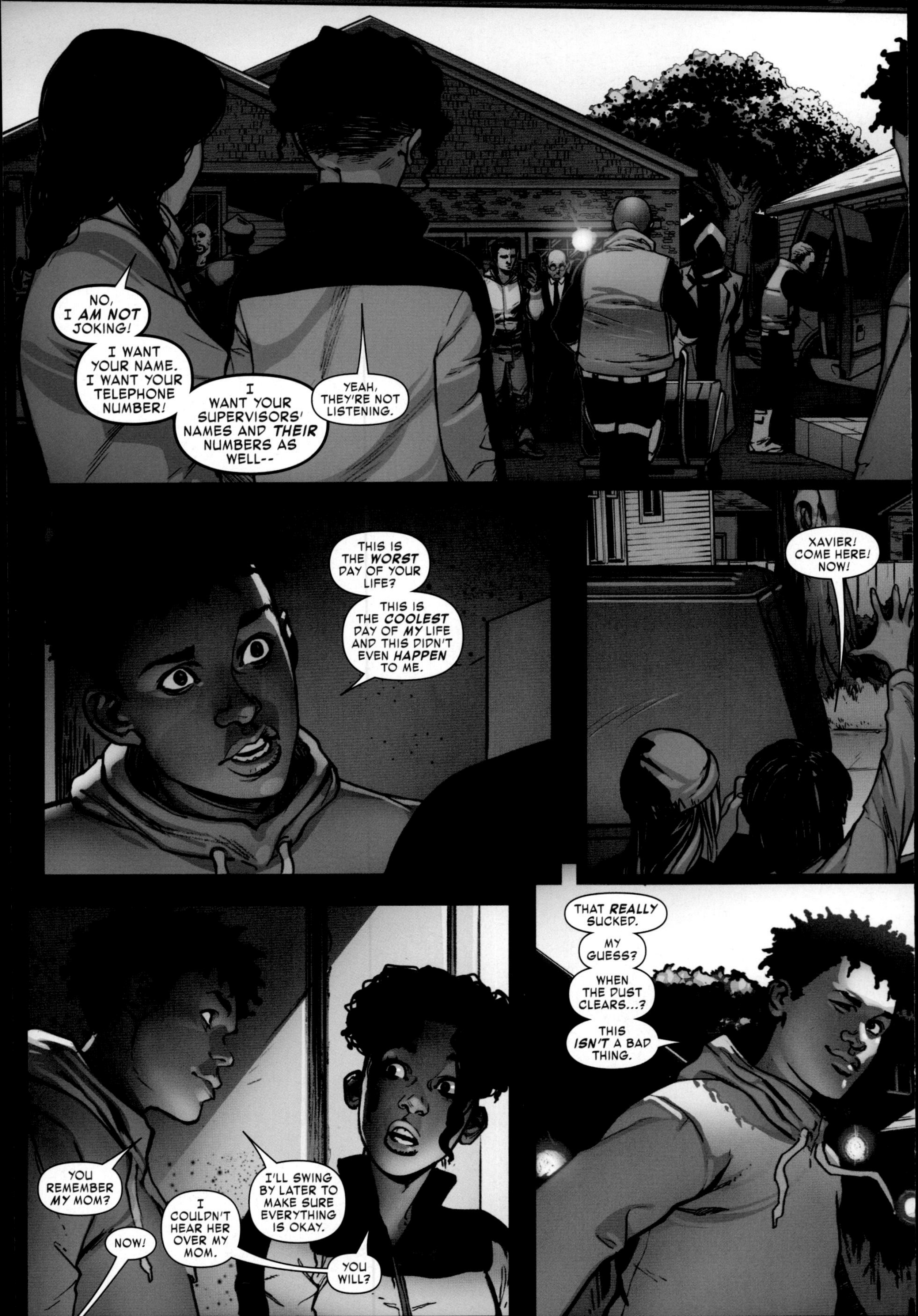
NO, I AM NOT JOKING!
I WANT YOUR NAME. I WANT YOUR TELEPHONE NUMBER!
I WANT YOUR SUPERVISORS' NAMES AND THEIR NUMBERS AS WELL--
YEAH, THEY'RE NOT LISTENING.
THIS IS THE WORST DAY OF YOUR LIFE?
THIS IS THE COOLEST DAY OF MY LIFE AND THIS DIDN'T EVEN HAPPEN TO ME.
XAVIER! COME HERE! NOW!
YOU REMEMBER MY MOM?
NOW!
I COULDN'T HEAR HER OVER MY MOM.
I'LL SWING BY LATER TO MAKE SURE EVERYTHING IS OKAY.
YOU WILL?
THAT REALLY SUCKED.
MY GUESS?
WHEN THE DUST CLEARS...?
THIS ISN'T A BAD THING.

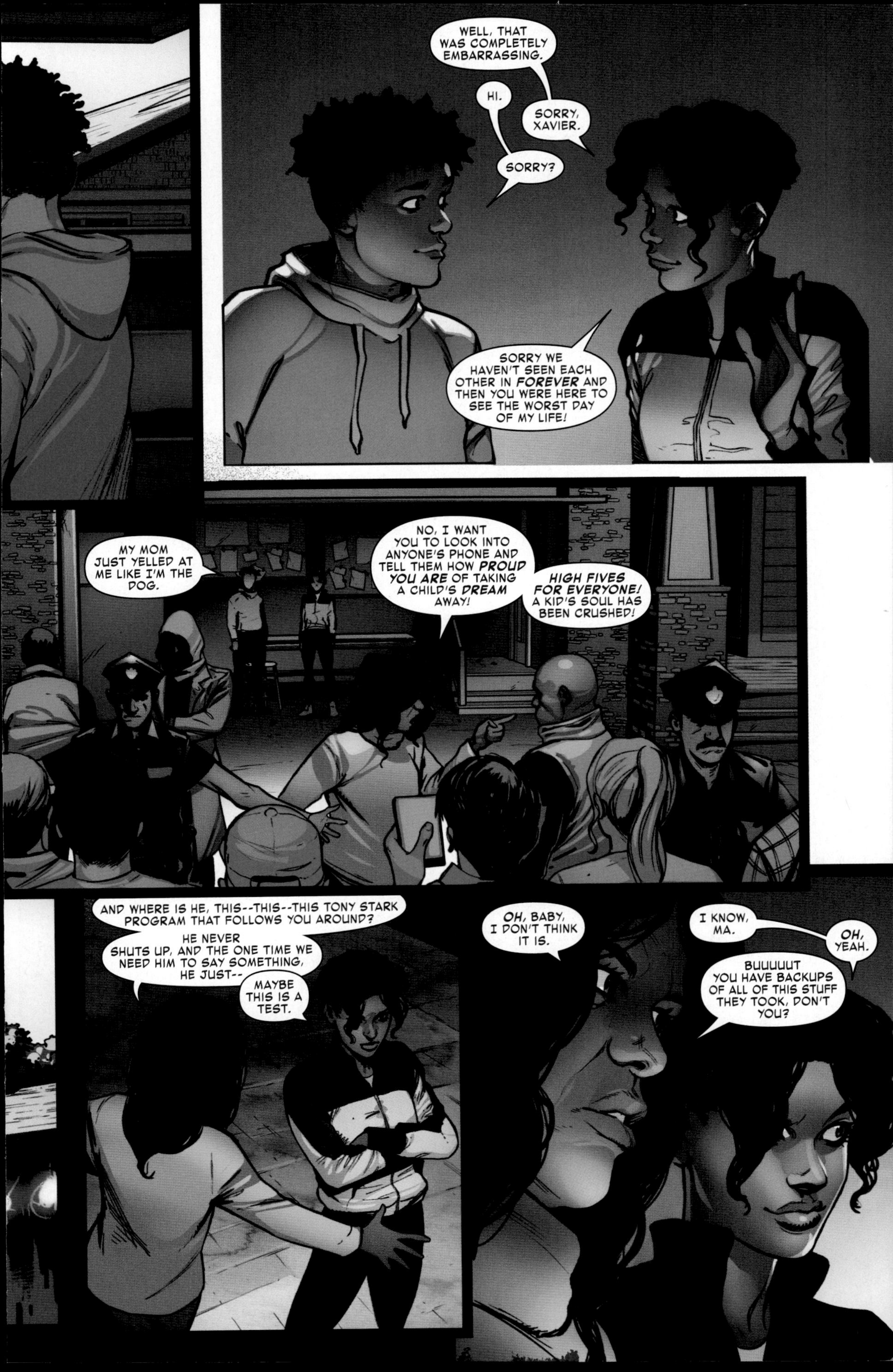
WELL, THAT WAS COMPLETELY EMBARRASSING.
HI.
SORRY, XAVIER.
SORRY?
SORRY WE HAVEN'T SEEN EACH OTHER IN FOREVER AND THEN YOU WERE HERE TO SEE THE WORST DAY OF MY LIFE!
MY MOM JUST YELLED AT ME LIKE I'M THE DOG.
NO, I WANT YOU TO LOOK INTO ANYONE'S PHONE AND TELL THEM HOW PROUD YOU ARE OF TAKING A CHILD'S DREAM AWAY!
HIGH FIVES FOR EVERYONE! A KID'S SOUL HAS BEEN CRUSHED!
AND WHERE IS HE, THIS--THIS--THIS TONY STARK PROGRAM THAT FOLLOWS YOU AROUND?
HE NEVER SHUTS UP, AND THE ONE TIME WE NEED HIM TO SAY SOMETHING, HE JUST--
MAYBE THIS IS A TEST.
OH, BABY, I DON'T THINK IT IS.
I KNOW, MA.
OH, YEAH.
BUUUUUT YOU HAVE BACKUPS OF ALL OF THIS STUFF THEY TOOK, DON'T YOU?

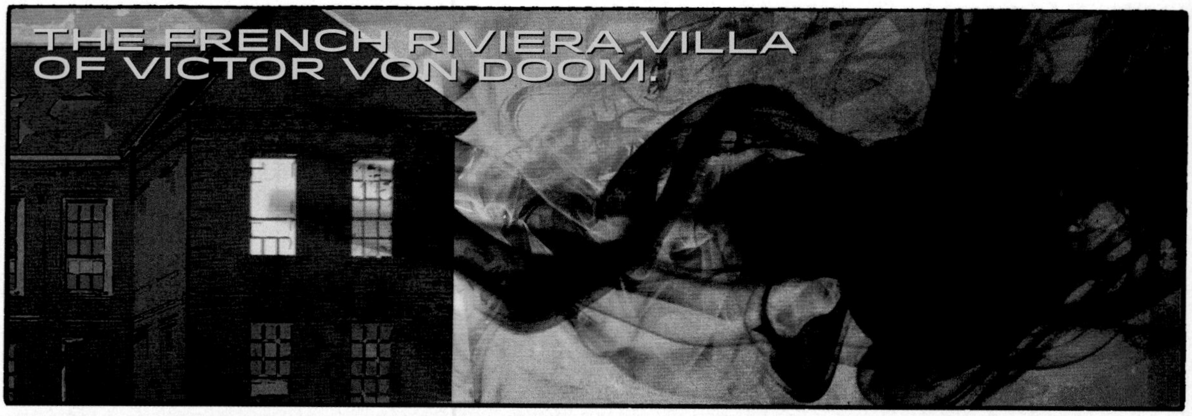
THE FRENCH RIVIERA VILLA OF VICTOR VON DOOM.

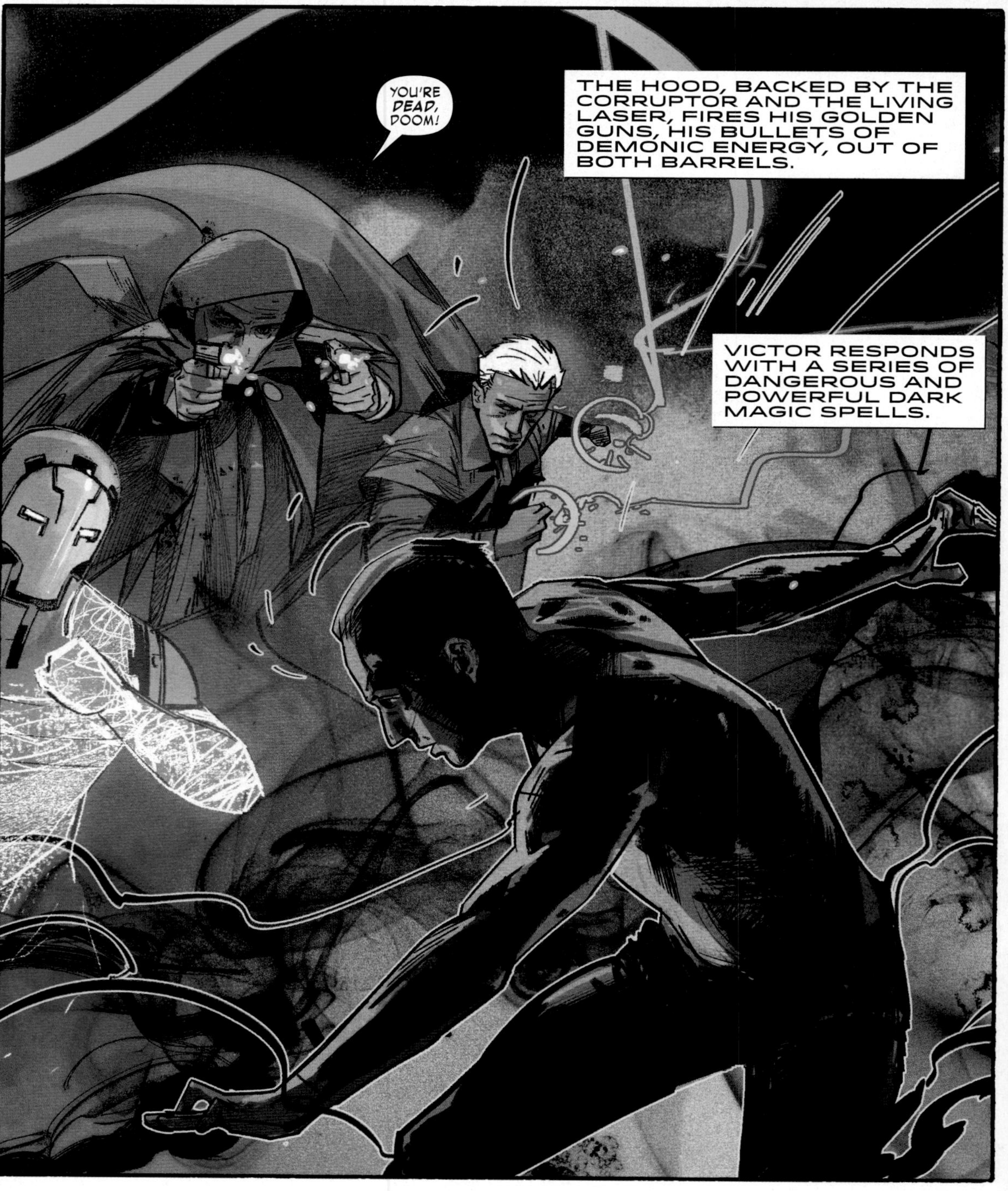
YOU'RE DEAD, DOOM!
THE HOOD, BACKED BY THE CORRUPTOR AND THE LIVING LASER, FIRES HIS GOLDEN GUNS, HIS BULLETS OF DEMONIC ENERGY, OUT OF BOTH BARRELS.
VICTOR RESPONDS WITH A SERIES OF DANGEROUS AND POWERFUL DARK MAGIC SPELLS.

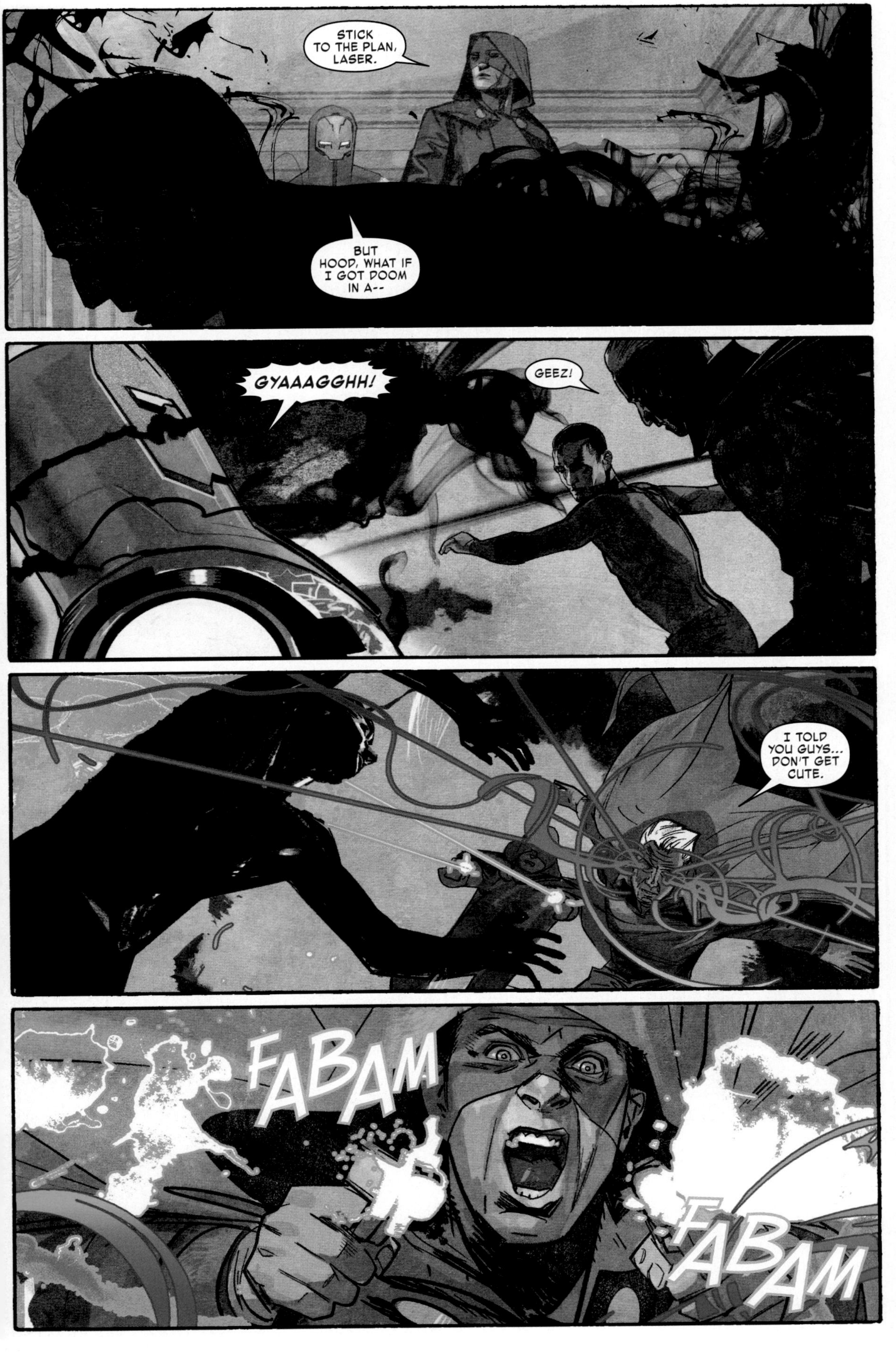
STICK TO THE PLAN, LASER.
BUT HOOD, WHAT IF I GOT DOOM IN A--
GYAAAGGHH!
GEEZ!
I TOLD YOU GUYS... DON'T GET CUTE.
FABAM
FABAM

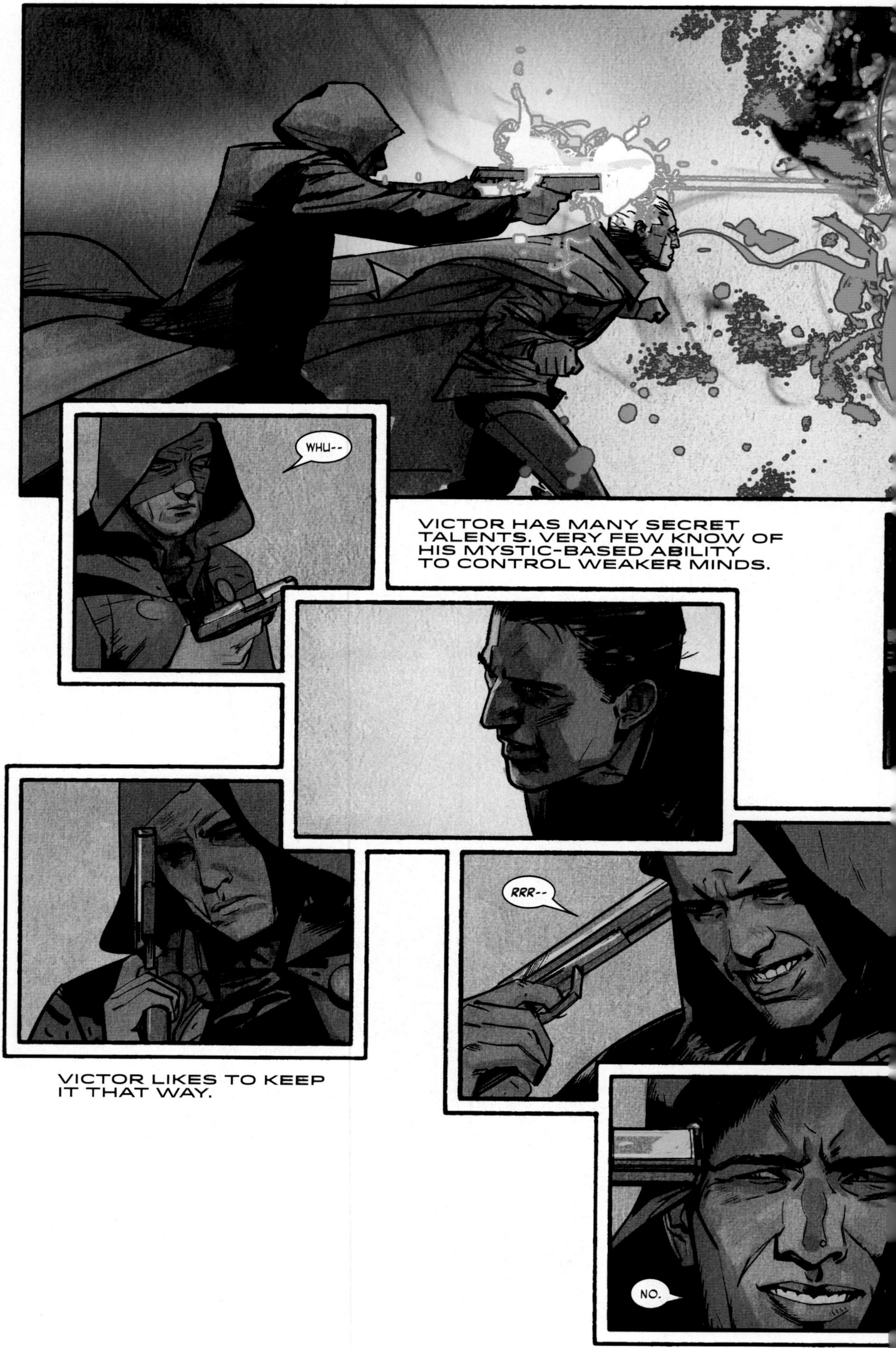
WHU--
VICTOR HAS MANY SECRET TALENTS. VERY FEW KNOW OF HIS MYSTIC-BASED ABILITY TO CONTROL WEAKER MINDS.
VICTOR LIKES TO KEEP IT THAT WAY.
RRR--
NO.

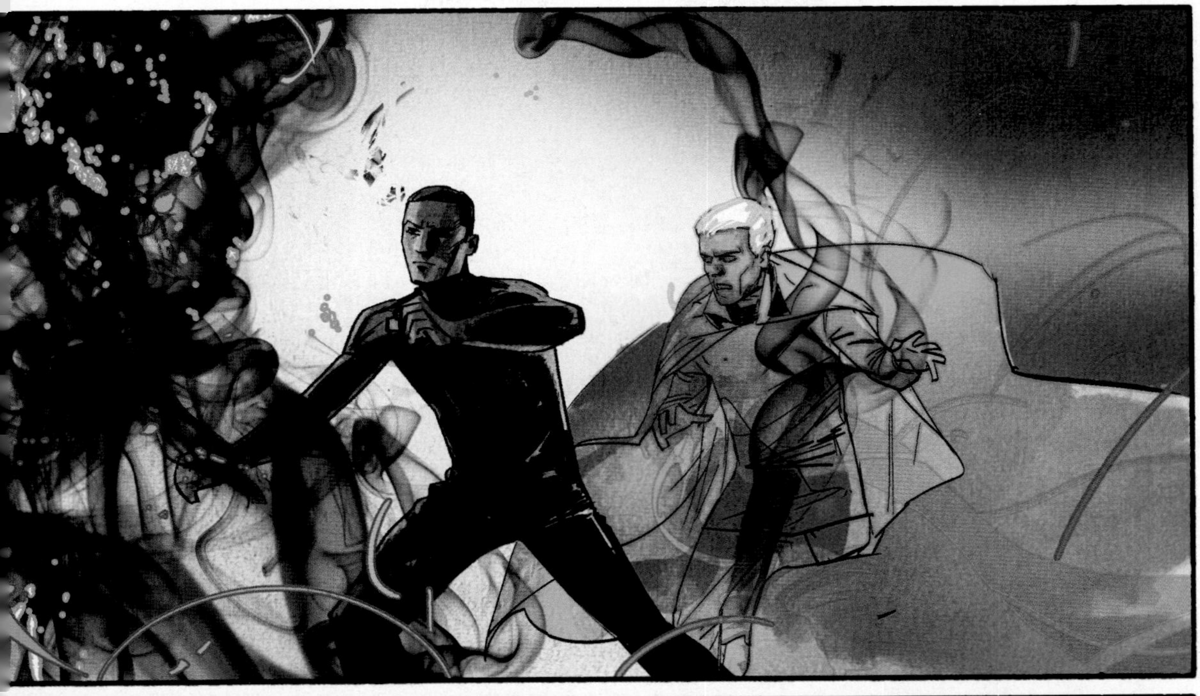

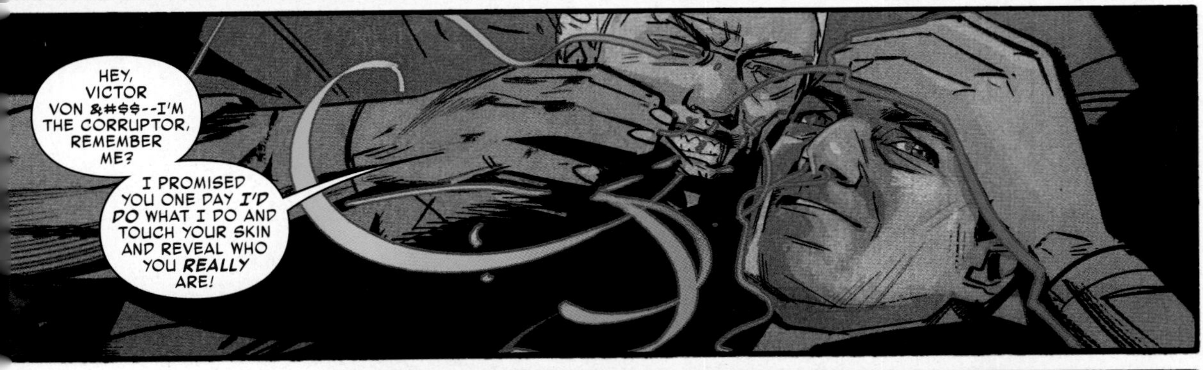
HEY, VICTOR VON &#$$--I'M THE CORRUPTOR, REMEMBER ME?
I PROMISED YOU ONE DAY I'D DO WHAT I DO AND TOUCH YOUR SKIN AND REVEAL WHO YOU REALLY ARE!

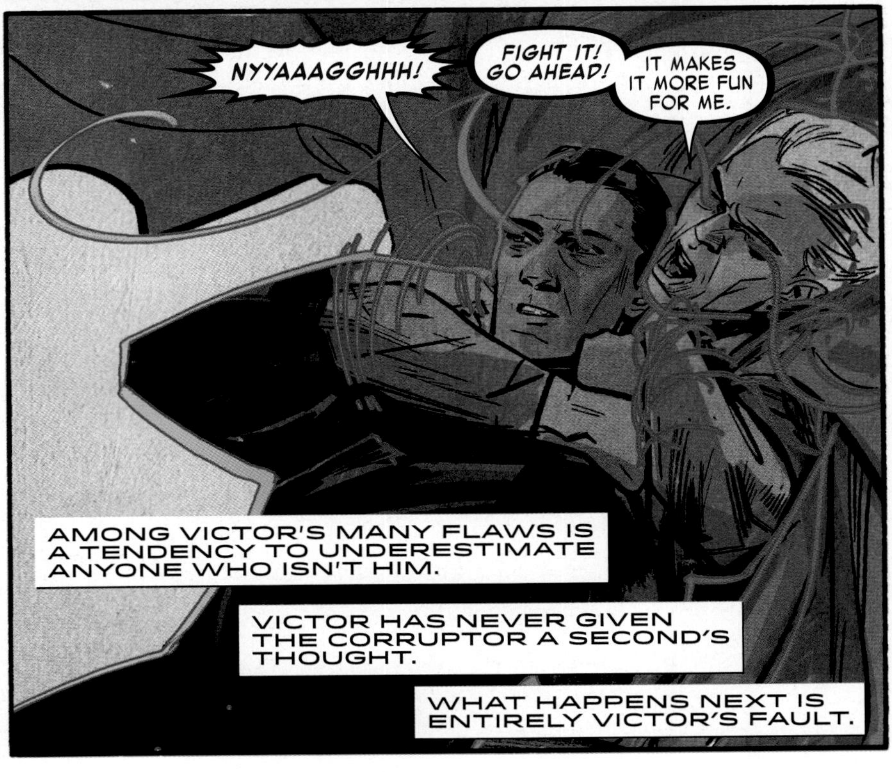
NYYAAAGGHHH!
FIGHT IT! GO AHEAD!
IT MAKES IT MORE FUN FOR ME.
AMONG VICTOR'S MANY FLAWS IS A TENDENCY TO UNDERESTIMATE ANYONE WHO ISN'T HIM.
VICTOR HAS NEVER GIVEN THE CORRUPTOR A SECOND'S THOUGHT.
WHAT HAPPENS NEXT IS ENTIRELY VICTOR'S FAULT.

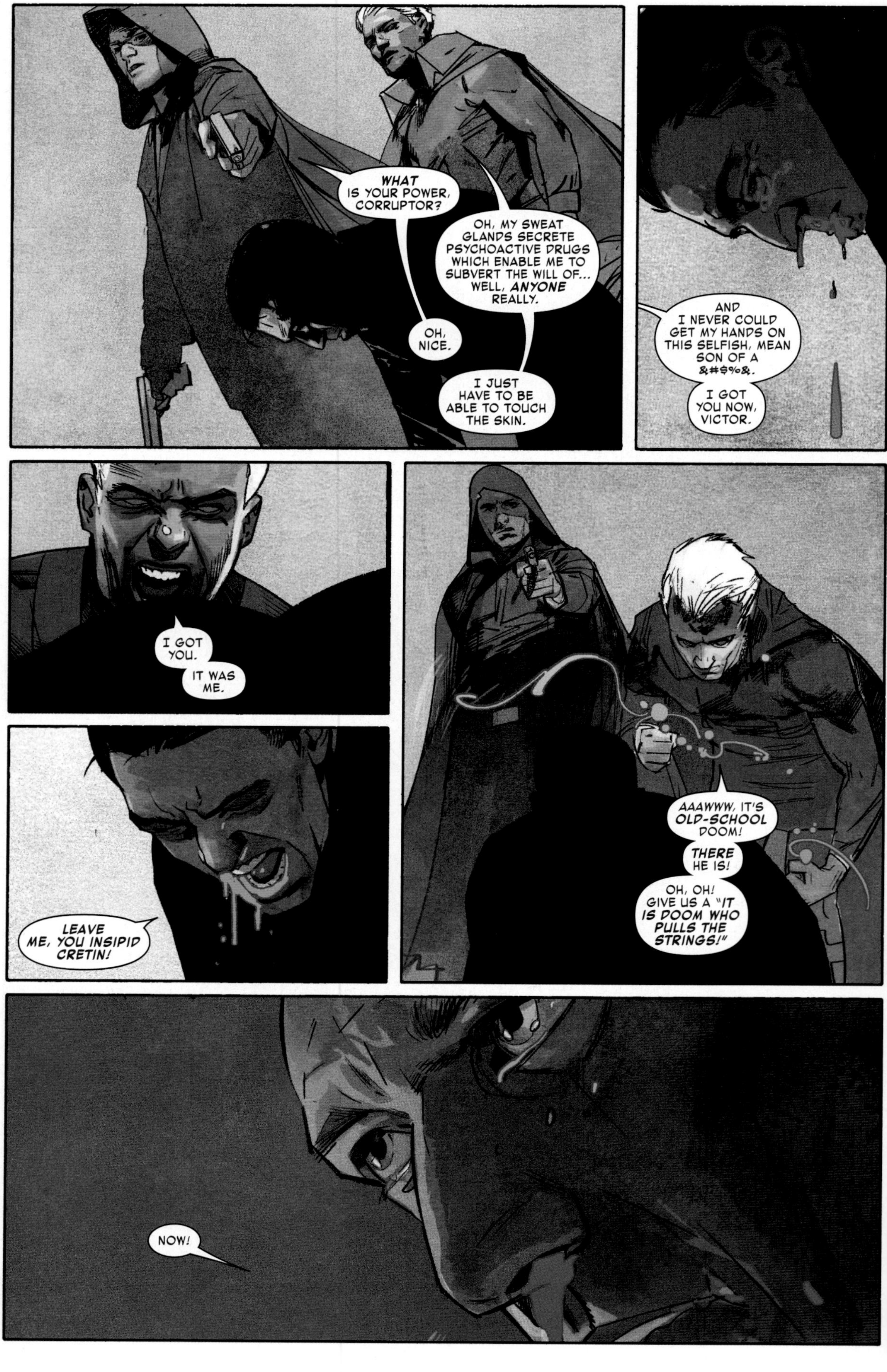
WHAT IS YOUR POWER, CORRUPTOR?
OH, MY SWEAT GLANDS SECRETE PSYCHOACTIVE DRUGS WHICH ENABLE ME TO SUBVERT THE WILL OF... WELL, ANYONE REALLY.
OH, NICE.
I JUST HAVE TO BE ABLE TO TOUCH THE SKIN.
AND I NEVER COULD GET MY HANDS ON THIS SELFISH, MEAN SON OF A &#$%&.
I GOT YOU NOW, VICTOR.
I GOT YOU.
IT WAS ME.
LEAVE ME, YOU INSIPID CRETIN!
AAAWWW, IT'S OLD-SCHOOL DOOM!
THERE HE IS!
OH, OH! GIVE US A "IT IS DOOM WHO PULLS THE STRINGS!"
NOW!

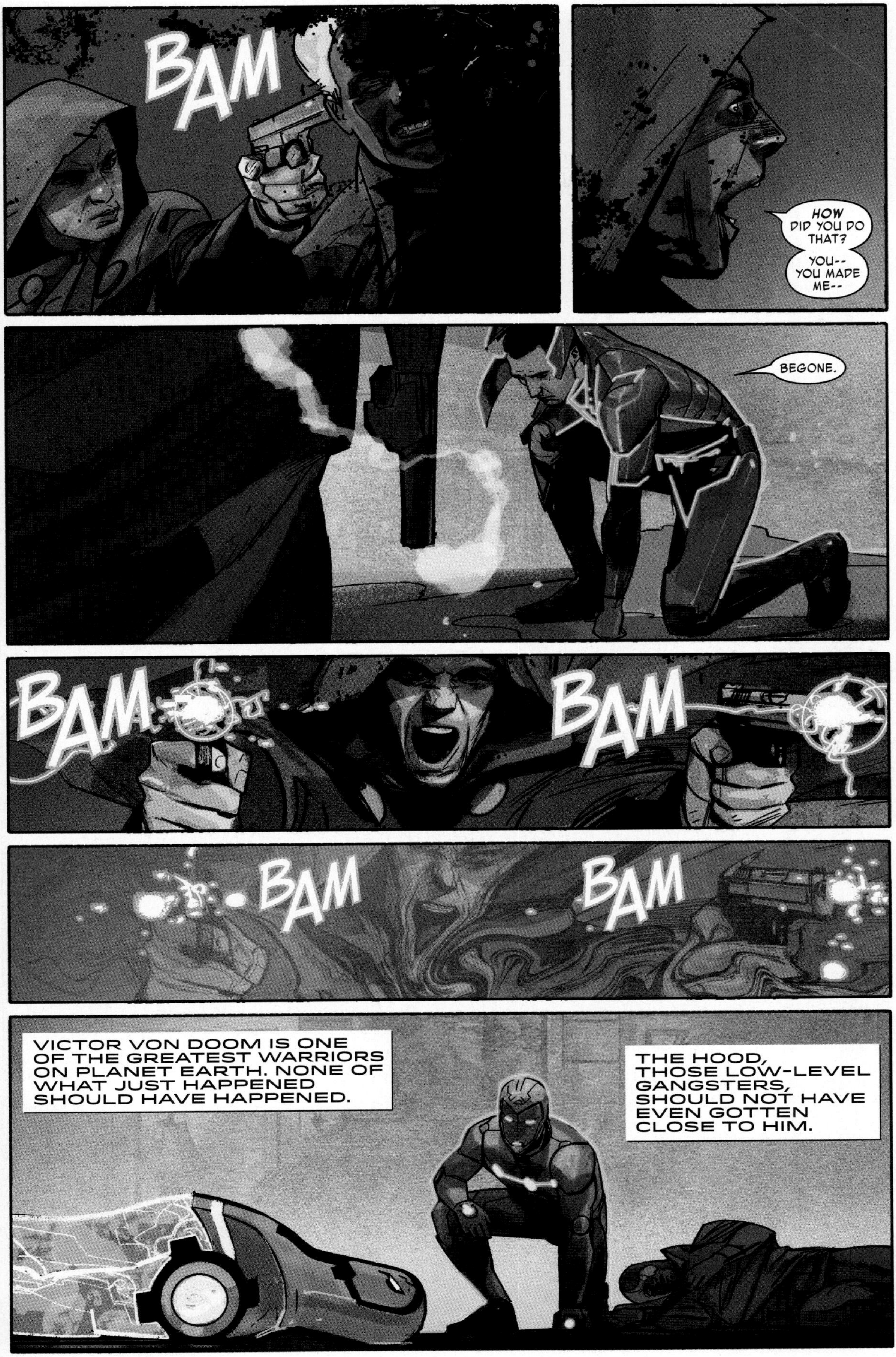

BAM
HOW DID YOU DO THAT?
YOU-- YOU MADE ME--
BEGONE.
BAM
BAM
BAM
BAM
VICTOR VON DOOM IS ONE OF THE GREATEST WARRIORS ON PLANET EARTH. NONE OF WHAT JUST HAPPENED SHOULD HAVE HAPPENED.
THE HOOD, THOSE LOW-LEVEL GANGSTERS, SHOULD NOT HAVE EVEN GOTTEN CLOSE TO HIM.

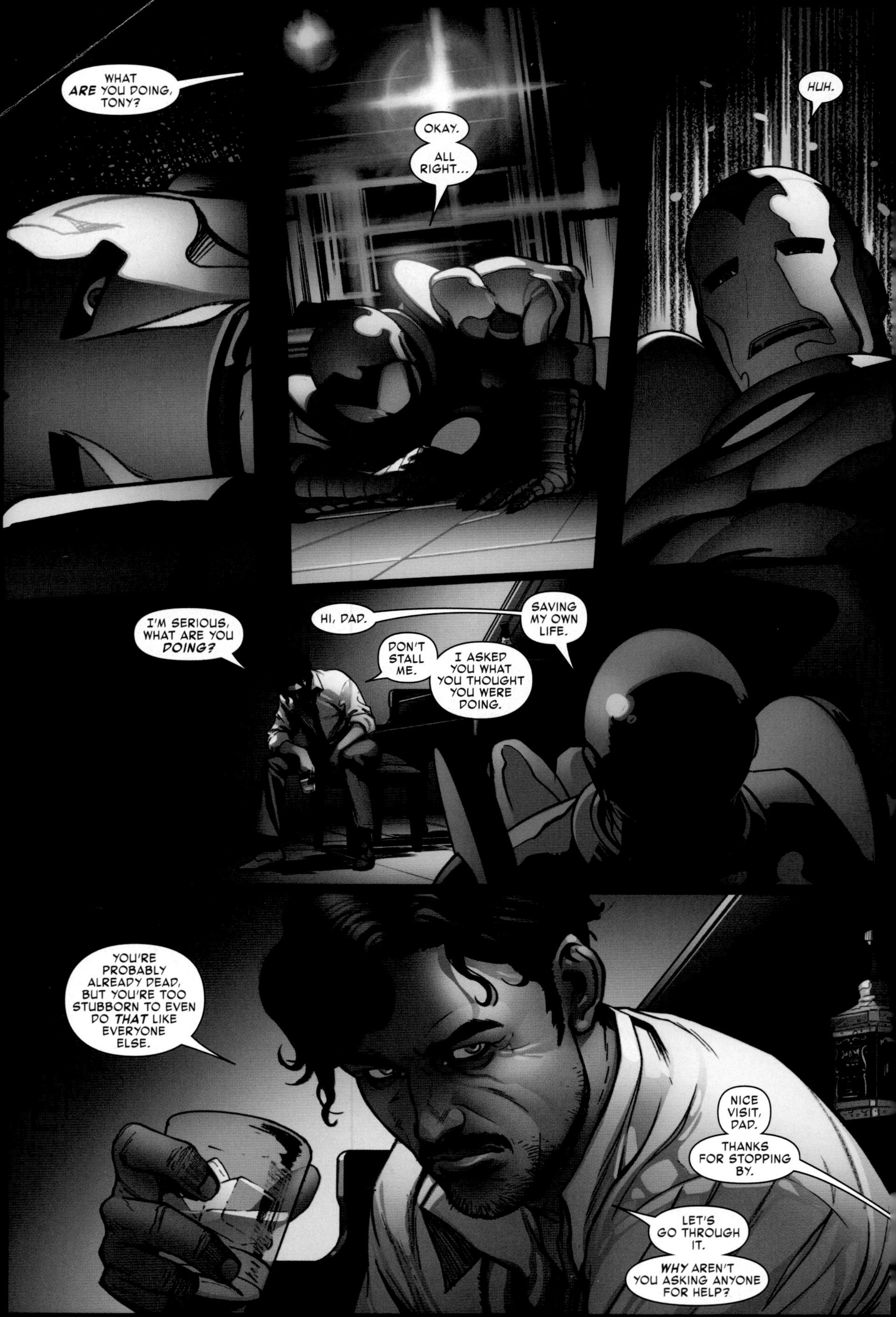
WHAT ARE YOU DOING, TONY?
OKAY.
ALL RIGHT...
HUH.
I'M SERIOUS, WHAT ARE YOU DOING?
HI, DAD.
SAVING MY OWN LIFE.
DON'T STALL ME.
I ASKED YOU WHAT YOU THOUGHT YOU WERE DOING.
YOU'RE PROBABLY ALREADY DEAD, BUT YOU'RE TOO STUBBORN TO EVEN DO THAT LIKE EVERYONE ELSE.
NICE VISIT, DAD.
THANKS FOR STOPPING BY.
LET'S GO THROUGH IT.
WHY AREN'T YOU ASKING ANYONE FOR HELP?

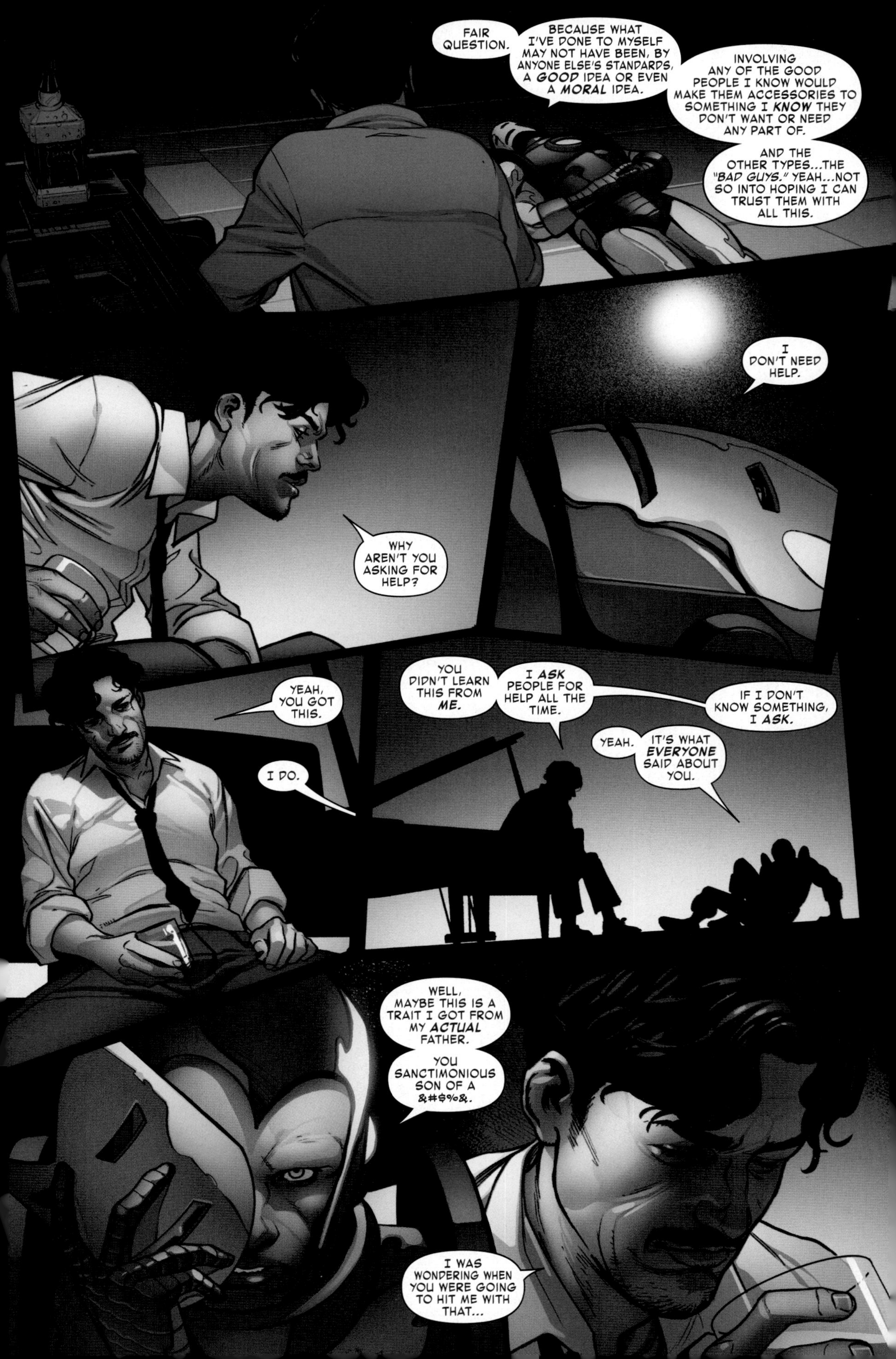
FAIR QUESTION.
BECAUSE WHAT I'VE DONE TO MYSELF MAY NOT HAVE BEEN, BY ANYONE ELSE'S STANDARDS, A GOOD IDEA OR EVEN A MORAL IDEA.
INVOLVING ANY OF THE GOOD PEOPLE I KNOW WOULD MAKE THEM ACCESSORIES TO SOMETHING I KNOW THEY DON'T WANT OR NEED ANY PART OF.
AND THE OTHER TYPES...THE "BAD GUYS." YEAH...NOT SO INTO HOPING I CAN TRUST THEM WITH ALL THIS.
WHY AREN'T YOU ASKING FOR HELP?
I DON'T NEED HELP.
YEAH, YOU GOT THIS.
I DO.
YOU DIDN'T LEARN THIS FROM ME.
I ASK PEOPLE FOR HELP ALL THE TIME.
IF I DON'T KNOW SOMETHING, I ASK.
YEAH.
IT'S WHAT EVERYONE SAID ABOUT YOU.
WELL, MAYBE THIS IS A TRAIT I GOT FROM MY ACTUAL FATHER.
YOU SANCTIMONIOUS SON OF A &#$%&.
I WAS WONDERING WHEN YOU WERE GOING TO HIT ME WITH THAT...

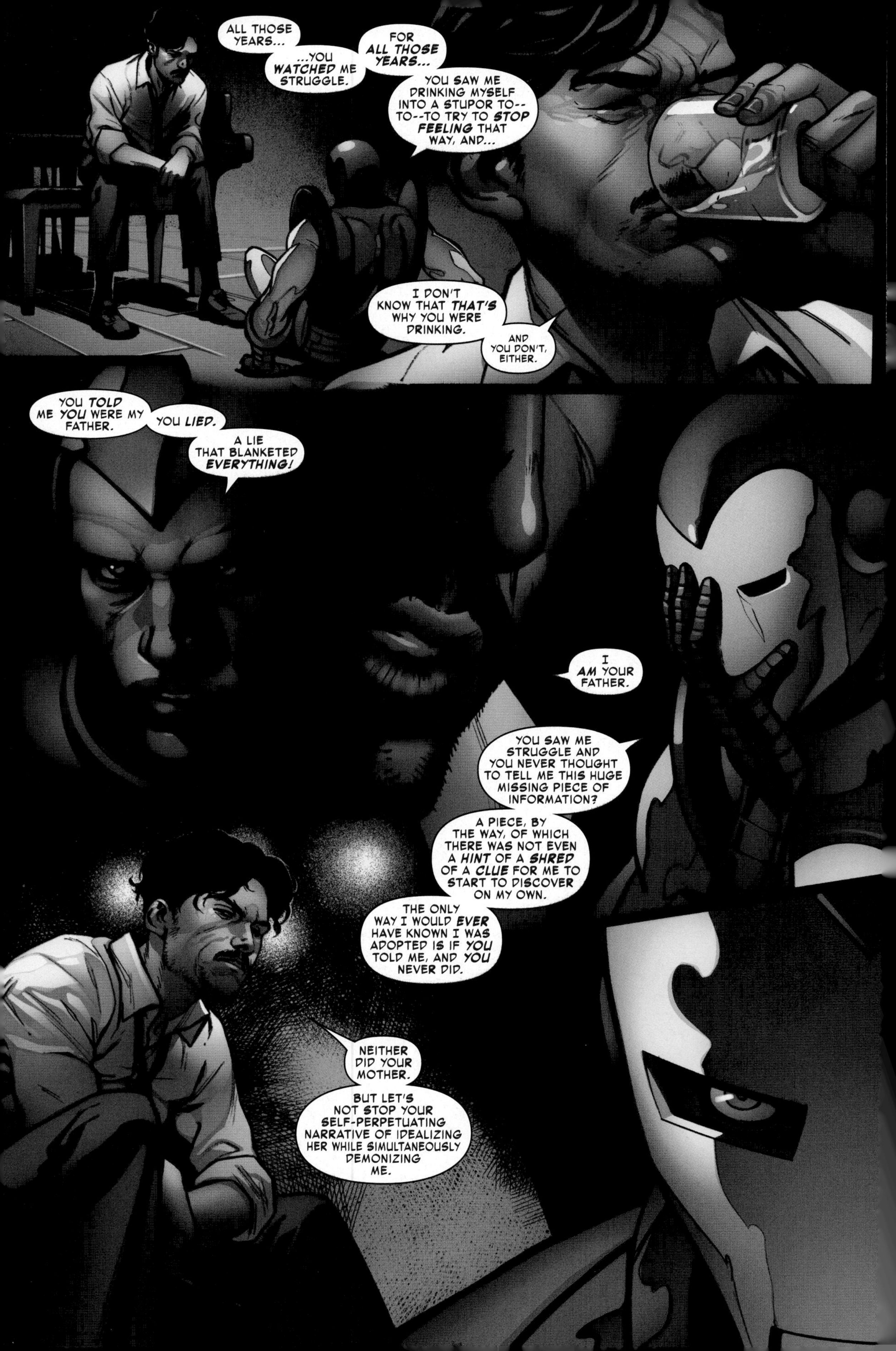
ALL THOSE YEARS...
...YOU WATCHED ME STRUGGLE.
FOR ALL THOSE YEARS...
YOU SAW ME DRINKING MYSELF INTO A STUPOR TO--TO--TO TRY TO STOP FEELING THAT WAY, AND...
I DON'T KNOW THAT THAT'S WHY YOU WERE DRINKING.
AND YOU DON'T, EITHER.
YOU TOLD ME YOU WERE MY FATHER.
YOU LIED.
A LIE THAT BLANKETED EVERYTHING!
I AM YOUR FATHER.
YOU SAW ME STRUGGLE AND YOU NEVER THOUGHT TO TELL ME THIS HUGE MISSING PIECE OF INFORMATION?
A PIECE, BY THE WAY, OF WHICH THERE WAS NOT EVEN A HINT OF A SHRED OF A CLUE FOR ME TO START TO DISCOVER ON MY OWN.
THE ONLY WAY I WOULD EVER HAVE KNOWN I WAS ADOPTED IS IF YOU TOLD ME, AND YOU NEVER DID.
NEITHER DID YOUR MOTHER.
BUT LET'S NOT STOP YOUR SELF-PERPETUATING NARRATIVE OF IDEALIZING HER WHILE SIMULTANEOUSLY DEMONIZING ME.

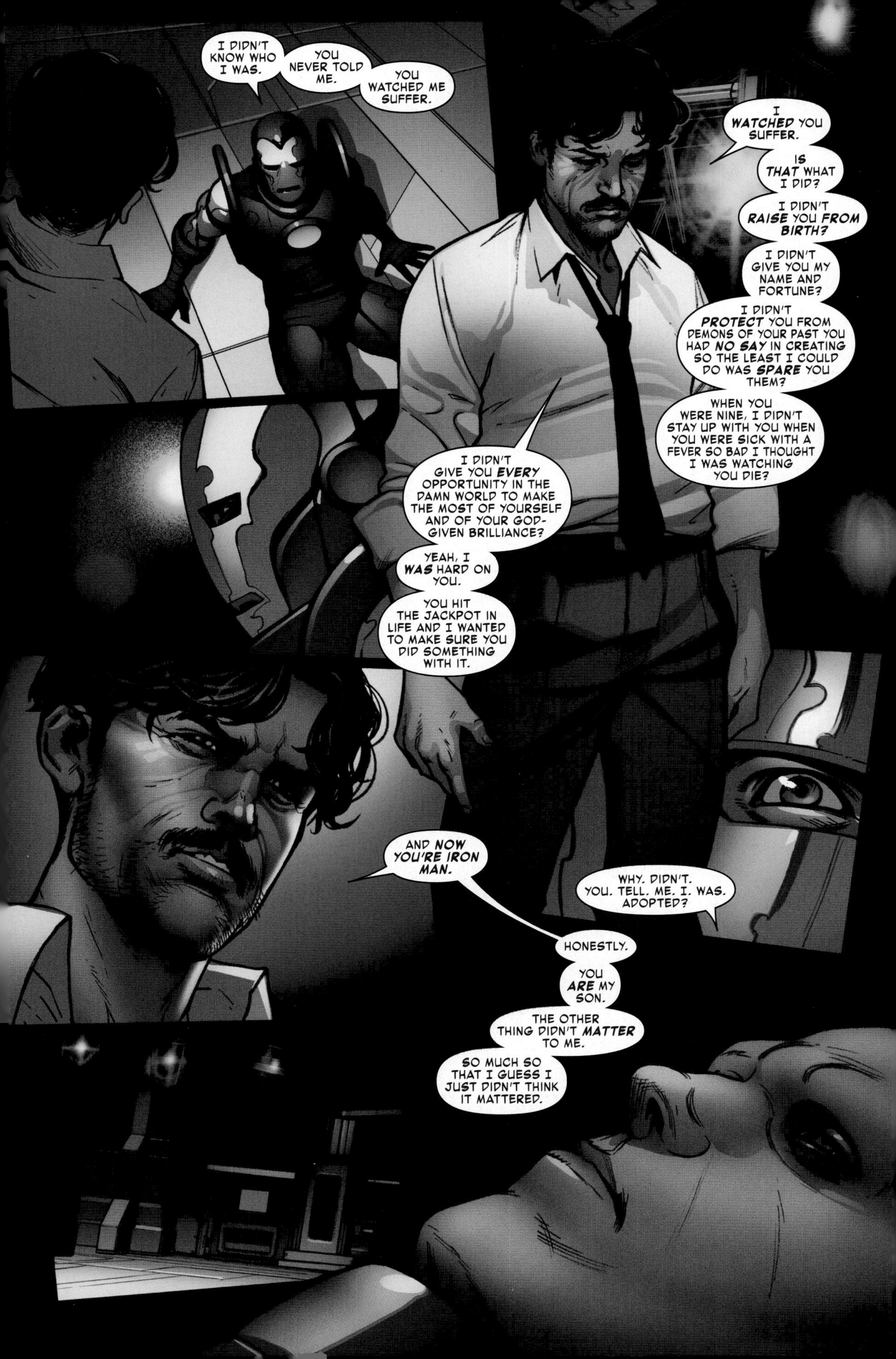
I DIDN'T KNOW WHO I WAS.
YOU NEVER TOLD ME.
YOU WATCHED ME SUFFER.
I WATCHED YOU SUFFER.
IS THAT WHAT I DID?
I DIDN'T RAISE YOU FROM BIRTH?
I DIDN'T GIVE YOU MY NAME AND FORTUNE?
I DIDN'T PROTECT YOU FROM DEMONS OF YOUR PAST YOU HAD NO SAY IN CREATING SO THE LEAST I COULD DO WAS SPARE YOU THEM?
WHEN YOU WERE NINE, I DIDN'T STAY UP WITH YOU WHEN YOU WERE SICK WITH A FEVER SO BAD I THOUGHT I WAS WATCHING YOU DIE?
I DIDN'T GIVE YOU EVERY OPPORTUNITY IN THE DAMN WORLD TO MAKE THE MOST OF YOURSELF AND OF YOUR GOD-GIVEN BRILLIANCE?
YEAH, I WAS HARD ON YOU.
YOU HIT THE JACKPOT IN LIFE AND I WANTED TO MAKE SURE YOU DID SOMETHING WITH IT.
AND NOW YOU'RE IRON MAN.
WHY. DIDN'T. YOU. TELL. ME. I. WAS. ADOPTED?
HONESTLY.
YOU ARE MY SON.
THE OTHER THING DIDN'T MATTER TO ME.
SO MUCH SO THAT I GUESS I JUST DIDN'T THINK IT MATTERED.

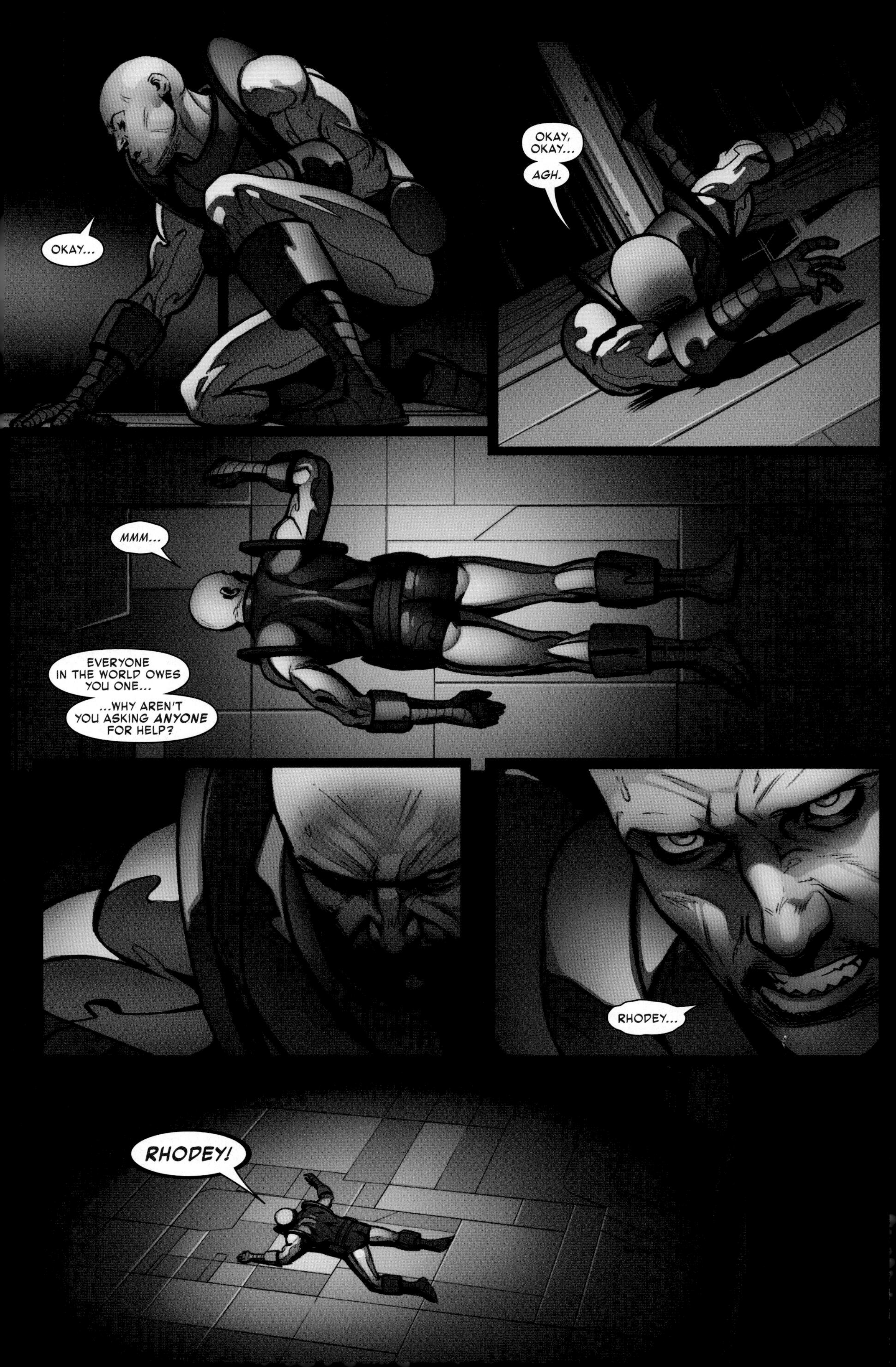
OKAY...
OKAY, OKAY...
AGH.
MMM...
EVERYONE IN THE WORLD OWES YOU ONE...
...WHY AREN'T YOU ASKING ANYONE FOR HELP?
RHODEY...
RHODEY!

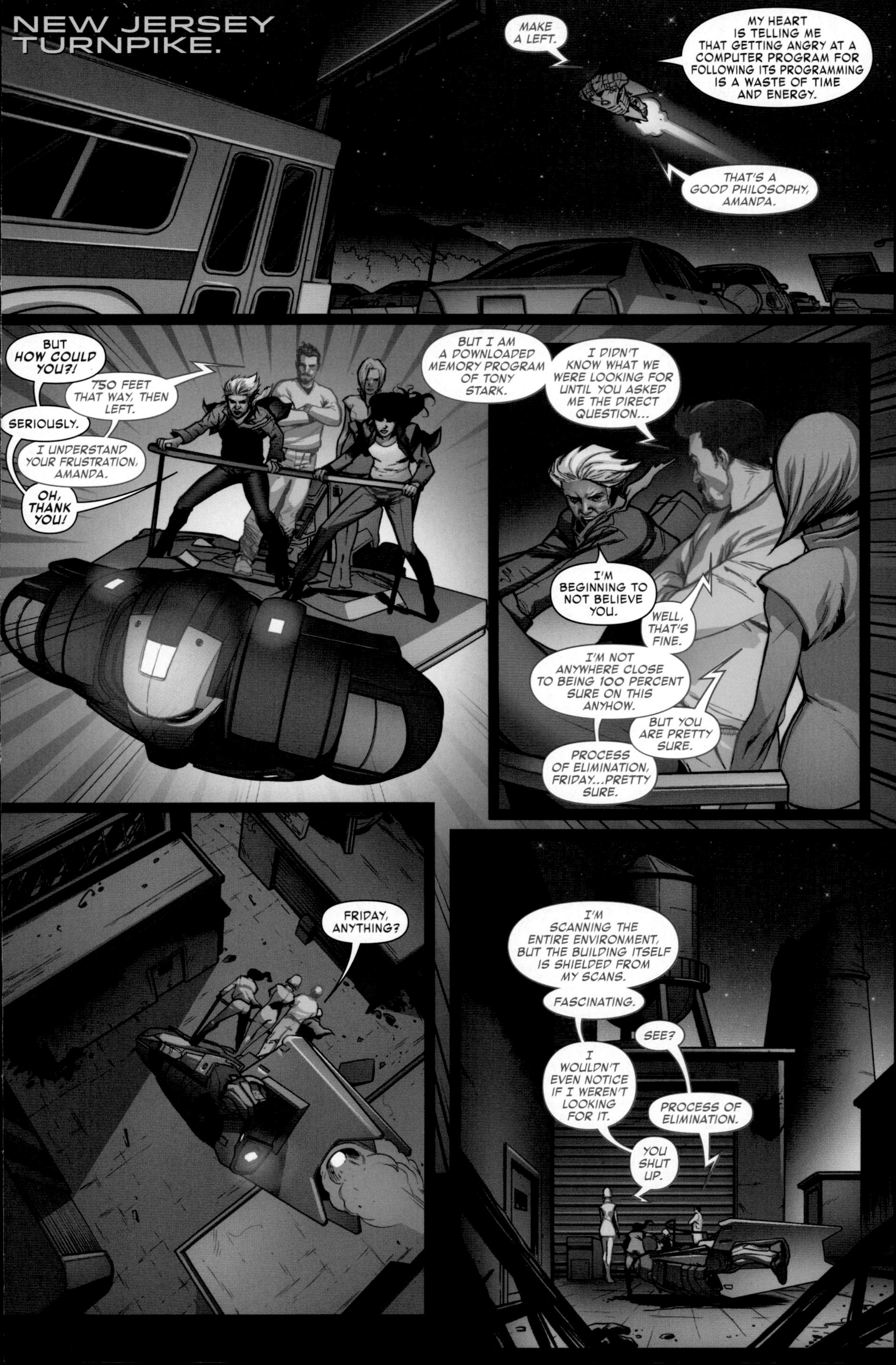
NEW JERSEY TURNPIKE.
MAKE A LEFT.
MY HEART IS TELLING ME THAT GETTING ANGRY AT A COMPUTER PROGRAM FOR FOLLOWING ITS PROGRAMMING IS A WASTE OF TIME AND ENERGY.
THAT'S A GOOD PHILOSOPHY, AMANDA.
BUT HOW COULD YOU?!
750 FEET THAT WAY, THEN LEFT.
SERIOUSLY.
I UNDERSTAND YOUR FRUSTRATION, AMANDA.
OH, THANK YOU!
BUT I AM A DOWNLOADED MEMORY PROGRAM OF TONY STARK.
I DIDN'T KNOW WHAT WE WERE LOOKING FOR UNTIL YOU ASKED ME THE DIRECT QUESTION...
I'M BEGINNING TO NOT BELIEVE YOU.
WELL, THAT'S FINE.
I'M NOT ANYWHERE CLOSE TO BEING 100 PERCENT SURE ON THIS ANYHOW.
BUT YOU ARE PRETTY SURE.
PROCESS OF ELIMINATION, FRIDAY...PRETTY SURE.
FRIDAY, ANYTHING?
I'M SCANNING THE ENTIRE ENVIRONMENT, BUT THE BUILDING ITSELF IS SHIELDED FROM MY SCANS.
FASCINATING.
SEE?
I WOULDN'T EVEN NOTICE IF I WEREN'T LOOKING FOR IT.
PROCESS OF ELIMINATION.
YOU SHUT UP.

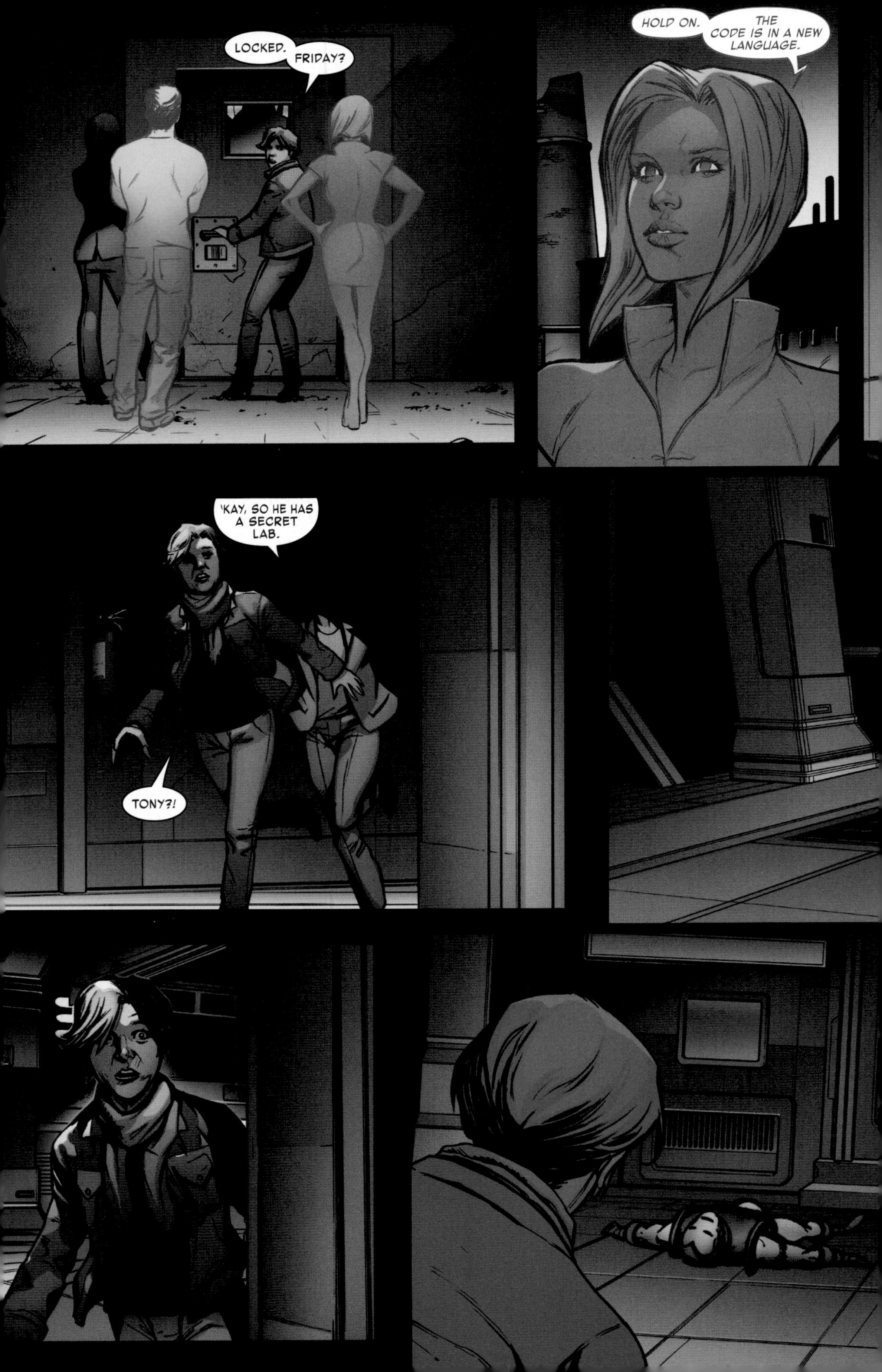

LOCKED.
FRIDAY?
HOLD ON.
THE CODE IS IN A NEW LANGUAGE.
'KAY, SO HE HAS A SECRET LAB.
TONY?!

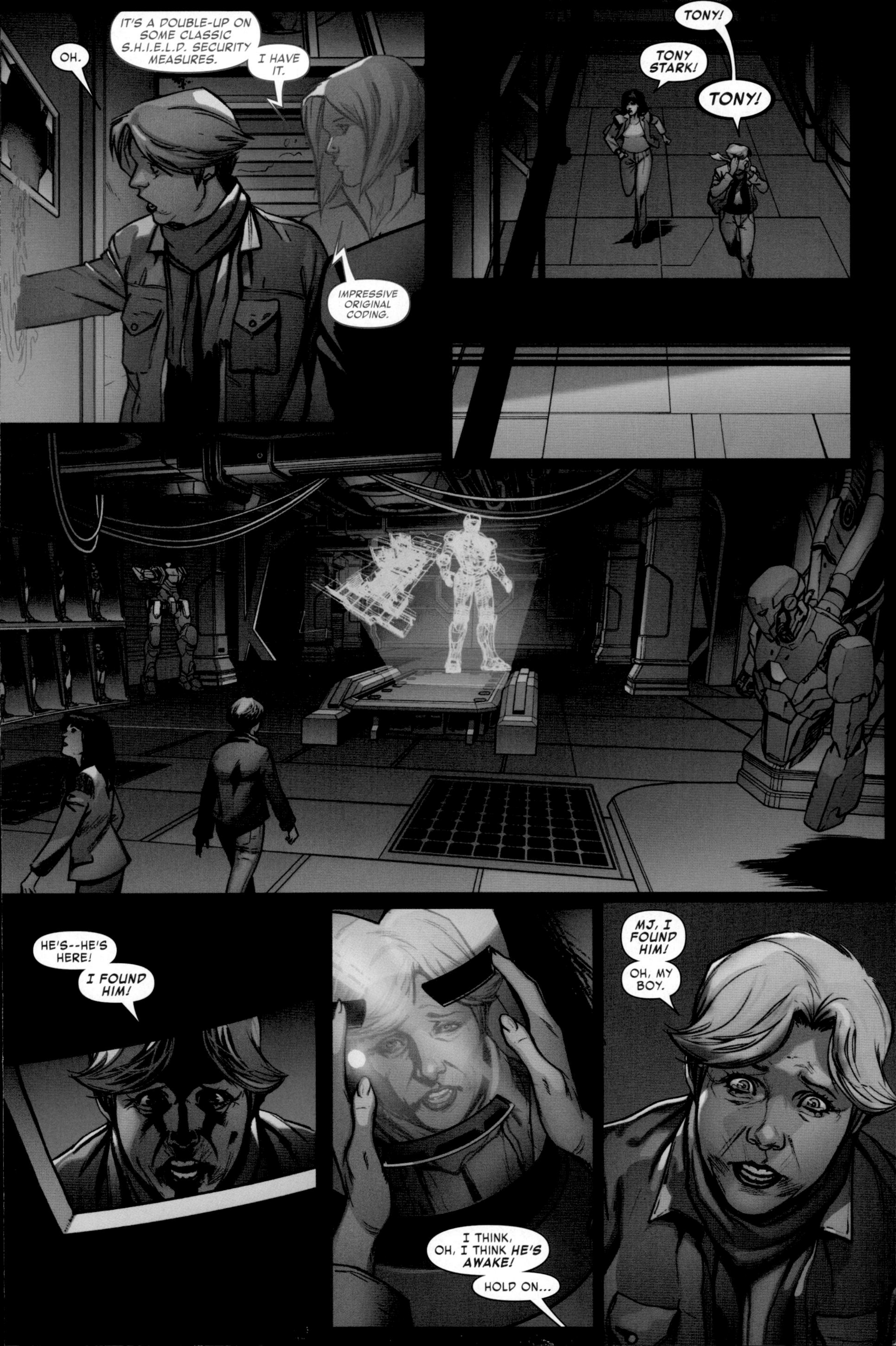
OH.
IT'S A DOUBLE-UP ON SOME CLASSIC S.H.I.E.L.D. SECURITY MEASURES.
I HAVE IT.
IMPRESSIVE ORIGINAL CODING.
TONY!
TONY STARK!
TONY!
HE'S--HE'S HERE!
I FOUND HIM!
I THINK, OH, I THINK HE'S AWAKE!
HOLD ON...
MJ, I FOUND HIM!
OH, MY BOY.

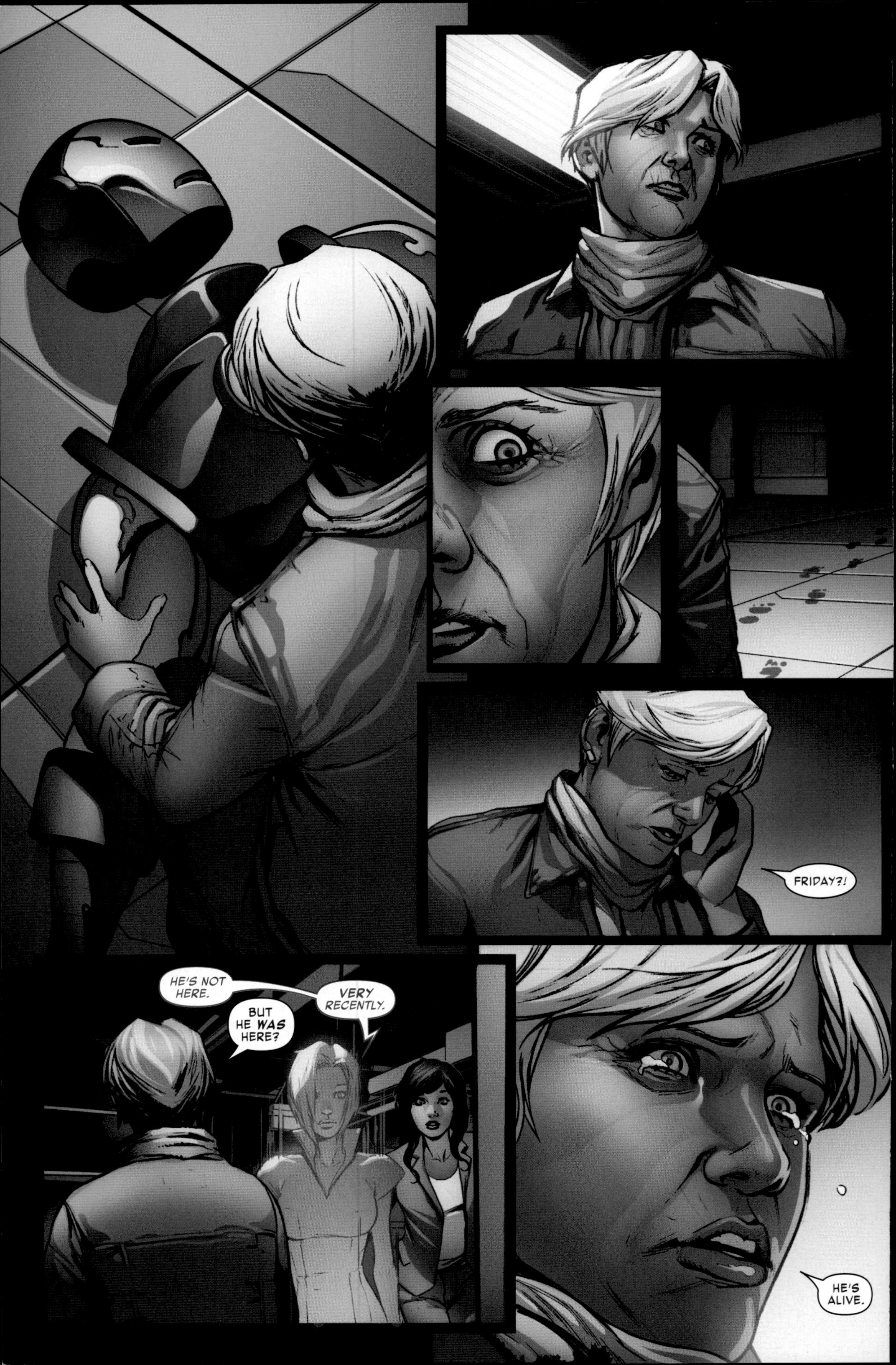
FRIDAY?!
HE'S NOT HERE.
BUT HE WAS HERE?
VERY RECENTLY.
HE'S ALIVE.

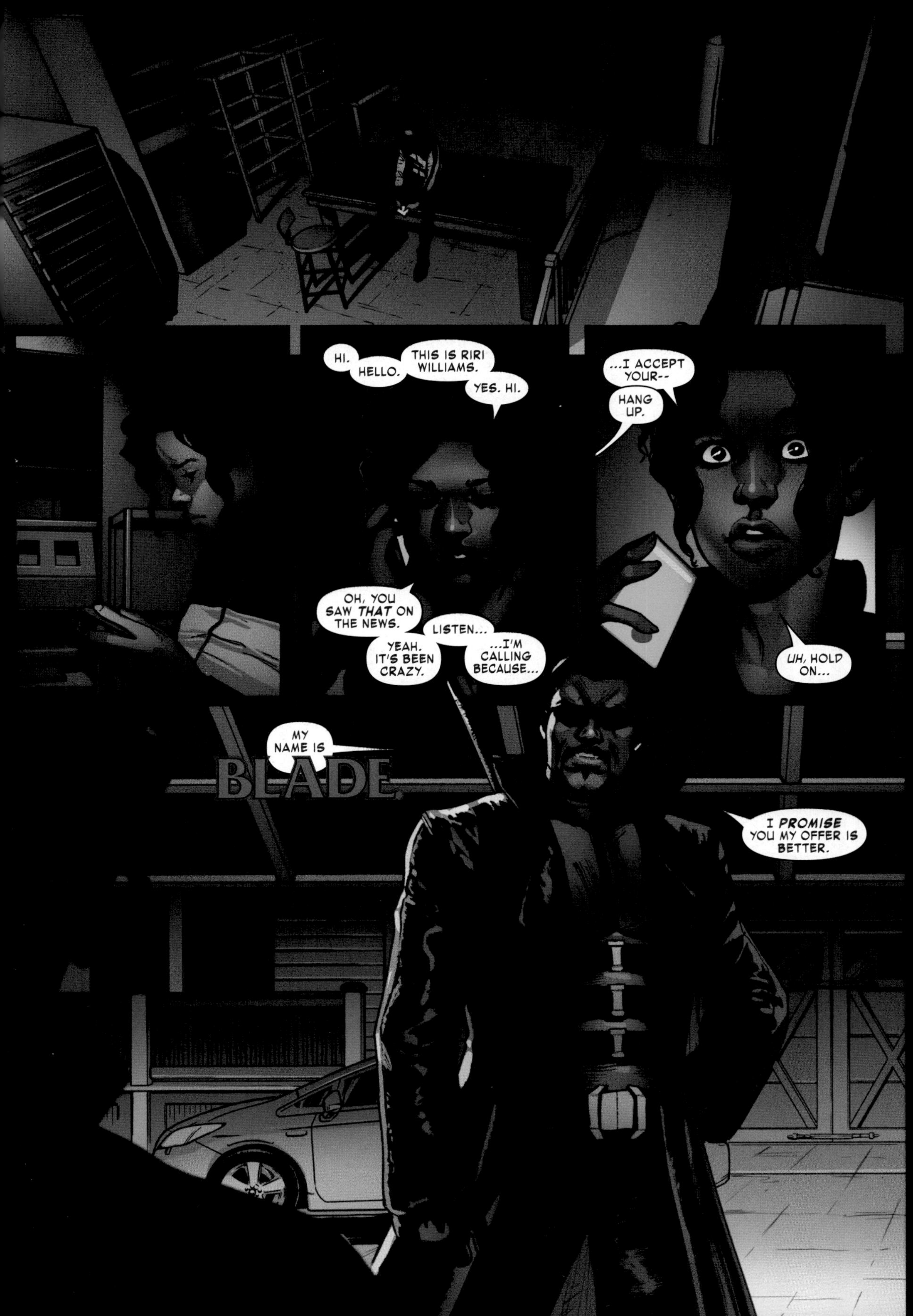
HI.
HELLO.
THIS IS RIRI WILLIAMS.
YES. HI.
OH, YOU SAW THAT ON THE NEWS.
YEAH. IT'S BEEN CRAZY.
LISTEN...
...I'M CALLING BECAUSE...
...I ACCEPT YOUR--
HANG UP.
UH, HOLD ON...
MY NAME IS
BLADE.
I PROMISE YOU MY OFFER IS BETTER.

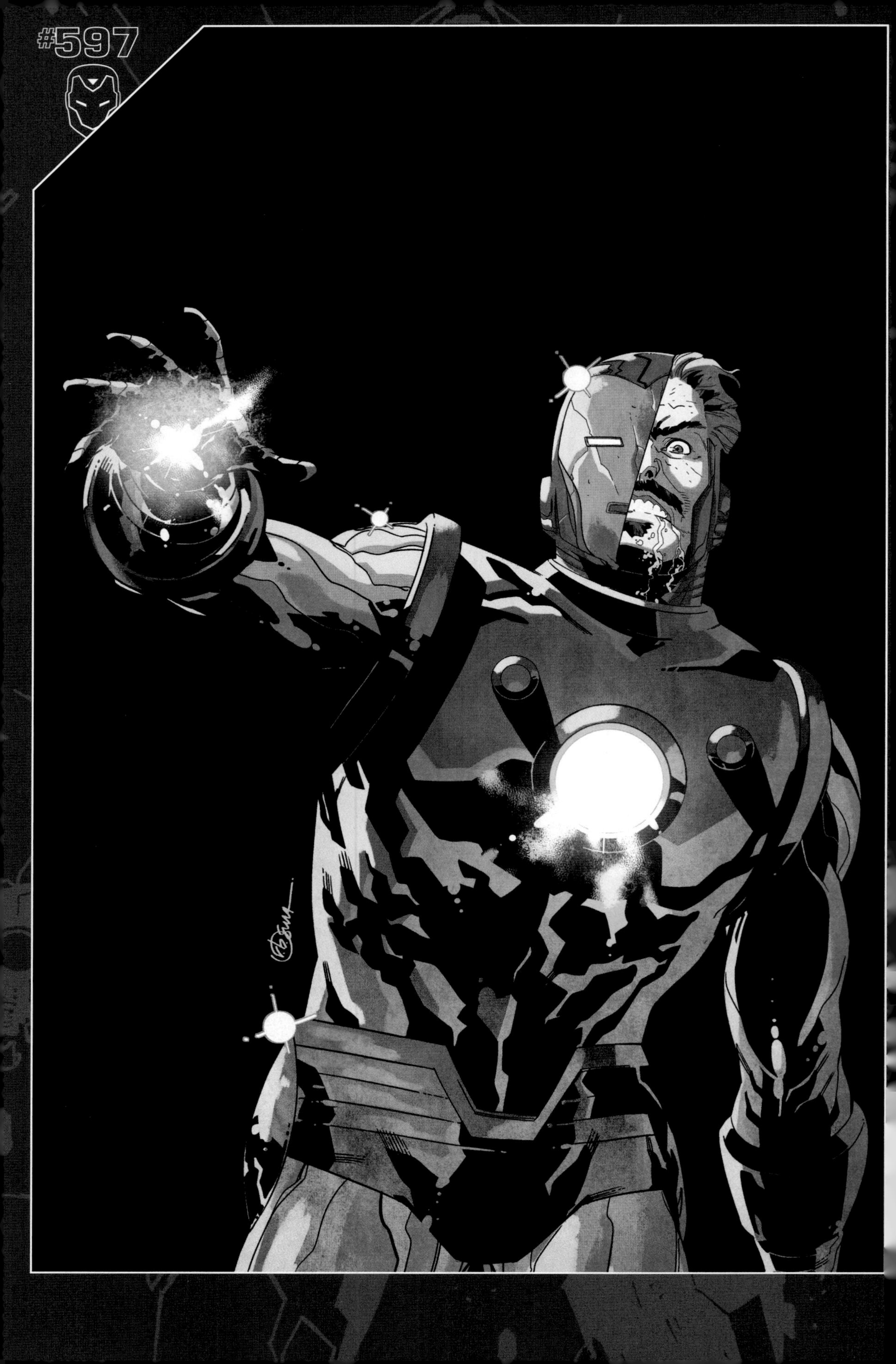
#597

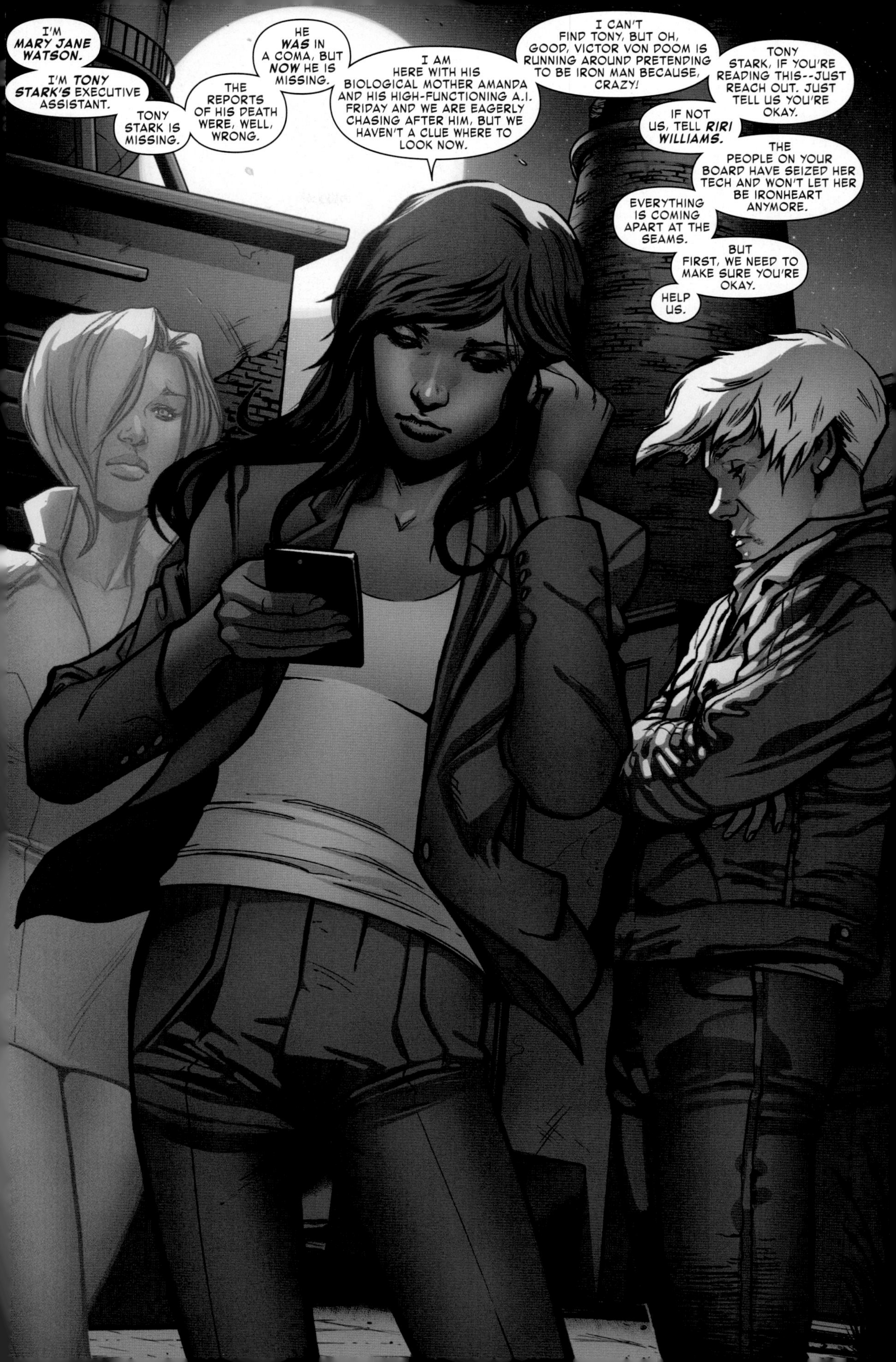
I'M MARY JANE WATSON.
I'M TONY STARK'S EXECUTIVE ASSISTANT.
TONY STARK IS MISSING.
THE REPORTS OF HIS DEATH WERE, WELL, WRONG.
HE WAS IN A COMA, BUT NOW HE IS MISSING.
I AM HERE WITH HIS BIOLOGICAL MOTHER AMANDA AND HIS HIGH-FUNCTIONING A.I. FRIDAY AND WE ARE EAGERLY CHASING AFTER HIM, BUT WE HAVEN'T A CLUE WHERE TO LOOK NOW.
I CAN'T FIND TONY, BUT OH, GOOD, VICTOR VON DOOM IS RUNNING AROUND PRETENDING TO BE IRON MAN BECAUSE, CRAZY!
TONY STARK, IF YOU'RE READING THIS--JUST REACH OUT. JUST TELL US YOU'RE OKAY.
IF NOT US, TELL RIRI WILLIAMS.
THE PEOPLE ON YOUR BOARD HAVE SEIZED HER TECH AND WON'T LET HER BE IRONHEART ANYMORE.
EVERYTHING IS COMING APART AT THE SEAMS.
BUT FIRST, WE NEED TO MAKE SURE YOU'RE OKAY.
HELP US.

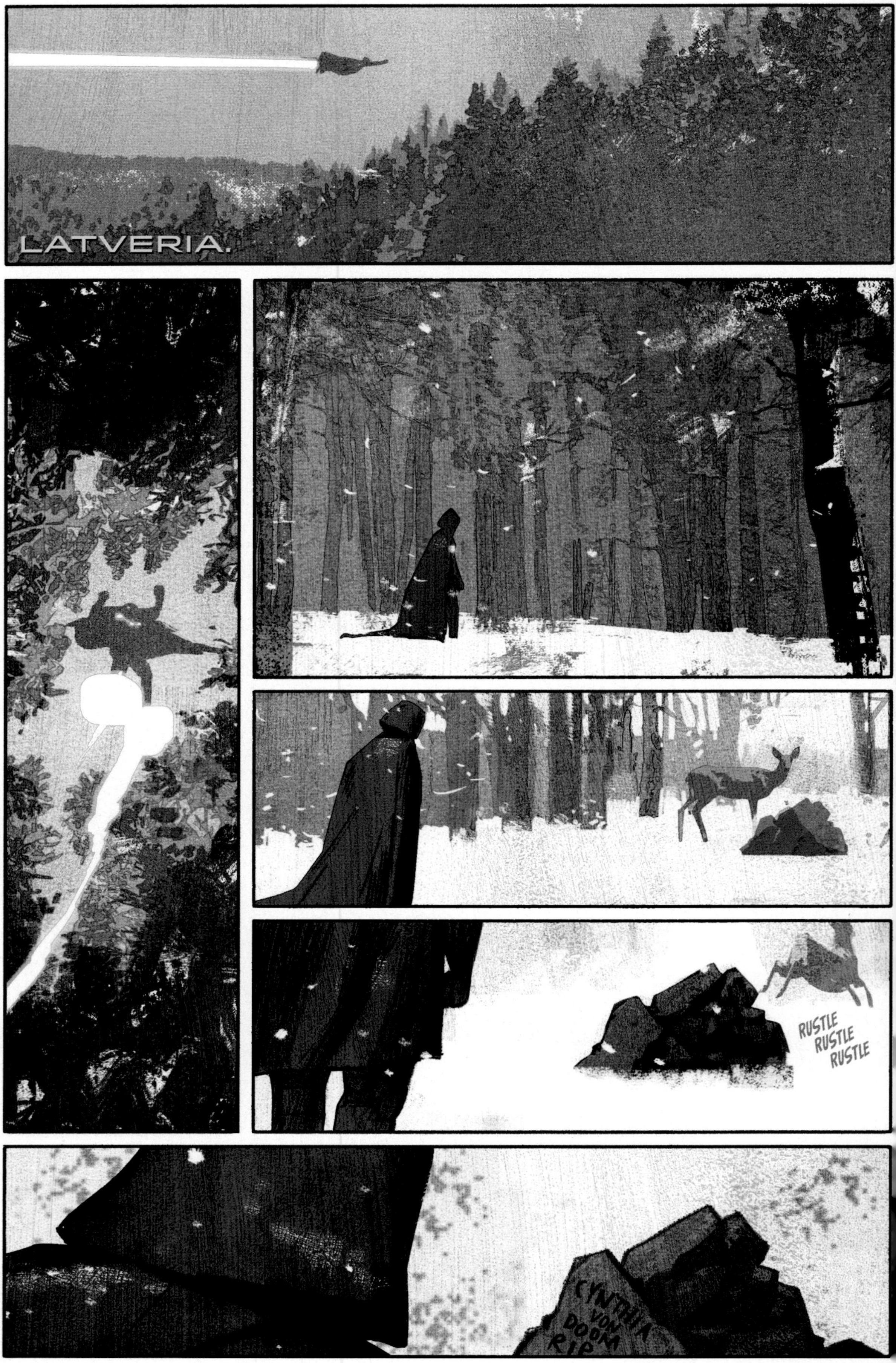
LATVERIA.
RUSTLE
RUSTLE
RUSTLE
CYNTHIA
VON
DOOM
RIP

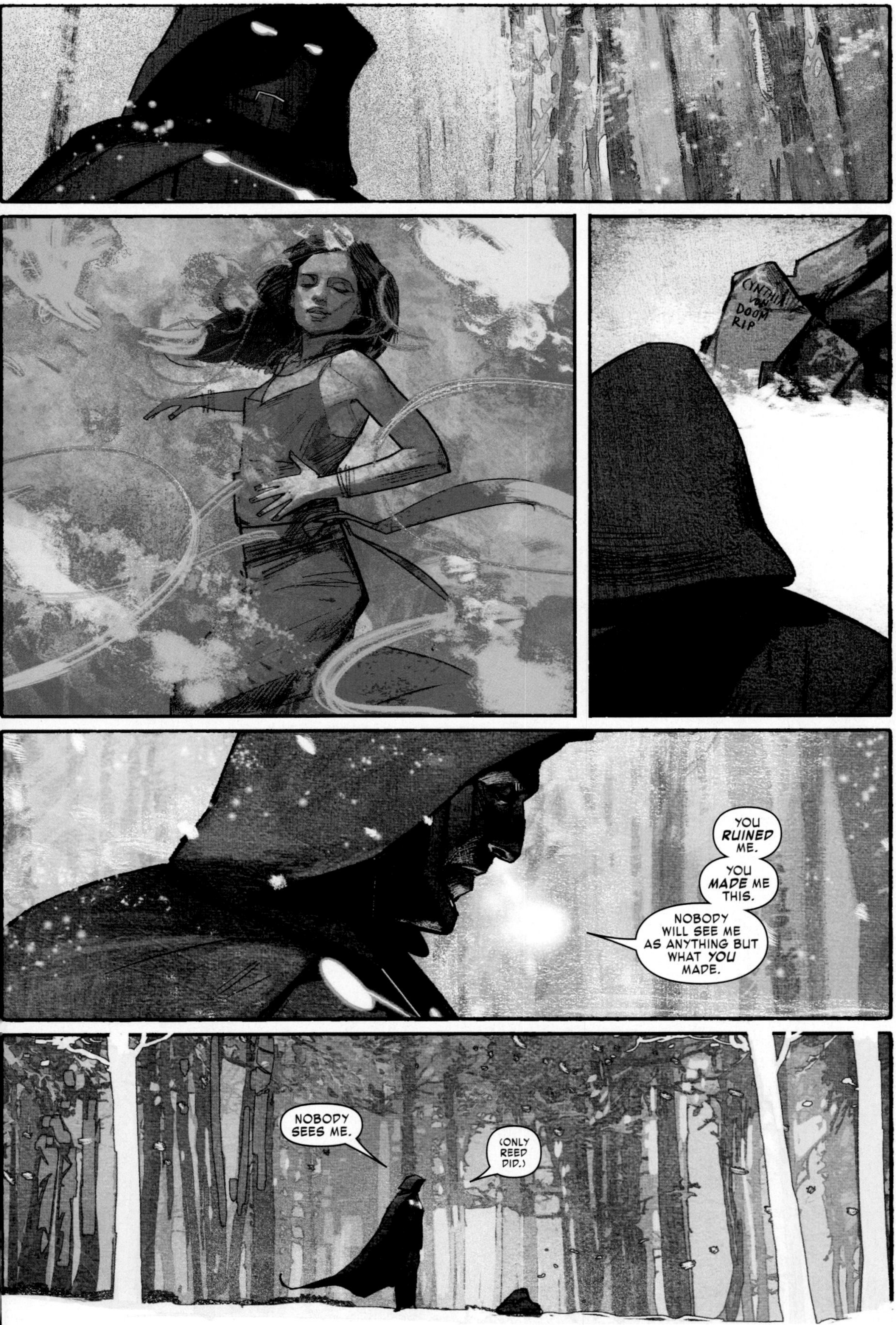
CYNTHIA VON DOOM RIP
YOU RUINED ME.
YOU MADE ME THIS.
NOBODY WILL SEE ME AS ANYTHING BUT WHAT YOU MADE.
NOBODY SEES ME.
(ONLY REED DID.)

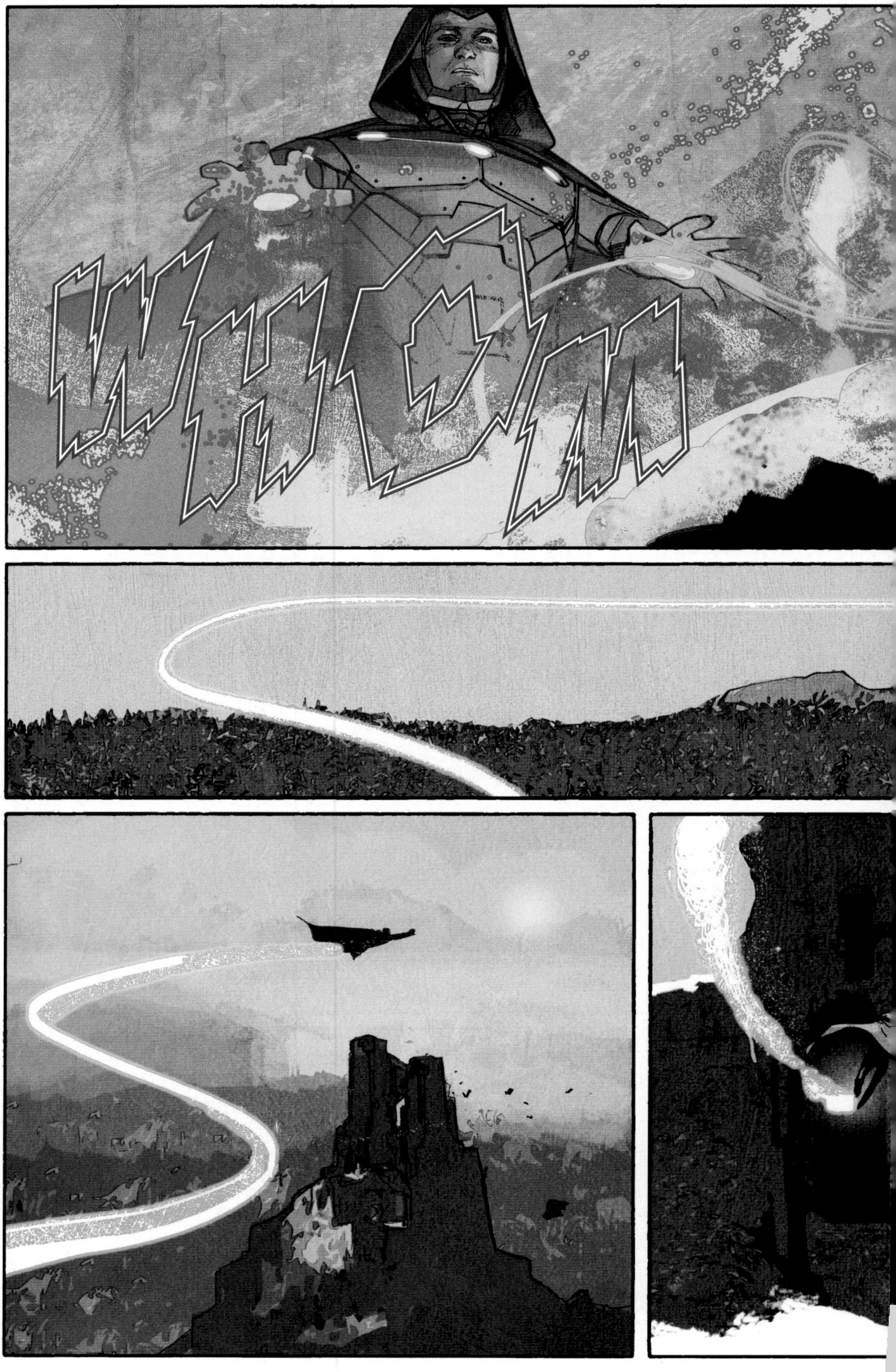
WHOOM

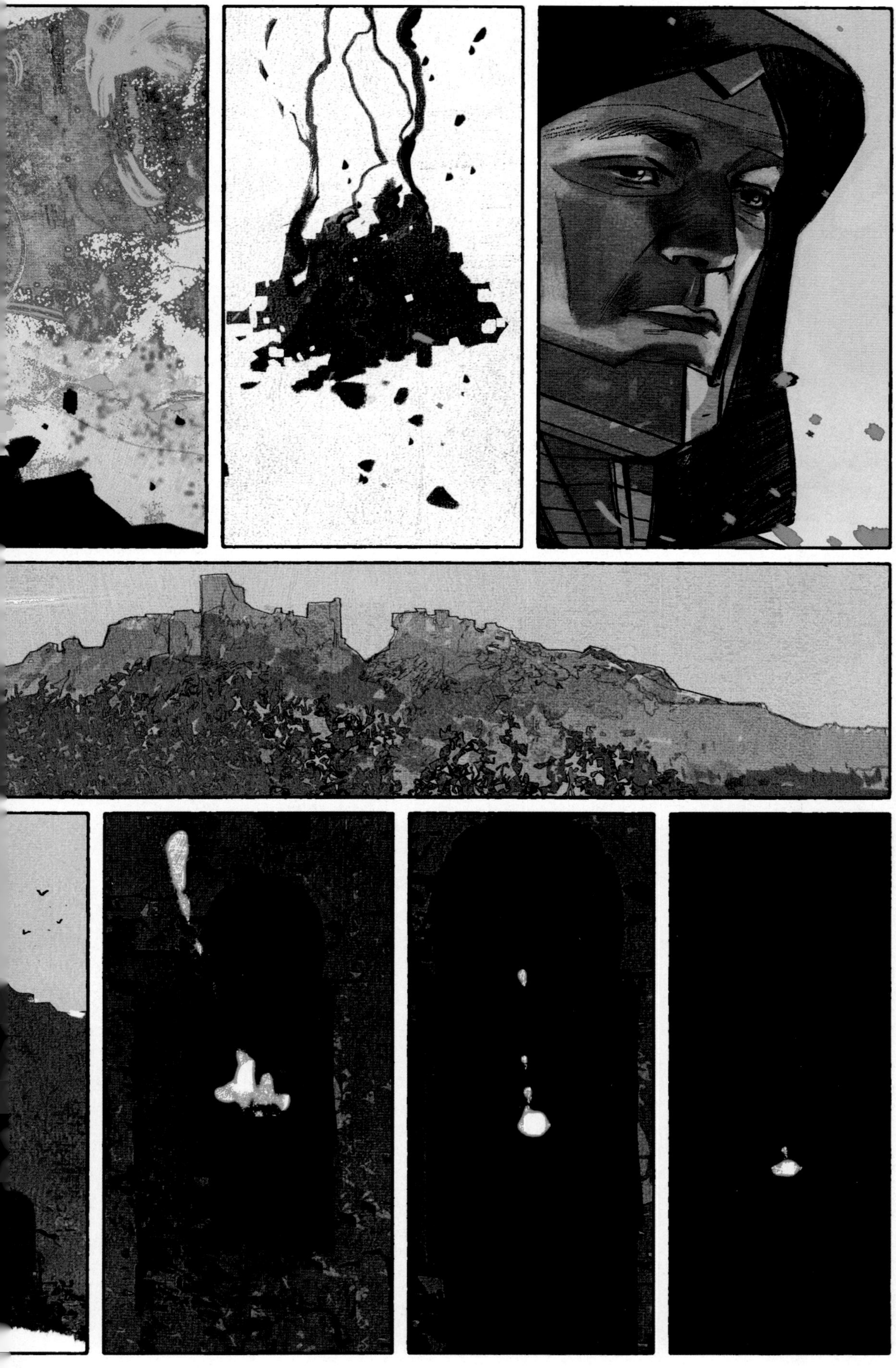

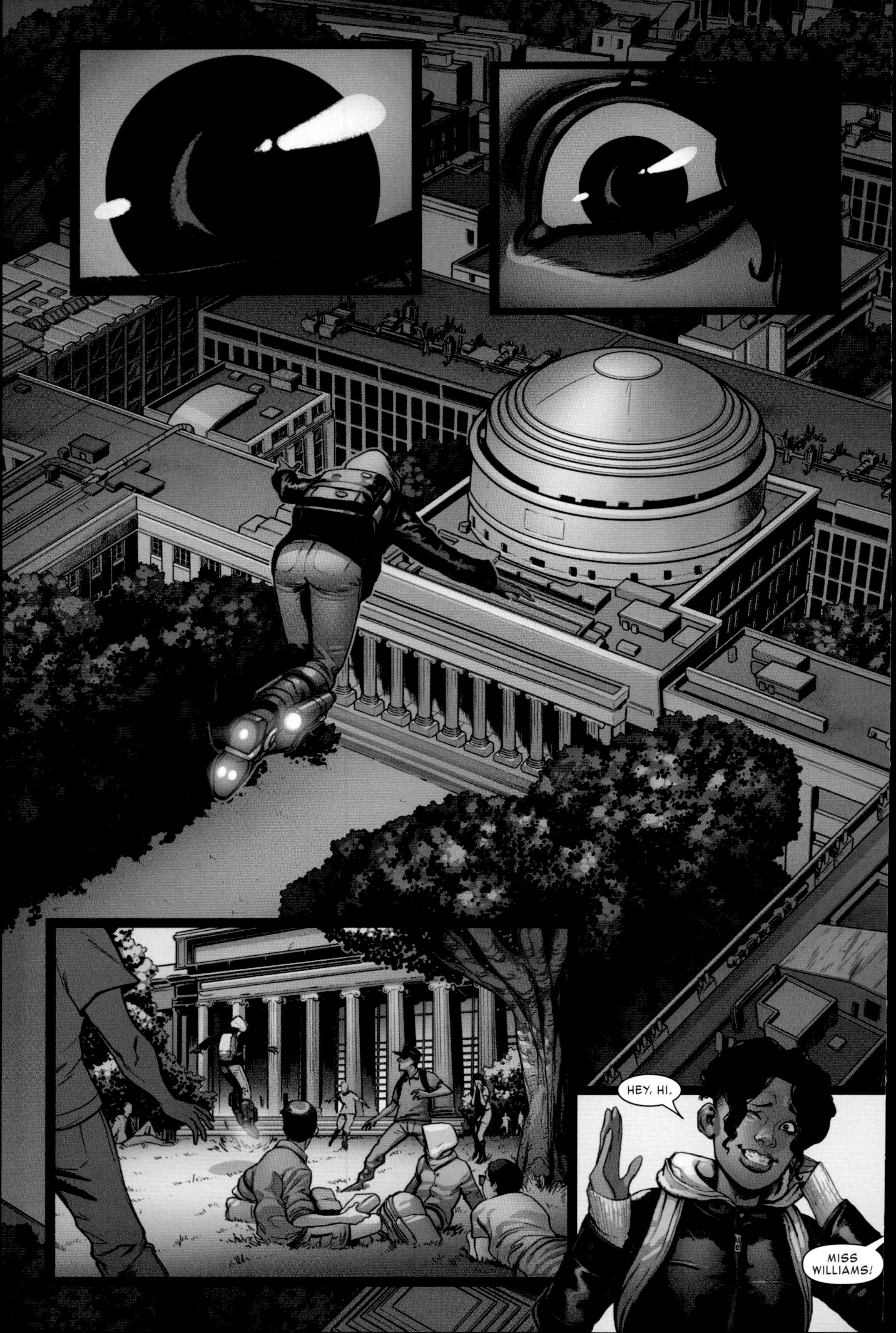
HEY, HI.
MISS WILLIAMS!

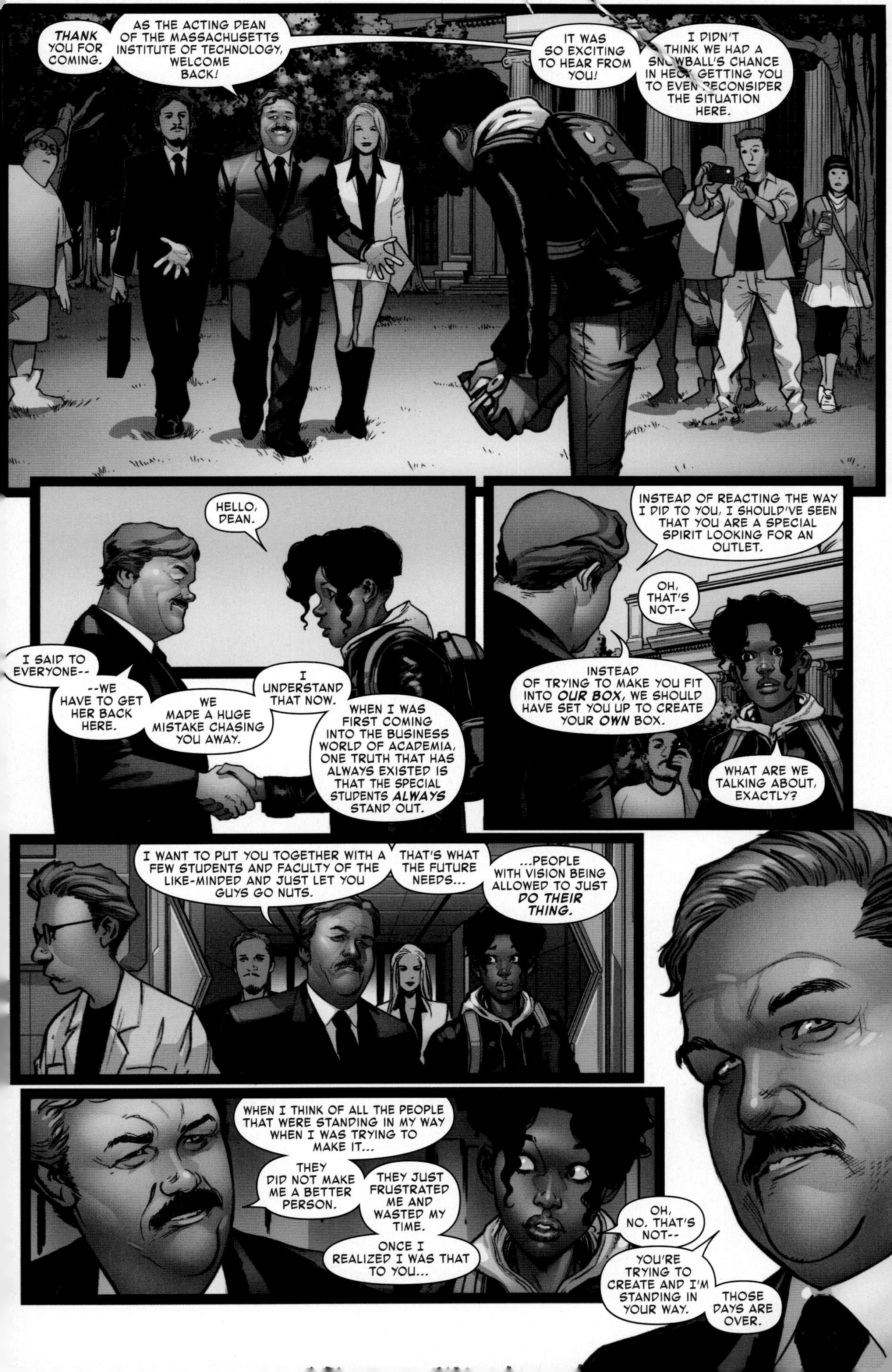
THANK YOU FOR COMING.
AS THE ACTING DEAN OF THE MASSACHUSETTS INSTITUTE OF TECHNOLOGY, WELCOME BACK!
IT WAS SO EXCITING TO HEAR FROM YOU!
I DIDN'T THINK WE HAD A SNOWBALL'S CHANCE IN HECK GETTING YOU TO EVEN RECONSIDER THE SITUATION HERE.
HELLO, DEAN.
I SAID TO EVERYONE--
--WE HAVE TO GET HER BACK HERE.
WE MADE A HUGE MISTAKE CHASING YOU AWAY.
I UNDERSTAND THAT NOW.
WHEN I WAS FIRST COMING INTO THE BUSINESS WORLD OF ACADEMIA, ONE TRUTH THAT HAS ALWAYS EXISTED IS THAT THE SPECIAL STUDENTS ALWAYS STAND OUT.
INSTEAD OF REACTING THE WAY I DID TO YOU, I SHOULD'VE SEEN THAT YOU ARE A SPECIAL SPIRIT LOOKING FOR AN OUTLET.
OH, THAT'S NOT--
INSTEAD OF TRYING TO MAKE YOU FIT INTO OUR BOX, WE SHOULD HAVE SET YOU UP TO CREATE YOUR OWN BOX.
WHAT ARE WE TALKING ABOUT, EXACTLY?
I WANT TO PUT YOU TOGETHER WITH A FEW STUDENTS AND FACULTY OF THE LIKE-MINDED AND JUST LET YOU GUYS GO NUTS.
THAT'S WHAT THE FUTURE NEEDS...
...PEOPLE WITH VISION BEING ALLOWED TO JUST DO THEIR THING.
WHEN I THINK OF ALL THE PEOPLE THAT WERE STANDING IN MY WAY WHEN I WAS TRYING TO MAKE IT...
THEY DID NOT MAKE ME A BETTER PERSON.
THEY JUST FRUSTRATED ME AND WASTED MY TIME.
ONCE I REALIZED I WAS THAT TO YOU...
OH, NO. THAT'S NOT--
YOU'RE TRYING TO CREATE AND I'M STANDING IN YOUR WAY.
THOSE DAYS ARE OVER.

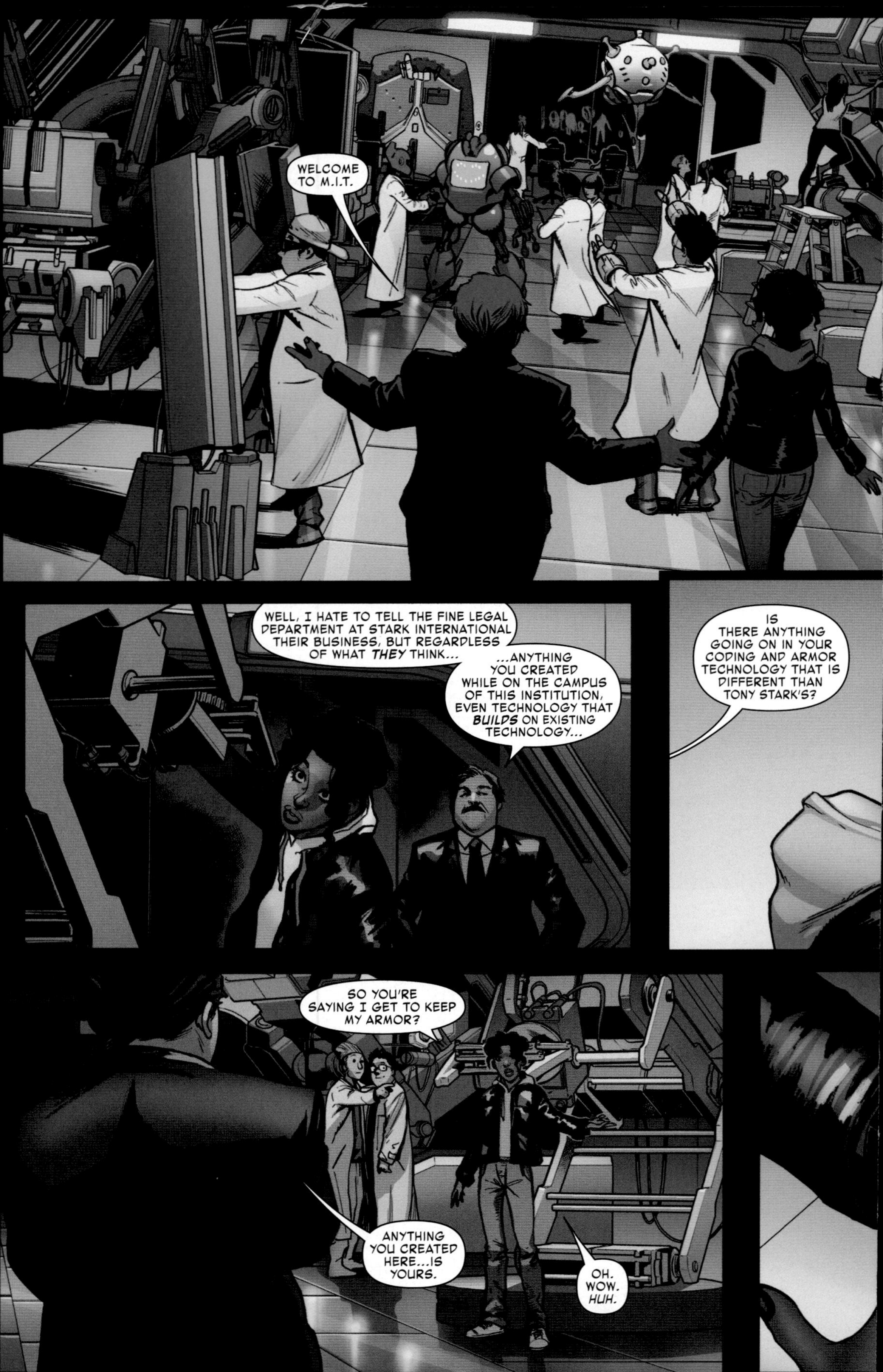

WELCOME TO M.I.T.
WELL, I HATE TO TELL THE FINE LEGAL DEPARTMENT AT STARK INTERNATIONAL THEIR BUSINESS, BUT REGARDLESS OF WHAT THEY THINK...
...ANYTHING YOU CREATED WHILE ON THE CAMPUS OF THIS INSTITUTION, EVEN TECHNOLOGY THAT BUILDS ON EXISTING TECHNOLOGY...
IS THERE ANYTHING GOING ON IN YOUR CODING AND ARMOR TECHNOLOGY THAT IS DIFFERENT THAN TONY STARK'S?
SO YOU'RE SAYING I GET TO KEEP MY ARMOR?
ANYTHING YOU CREATED HERE...IS YOURS.
OH. WOW. HUH.

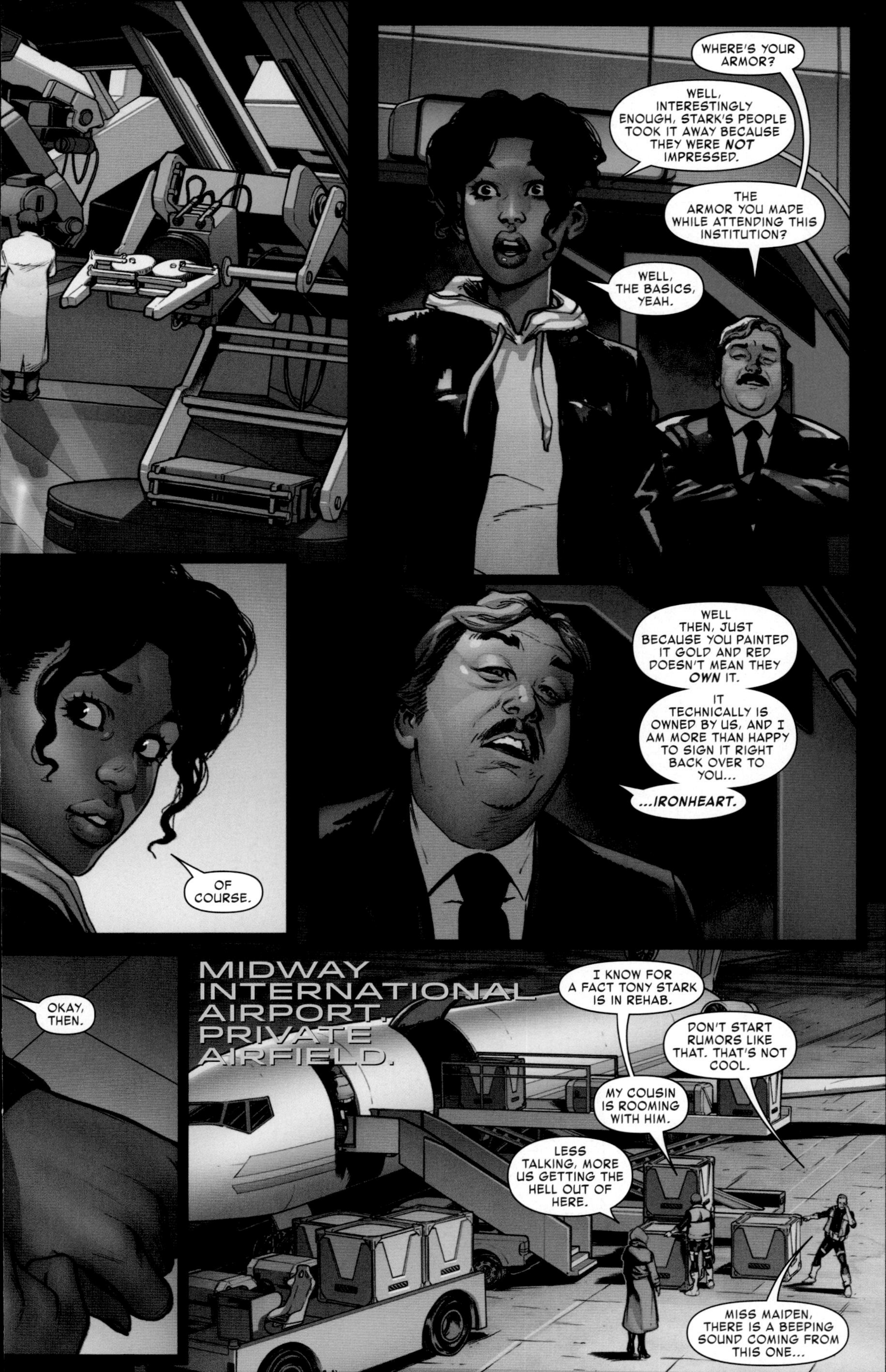
WHERE'S YOUR ARMOR?
WELL, INTERESTINGLY ENOUGH, STARK'S PEOPLE TOOK IT AWAY BECAUSE THEY WERE NOT IMPRESSED.
THE ARMOR YOU MADE WHILE ATTENDING THIS INSTITUTION?
WELL, THE BASICS, YEAH.
WELL THEN, JUST BECAUSE YOU PAINTED IT GOLD AND RED DOESN'T MEAN THEY OWN IT.
IT TECHNICALLY IS OWNED BY US, AND I AM MORE THAN HAPPY TO SIGN IT RIGHT BACK OVER TO YOU...
...IRONHEART.
OF COURSE.
OKAY, THEN.
MIDWAY INTERNATIONAL AIRPORT. PRIVATE AIRFIELD.
I KNOW FOR A FACT TONY STARK IS IN REHAB.
DON'T START RUMORS LIKE THAT. THAT'S NOT COOL.
MY COUSIN IS ROOMING WITH HIM.
LESS TALKING, MORE US GETTING THE HELL OUT OF HERE.
MISS MAIDEN, THERE IS A BEEPING SOUND COMING FROM THIS ONE...

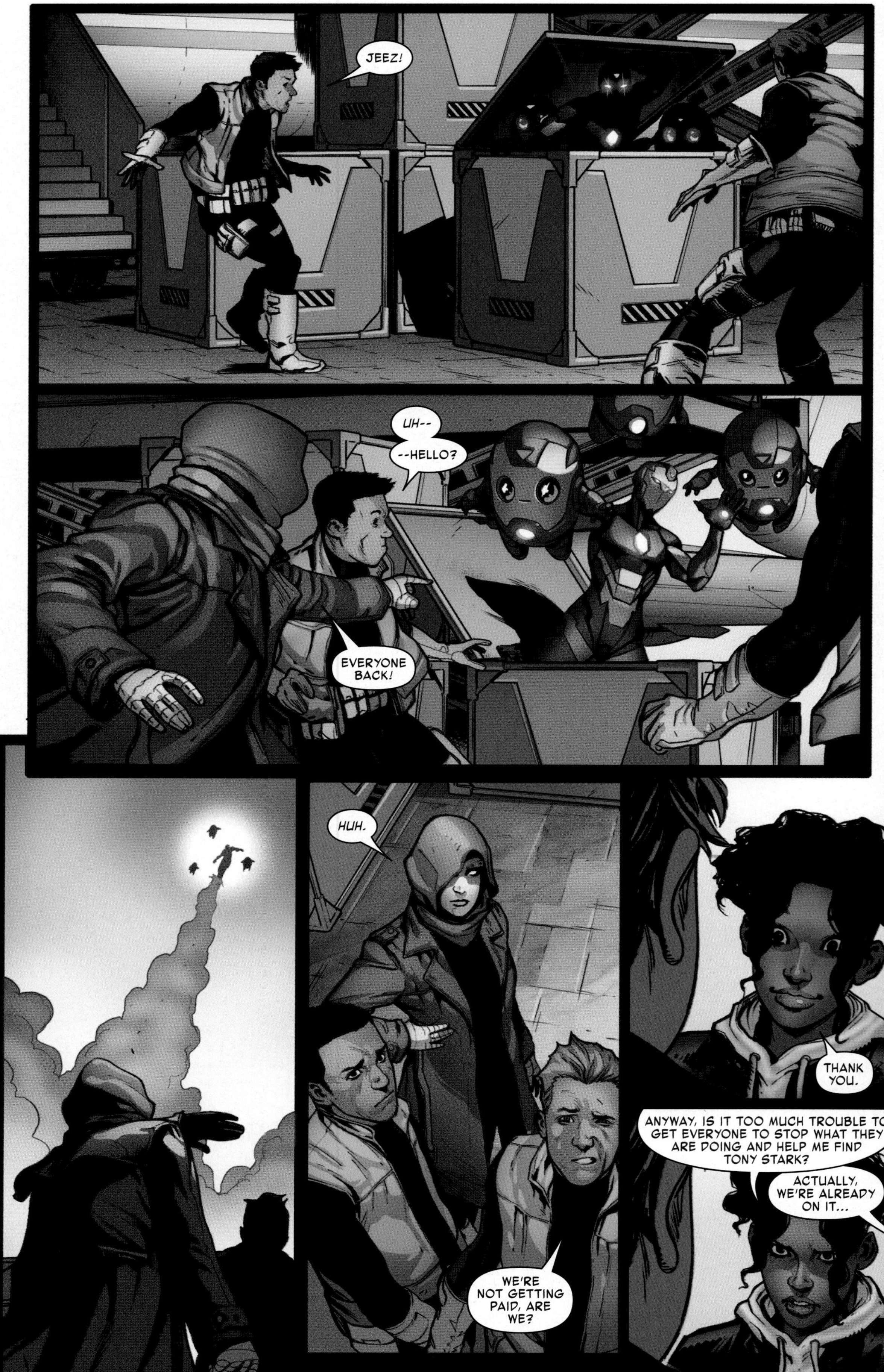
JEEZ!
UH--
--HELLO?
EVERYONE BACK!
HUH.
WE'RE NOT GETTING PAID, ARE WE?
THANK YOU.
ANYWAY, IS IT TOO MUCH TROUBLE TO GET EVERYONE TO STOP WHAT THEY ARE DOING AND HELP ME FIND TONY STARK?
ACTUALLY, WE'RE ALREADY ON IT...

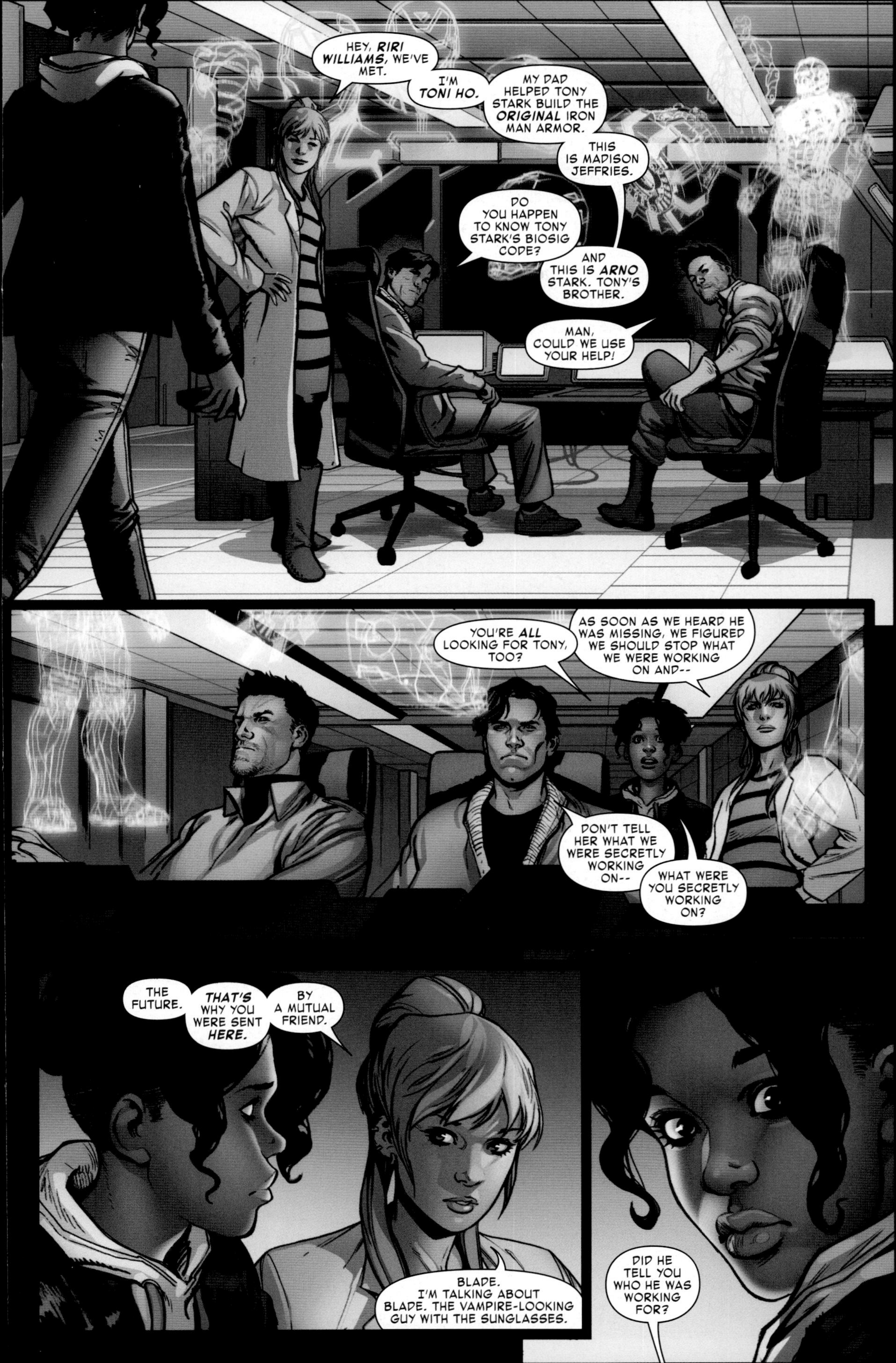
HEY, **RIRI WILLIAMS,** WE'VE MET.
I'M ***TONI HO.***
MY DAD HELPED TONY STARK BUILD THE ***ORIGINAL*** IRON MAN ARMOR.
THIS IS MADISON JEFFRIES.
DO YOU HAPPEN TO KNOW TONY STARK'S BIOSIG CODE?
AND THIS IS ***ARNO*** STARK. TONY'S BROTHER.
MAN, COULD WE USE YOUR HELP!
YOU'RE ***ALL*** LOOKING FOR TONY, TOO?
AS SOON AS WE HEARD HE WAS MISSING, WE FIGURED WE SHOULD STOP WHAT WE WERE WORKING ON AND--
DON'T TELL HER WHAT WE WERE SECRETLY WORKING ON--
WHAT WERE YOU SECRETLY WORKING ON?
THE FUTURE.
***THAT'S*** WHY YOU WERE SENT ***HERE.***
BY A MUTUAL FRIEND.
BLADE. I'M TALKING ABOUT BLADE. THE VAMPIRE-LOOKING GUY WITH THE SUNGLASSES.
DID HE TELL YOU WHO HE WAS WORKING FOR?

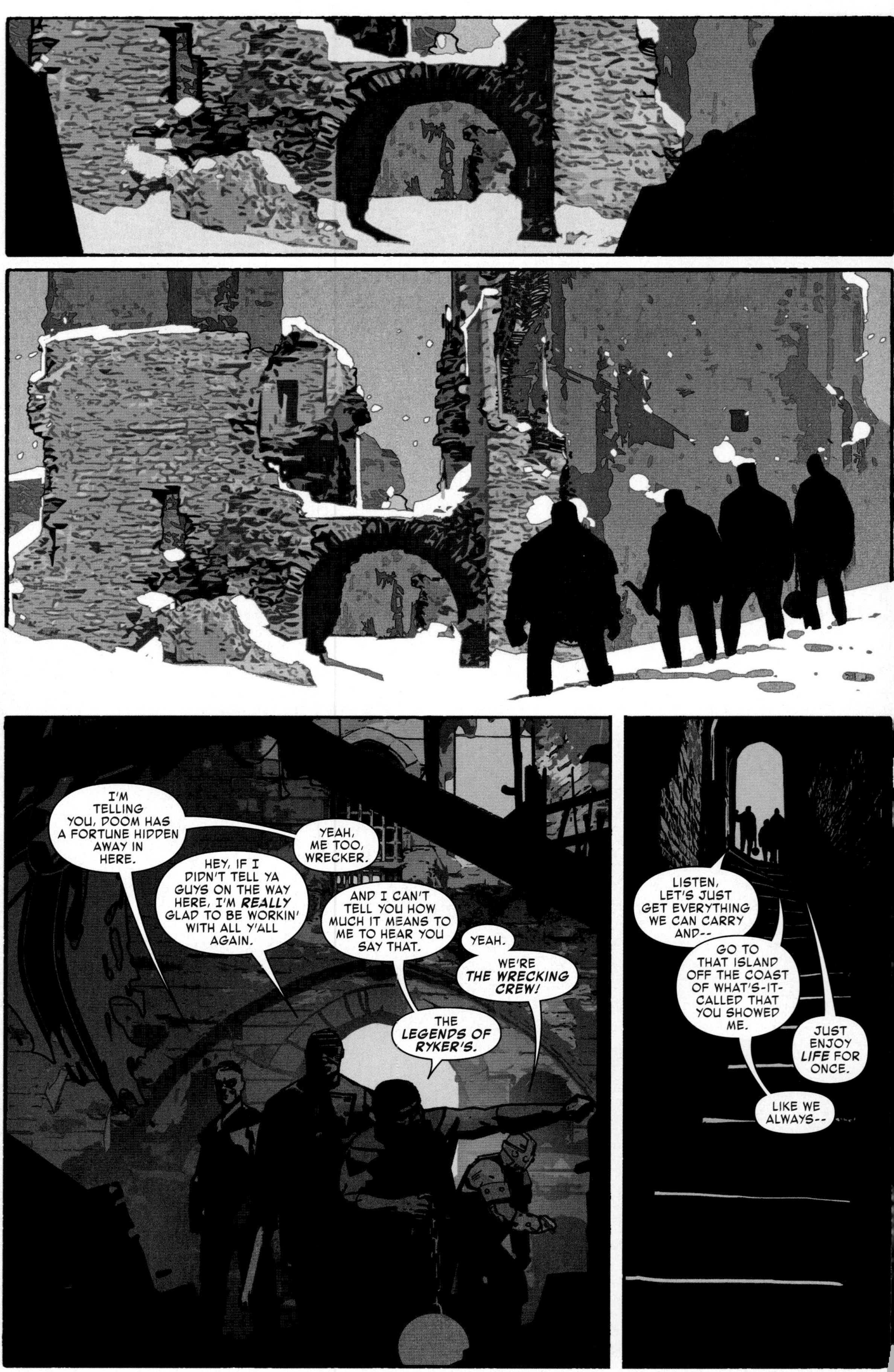
I'M TELLING YOU, DOOM HAS A FORTUNE HIDDEN AWAY IN HERE.
YEAH, ME TOO, WRECKER.
HEY, IF I DIDN'T TELL YA GUYS ON THE WAY HERE, I'M REALLY GLAD TO BE WORKIN' WITH ALL Y'ALL AGAIN.
AND I CAN'T TELL YOU HOW MUCH IT MEANS TO ME TO HEAR YOU SAY THAT.
YEAH.
WE'RE THE WRECKING CREW!
THE LEGENDS OF RYKER'S.
LISTEN, LET'S JUST GET EVERYTHING WE CAN CARRY AND--
GO TO THAT ISLAND OFF THE COAST OF WHAT'S-IT-CALLED THAT YOU SHOWED ME.
JUST ENJOY LIFE FOR ONCE.
LIKE WE ALWAYS--

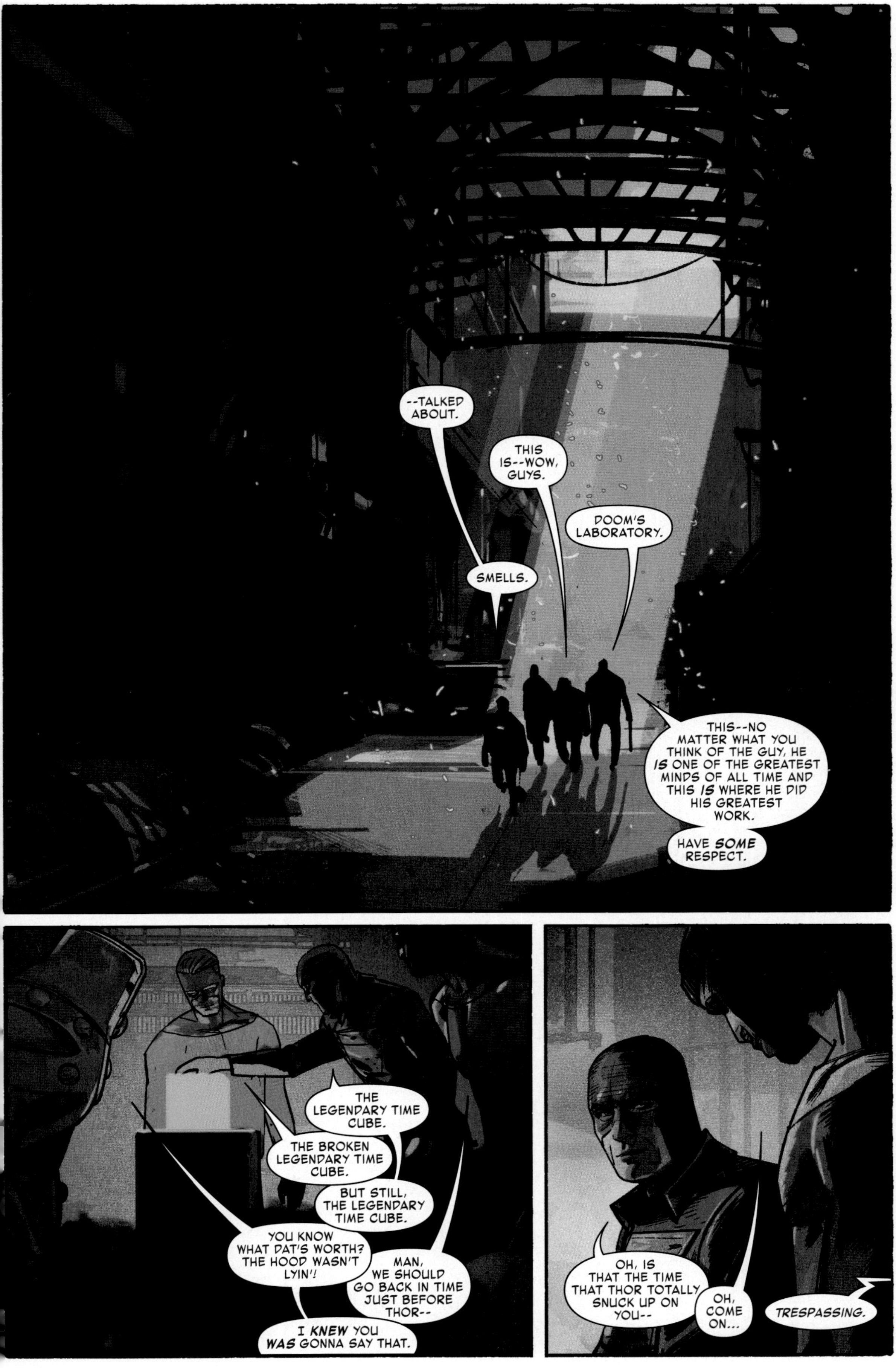
--TALKED ABOUT.
SMELLS.
THIS IS--WOW, GUYS.
DOOM'S LABORATORY.
THIS--NO MATTER WHAT YOU THINK OF THE GUY, HE IS ONE OF THE GREATEST MINDS OF ALL TIME AND THIS IS WHERE HE DID HIS GREATEST WORK.
HAVE SOME RESPECT.
THE LEGENDARY TIME CUBE.
THE BROKEN LEGENDARY TIME CUBE.
BUT STILL, THE LEGENDARY TIME CUBE.
YOU KNOW WHAT DAT'S WORTH? THE HOOD WASN'T LYIN'!
MAN, WE SHOULD GO BACK IN TIME JUST BEFORE THOR--
I KNEW YOU WAS GONNA SAY THAT.
OH, IS THAT THE TIME THAT THOR TOTALLY SNUCK UP ON YOU--
OH, COME ON...
TRESPASSING.

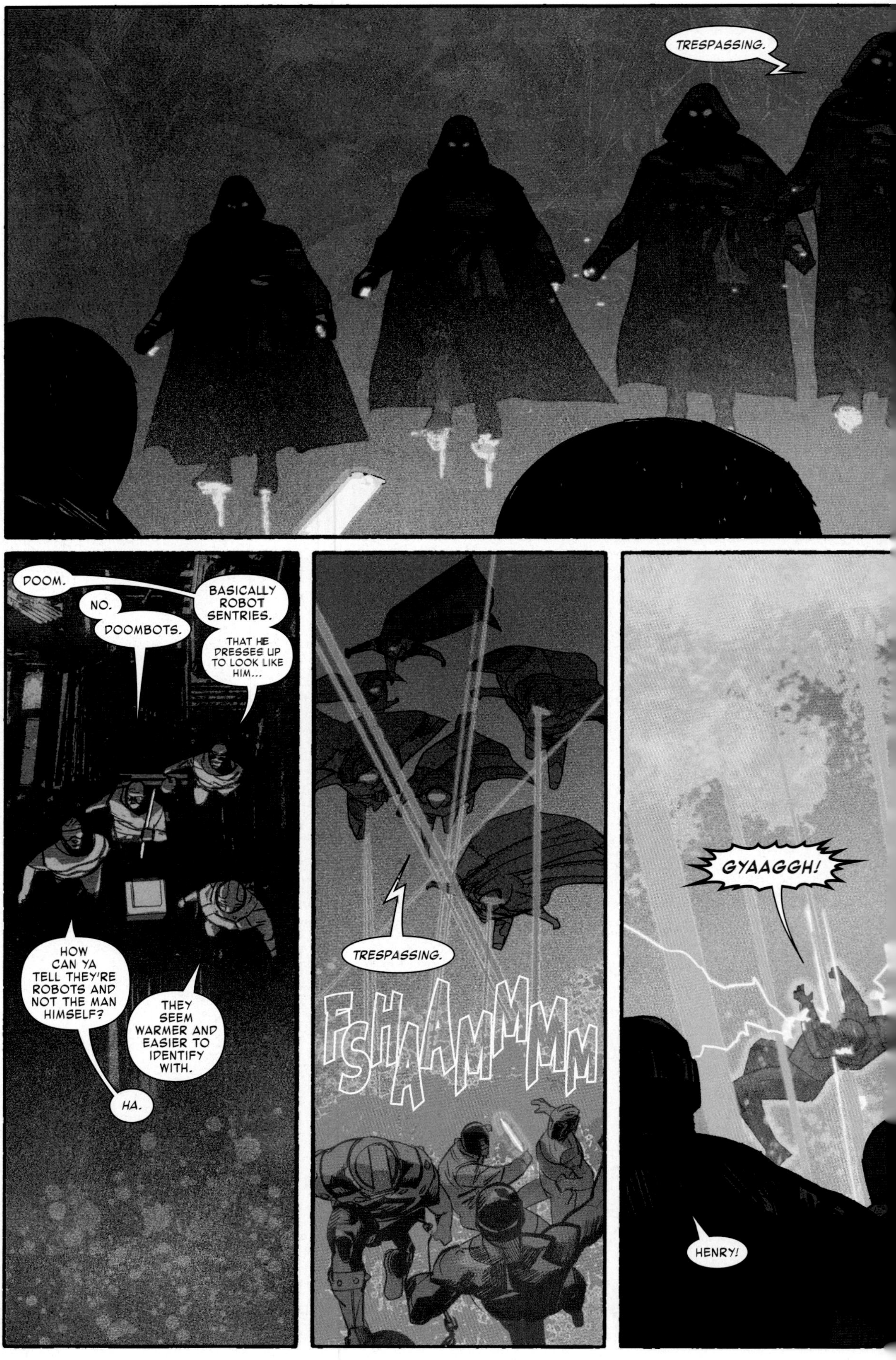
TRESPASSING.
DOOM.
NO.
DOOMBOTS.
BASICALLY ROBOT SENTRIES.
THAT HE DRESSES UP TO LOOK LIKE HIM...
HOW CAN YA TELL THEY'RE ROBOTS AND NOT THE MAN HIMSELF?
THEY SEEM WARMER AND EASIER TO IDENTIFY WITH.
HA.
TRESPASSING.
FSHAMMMM
GYAAGGH!
HENRY!

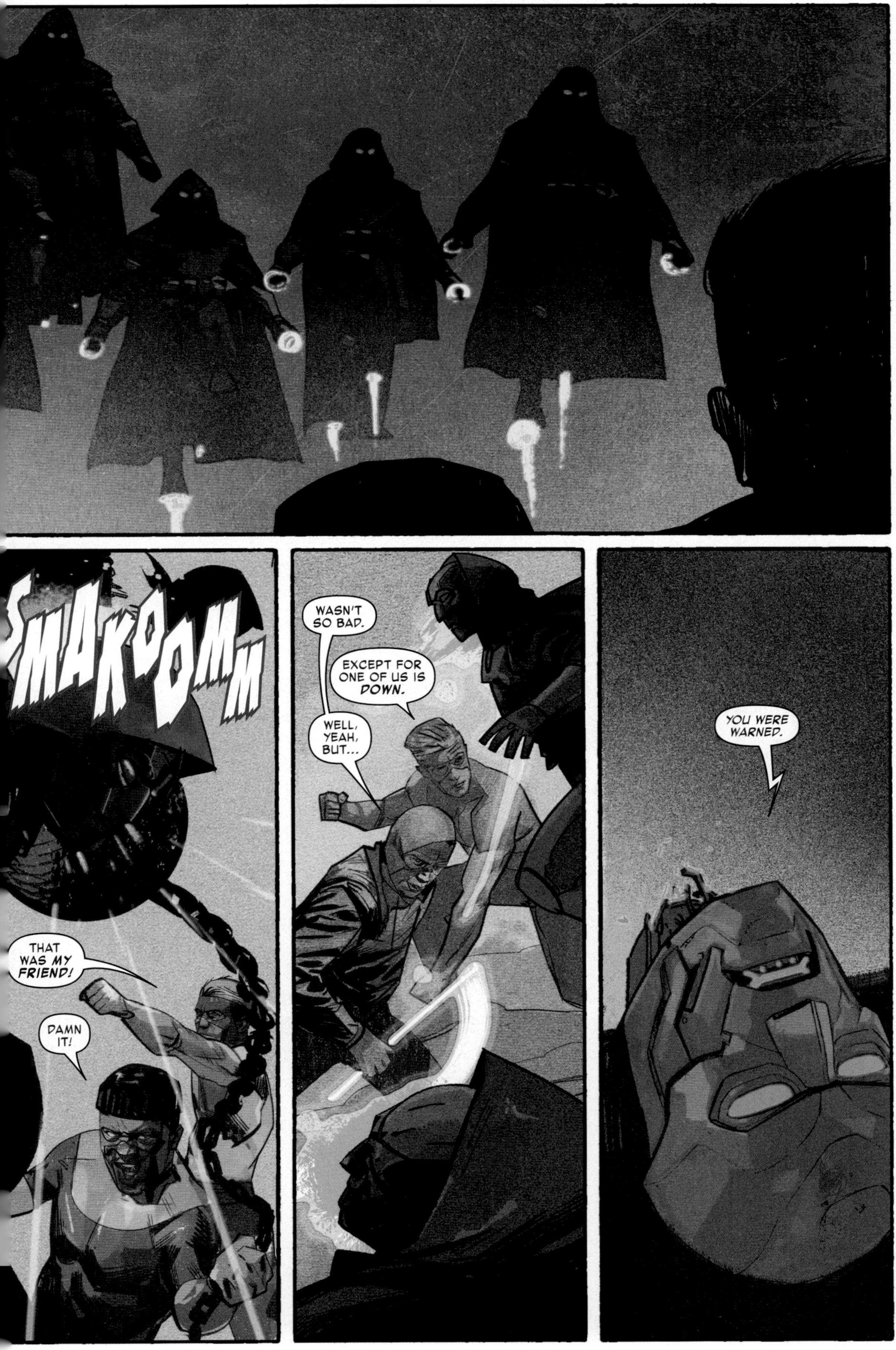
SMAKOOMM
THAT WAS MY FRIEND!
DAMN IT!
WASN'T SO BAD.
EXCEPT FOR ONE OF US IS DOWN.
WELL, YEAH, BUT...
YOU WERE WARNED.

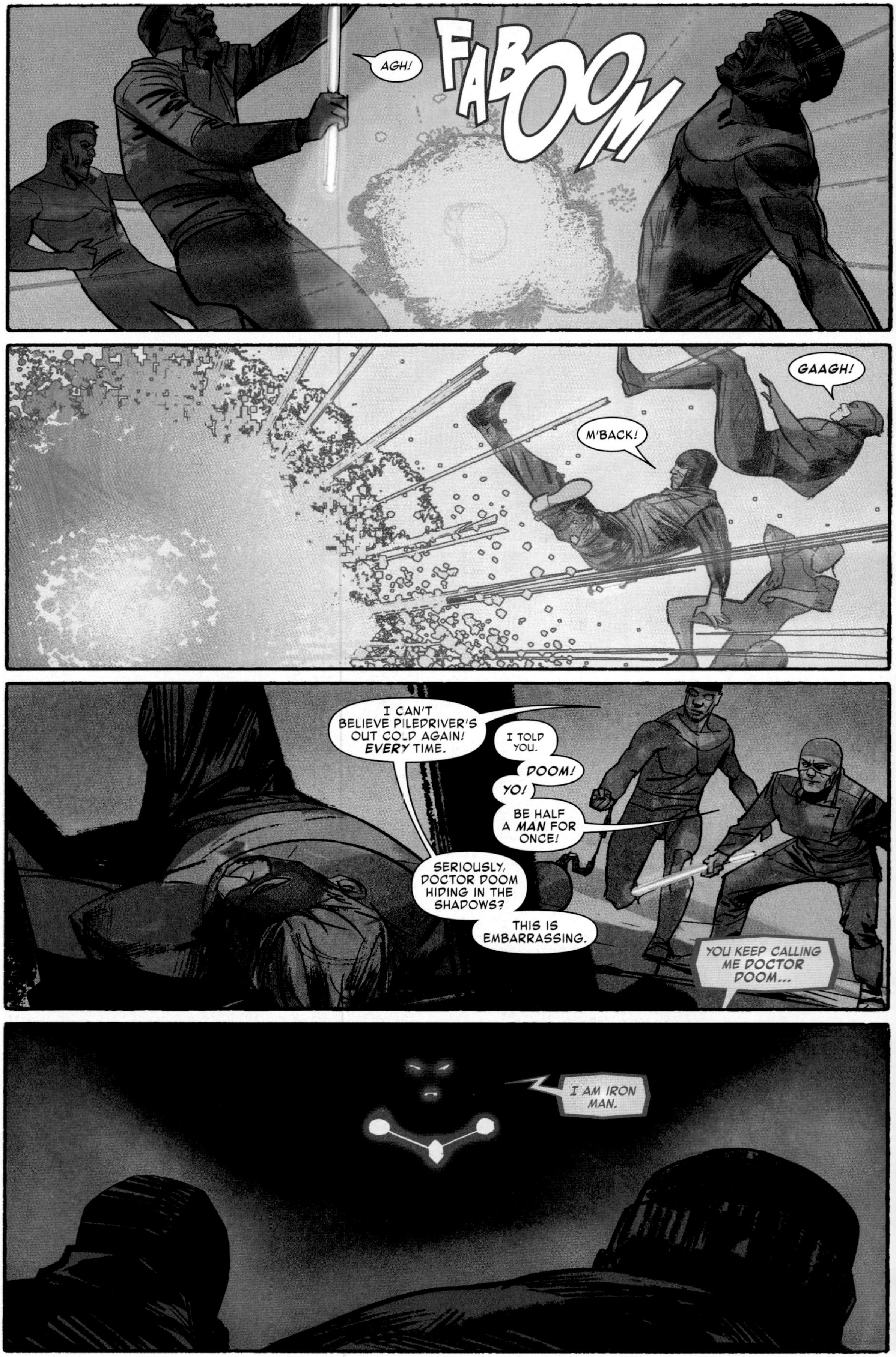
AGH!
FABOOM
GAAGH!
M'BACK!
I CAN'T BELIEVE PILEDRIVER'S OUT COLD AGAIN! EVERY TIME.
I TOLD YOU.
DOOM!
YO!
BE HALF A MAN FOR ONCE!
SERIOUSLY, DOCTOR DOOM HIDING IN THE SHADOWS?
THIS IS EMBARRASSING.
YOU KEEP CALLING ME DOCTOR DOOM...
I AM IRON MAN.

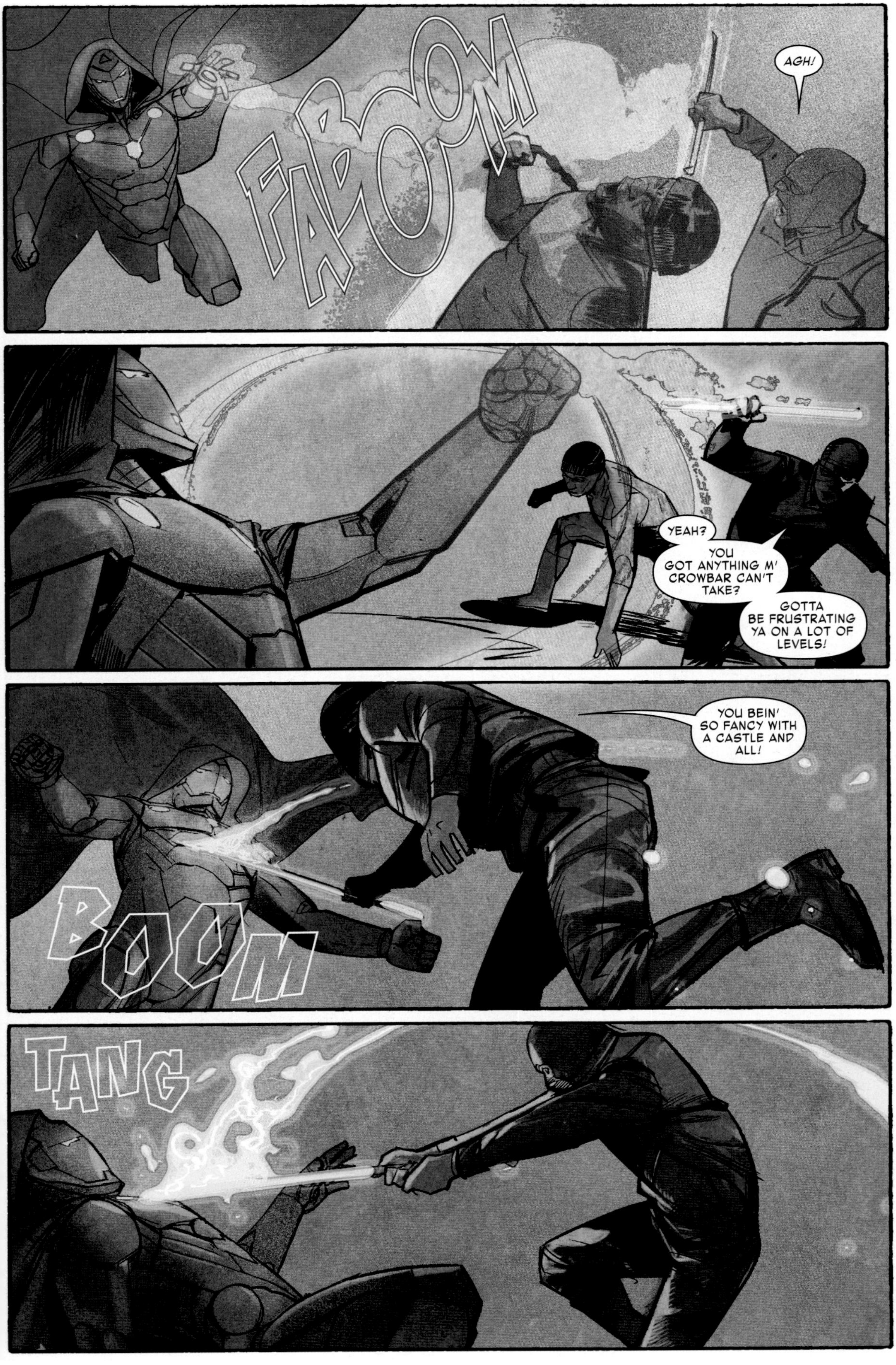
FABOOM
AGH!
YEAH?
YOU GOT ANYTHING M' CROWBAR CAN'T TAKE?
GOTTA BE FRUSTRATING YA ON A LOT OF LEVELS!
YOU BEIN' SO FANCY WITH A CASTLE AND ALL!
BOOM
TANG

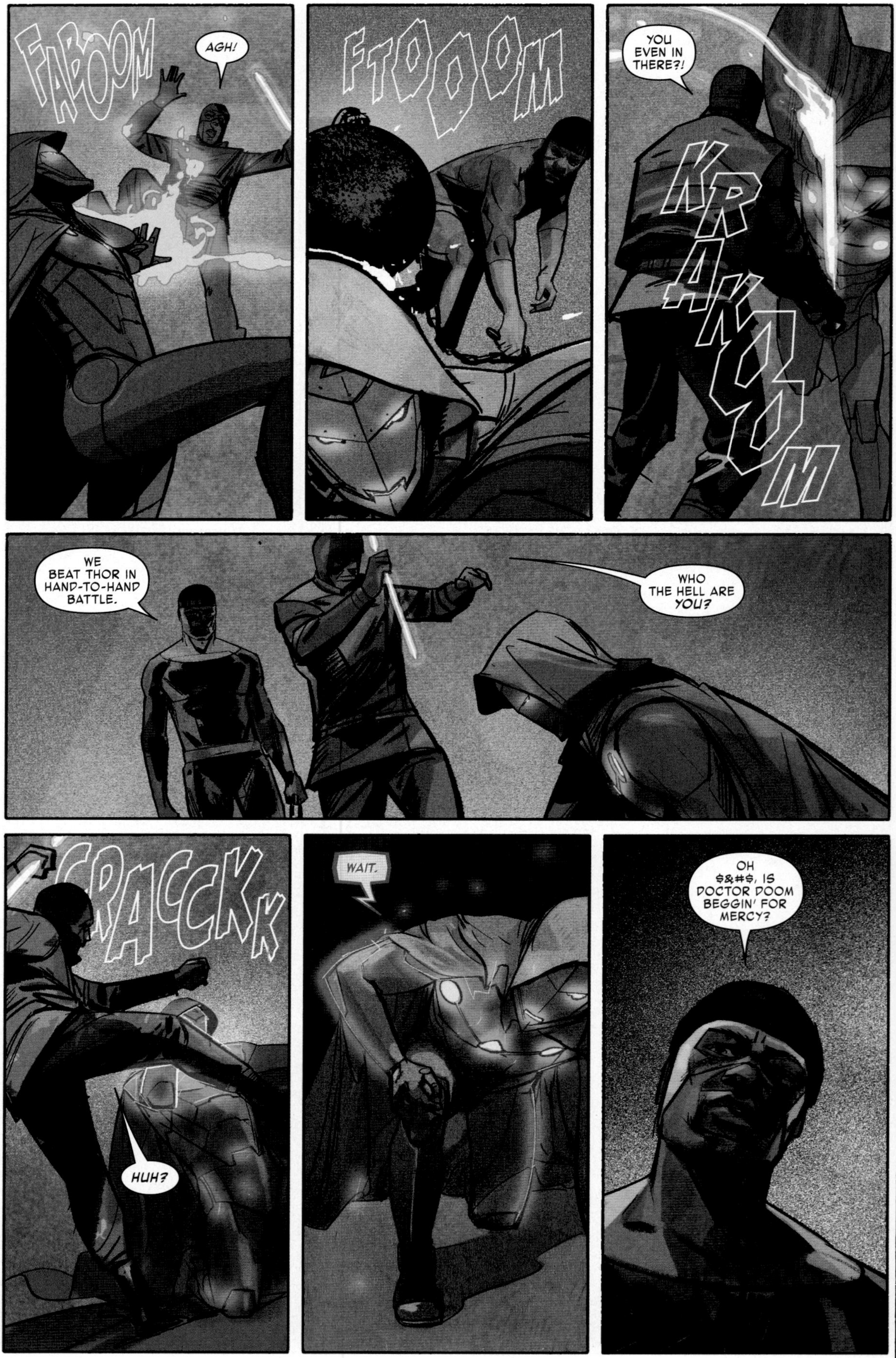
FABOOM
AGH!
FTOOOM
YOU EVEN IN THERE?!
KRAKOOM
WE BEAT THOR IN HAND-TO-HAND BATTLE.
WHO THE HELL ARE YOU?
CRACCKK
HUH?
WAIT.
OH $&#$, IS DOCTOR DOOM BEGGIN' FOR MERCY?

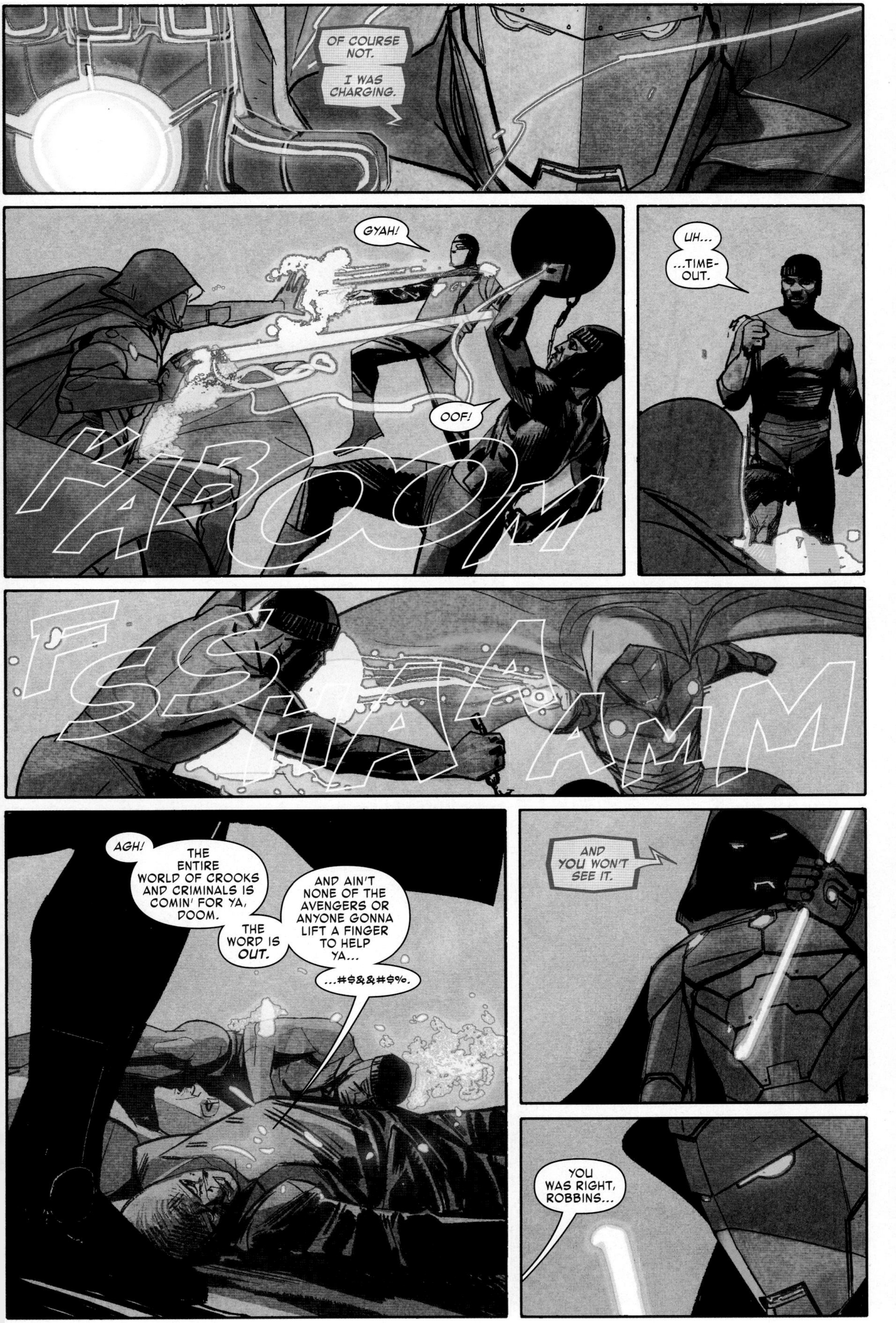
OF COURSE NOT.
I WAS CHARGING.
GYAH!
OOF!
KABOOM
UH...
...TIME-OUT.
FSSHAAAMM
AGH!
THE ENTIRE WORLD OF CROOKS AND CRIMINALS IS COMIN' FOR YA, DOOM.
THE WORD IS OUT.
AND AIN'T NONE OF THE AVENGERS OR ANYONE GONNA LIFT A FINGER TO HELP YA...
...#$&#$%.
AND YOU WON'T SEE IT.
YOU WAS RIGHT, ROBBINS...

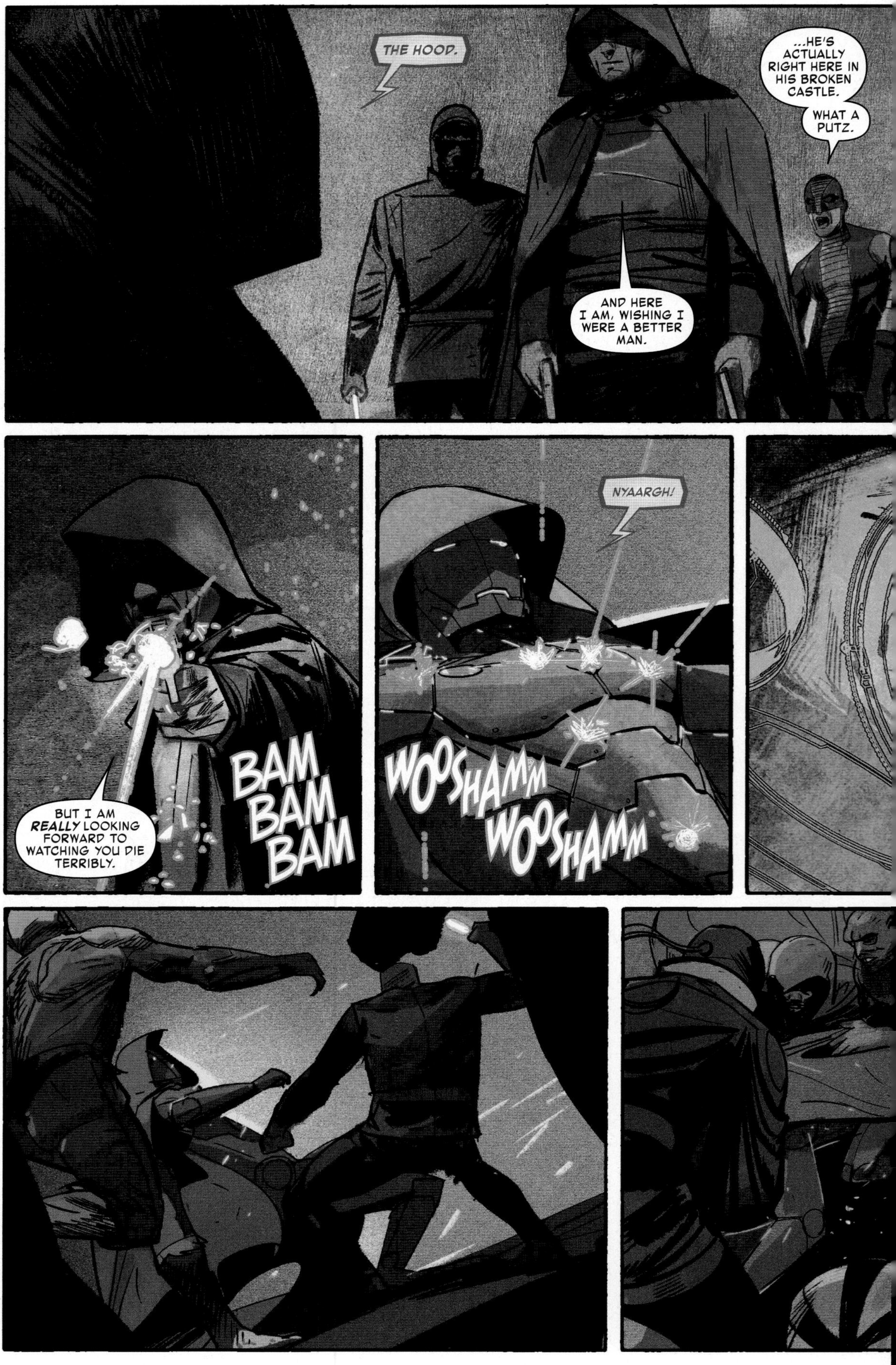
THE HOOD.
...HE'S ACTUALLY RIGHT HERE IN HIS BROKEN CASTLE.
WHAT A PUTZ.
AND HERE I AM, WISHING I WERE A BETTER MAN.
BUT I AM REALLY LOOKING FORWARD TO WATCHING YOU DIE TERRIBLY.
BAM BAM BAM
NYAARGH!
WOOSHAMM WOOSHAMM

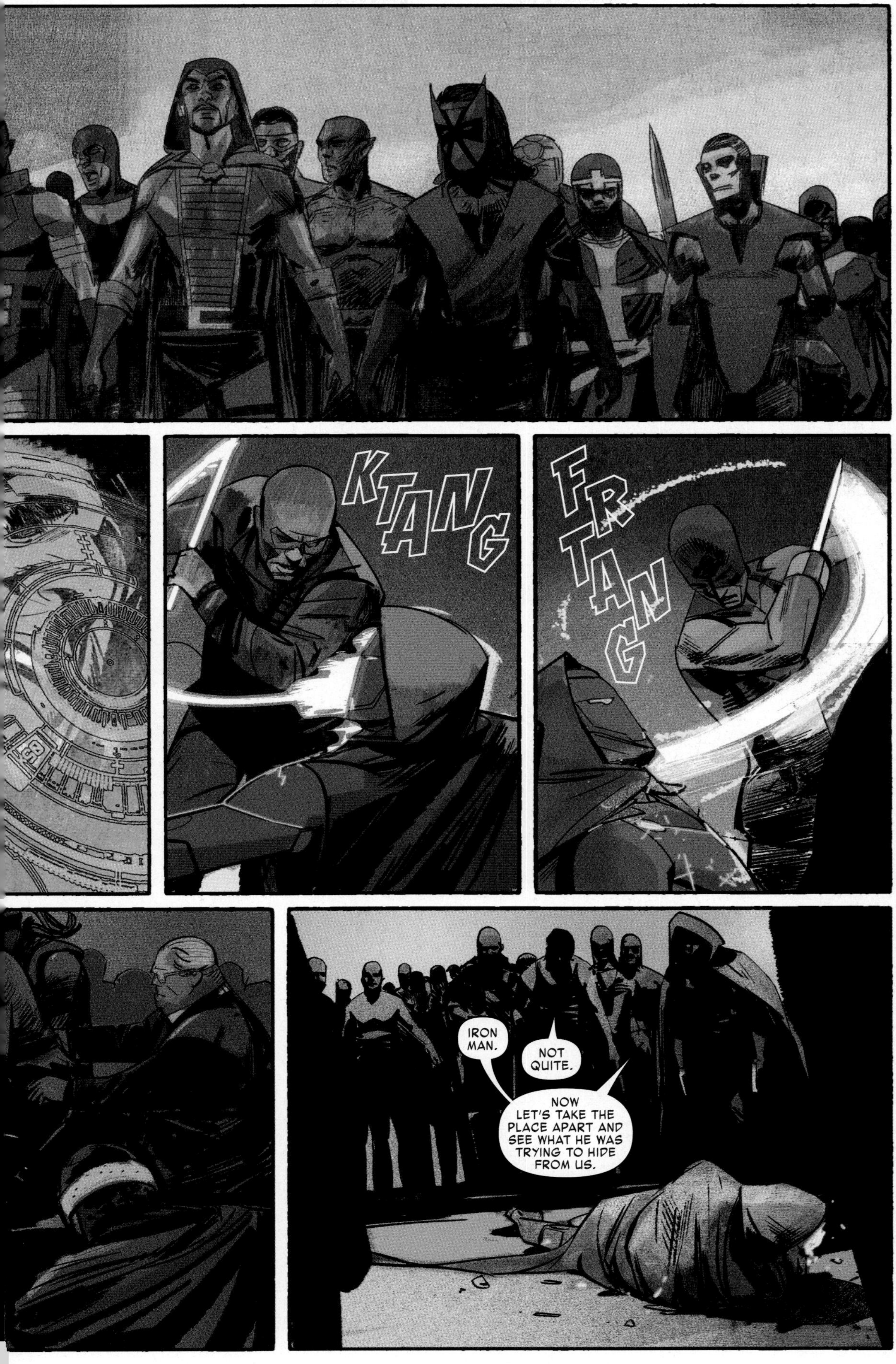
KTANG
FRTANG
IRON MAN.
NOT QUITE.
NOW LET'S TAKE THE PLACE APART AND SEE WHAT HE WAS TRYING TO HIDE FROM US.

#598

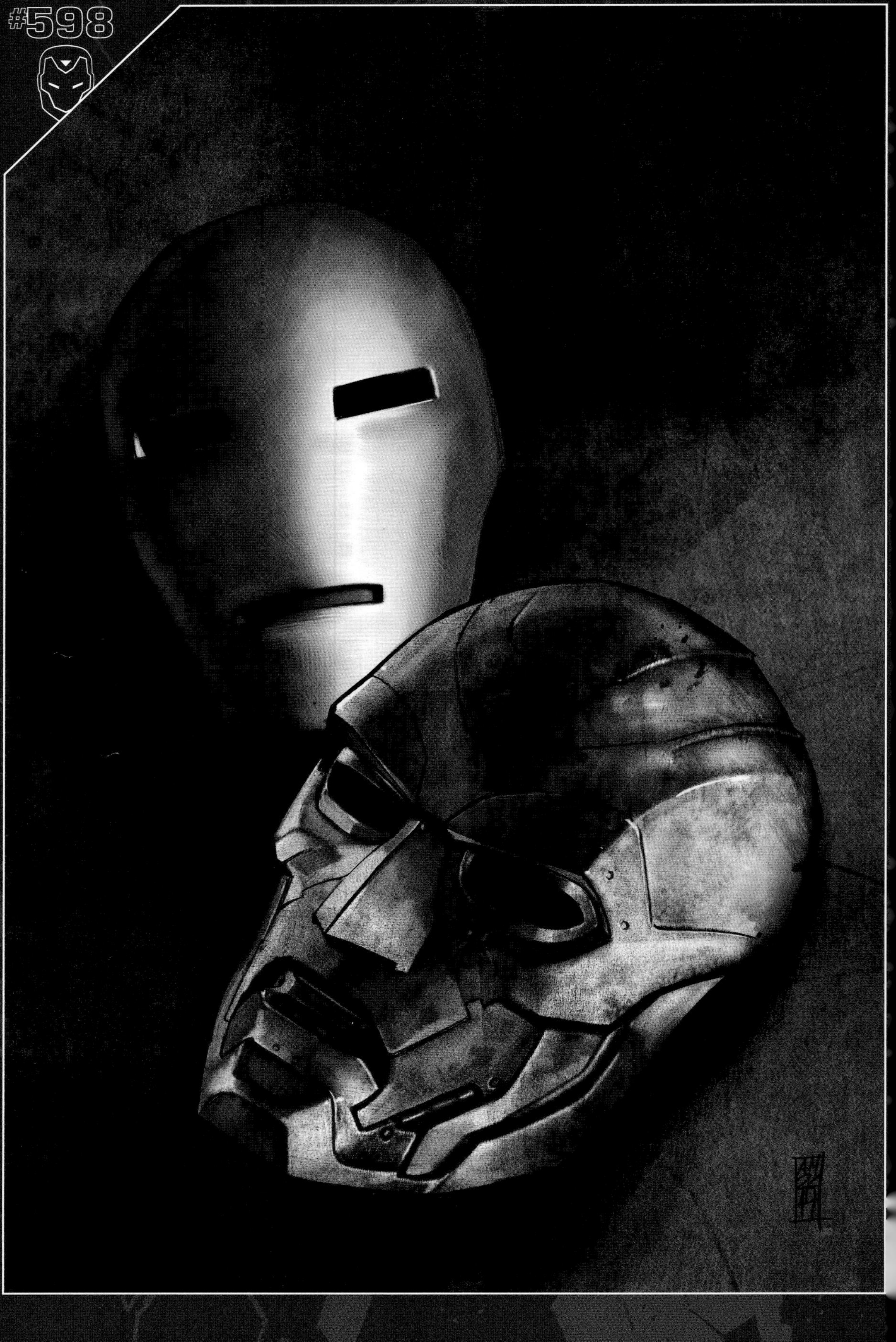

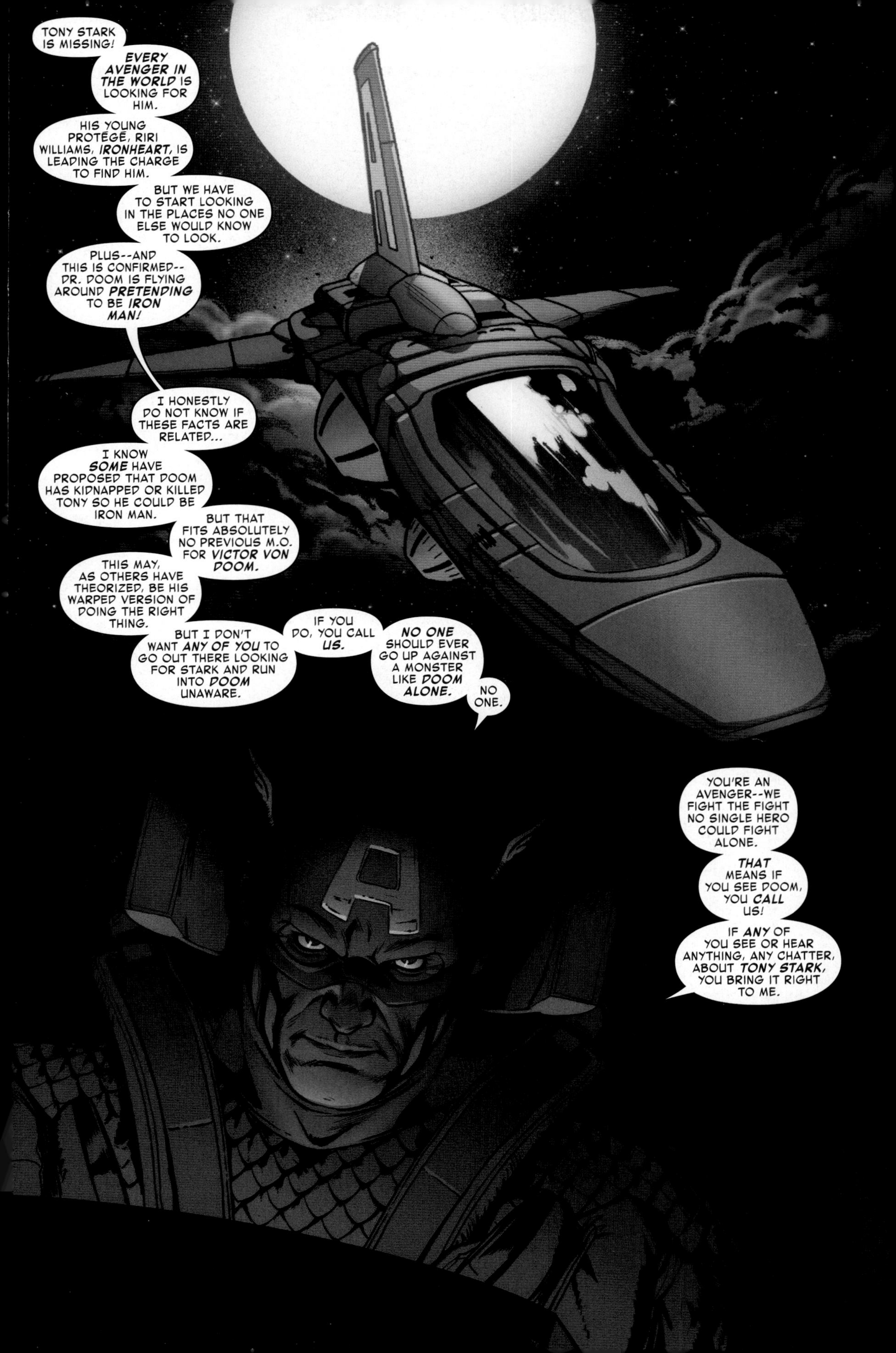
TONY STARK IS MISSING!
EVERY AVENGER IN THE WORLD IS LOOKING FOR HIM.
HIS YOUNG PROTÉGÉ, RIRI WILLIAMS, IRONHEART, IS LEADING THE CHARGE TO FIND HIM.
BUT WE HAVE TO START LOOKING IN THE PLACES NO ONE ELSE WOULD KNOW TO LOOK.
PLUS--AND THIS IS CONFIRMED--DR. DOOM IS FLYING AROUND PRETENDING TO BE IRON MAN!
I HONESTLY DO NOT KNOW IF THESE FACTS ARE RELATED...
I KNOW SOME HAVE PROPOSED THAT DOOM HAS KIDNAPPED OR KILLED TONY SO HE COULD BE IRON MAN.
BUT THAT FITS ABSOLUTELY NO PREVIOUS M.O. FOR VICTOR VON DOOM.
THIS MAY, AS OTHERS HAVE THEORIZED, BE HIS WARPED VERSION OF DOING THE RIGHT THING.
BUT I DON'T WANT ANY OF YOU TO GO OUT THERE LOOKING FOR STARK AND RUN INTO DOOM UNAWARE.
IF YOU DO, YOU CALL US.
NO ONE SHOULD EVER GO UP AGAINST A MONSTER LIKE DOOM ALONE.
NO ONE.
YOU'RE AN AVENGER--WE FIGHT THE FIGHT NO SINGLE HERO COULD FIGHT ALONE.
THAT MEANS IF YOU SEE DOOM, YOU CALL US!
IF ANY OF YOU SEE OR HEAR ANYTHING, ANY CHATTER, ABOUT TONY STARK, YOU BRING IT RIGHT TO ME.

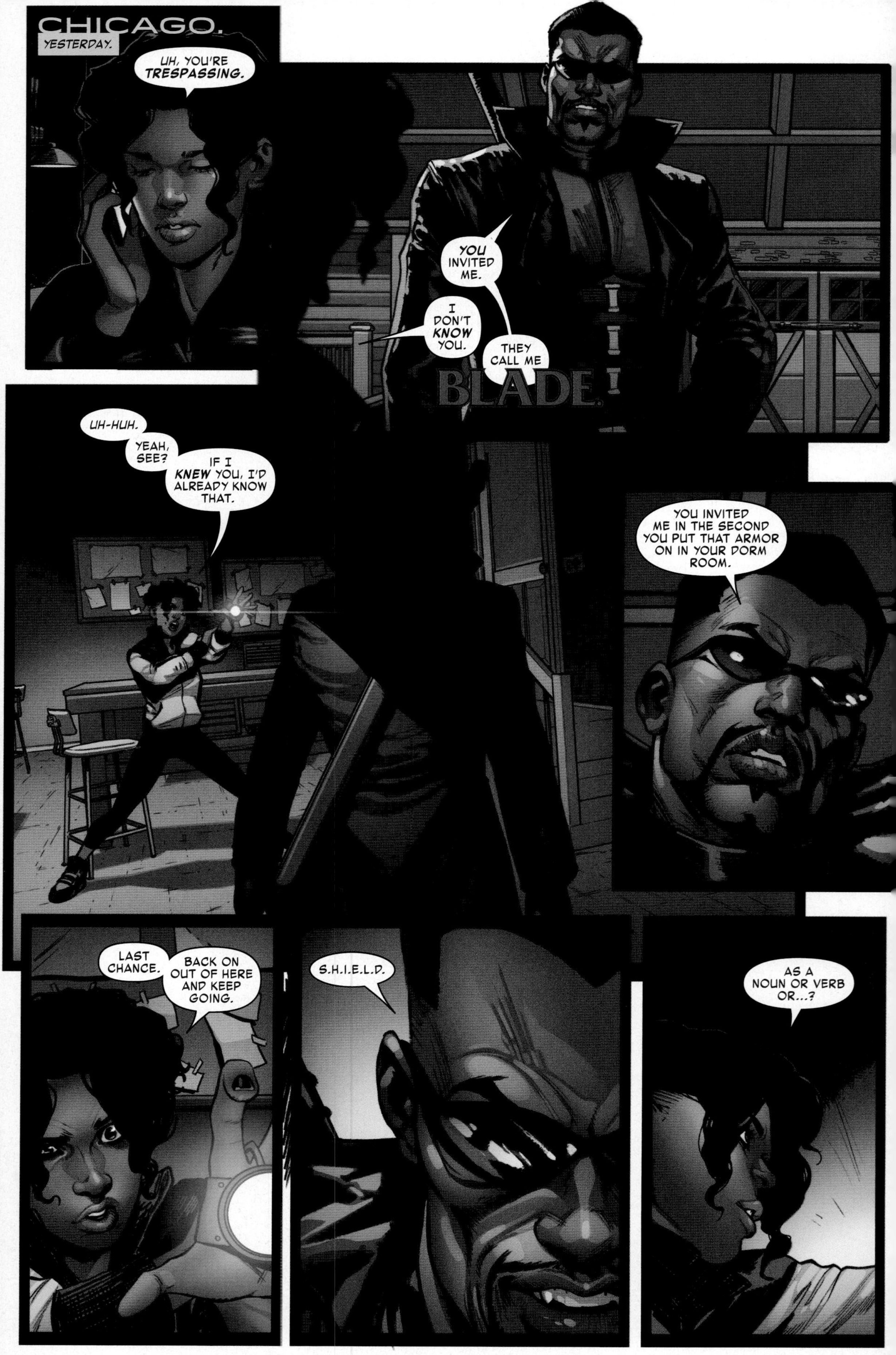
CHICAGO.
YESTERDAY.
UH, YOU'RE TRESPASSING.
YOU INVITED ME.
I DON'T KNOW YOU.
THEY CALL ME
BLADE.
UH-HUH.
YEAH, SEE?
IF I KNEW YOU, I'D ALREADY KNOW THAT.
YOU INVITED ME IN THE SECOND YOU PUT THAT ARMOR ON IN YOUR DORM ROOM.
LAST CHANCE.
BACK ON OUT OF HERE AND KEEP GOING.
S.H.I.E.L.D.
AS A NOUN OR VERB OR...?

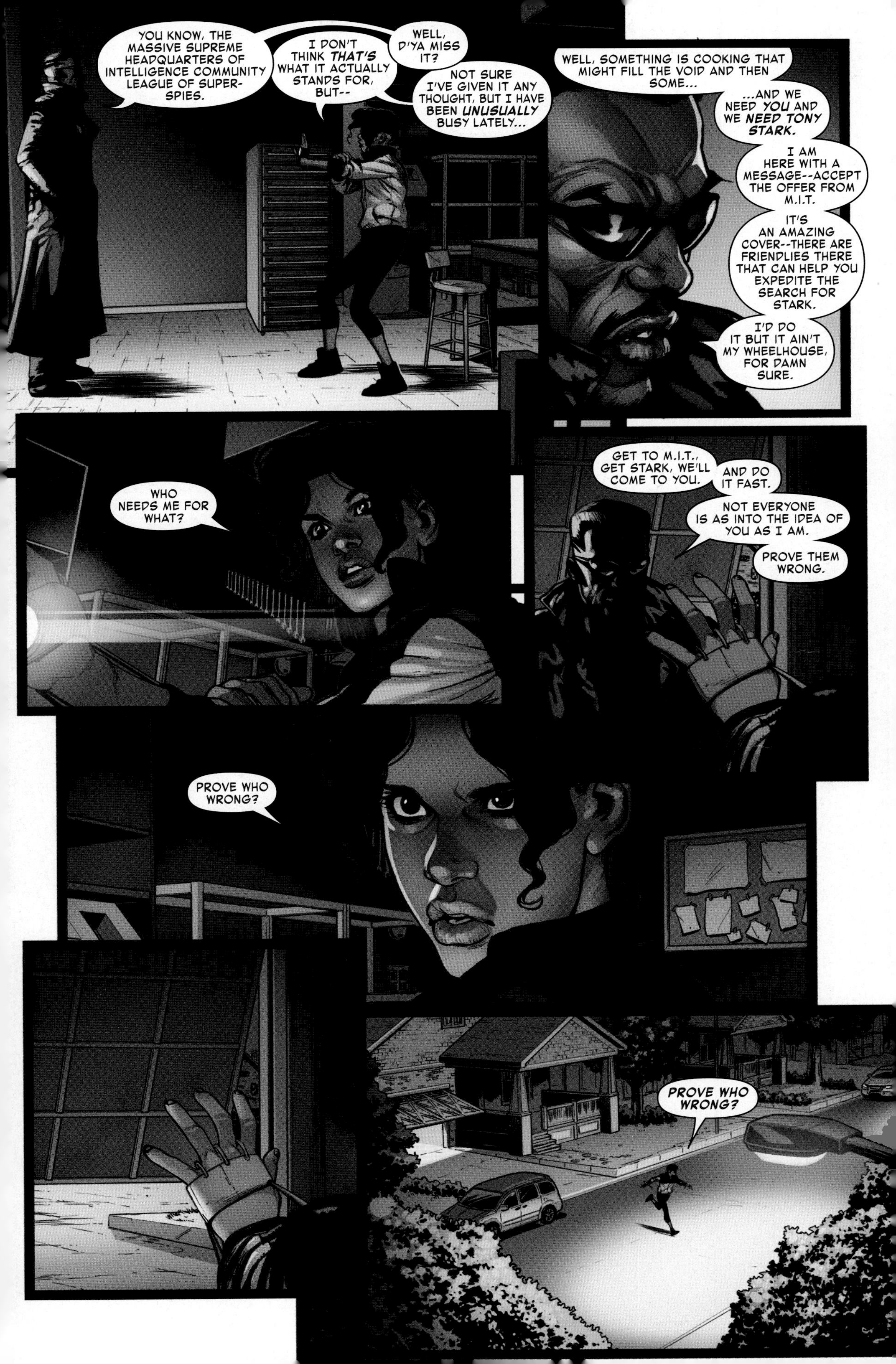
YOU KNOW, THE MASSIVE SUPREME HEADQUARTERS OF INTELLIGENCE COMMUNITY LEAGUE OF SUPER-SPIES.
I DON'T THINK THAT'S WHAT IT ACTUALLY STANDS FOR, BUT--
WELL, D'YA MISS IT?
NOT SURE I'VE GIVEN IT ANY THOUGHT, BUT I HAVE BEEN UNUSUALLY BUSY LATELY...
WELL, SOMETHING IS COOKING THAT MIGHT FILL THE VOID AND THEN SOME...
...AND WE NEED YOU AND WE NEED TONY STARK.
I AM HERE WITH A MESSAGE--ACCEPT THE OFFER FROM M.I.T.
IT'S AN AMAZING COVER--THERE ARE FRIENDLIES THERE THAT CAN HELP YOU EXPEDITE THE SEARCH FOR STARK.
I'D DO IT BUT IT AIN'T MY WHEELHOUSE, FOR DAMN SURE.
WHO NEEDS ME FOR WHAT?
GET TO M.I.T., GET STARK, WE'LL COME TO YOU.
AND DO IT FAST.
NOT EVERYONE IS AS INTO THE IDEA OF YOU AS I AM.
PROVE THEM WRONG.
PROVE WHO WRONG?
PROVE WHO WRONG?

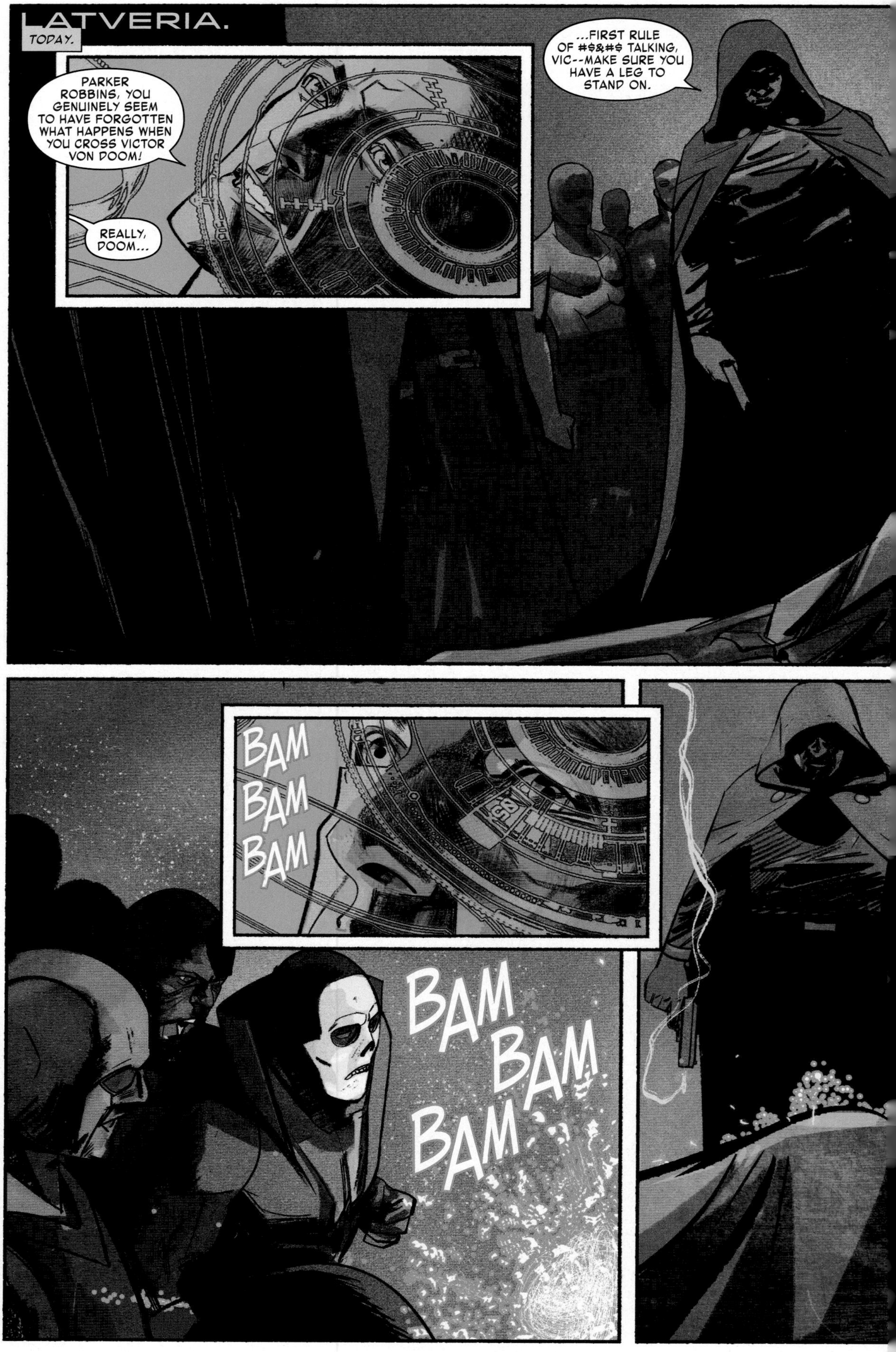
LATVERIA.
TODAY.
PARKER ROBBINS, YOU GENUINELY SEEM TO HAVE FORGOTTEN WHAT HAPPENS WHEN YOU CROSS VICTOR VON DOOM!
REALLY, DOOM...
...FIRST RULE OF #$&#$ TALKING, VIC--MAKE SURE YOU HAVE A LEG TO STAND ON.
BAM BAM BAM
BAM BAM BAM

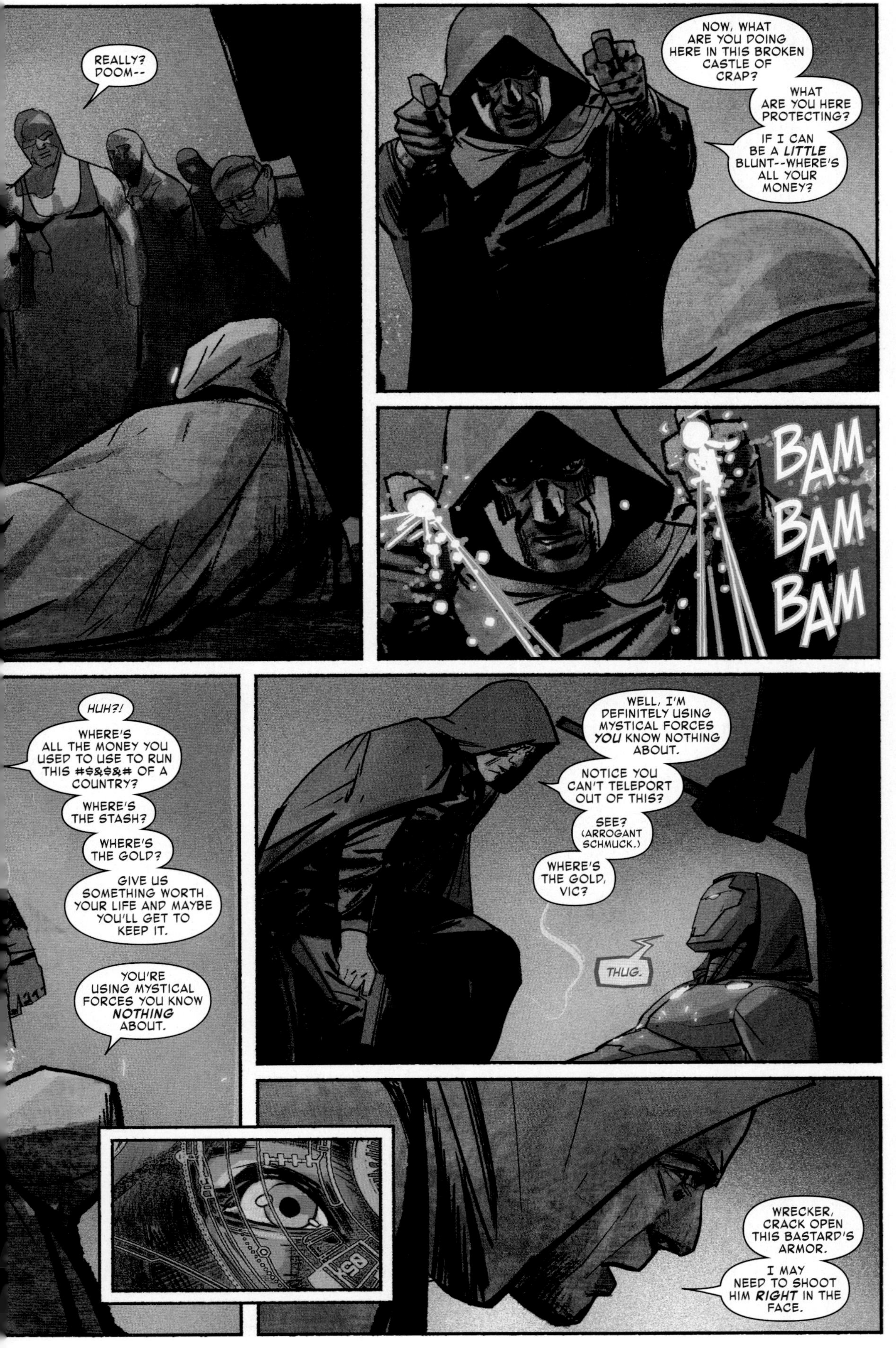

REALLY? DOOM--
NOW, WHAT ARE YOU DOING HERE IN THIS BROKEN CASTLE OF CRAP?
WHAT ARE YOU HERE PROTECTING?
IF I CAN BE A *LITTLE* BLUNT--WHERE'S ALL YOUR MONEY?
BAM BAM BAM
*HUH?!*
WHERE'S ALL THE MONEY YOU USED TO USE TO RUN THIS #$&$&# OF A COUNTRY?
WHERE'S THE STASH?
WHERE'S THE GOLD?
GIVE US SOMETHING WORTH YOUR LIFE AND MAYBE YOU'LL GET TO KEEP IT.
YOU'RE USING MYSTICAL FORCES YOU KNOW *NOTHING* ABOUT.
WELL, I'M DEFINITELY USING MYSTICAL FORCES *YOU* KNOW NOTHING ABOUT.
NOTICE YOU CAN'T TELEPORT OUT OF THIS?
SEE? (ARROGANT SCHMUCK.)
WHERE'S THE GOLD, VIC?
*THUG.*
WRECKER, CRACK OPEN THIS BASTARD'S ARMOR.
I MAY NEED TO SHOOT HIM *RIGHT* IN THE FACE.

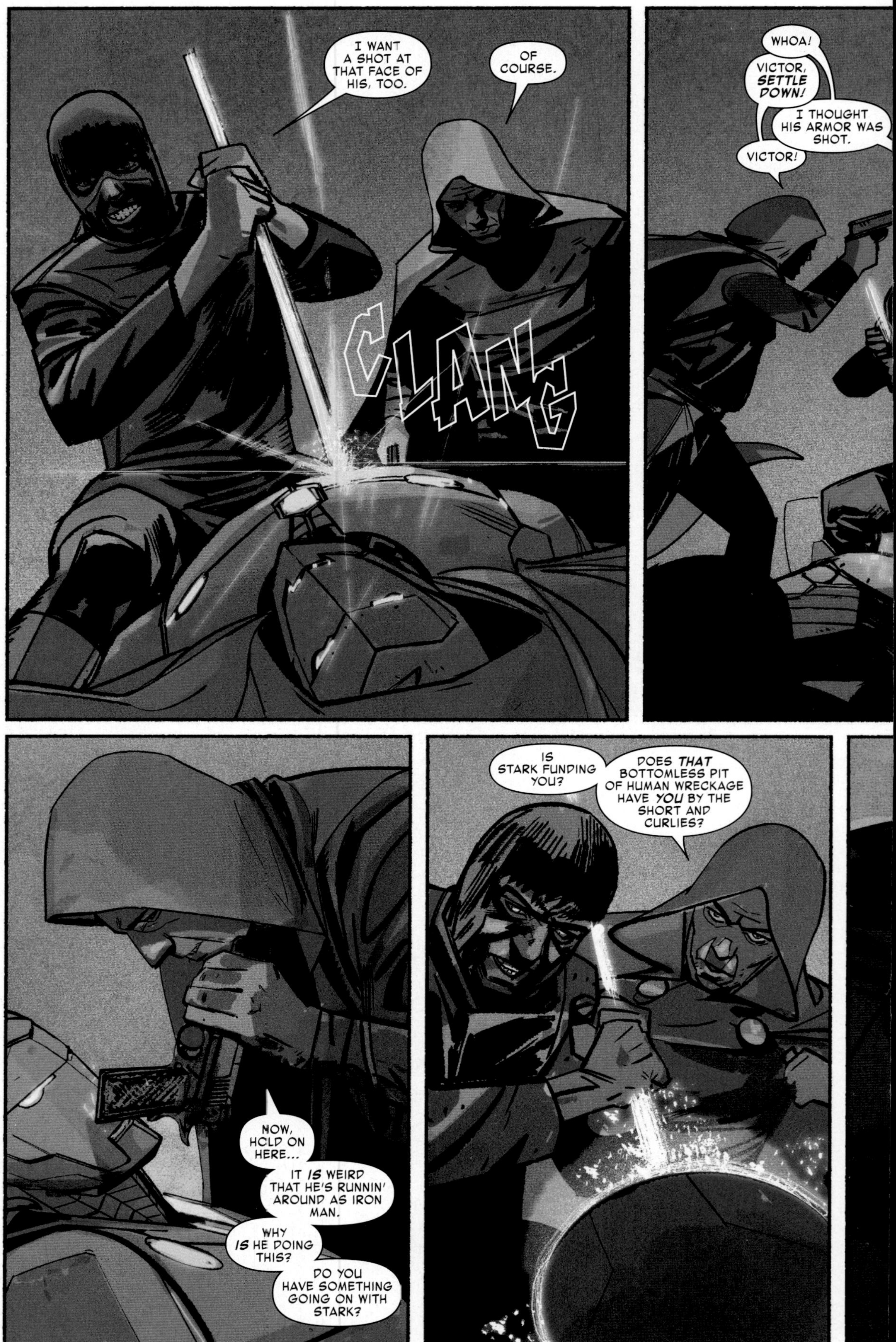

I WANT A SHOT AT THAT FACE OF HIS, TOO.
OF COURSE.
CLANG
WHOA!
VICTOR, SETTLE DOWN!
I THOUGHT HIS ARMOR WAS SHOT.
VICTOR!
NOW, HOLD ON HERE...
IT IS WEIRD THAT HE'S RUNNIN' AROUND AS IRON MAN.
WHY IS HE DOING THIS?
DO YOU HAVE SOMETHING GOING ON WITH STARK?
IS STARK FUNDING YOU?
DOES THAT BOTTOMLESS PIT OF HUMAN WRECKAGE HAVE YOU BY THE SHORT AND CURLIES?

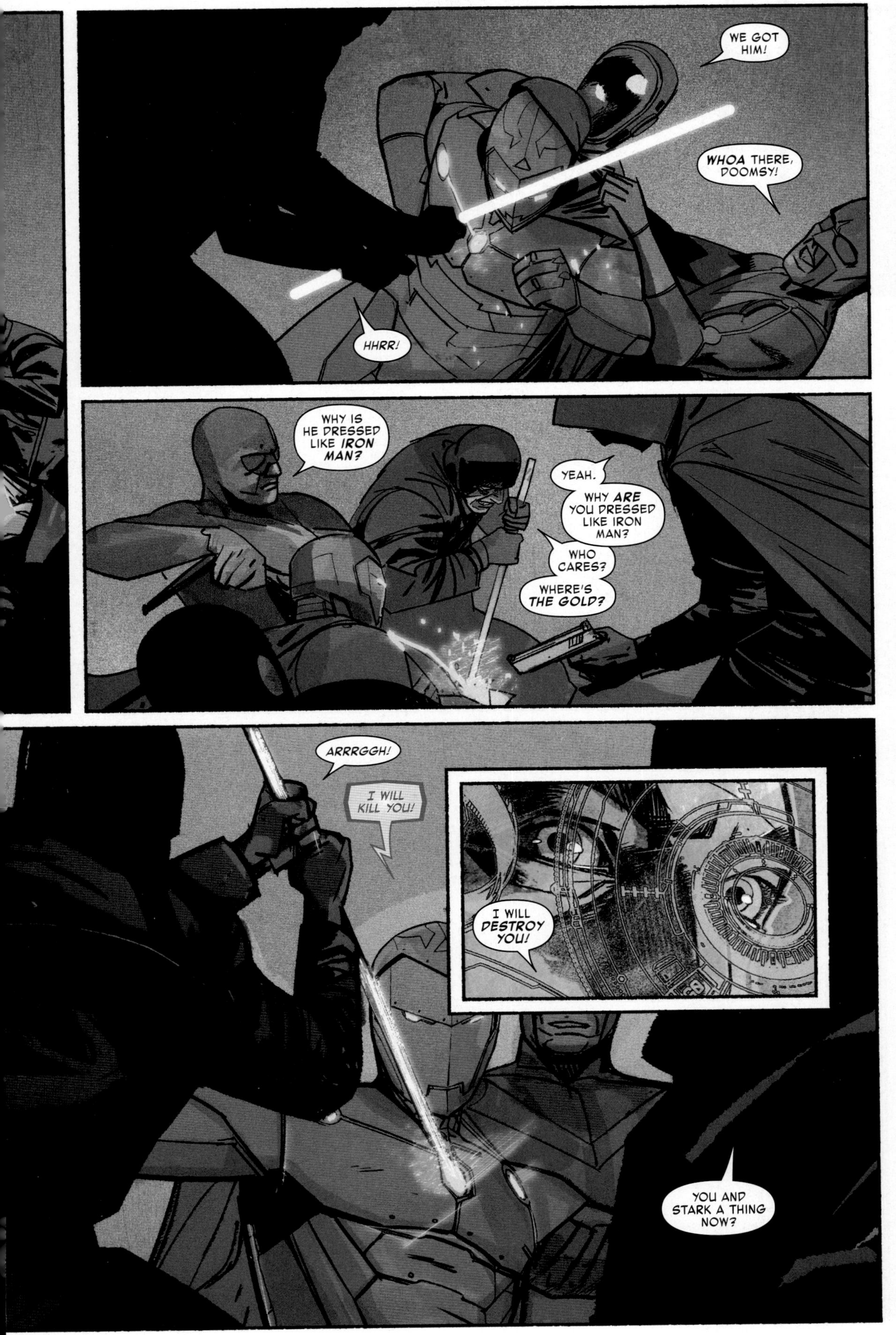
WE GOT HIM!
WHOA THERE, DOOMSY!
HHRR!
WHY IS HE DRESSED LIKE IRON MAN?
YEAH.
WHY ARE YOU DRESSED LIKE IRON MAN?
WHO CARES?
WHERE'S THE GOLD?
ARRRGGH!
I WILL KILL YOU!
I WILL DESTROY YOU!
YOU AND STARK A THING NOW?

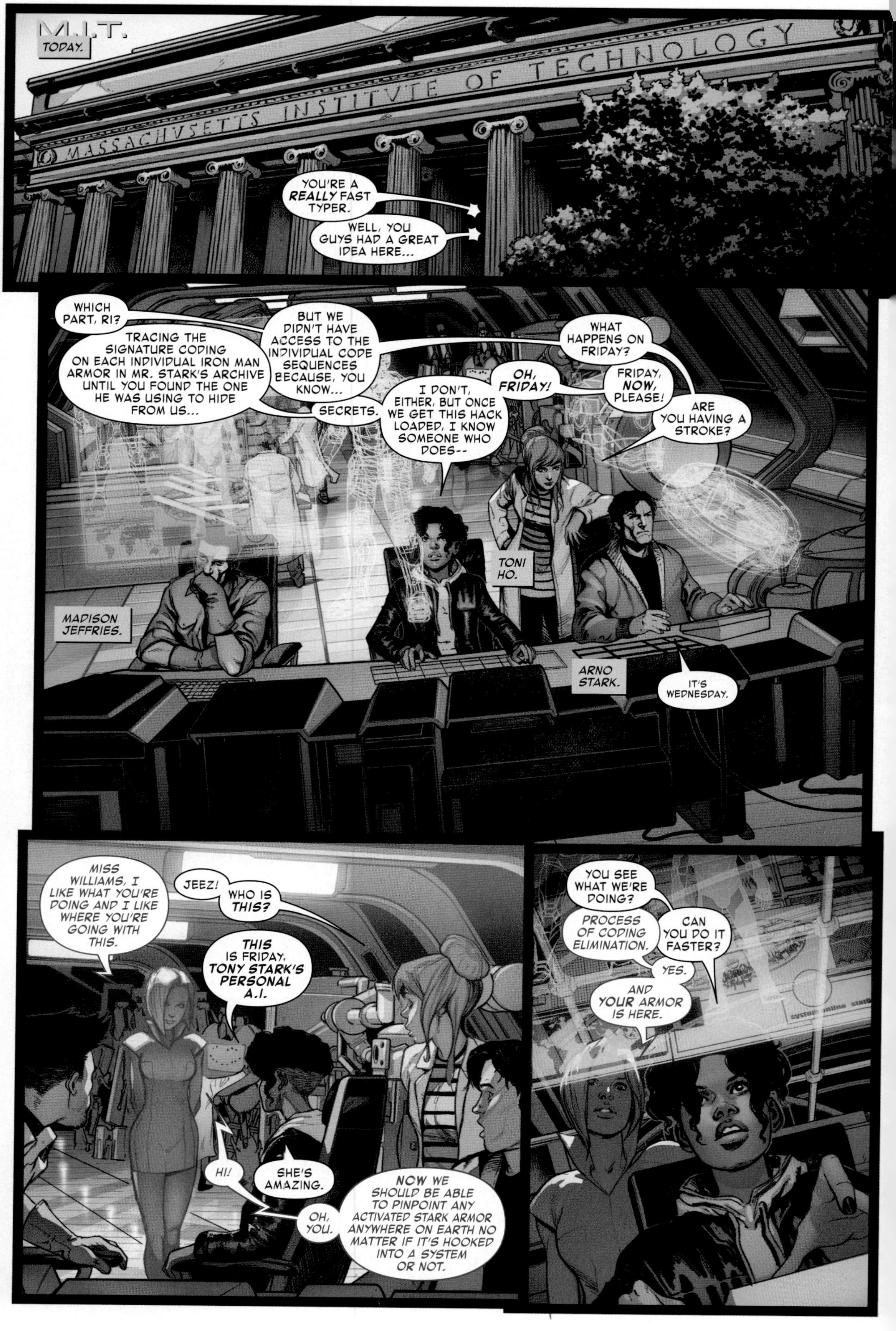
M.I.T.
TODAY.
MASSACHVSETTS INSTITVTE OF TECHNOLOGY
YOU'RE A REALLY FAST TYPER.
WELL, YOU GUYS HAD A GREAT IDEA HERE...
WHICH PART, RI?
TRACING THE SIGNATURE CODING ON EACH INDIVIDUAL IRON MAN ARMOR IN MR. STARK'S ARCHIVE UNTIL YOU FOUND THE ONE HE WAS USING TO HIDE FROM US...
BUT WE DIDN'T HAVE ACCESS TO THE INDIVIDUAL CODE SEQUENCES BECAUSE, YOU KNOW...
SECRETS.
WHAT HAPPENS ON FRIDAY?
I DON'T, EITHER, BUT ONCE WE GET THIS HACK LOADED, I KNOW SOMEONE WHO DOES--
OH, FRIDAY!
FRIDAY, NOW, PLEASE!
ARE YOU HAVING A STROKE?
TONI HO.
MADISON JEFFRIES.
ARNO STARK.
IT'S WEDNESDAY.
MISS WILLIAMS, I LIKE WHAT YOU'RE DOING AND I LIKE WHERE YOU'RE GOING WITH THIS.
JEEZ!
WHO IS THIS?
THIS IS FRIDAY, TONY STARK'S PERSONAL A.I.
HI!
SHE'S AMAZING.
OH, YOU.
NOW WE SHOULD BE ABLE TO PINPOINT ANY ACTIVATED STARK ARMOR ANYWHERE ON EARTH NO MATTER IF IT'S HOOKED INTO A SYSTEM OR NOT.
YOU SEE WHAT WE'RE DOING?
PROCESS OF CODING ELIMINATION.
CAN YOU DO IT FASTER?
YES.
AND YOUR ARMOR IS HERE.

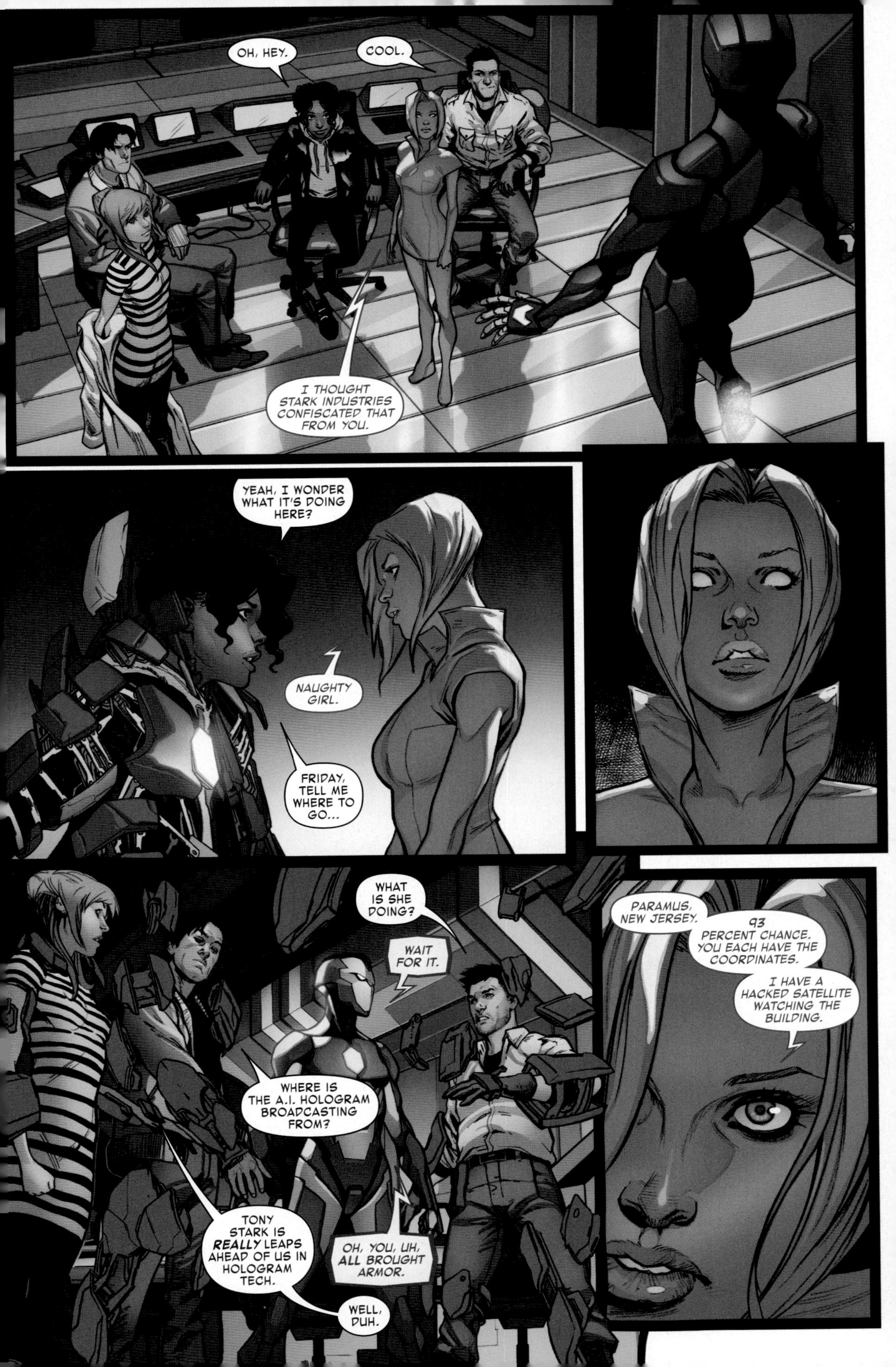
OH, HEY.
COOL.
I THOUGHT STARK INDUSTRIES CONFISCATED THAT FROM YOU.
YEAH, I WONDER WHAT IT'S DOING HERE?
NAUGHTY GIRL.
FRIDAY, TELL ME WHERE TO GO...
WHAT IS SHE DOING?
WAIT FOR IT.
WHERE IS THE A.I. HOLOGRAM BROADCASTING FROM?
TONY STARK IS REALLY LEAPS AHEAD OF US IN HOLOGRAM TECH.
WELL, DUH.
OH, YOU, UH, ALL BROUGHT ARMOR.
PARAMUS, NEW JERSEY.
93 PERCENT CHANCE. YOU EACH HAVE THE COORDINATES.
I HAVE A HACKED SATELLITE WATCHING THE BUILDING.

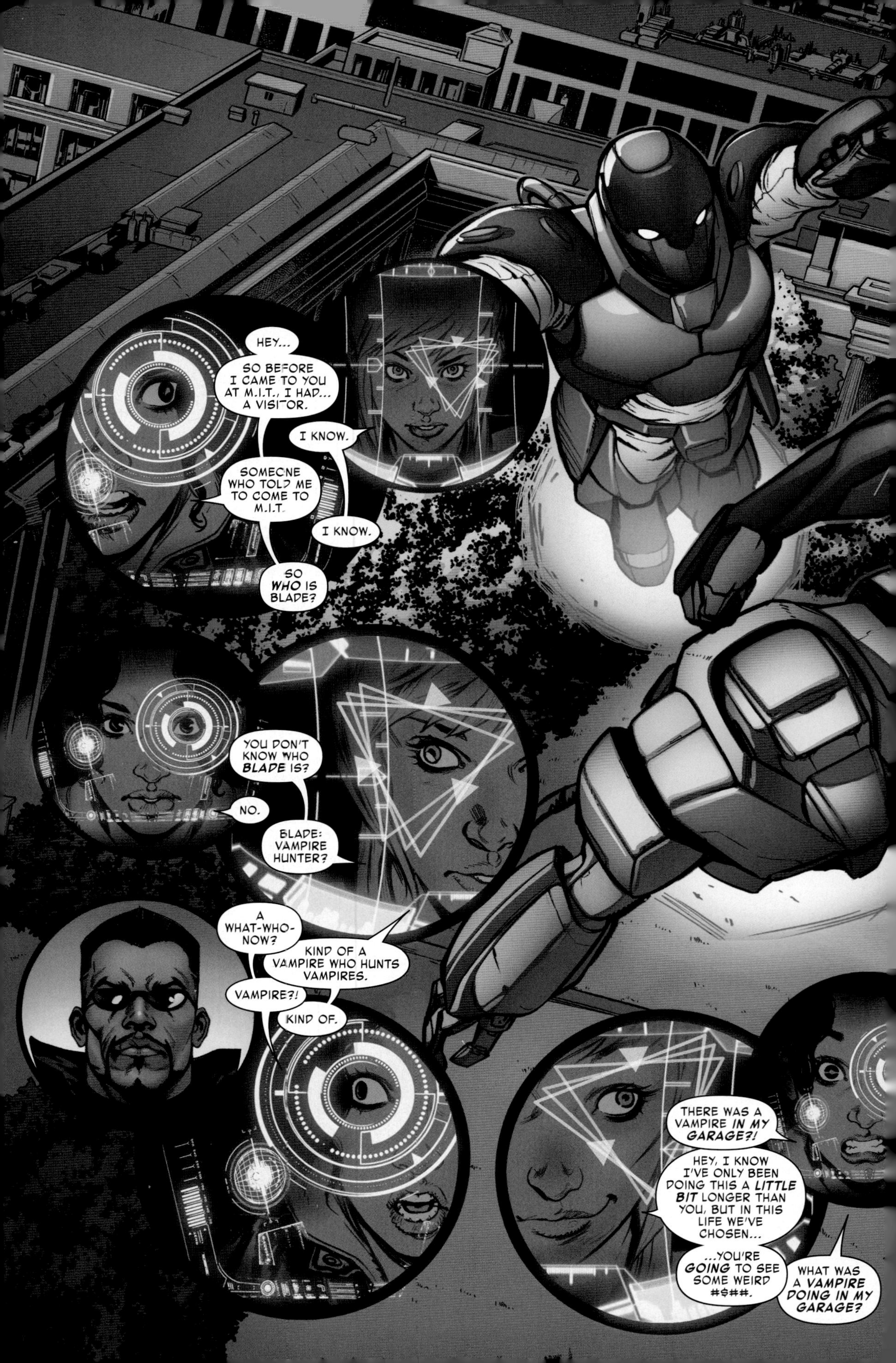
HEY...
SO BEFORE I CAME TO YOU AT M.I.T., I HAD... A VISITOR.
I KNOW.
SOMEONE WHO TOLD ME TO COME TO M.I.T.
I KNOW.
SO WHO IS BLADE?
YOU DON'T KNOW WHO BLADE IS?
NO.
BLADE: VAMPIRE HUNTER?
A WHAT-WHO-NOW?
KIND OF A VAMPIRE WHO HUNTS VAMPIRES.
VAMPIRE?!
KIND OF.
THERE WAS A VAMPIRE IN MY GARAGE?!
HEY, I KNOW I'VE ONLY BEEN DOING THIS A LITTLE BIT LONGER THAN YOU, BUT IN THIS LIFE WE'VE CHOSEN...
...YOU'RE GOING TO SEE SOME WEIRD #$##.
WHAT WAS A VAMPIRE DOING IN MY GARAGE?

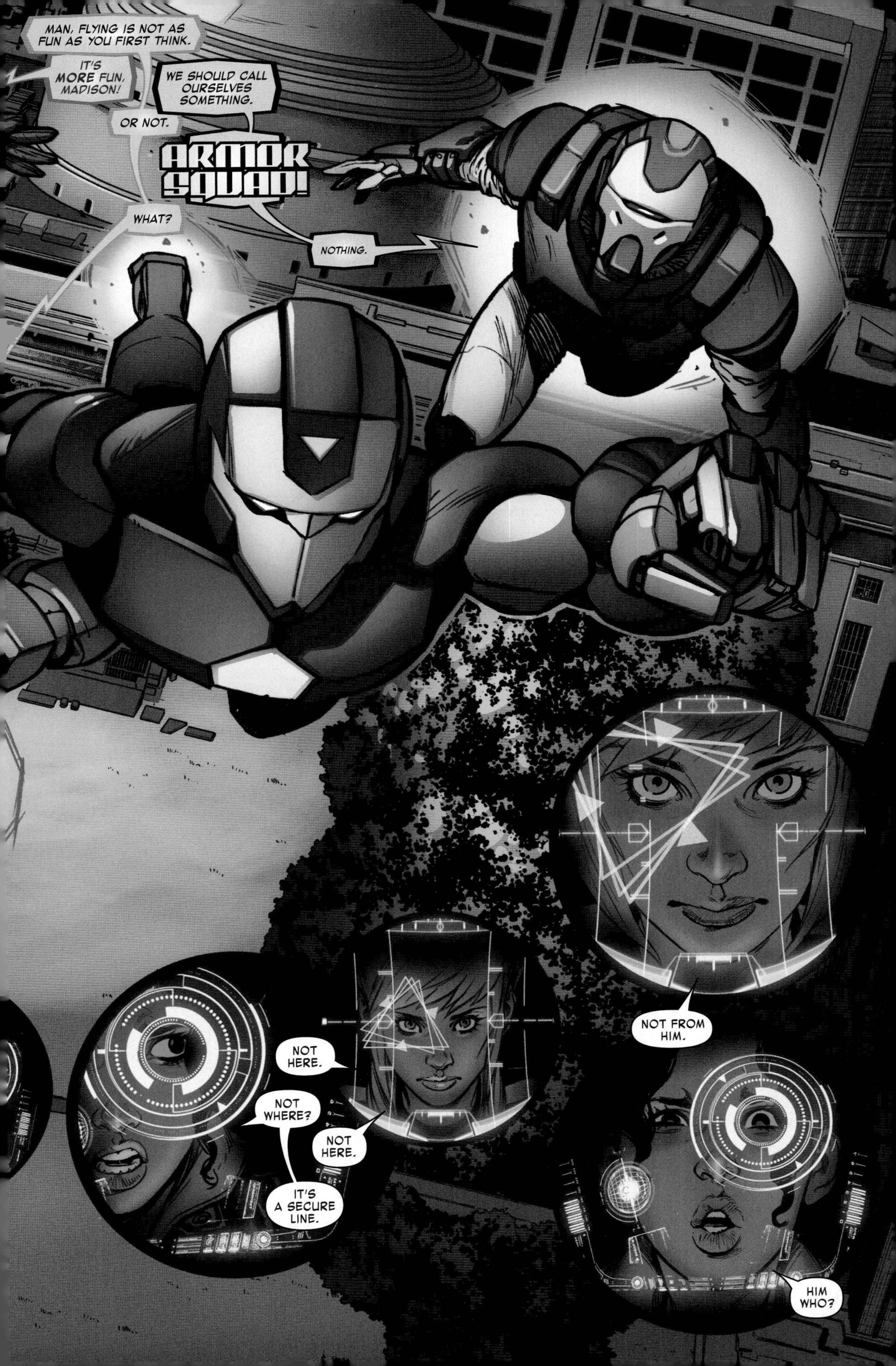
MAN, FLYING IS NOT AS FUN AS YOU FIRST THINK.
IT'S MORE FUN, MADISON!
OR NOT.
WE SHOULD CALL OURSELVES SOMETHING.
ARMOR SQUAD!
WHAT?
NOTHING.
NOT FROM HIM.
NOT HERE.
NOT WHERE?
NOT HERE.
IT'S A SECURE LINE.
HIM WHO?

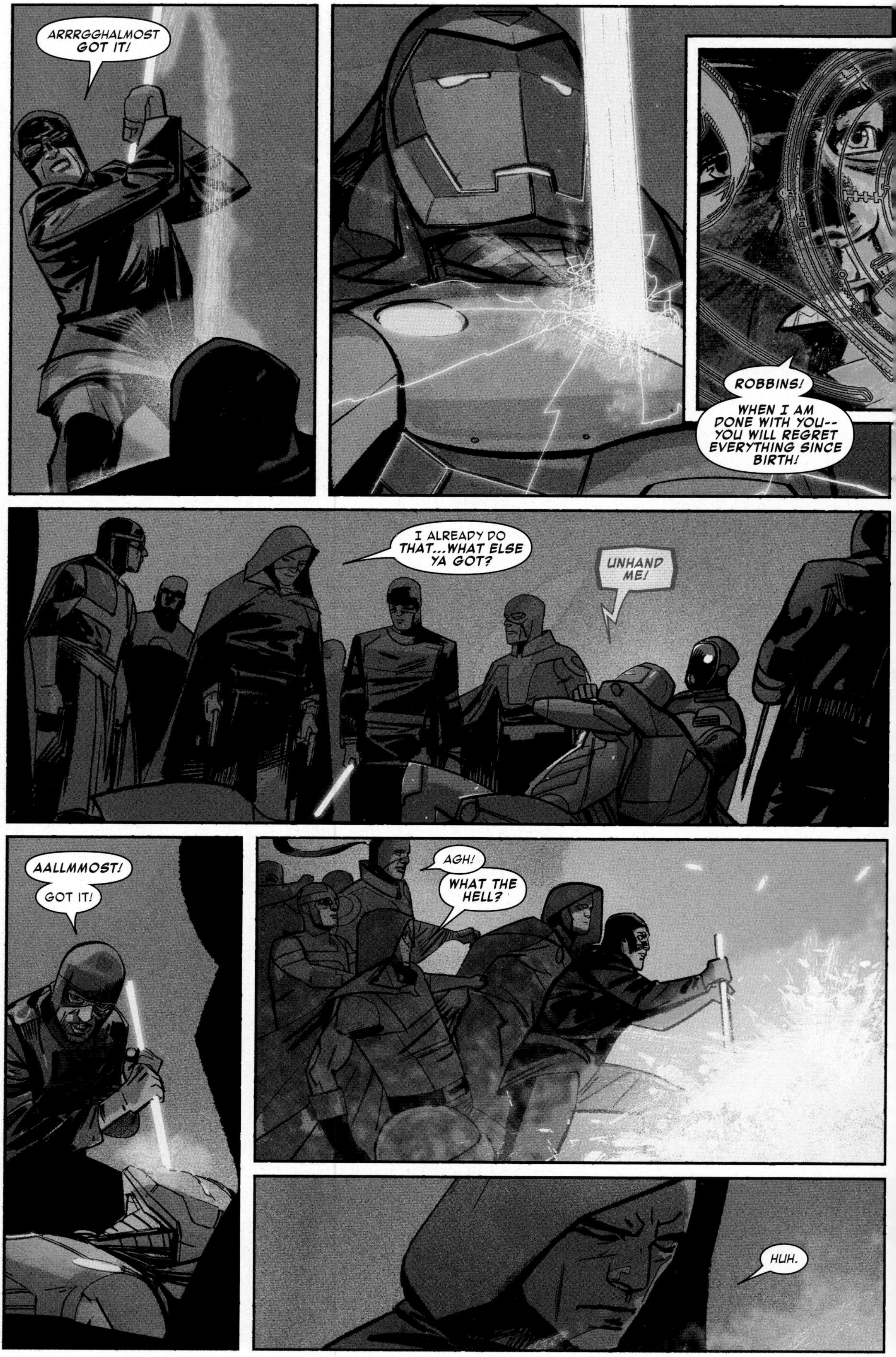
ARRRGGHALMOST GOT IT!
ROBBINS!
WHEN I AM DONE WITH YOU-- YOU WILL REGRET EVERYTHING SINCE BIRTH!
I ALREADY DO THAT...WHAT ELSE YA GOT?
UNHAND ME!
AALLMMOST!
GOT IT!
AGH!
WHAT THE HELL?
HUH.

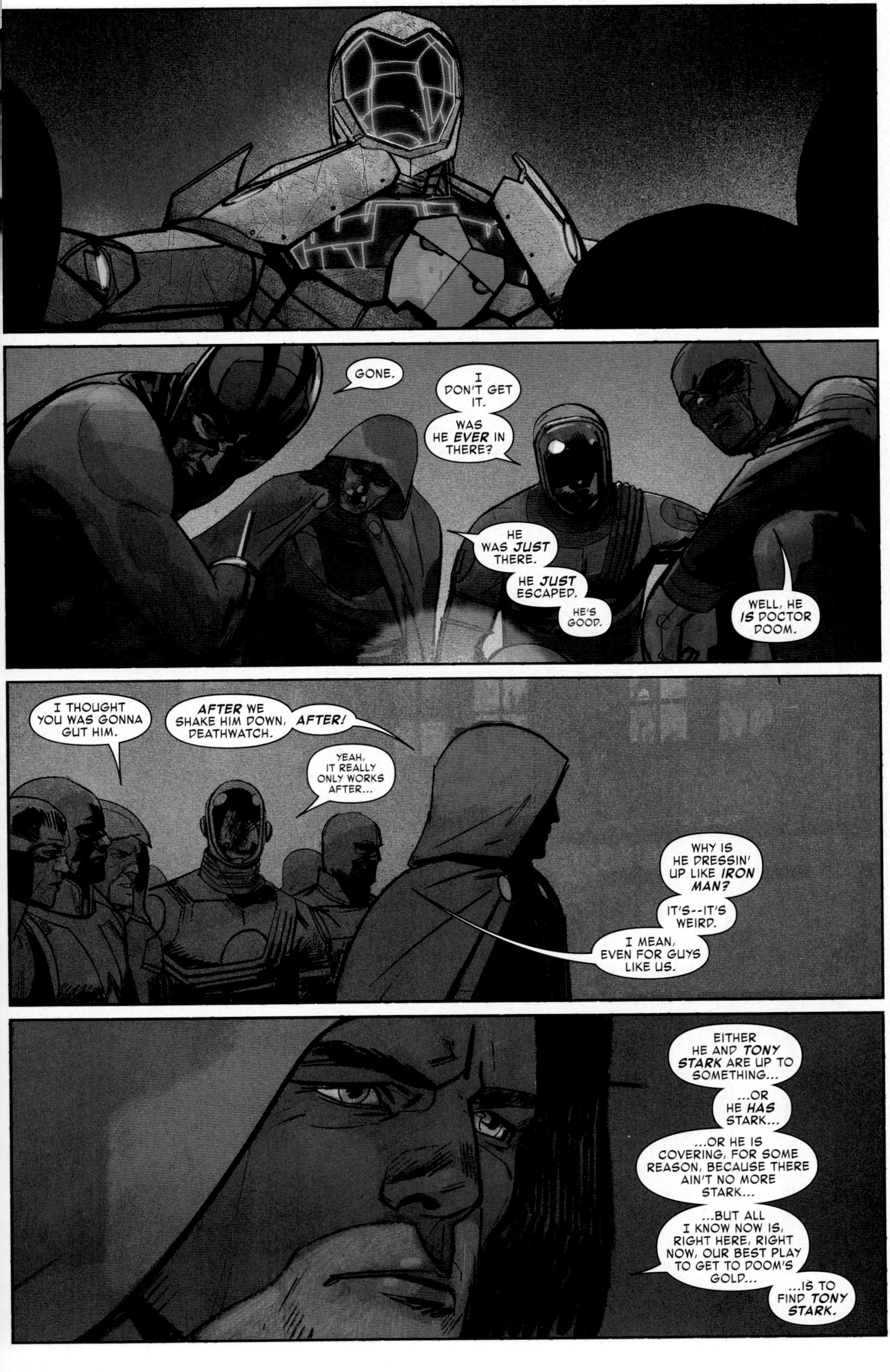
GONE.
I DON'T GET IT.
WAS HE EVER IN THERE?
HE WAS JUST THERE.
HE JUST ESCAPED.
HE'S GOOD.
WELL, HE IS DOCTOR DOOM.
I THOUGHT YOU WAS GONNA GUT HIM.
AFTER WE SHAKE HIM DOWN, DEATHWATCH.
AFTER!
YEAH, IT REALLY ONLY WORKS AFTER...
WHY IS HE DRESSIN' UP LIKE IRON MAN?
IT'S--IT'S WEIRD.
I MEAN, EVEN FOR GUYS LIKE US.
EITHER HE AND TONY STARK ARE UP TO SOMETHING...
...OR HE HAS STARK...
...OR HE IS COVERING, FOR SOME REASON, BECAUSE THERE AIN'T NO MORE STARK...
...BUT ALL I KNOW NOW IS, RIGHT HERE, RIGHT NOW, OUR BEST PLAY TO GET TO DOOM'S GOLD...
...IS TO FIND TONY STARK.

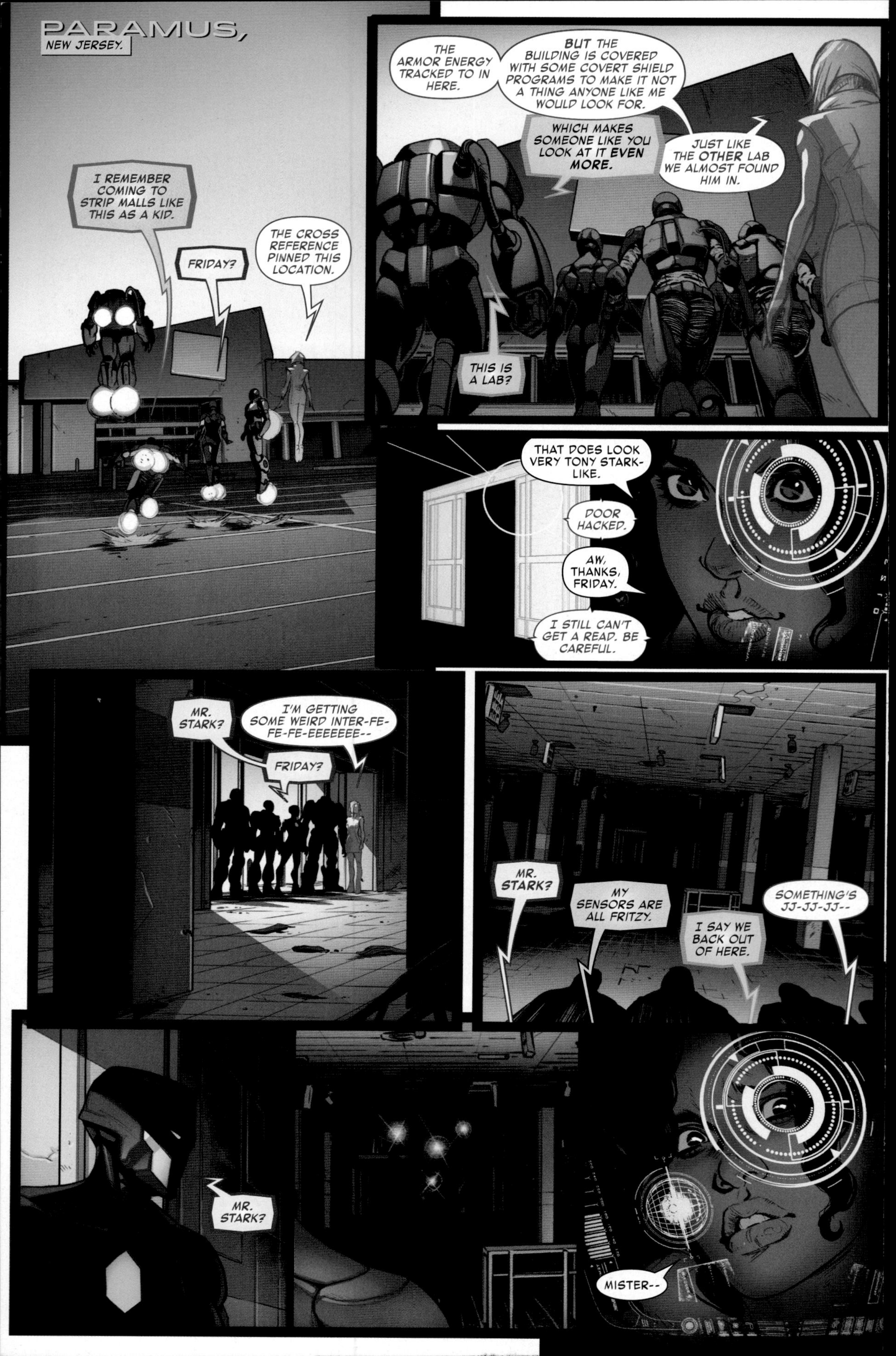
PARAMUS,
NEW JERSEY.
I REMEMBER COMING TO STRIP MALLS LIKE THIS AS A KID.
FRIDAY?
THE CROSS REFERENCE PINNED THIS LOCATION.
THE ARMOR ENERGY TRACKED TO IN HERE.
BUT THE BUILDING IS COVERED WITH SOME COVERT SHIELD PROGRAMS TO MAKE IT NOT A THING ANYONE LIKE ME WOULD LOOK FOR.
WHICH MAKES SOMEONE LIKE YOU LOOK AT IT EVEN MORE.
JUST LIKE THE OTHER LAB WE ALMOST FOUND HIM IN.
THIS IS A LAB?
THAT DOES LOOK VERY TONY STARK-LIKE.
DOOR HACKED.
AW, THANKS, FRIDAY.
I STILL CAN'T GET A READ. BE CAREFUL.
MR. STARK?
I'M GETTING SOME WEIRD INTER-FE-FE-FE-EEEEEEE--
FRIDAY?
MR. STARK?
MY SENSORS ARE ALL FRITZY.
I SAY WE BACK OUT OF HERE.
SOMETHING'S JJ-JJ-JJ--
MR. STARK?
MISTER--

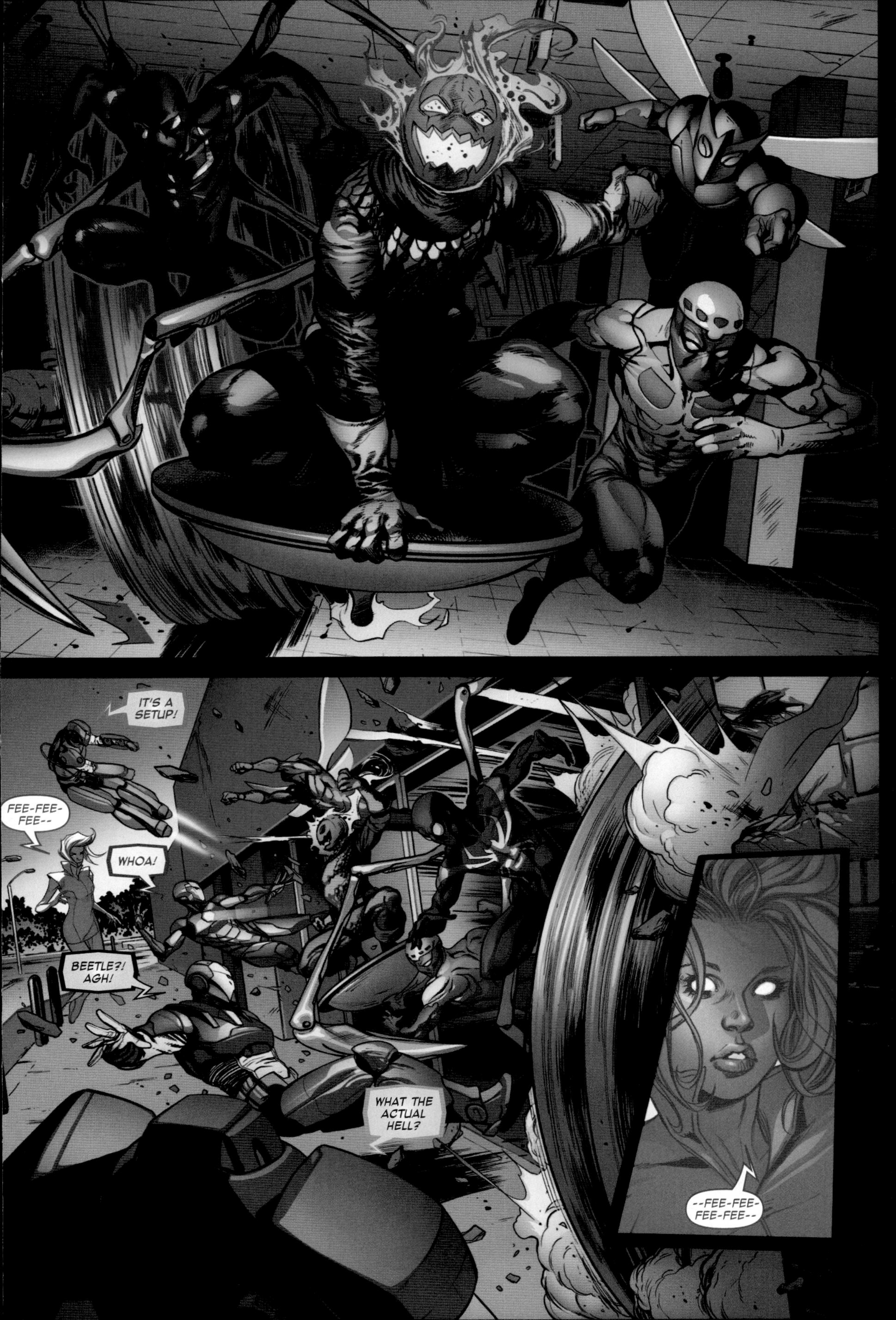
IT'S A SETUP!
FEE-FEE-FEE--
WHOA!
BEETLE?! AGH!
WHAT THE ACTUAL HELL?
--FEE-FEE-FEE-FEE--

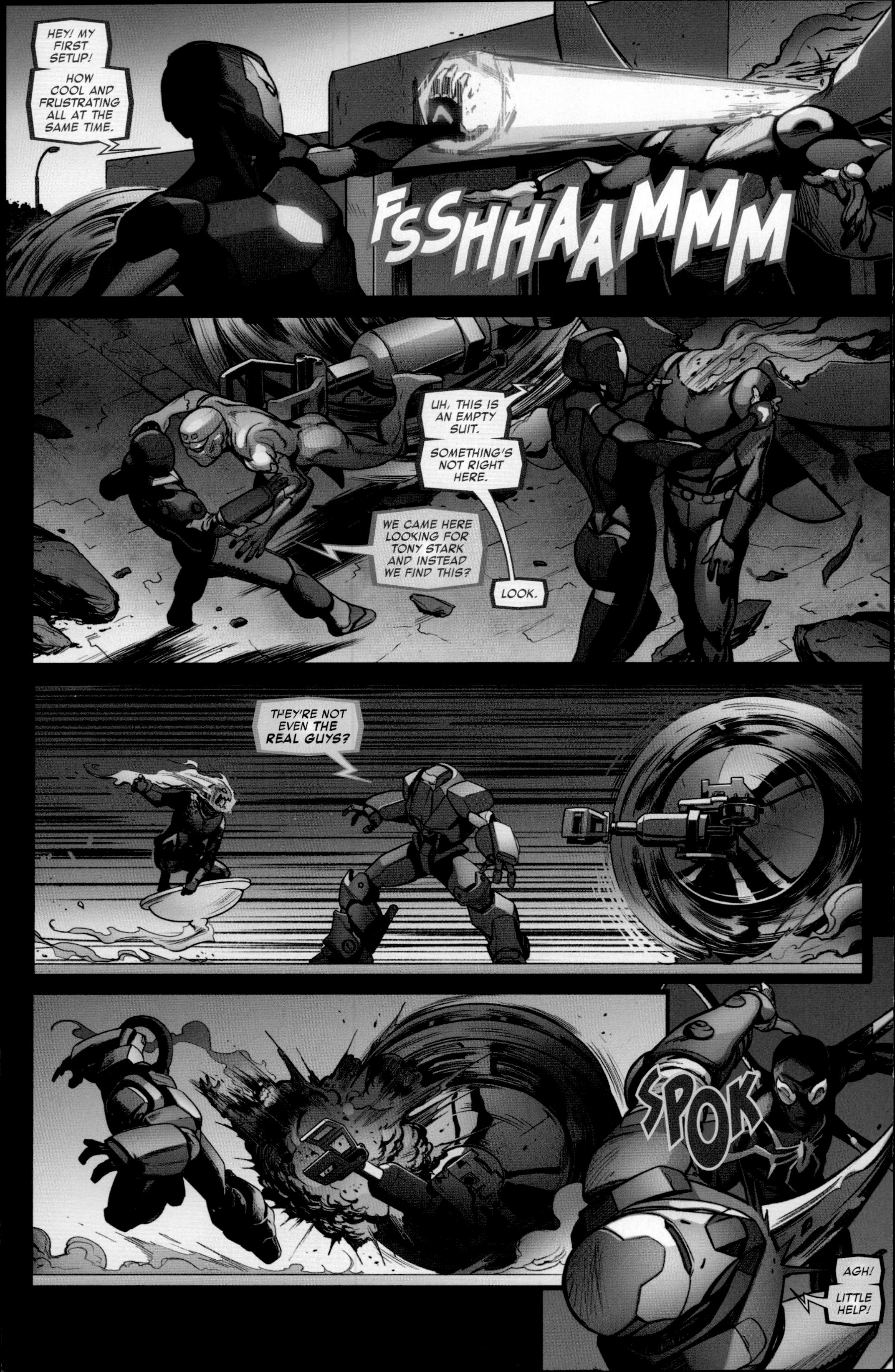
HEY! MY FIRST SETUP!
HOW COOL AND FRUSTRATING ALL AT THE SAME TIME.
FSSHHAAMMMM
UH, THIS IS AN EMPTY SUIT.
SOMETHING'S NOT RIGHT HERE.
WE CAME HERE LOOKING FOR TONY STARK AND INSTEAD WE FIND THIS?
LOOK.
THEY'RE NOT EVEN THE REAL GUYS?
SPOK
AGH!
LITTLE HELP!

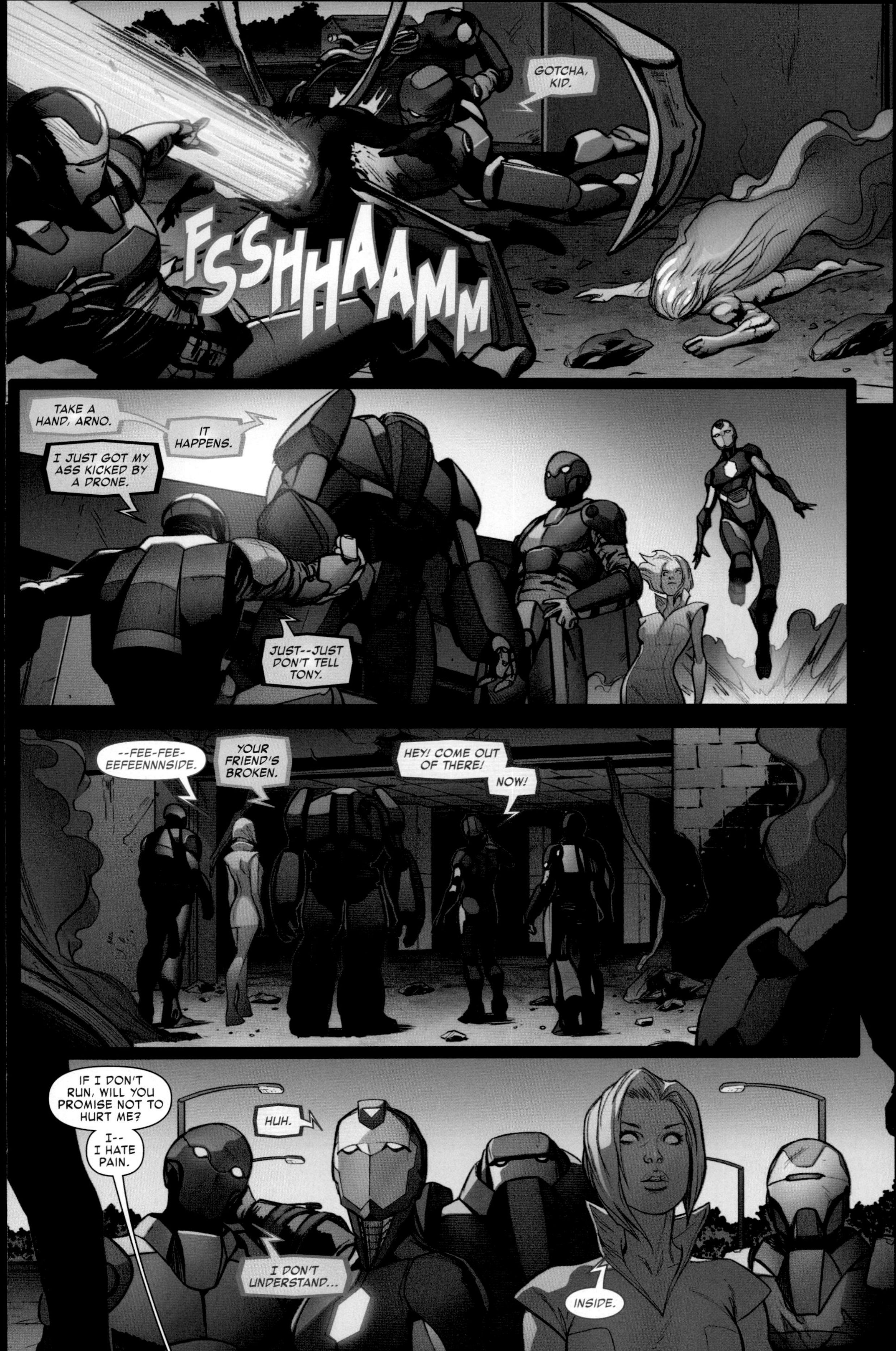
GOTCHA, KID.
FSSHHAAMM
TAKE A HAND, ARNO.
IT HAPPENS.
I JUST GOT MY ASS KICKED BY A DRONE.
JUST--JUST DON'T TELL TONY.
--FEE-FEE-EEFEENNNSIDE.
YOUR FRIEND'S BROKEN.
HEY! COME OUT OF THERE!
NOW!
IF I DON'T RUN, WILL YOU PROMISE NOT TO HURT ME?
I--I HATE PAIN.
HUH.
I DON'T UNDERSTAND...
INSIDE.

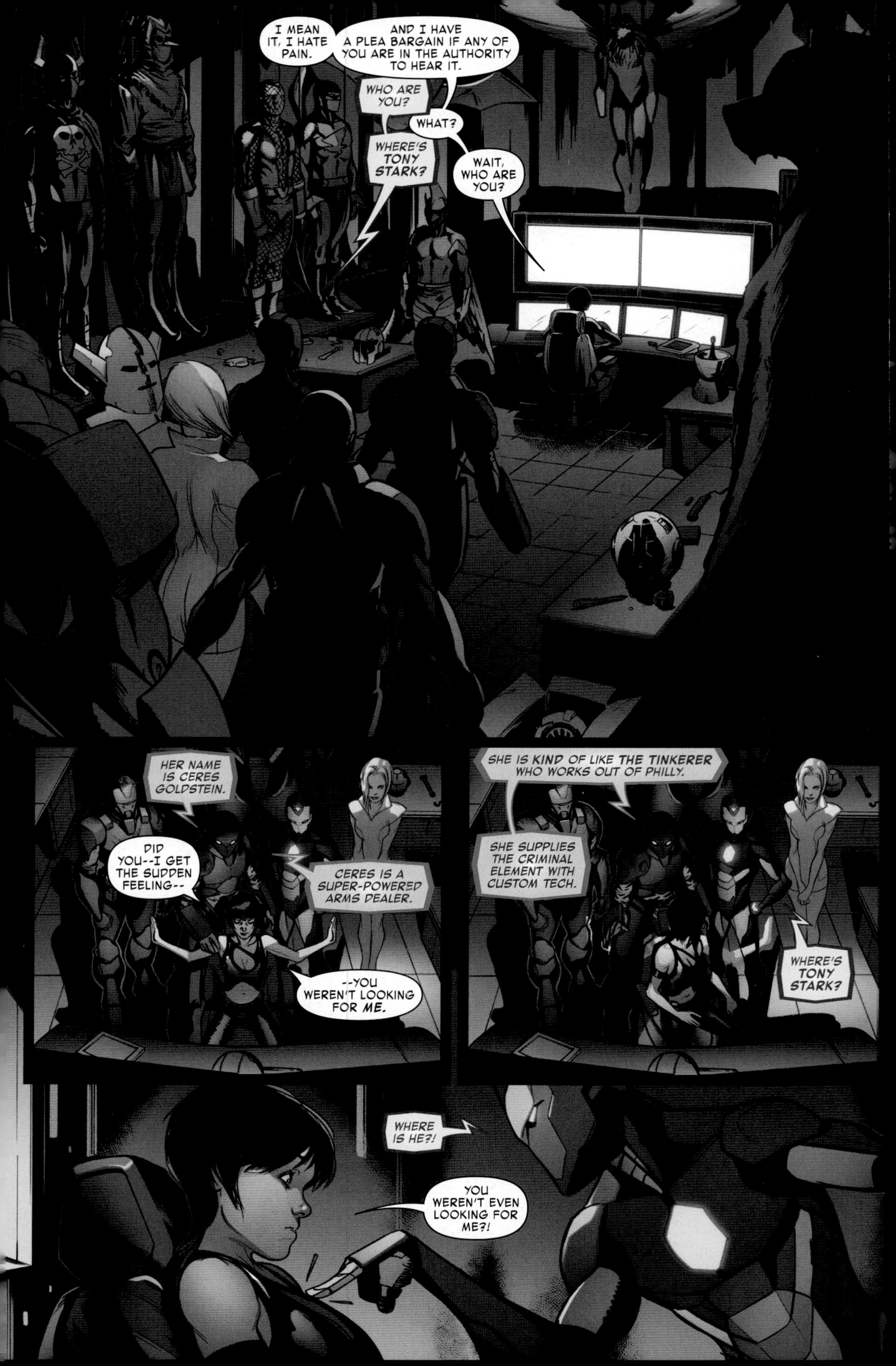
I MEAN IT, I HATE PAIN.
AND I HAVE A PLEA BARGAIN IF ANY OF YOU ARE IN THE AUTHORITY TO HEAR IT.
WHO ARE YOU?
WHAT?
WHERE'S TONY STARK?
WAIT, WHO ARE YOU?
HER NAME IS CERES GOLDSTEIN.
DID YOU--I GET THE SUDDEN FEELING--
CERES IS A SUPER-POWERED ARMS DEALER.
--YOU WEREN'T LOOKING FOR ME.
SHE IS KIND OF LIKE THE TINKERER WHO WORKS OUT OF PHILLY.
SHE SUPPLIES THE CRIMINAL ELEMENT WITH CUSTOM TECH.
WHERE'S TONY STARK?
WHERE IS HE?!
YOU WEREN'T EVEN LOOKING FOR ME?!

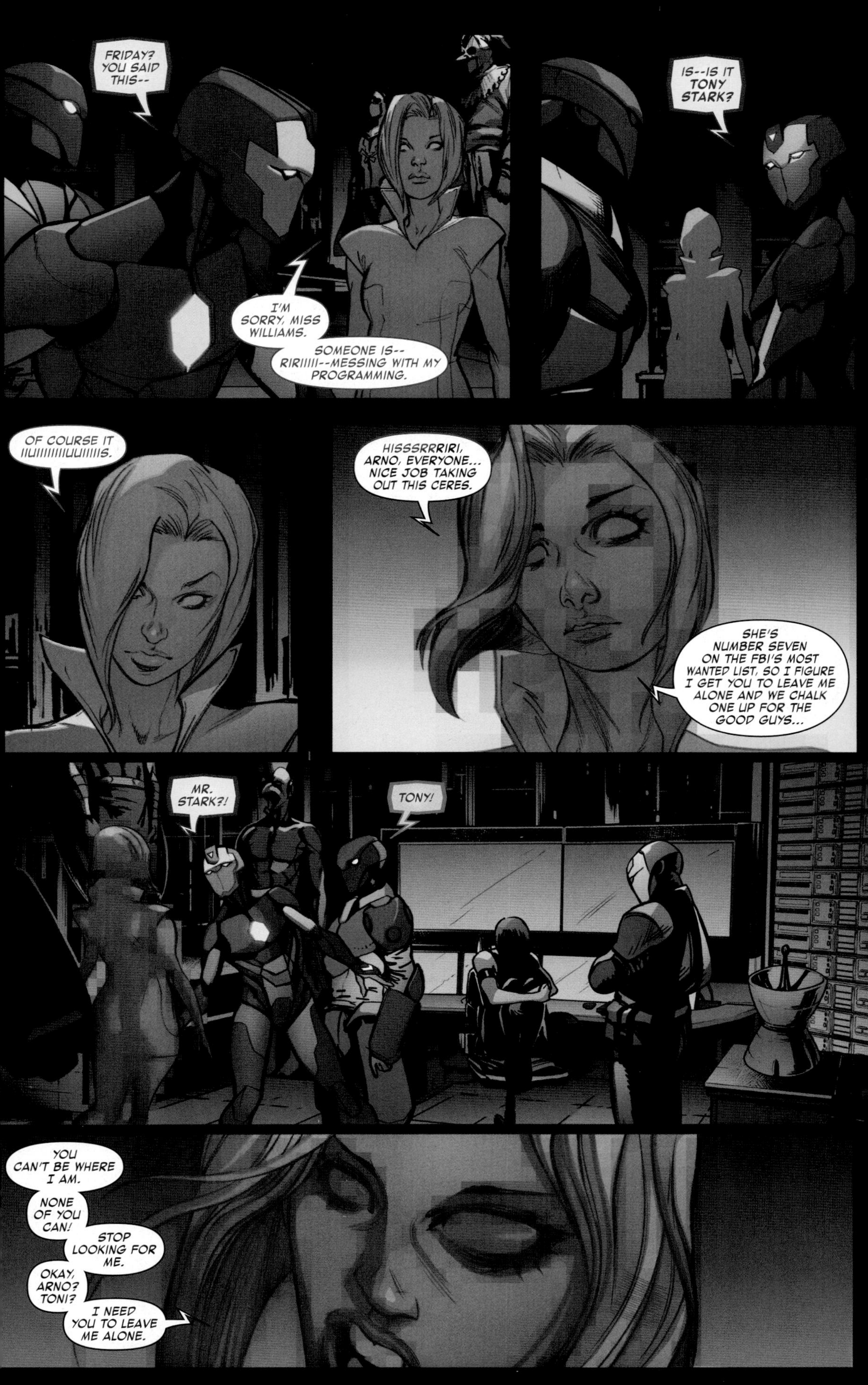
FRIDAY? YOU SAID THIS--
I'M SORRY, MISS WILLIAMS.
SOMEONE IS-- RIRIIIII--MESSING WITH MY PROGRAMMING.
IS--IS IT TONY STARK?
OF COURSE IT IIUIIIIIIIIUUIIIIIS.
HISSSRRRIRI, ARNO, EVERYONE... NICE JOB TAKING OUT THIS CERES.
SHE'S NUMBER SEVEN ON THE FBI'S MOST WANTED LIST, SO I FIGURE I GET YOU TO LEAVE ME ALONE AND WE CHALK ONE UP FOR THE GOOD GUYS...
MR. STARK?!
TONY!
YOU CAN'T BE WHERE I AM.
NONE OF YOU CAN!
STOP LOOKING FOR ME.
OKAY, ARNO? TONI?
I NEED YOU TO LEAVE ME ALONE.

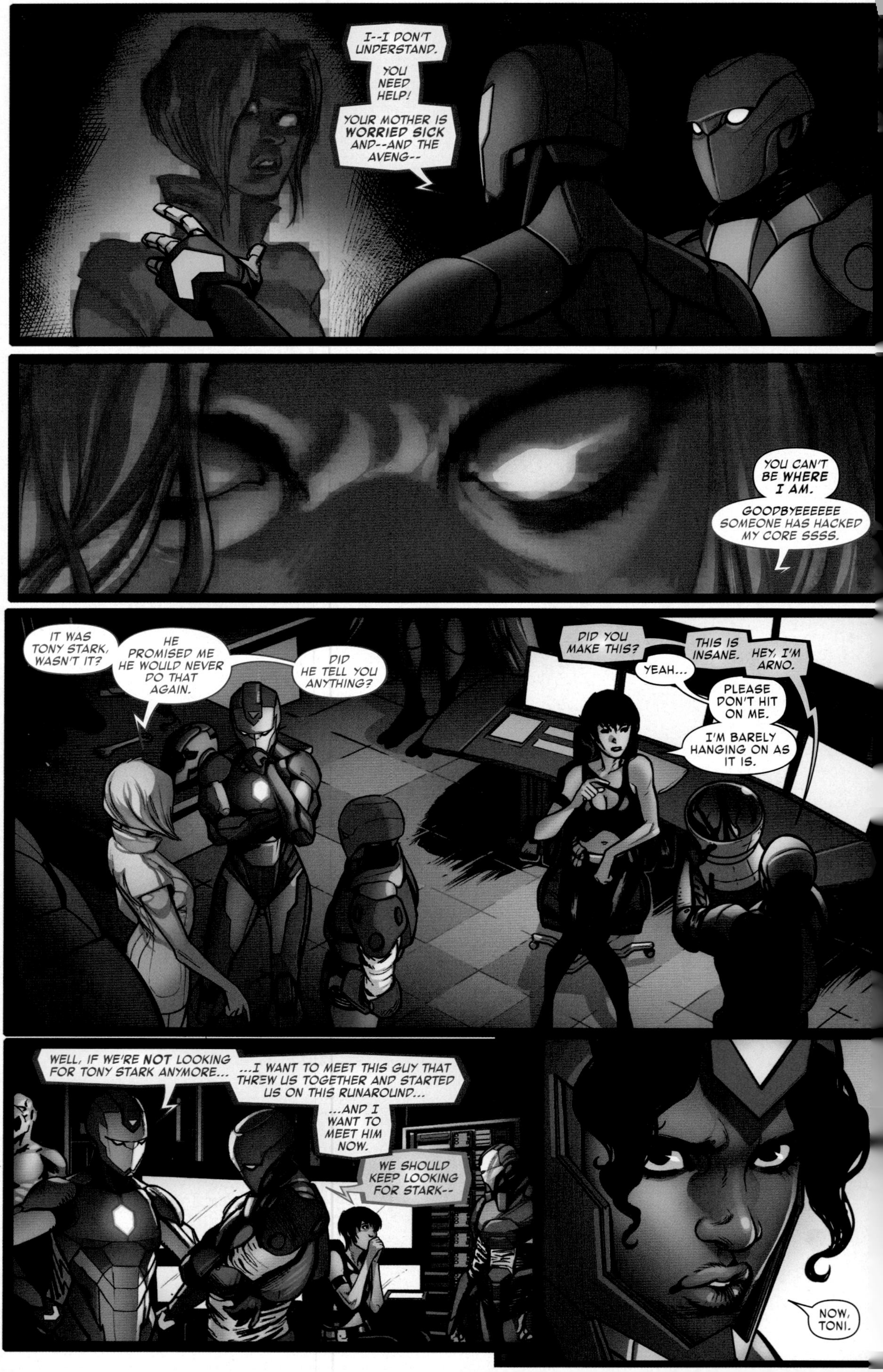
I--I DON'T UNDERSTAND.
YOU NEED HELP!
YOUR MOTHER IS WORRIED SICK AND--AND THE AVENG--
YOU CAN'T BE WHERE I AM.
GOODBYEEEEEE SOMEONE HAS HACKED MY CORE SSSS.
IT WAS TONY STARK, WASN'T IT?
HE PROMISED ME HE WOULD NEVER DO THAT AGAIN.
DID HE TELL YOU ANYTHING?
DID YOU MAKE THIS?
THIS IS INSANE.
YEAH...
HEY, I'M ARNO.
PLEASE DON'T HIT ON ME.
I'M BARELY HANGING ON AS IT IS.
WELL, IF WE'RE NOT LOOKING FOR TONY STARK ANYMORE...
...I WANT TO MEET THIS GUY THAT THREW US TOGETHER AND STARTED US ON THIS RUNAROUND...
...AND I WANT TO MEET HIM NOW.
WE SHOULD KEEP LOOKING FOR STARK--
NOW, TONI.

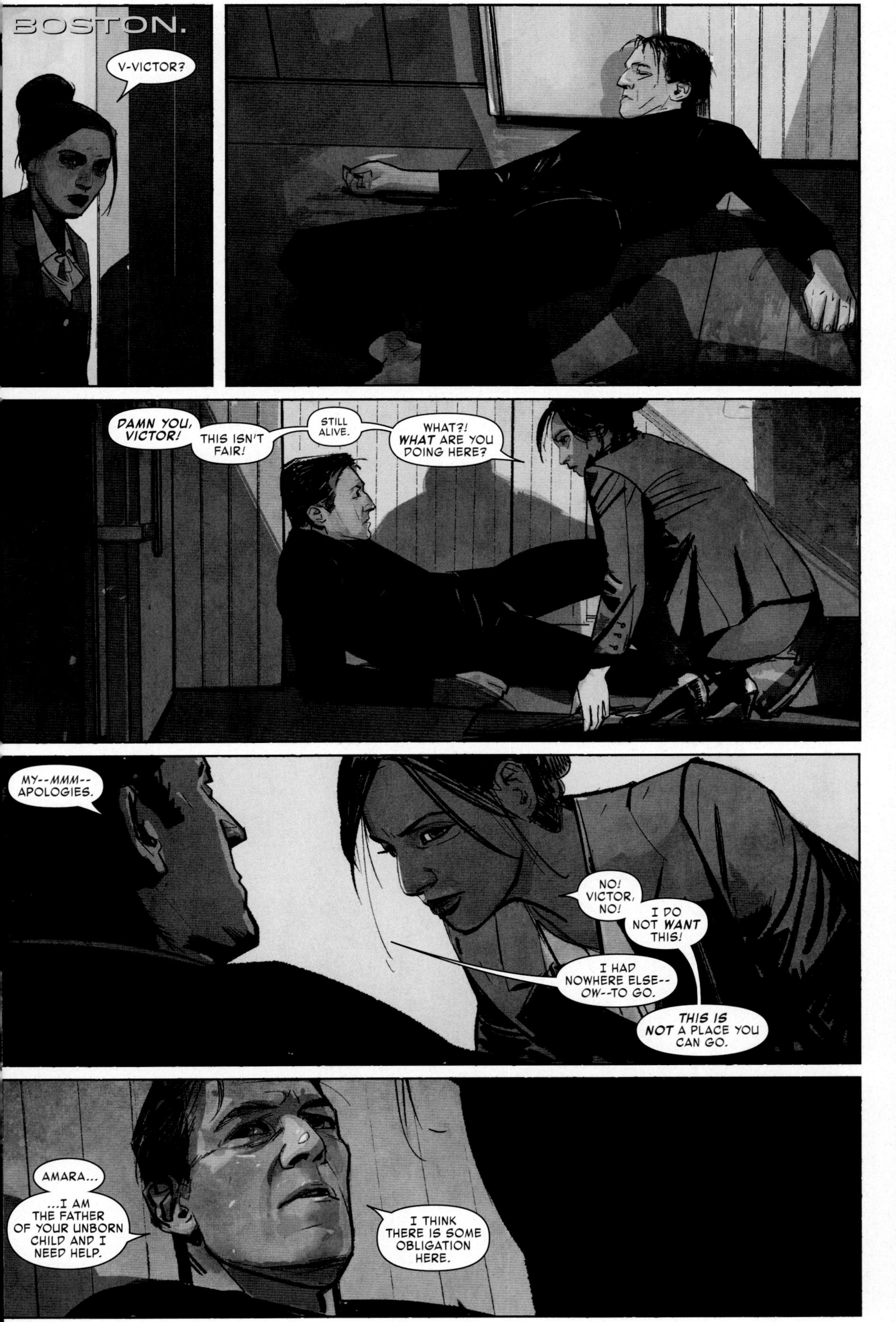
BOSTON.
V-VICTOR?
DAMN YOU, VICTOR!
THIS ISN'T FAIR!
STILL ALIVE.
WHAT?! WHAT ARE YOU DOING HERE?
MY--MMM--APOLOGIES.
NO! VICTOR, NO!
I DO NOT WANT THIS!
I HAD NOWHERE ELSE--OW--TO GO.
THIS IS NOT A PLACE YOU CAN GO.
AMARA...
...I AM THE FATHER OF YOUR UNBORN CHILD AND I NEED HELP.
I THINK THERE IS SOME OBLIGATION HERE.

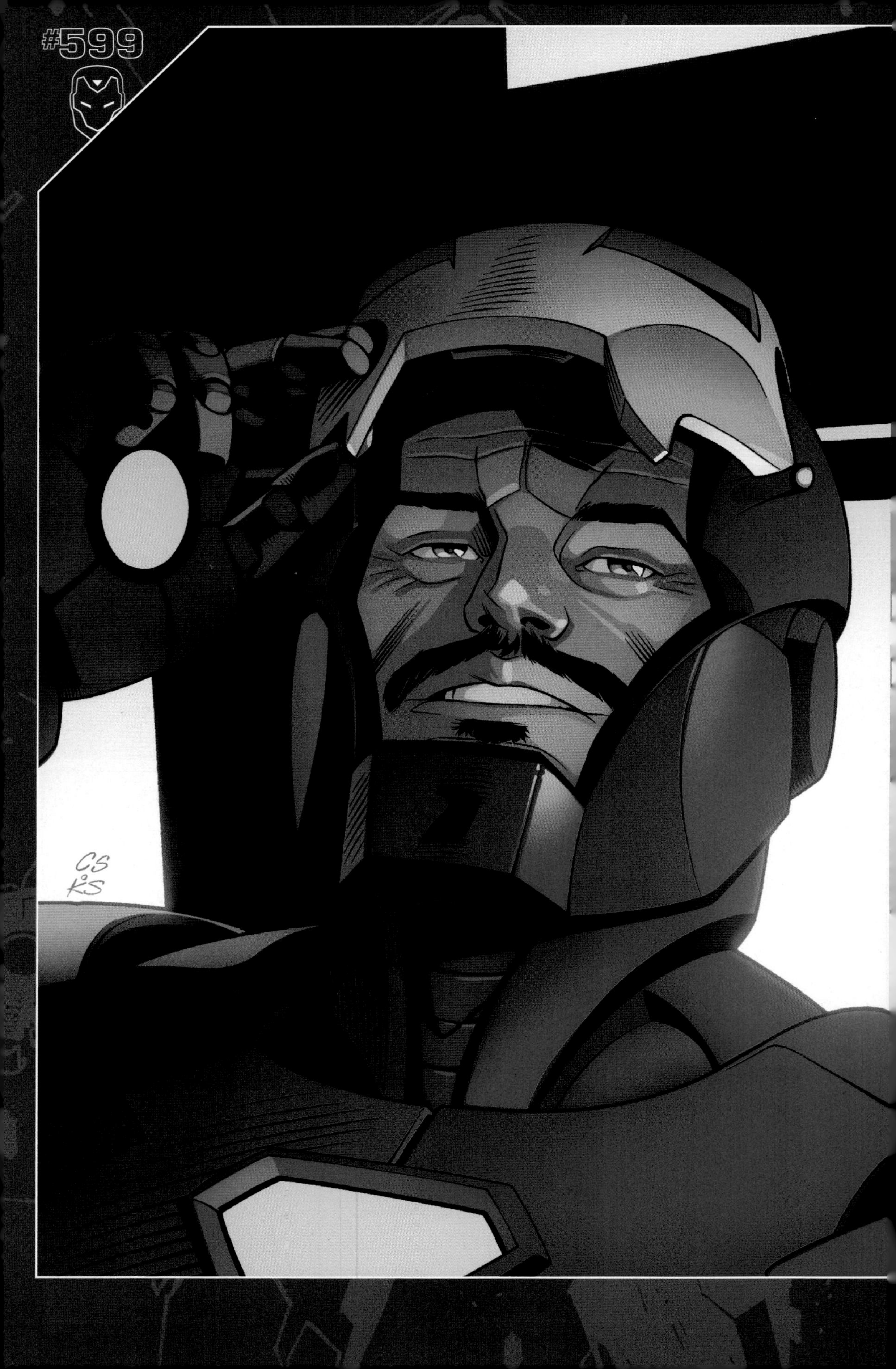
#599
CS
KS

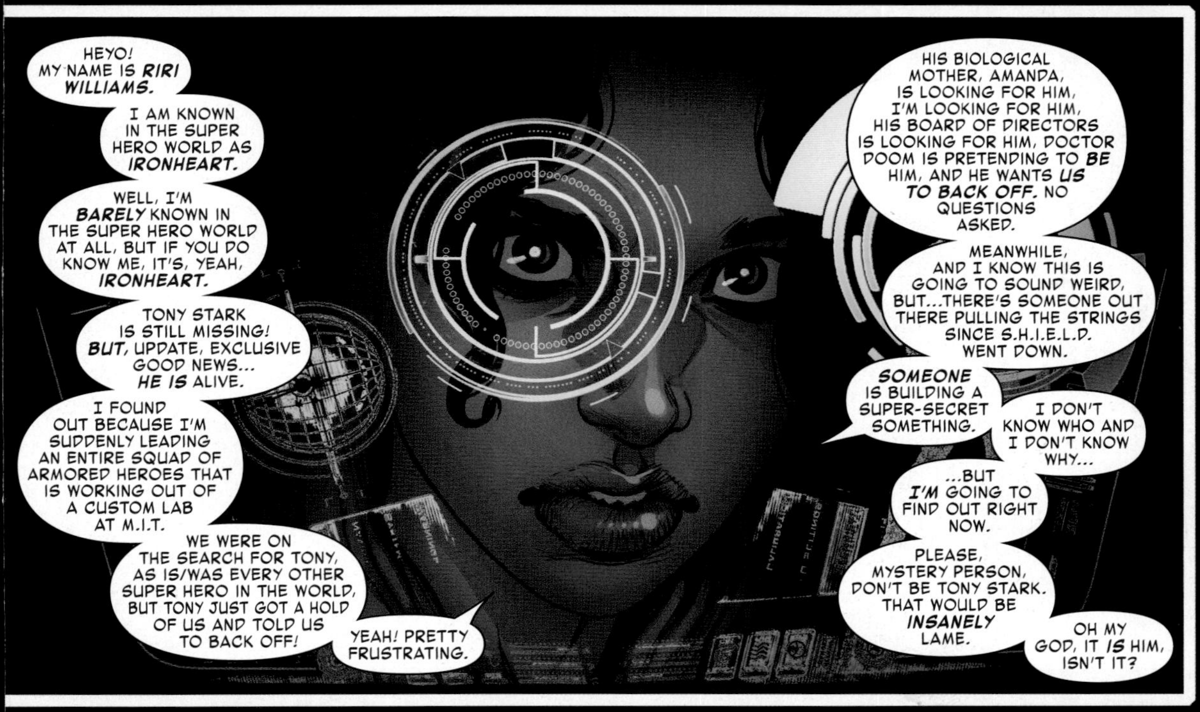

HEYO! MY NAME IS RIRI WILLIAMS.
I AM KNOWN IN THE SUPER HERO WORLD AS IRONHEART.
WELL, I'M BARELY KNOWN IN THE SUPER HERO WORLD AT ALL, BUT IF YOU DO KNOW ME, IT'S, YEAH, IRONHEART.
TONY STARK IS STILL MISSING! BUT, UPDATE, EXCLUSIVE GOOD NEWS... HE IS ALIVE.
I FOUND OUT BECAUSE I'M SUDDENLY LEADING AN ENTIRE SQUAD OF ARMORED HEROES THAT IS WORKING OUT OF A CUSTOM LAB AT M.I.T.
WE WERE ON THE SEARCH FOR TONY, AS IS/WAS EVERY OTHER SUPER HERO IN THE WORLD, BUT TONY JUST GOT A HOLD OF US AND TOLD US TO BACK OFF!
YEAH! PRETTY FRUSTRATING.
HIS BIOLOGICAL MOTHER, AMANDA, IS LOOKING FOR HIM, I'M LOOKING FOR HIM, HIS BOARD OF DIRECTORS IS LOOKING FOR HIM, DOCTOR DOOM IS PRETENDING TO BE HIM, AND HE WANTS US TO BACK OFF. NO QUESTIONS ASKED.
MEANWHILE, AND I KNOW THIS IS GOING TO SOUND WEIRD, BUT...THERE'S SOMEONE OUT THERE PULLING THE STRINGS SINCE S.H.I.E.L.D. WENT DOWN.
SOMEONE IS BUILDING A SUPER-SECRET SOMETHING.
I DON'T KNOW WHO AND I DON'T KNOW WHY...
...BUT I'M GOING TO FIND OUT RIGHT NOW.
PLEASE, MYSTERY PERSON, DON'T BE TONY STARK. THAT WOULD BE INSANELY LAME.
OH MY GOD, IT IS HIM, ISN'T IT?

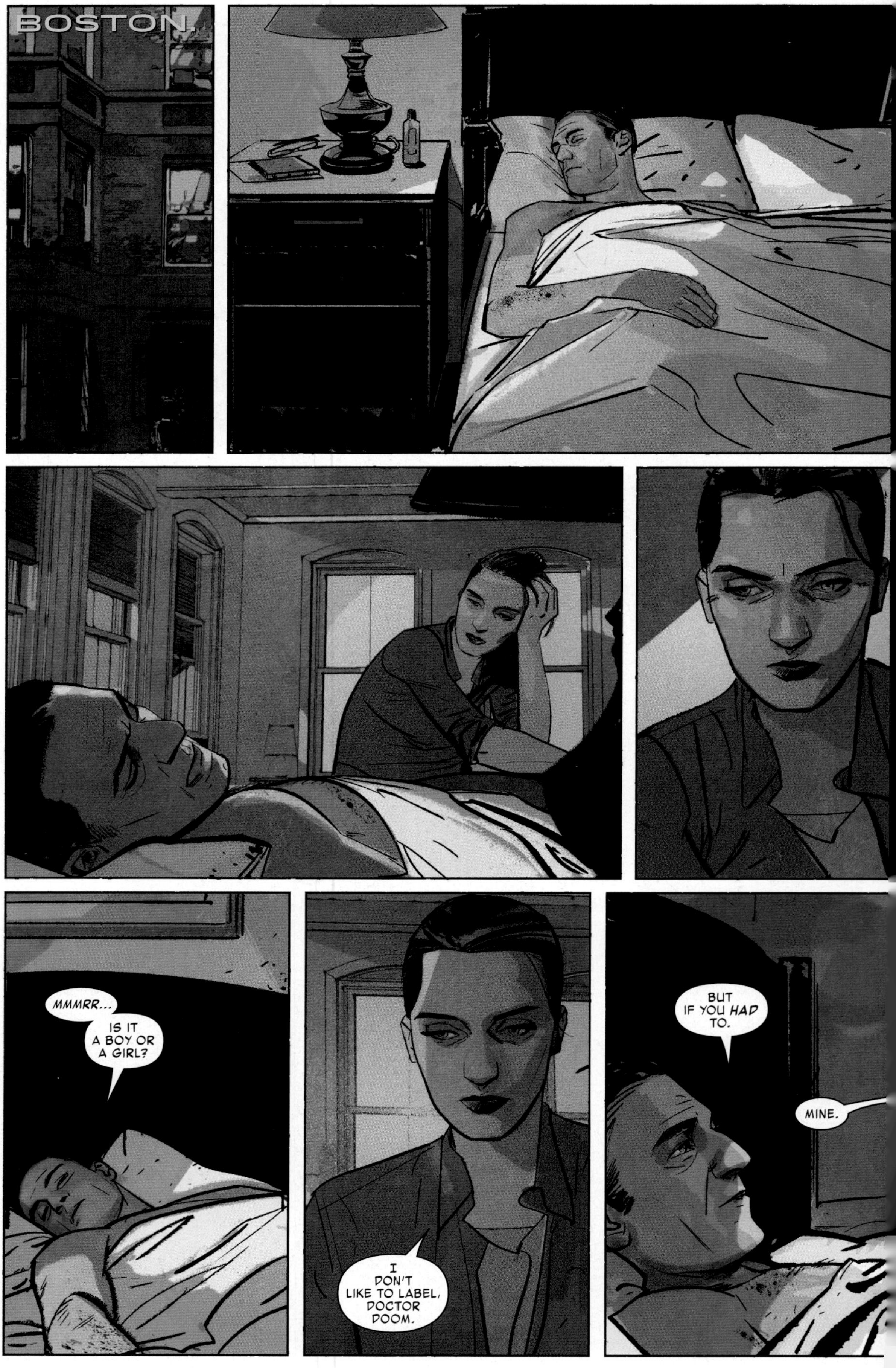
BOSTON.
MMMRR... IS IT A BOY OR A GIRL?
I DON'T LIKE TO LABEL, DOCTOR DOOM.
BUT IF YOU *HAD* TO.
MINE.

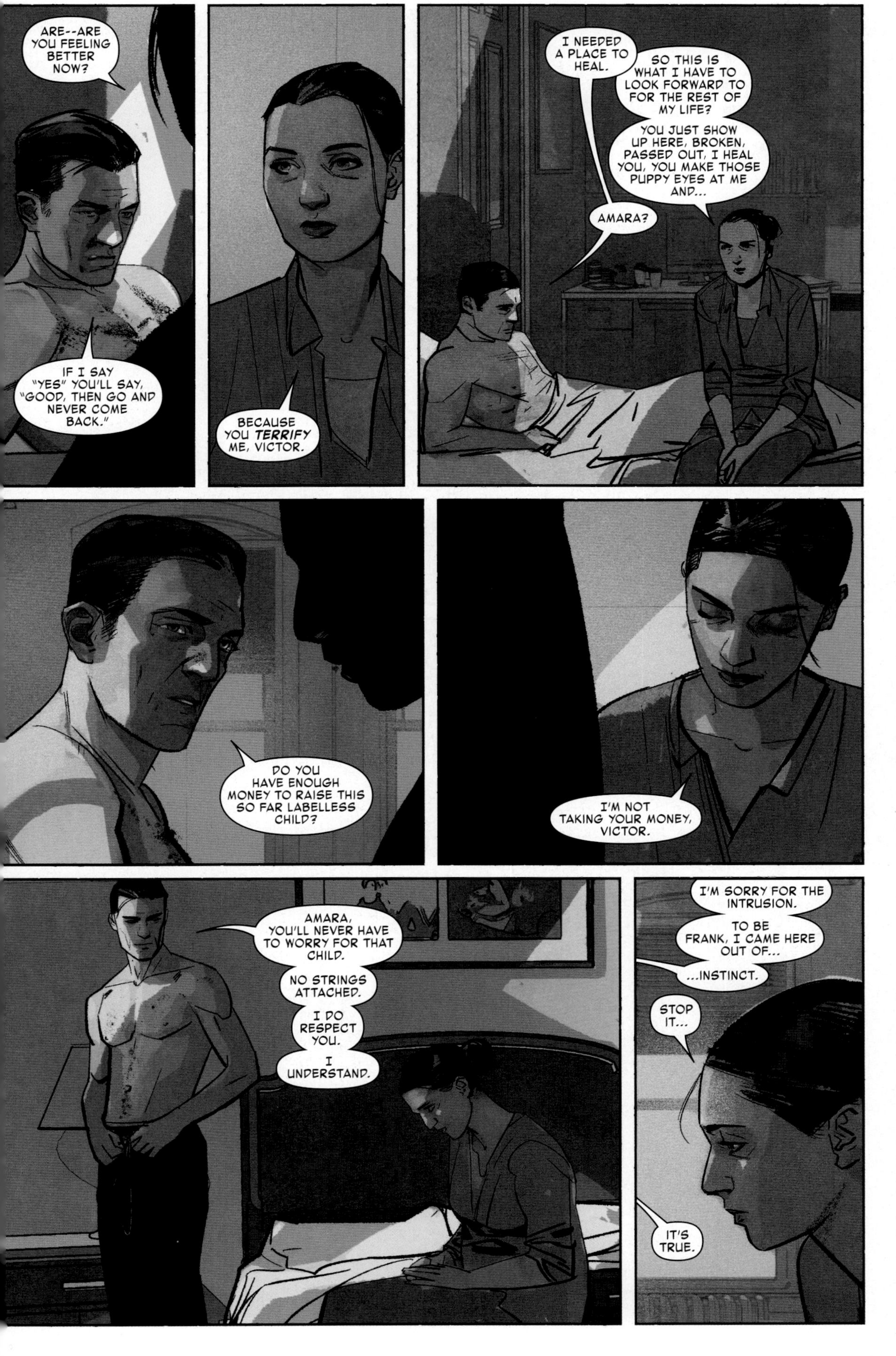
ARE--ARE YOU FEELING BETTER NOW?
IF I SAY "YES" YOU'LL SAY, "GOOD, THEN GO AND NEVER COME BACK."
BECAUSE YOU TERRIFY ME, VICTOR.
I NEEDED A PLACE TO HEAL.
SO THIS IS WHAT I HAVE TO LOOK FORWARD TO FOR THE REST OF MY LIFE?
YOU JUST SHOW UP HERE, BROKEN, PASSED OUT, I HEAL YOU, YOU MAKE THOSE PUPPY EYES AT ME AND...
AMARA?
DO YOU HAVE ENOUGH MONEY TO RAISE THIS SO FAR LABELLESS CHILD?
I'M NOT TAKING YOUR MONEY, VICTOR.
AMARA, YOU'LL NEVER HAVE TO WORRY FOR THAT CHILD.
NO STRINGS ATTACHED.
I DO RESPECT YOU.
I UNDERSTAND.
I'M SORRY FOR THE INTRUSION.
TO BE FRANK, I CAME HERE OUT OF...
...INSTINCT.
STOP IT...
IT'S TRUE.

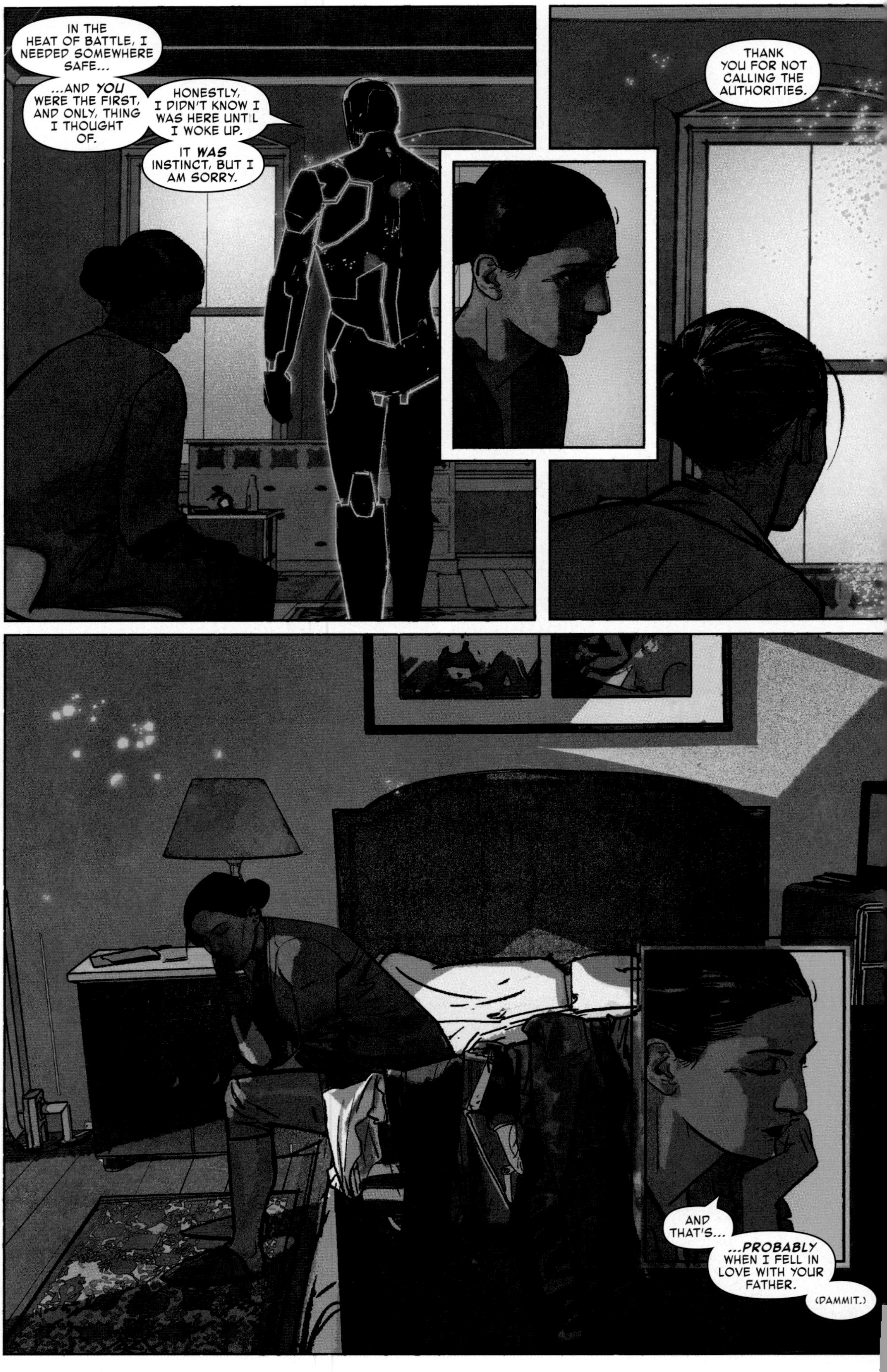

IN THE HEAT OF BATTLE, I NEEDED SOMEWHERE SAFE...
...AND YOU WERE THE FIRST, AND ONLY, THING I THOUGHT OF.
HONESTLY, I DIDN'T KNOW I WAS HERE UNTIL I WOKE UP.
IT WAS INSTINCT, BUT I AM SORRY.
THANK YOU FOR NOT CALLING THE AUTHORITIES.
AND THAT'S...
...PROBABLY WHEN I FELL IN LOVE WITH YOUR FATHER.
(DAMMIT.)

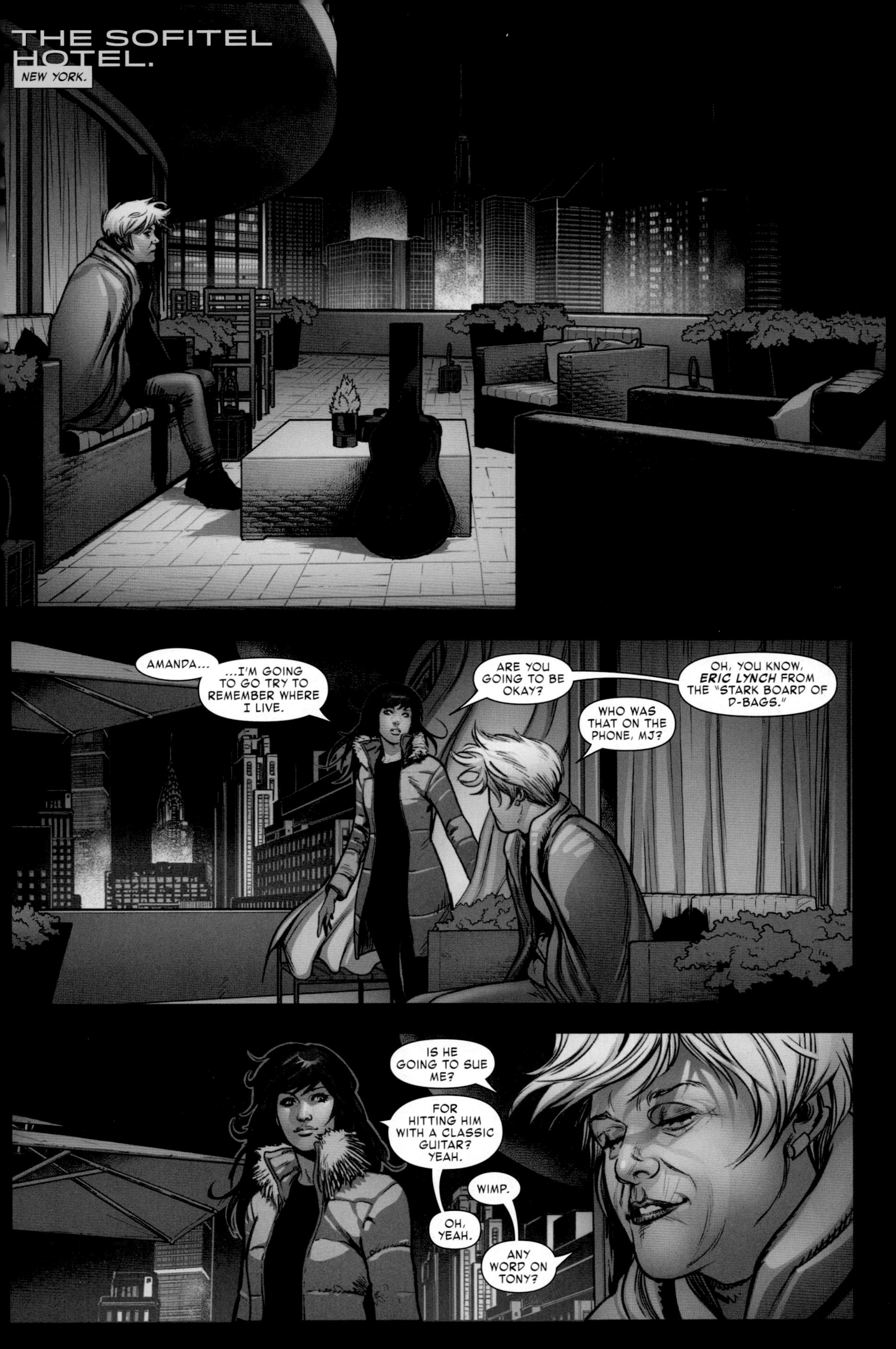
THE SOFITEL HOTEL.
NEW YORK.
AMANDA...
...I'M GOING TO GO TRY TO REMEMBER WHERE I LIVE.
ARE YOU GOING TO BE OKAY?
WHO WAS THAT ON THE PHONE, MJ?
OH, YOU KNOW, ERIC LYNCH FROM THE "STARK BOARD OF D-BAGS."
IS HE GOING TO SUE ME?
FOR HITTING HIM WITH A CLASSIC GUITAR? YEAH.
WIMP.
OH, YEAH.
ANY WORD ON TONY?

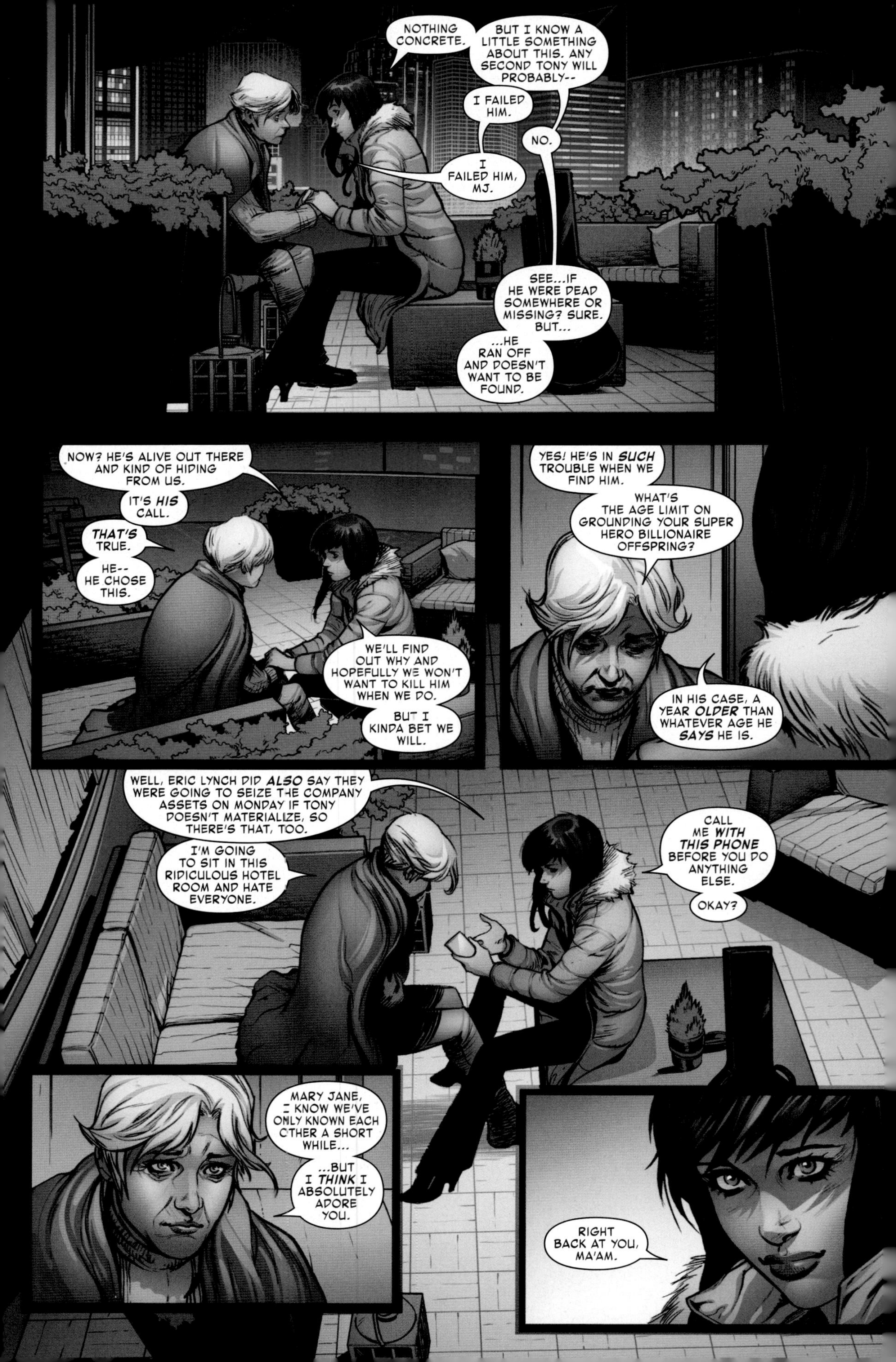
NOTHING CONCRETE.
BUT I KNOW A LITTLE SOMETHING ABOUT THIS. ANY SECOND TONY WILL PROBABLY--
I FAILED HIM.
NO.
I FAILED HIM, MJ.
SEE...IF HE WERE DEAD SOMEWHERE OR MISSING? SURE. BUT...
...HE RAN OFF AND DOESN'T WANT TO BE FOUND.
NOW? HE'S ALIVE OUT THERE AND KIND OF HIDING FROM US.
IT'S *HIS* CALL.
*THAT'S* TRUE.
HE-- HE CHOSE THIS.
WE'LL FIND OUT WHY AND HOPEFULLY WE WON'T WANT TO KILL HIM WHEN WE DO.
BUT I KINDA BET WE WILL.
YES! HE'S IN *SUCH* TROUBLE WHEN WE FIND HIM.
WHAT'S THE AGE LIMIT ON GROUNDING YOUR SUPER HERO BILLIONAIRE OFFSPRING?
IN HIS CASE, A YEAR *OLDER* THAN WHATEVER AGE HE *SAYS* HE IS.
WELL, ERIC LYNCH DID *ALSO* SAY THEY WERE GOING TO SEIZE THE COMPANY ASSETS ON MONDAY IF TONY DOESN'T MATERIALIZE, SO THERE'S THAT, TOO.
I'M GOING TO SIT IN THIS RIDICULOUS HOTEL ROOM AND HATE EVERYONE.
CALL ME *WITH THIS PHONE* BEFORE YOU DO ANYTHING ELSE.
OKAY?
MARY JANE, I KNOW WE'VE ONLY KNOWN EACH OTHER A SHORT WHILE...
...BUT I *THINK* I ABSOLUTELY ADORE YOU.
RIGHT BACK AT YOU, MA'AM.

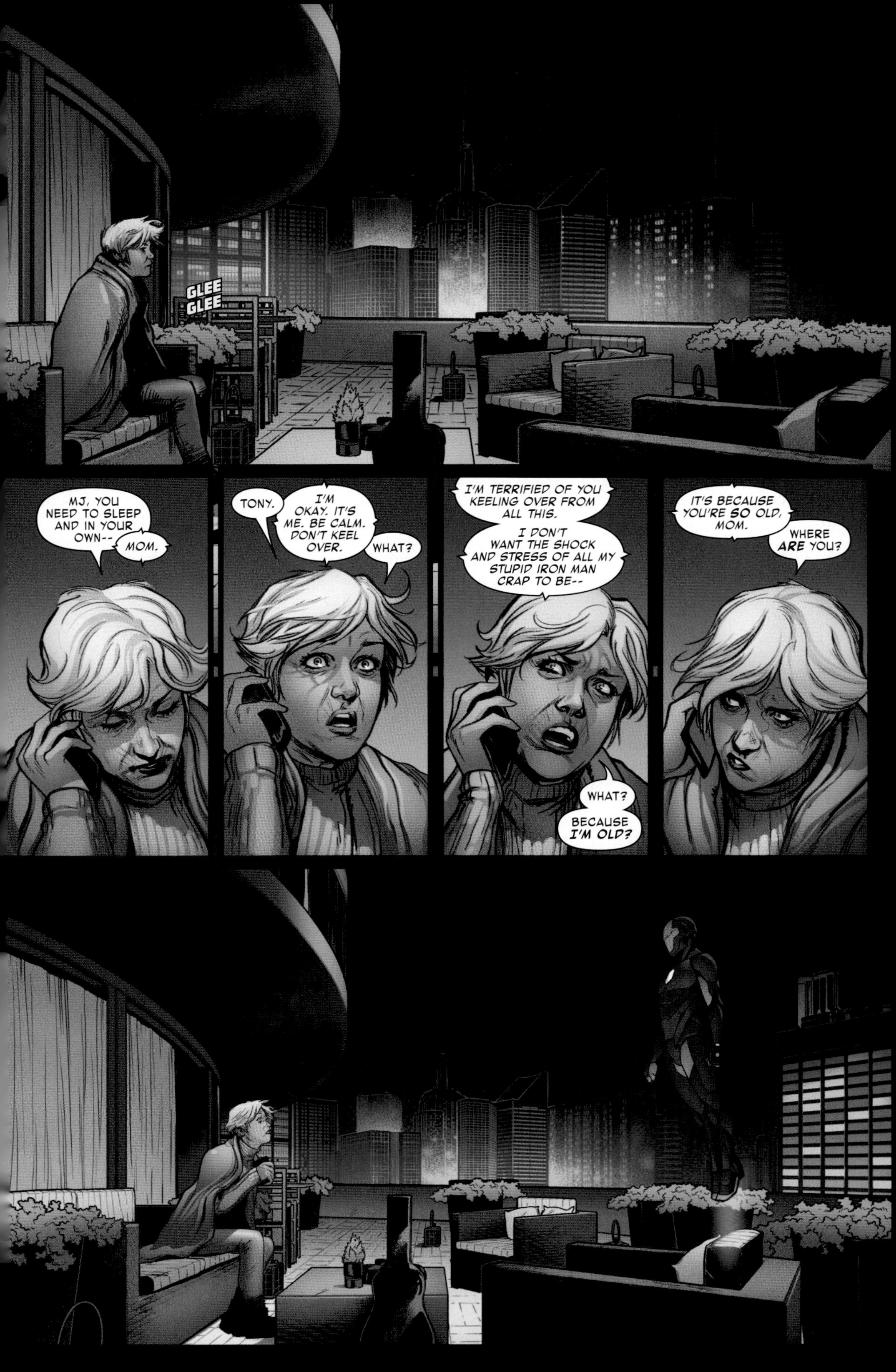
GLEE GLEE
MJ, YOU NEED TO SLEEP AND IN YOUR OWN--
MOM.
TONY.
I'M OKAY. IT'S ME. BE CALM. DON'T KEEL OVER.
WHAT?
I'M TERRIFIED OF YOU KEELING OVER FROM ALL THIS.
I DON'T WANT THE SHOCK AND STRESS OF ALL MY STUPID IRON MAN CRAP TO BE--
WHAT?
BECAUSE I'M OLD?
IT'S BECAUSE YOU'RE SO OLD, MOM.
WHERE ARE YOU?

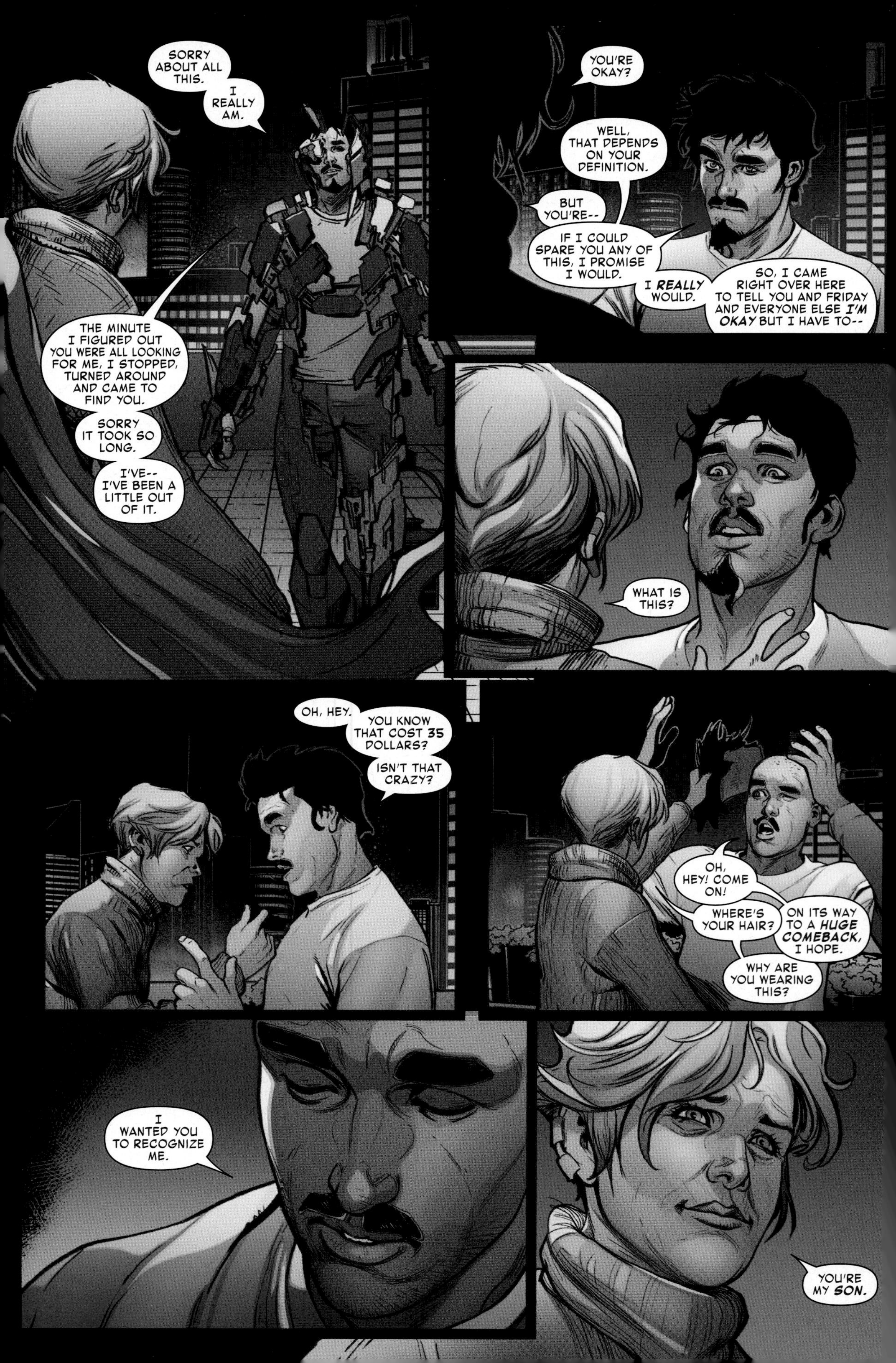
SORRY ABOUT ALL THIS.
I REALLY AM.
THE MINUTE I FIGURED OUT YOU WERE ALL LOOKING FOR ME, I STOPPED, TURNED AROUND AND CAME TO FIND YOU.
SORRY IT TOOK SO LONG.
I'VE-- I'VE BEEN A LITTLE OUT OF IT.
YOU'RE OKAY?
WELL, THAT DEPENDS ON YOUR DEFINITION.
BUT YOU'RE--
IF I COULD SPARE YOU ANY OF THIS, I PROMISE I WOULD.
I REALLY WOULD.
SO, I CAME RIGHT OVER HERE TO TELL YOU AND FRIDAY AND EVERYONE ELSE I'M OKAY BUT I HAVE TO--
WHAT IS THIS?
OH, HEY.
YOU KNOW THAT COST 35 DOLLARS?
ISN'T THAT CRAZY?
OH, HEY! COME ON!
WHERE'S YOUR HAIR?
ON ITS WAY TO A HUGE COMEBACK, I HOPE.
WHY ARE YOU WEARING THIS?
I WANTED YOU TO RECOGNIZE ME.
YOU'RE MY SON.

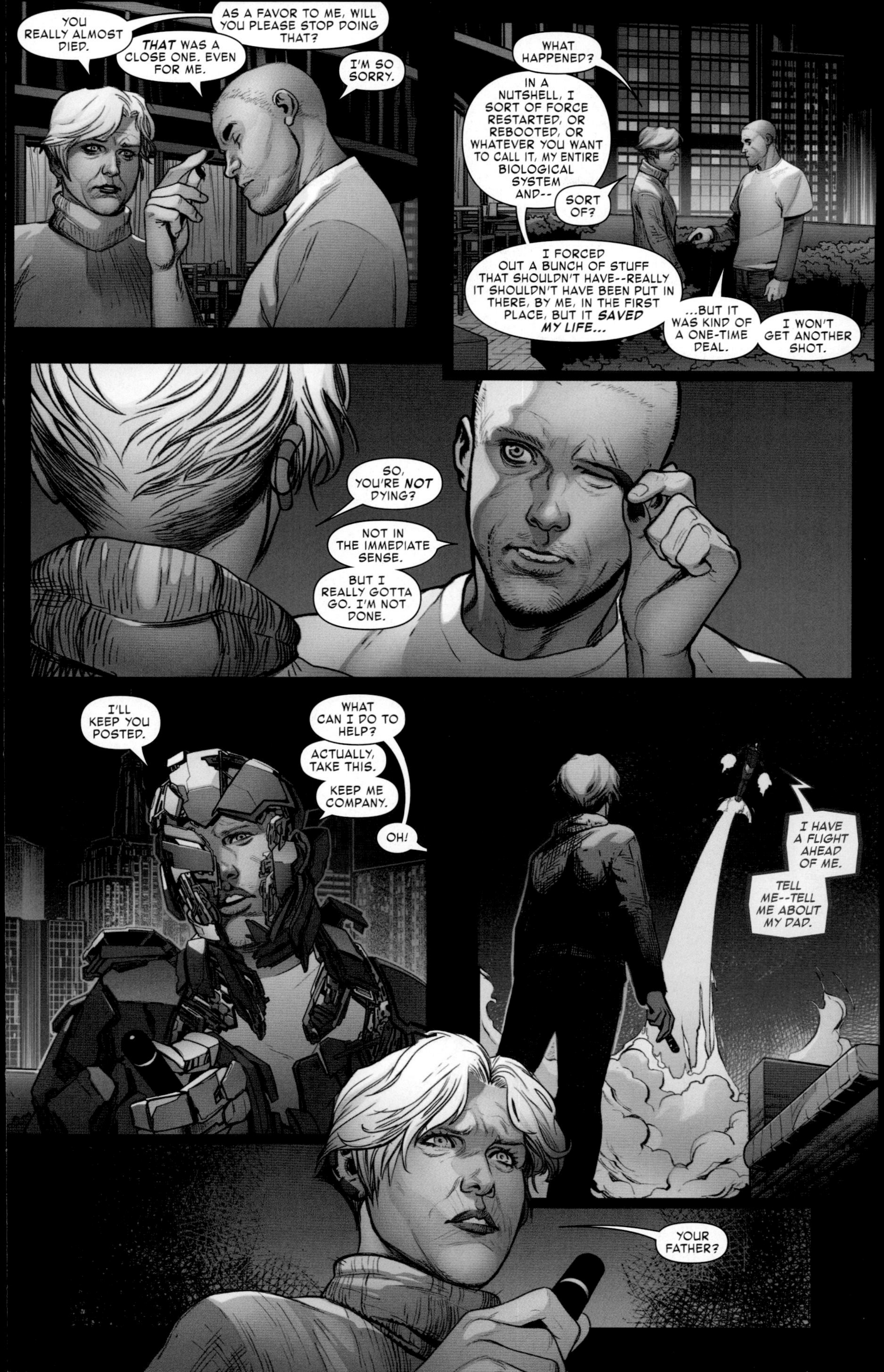
YOU REALLY ALMOST DIED.
AS A FAVOR TO ME, WILL YOU PLEASE STOP DOING THAT?
*THAT* WAS A CLOSE ONE. EVEN FOR ME.
I'M SO SORRY.
WHAT HAPPENED?
IN A NUTSHELL, I SORT OF FORCE RESTARTED, OR REBOOTED, OR WHATEVER YOU WANT TO CALL IT, MY ENTIRE BIOLOGICAL SYSTEM AND--
SORT OF?
I FORCED OUT A BUNCH OF STUFF THAT SHOULDN'T HAVE--REALLY IT SHOULDN'T HAVE BEEN PUT IN THERE, BY ME, IN THE FIRST PLACE, BUT IT *SAVED MY LIFE...*
...BUT IT WAS KIND OF A ONE-TIME DEAL.
I WON'T GET ANOTHER SHOT.
SO, YOU'RE *NOT* DYING?
NOT IN THE IMMEDIATE SENSE.
BUT I REALLY GOTTA GO. I'M NOT DONE.
I'LL KEEP YOU POSTED.
WHAT CAN I DO TO HELP?
ACTUALLY, TAKE THIS.
KEEP ME COMPANY.
OH!
I HAVE A FLIGHT AHEAD OF ME.
TELL ME--TELL ME ABOUT MY DAD.
YOUR FATHER?

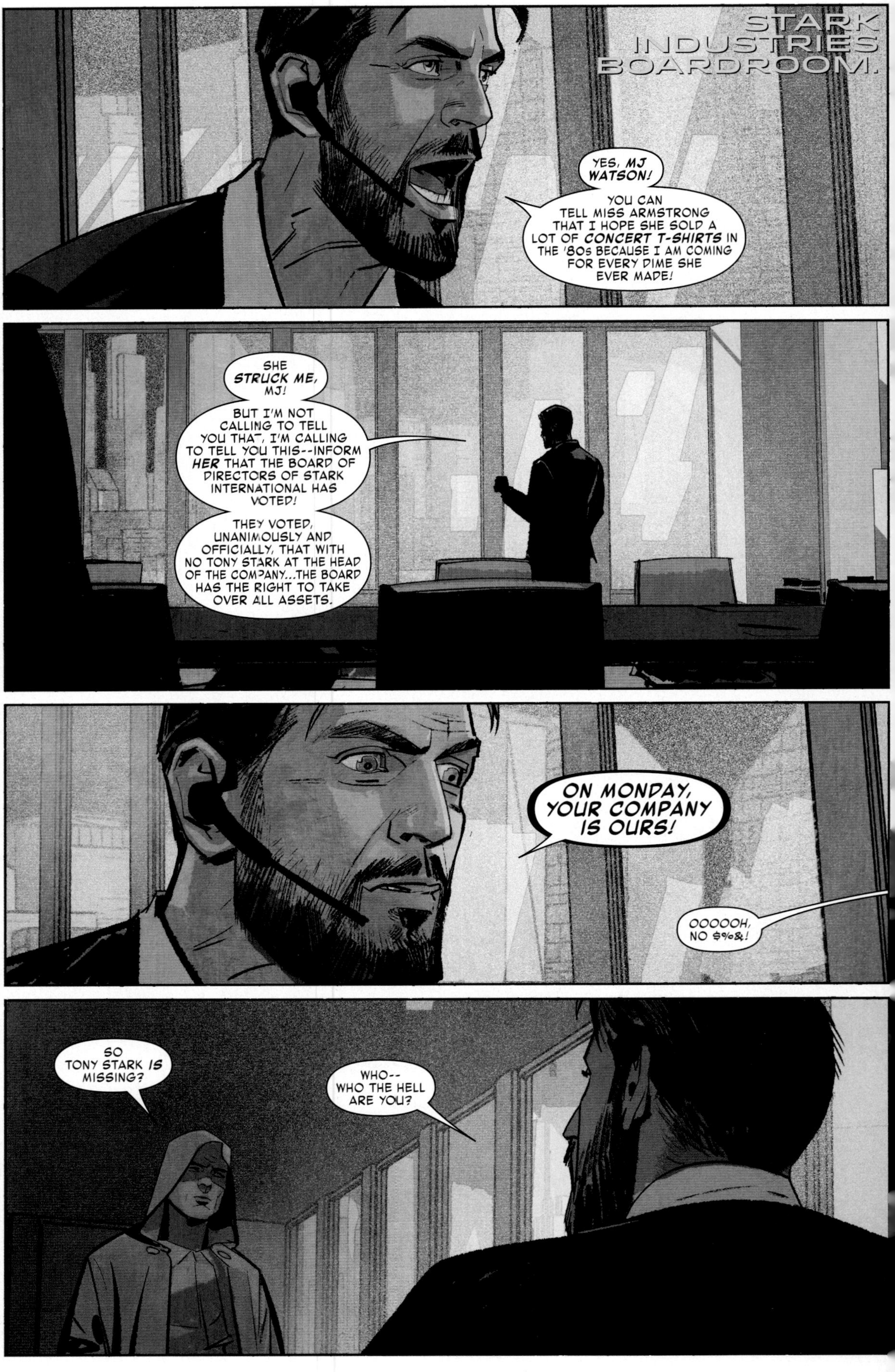
STARK INDUSTRIES BOARDROOM.
YES, MJ WATSON!
YOU CAN TELL MISS ARMSTRONG THAT I HOPE SHE SOLD A LOT OF CONCERT T-SHIRTS IN THE '80s BECAUSE I AM COMING FOR EVERY DIME SHE EVER MADE!
SHE STRUCK ME, MJ!
BUT I'M NOT CALLING TO TELL YOU THAT, I'M CALLING TO TELL YOU THIS--INFORM HER THAT THE BOARD OF DIRECTORS OF STARK INTERNATIONAL HAS VOTED!
THEY VOTED, UNANIMOUSLY AND OFFICIALLY, THAT WITH NO TONY STARK AT THE HEAD OF THE COMPANY...THE BOARD HAS THE RIGHT TO TAKE OVER ALL ASSETS.
ON MONDAY, YOUR COMPANY IS OURS!
OOOOOH, NO $%&!
SO TONY STARK IS MISSING?
WHO-- WHO THE HELL ARE YOU?

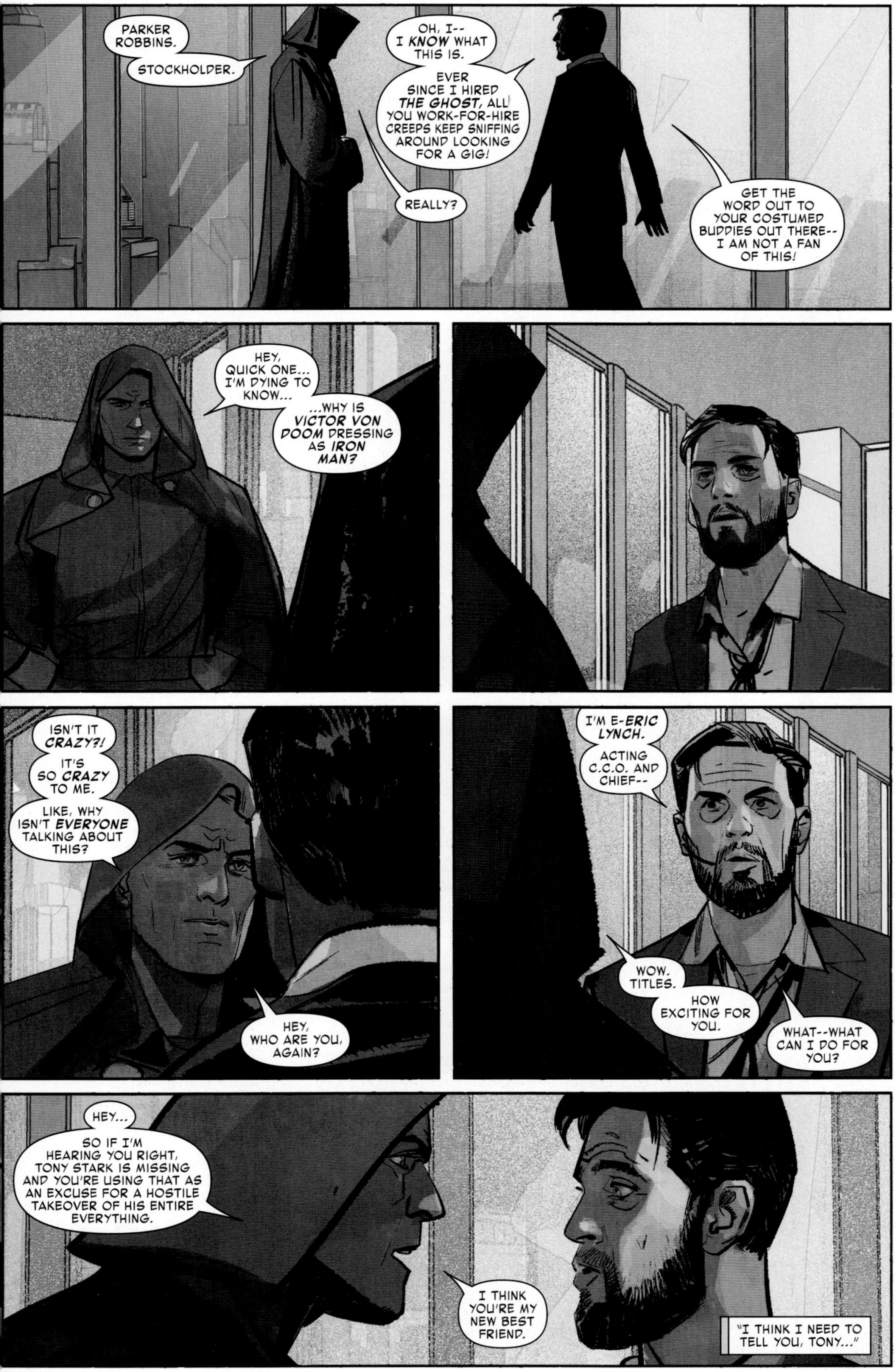
PARKER ROBBINS.
STOCKHOLDER.
OH, I-- I *KNOW* WHAT THIS IS.
EVER SINCE I HIRED ***THE GHOST,*** ALL YOU WORK-FOR-HIRE CREEPS KEEP SNIFFING AROUND LOOKING FOR A GIG!
REALLY?
GET THE WORD OUT TO YOUR COSTUMED BUDDIES OUT THERE-- I AM NOT A FAN OF THIS!
HEY, QUICK ONE... I'M DYING TO KNOW...
...WHY IS ***VICTOR VON DOOM*** DRESSING AS ***IRON MAN?***
ISN'T IT ***CRAZY?!***
IT'S SO ***CRAZY*** TO ME.
LIKE, WHY ISN'T ***EVERYONE*** TALKING ABOUT THIS?
HEY, WHO ARE YOU, AGAIN?
I'M E-***ERIC LYNCH.***
ACTING C.C.O. AND CHIEF--
WOW. TITLES.
HOW EXCITING FOR YOU.
WHAT--WHAT CAN I DO FOR YOU?
HEY...
SO IF I'M HEARING YOU RIGHT, TONY STARK IS MISSING AND YOU'RE USING THAT AS AN EXCUSE FOR A HOSTILE TAKEOVER OF HIS ENTIRE EVERYTHING.
I THINK YOU'RE MY NEW BEST FRIEND.
"I THINK I NEED TO TELL YOU, TONY..."

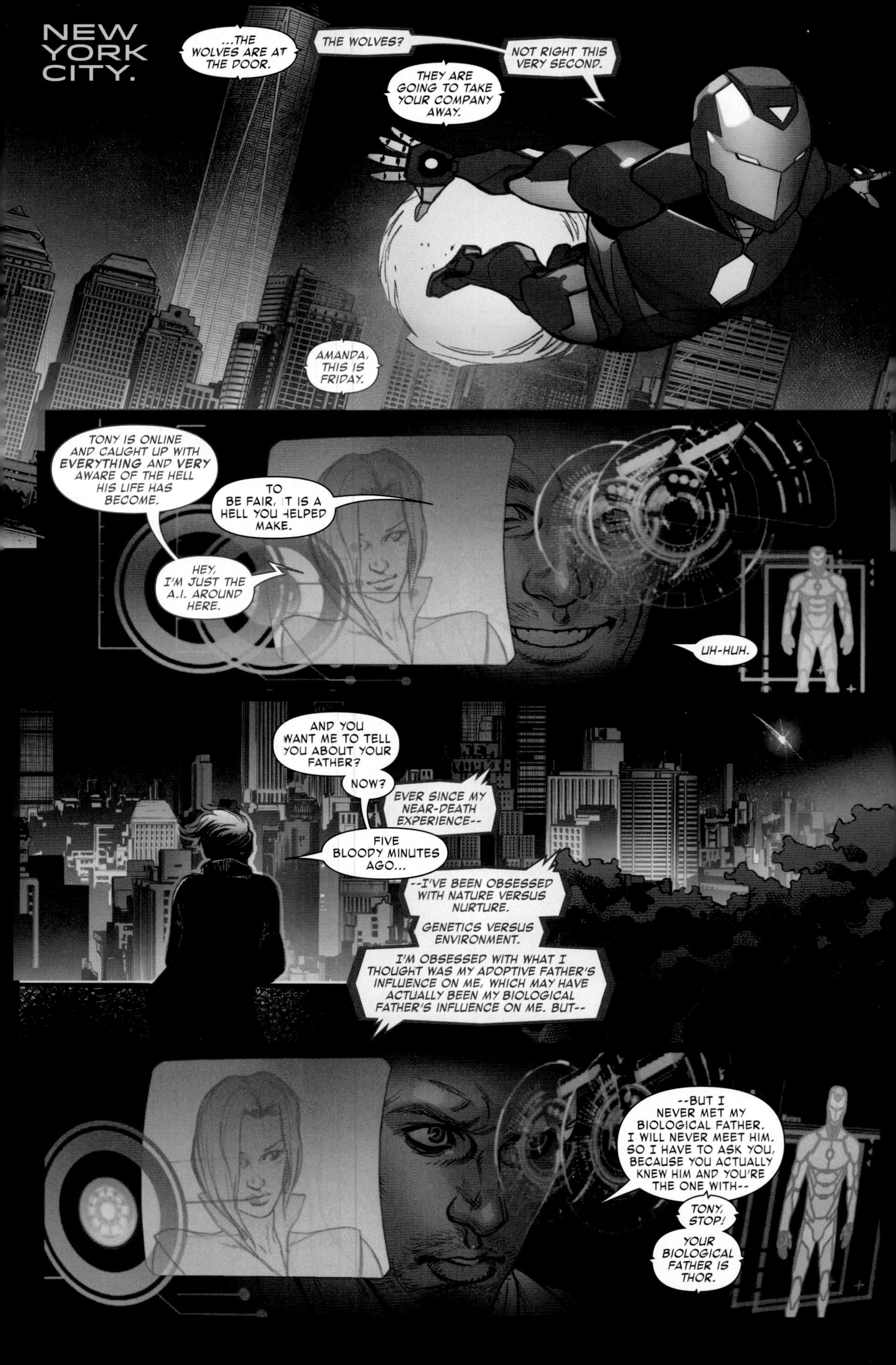
NEW YORK CITY.
...THE WOLVES ARE AT THE DOOR.
THE WOLVES?
NOT RIGHT THIS VERY SECOND.
THEY ARE GOING TO TAKE YOUR COMPANY AWAY.
AMANDA, THIS IS FRIDAY.
TONY IS ONLINE AND CAUGHT UP WITH EVERYTHING AND VERY AWARE OF THE HELL HIS LIFE HAS BECOME.
TO BE FAIR, IT IS A HELL YOU HELPED MAKE.
HEY, I'M JUST THE A.I. AROUND HERE.
UH-HUH.
AND YOU WANT ME TO TELL YOU ABOUT YOUR FATHER?
NOW?
EVER SINCE MY NEAR-DEATH EXPERIENCE--
FIVE BLOODY MINUTES AGO...
--I'VE BEEN OBSESSED WITH NATURE VERSUS NURTURE.
GENETICS VERSUS ENVIRONMENT.
I'M OBSESSED WITH WHAT I THOUGHT WAS MY ADOPTIVE FATHER'S INFLUENCE ON ME, WHICH MAY HAVE ACTUALLY BEEN MY BIOLOGICAL FATHER'S INFLUENCE ON ME. BUT--
--BUT I NEVER MET MY BIOLOGICAL FATHER. I WILL NEVER MEET HIM. SO I HAVE TO ASK YOU, BECAUSE YOU ACTUALLY KNEW HIM AND YOU'RE THE ONE WITH--
TONY, STOP!
YOUR BIOLOGICAL FATHER IS THOR.

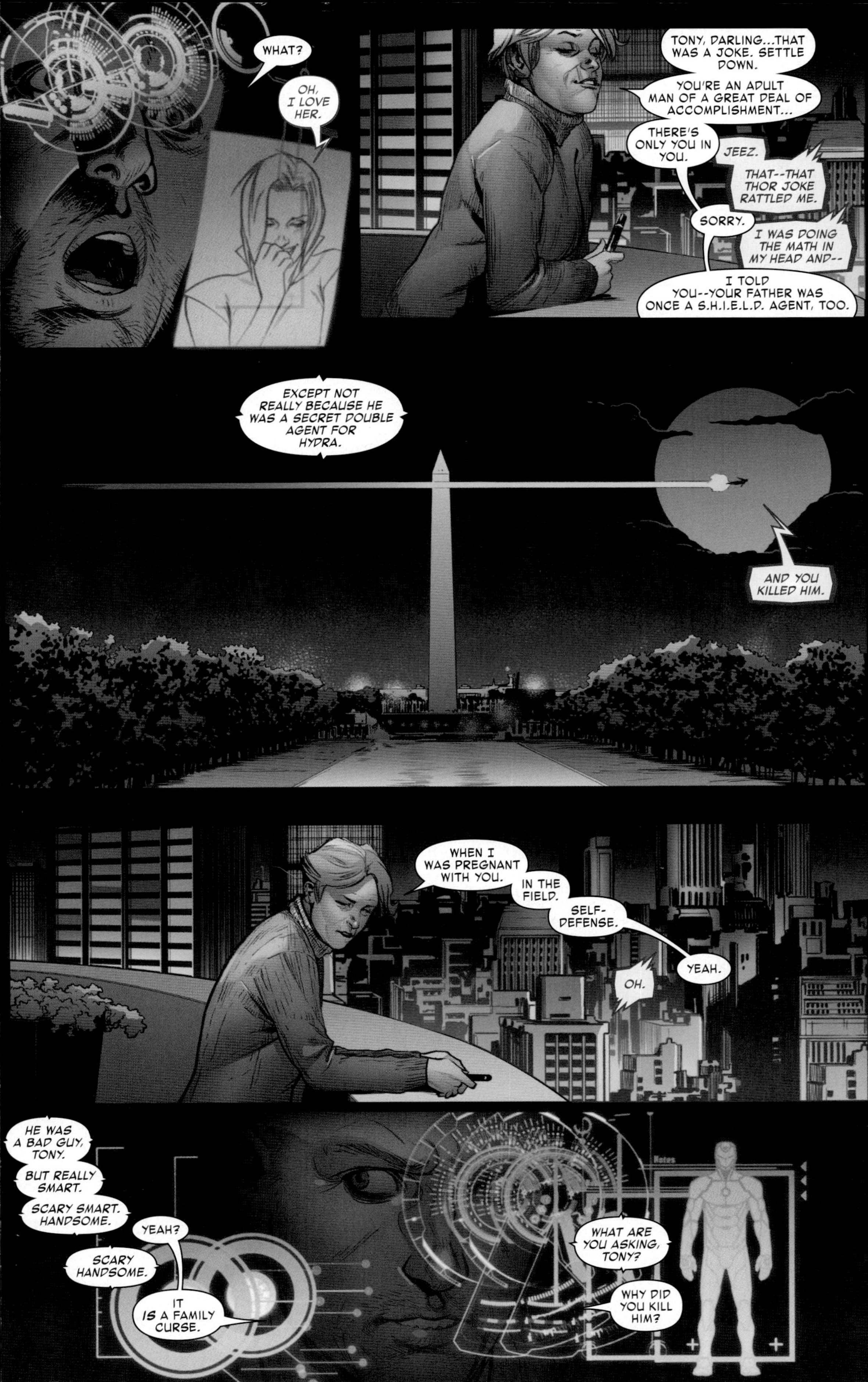

WHAT?
OH, I LOVE HER.
TONY, DARLING...THAT WAS A JOKE. SETTLE DOWN.
YOU'RE AN ADULT MAN OF A GREAT DEAL OF ACCOMPLISHMENT...
THERE'S ONLY YOU IN YOU.
JEEZ.
THAT--THAT THOR JOKE RATTLED ME.
SORRY.
I WAS DOING THE MATH IN MY HEAD AND--
I TOLD YOU--YOUR FATHER WAS ONCE A S.H.I.E.L.D. AGENT, TOO.
EXCEPT NOT REALLY BECAUSE HE WAS A SECRET DOUBLE AGENT FOR HYDRA.
AND YOU KILLED HIM.
WHEN I WAS PREGNANT WITH YOU.
IN THE FIELD.
SELF-DEFENSE.
YEAH.
OH.
HE WAS A BAD GUY, TONY.
BUT REALLY SMART.
SCARY SMART. HANDSOME.
YEAH?
SCARY HANDSOME.
IT IS A FAMILY CURSE.
WHAT ARE YOU ASKING, TONY?
WHY DID YOU KILL HIM?

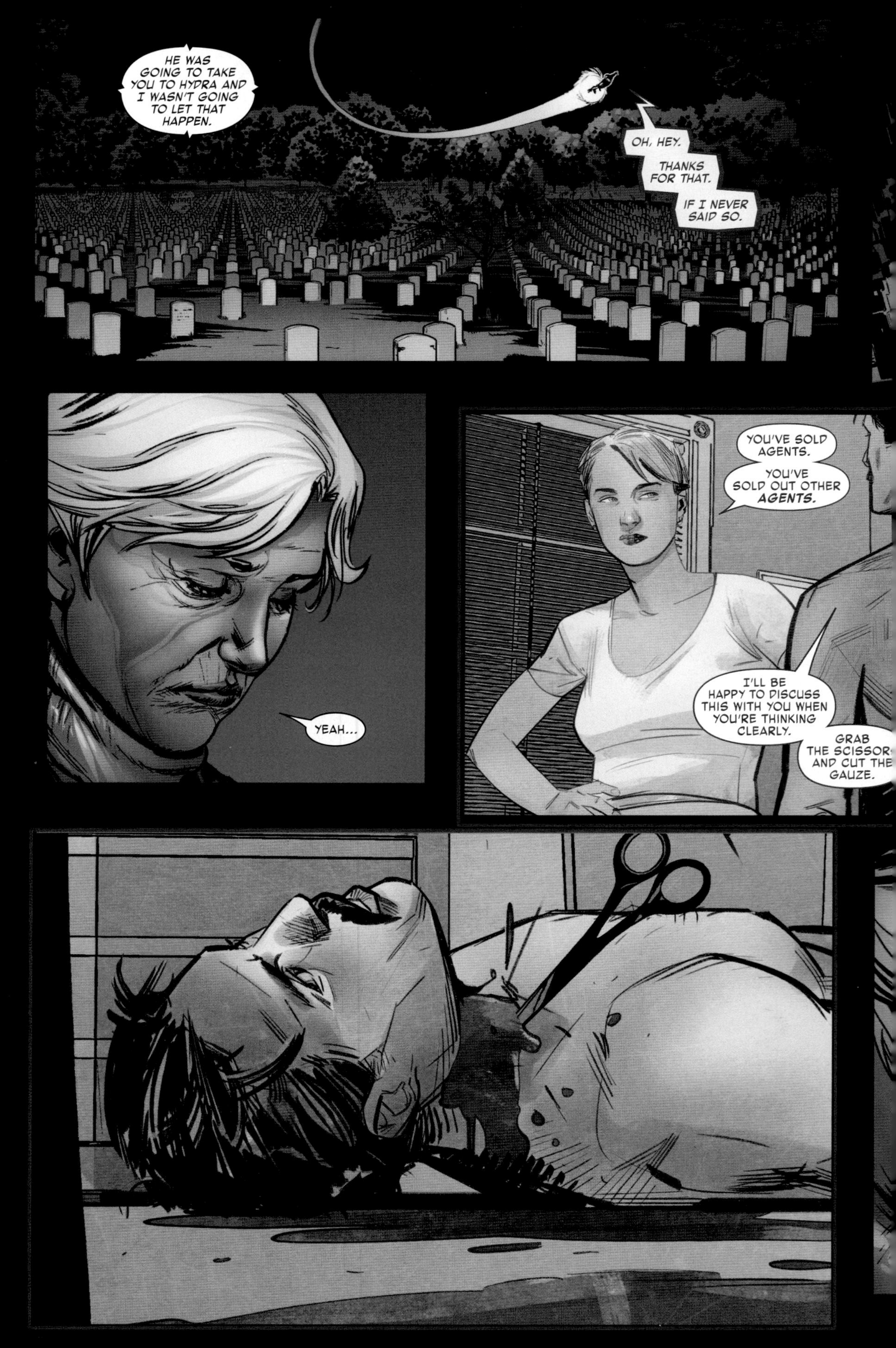
HE WAS GOING TO TAKE YOU TO HYDRA AND I WASN'T GOING TO LET THAT HAPPEN.
OH, HEY.
THANKS FOR THAT.
IF I NEVER SAID SO.
YEAH...
YOU'VE SOLD AGENTS.
YOU'VE SOLD OUT OTHER *AGENTS.*
I'LL BE HAPPY TO DISCUSS THIS WITH YOU WHEN YOU'RE THINKING CLEARLY.
GRAB THE SCISSOR AND CUT THE GAUZE.

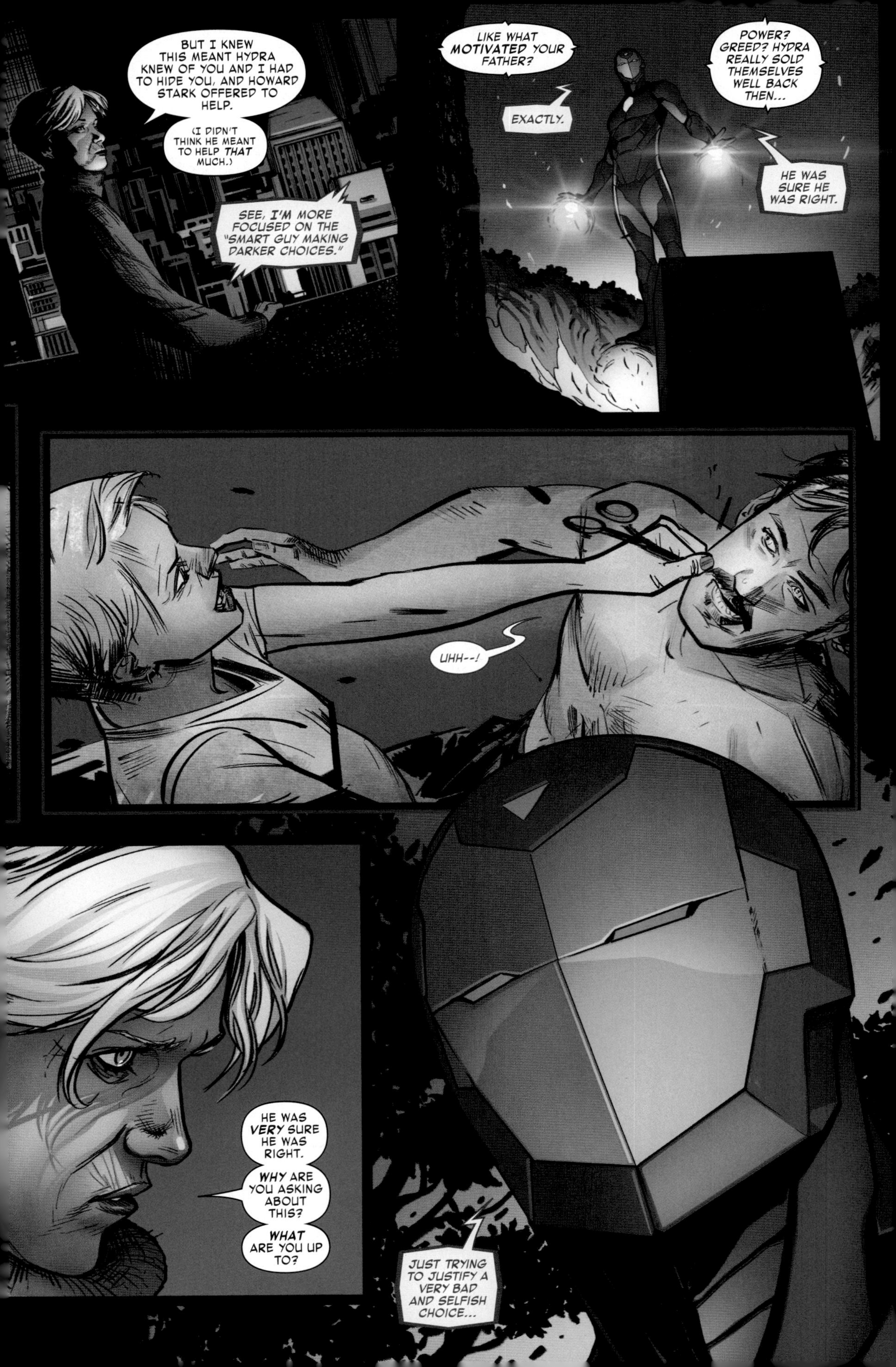
BUT I KNEW THIS MEANT HYDRA KNEW OF YOU AND I HAD TO HIDE YOU, AND HOWARD STARK OFFERED TO HELP.
(I DIDN'T THINK HE MEANT TO HELP *THAT* MUCH.)
SEE, *I'M* MORE FOCUSED ON THE "SMART GUY MAKING DARKER CHOICES."
LIKE WHAT *MOTIVATED* YOUR FATHER?
EXACTLY.
POWER? GREED? HYDRA REALLY SOLD THEMSELVES WELL BACK THEN...
HE WAS SURE HE WAS RIGHT.
UHH--!
HE WAS *VERY* SURE HE WAS RIGHT.
*WHY* ARE YOU ASKING ABOUT THIS?
*WHAT* ARE YOU UP TO?
JUST TRYING TO JUSTIFY A VERY BAD AND SELFISH CHOICE...

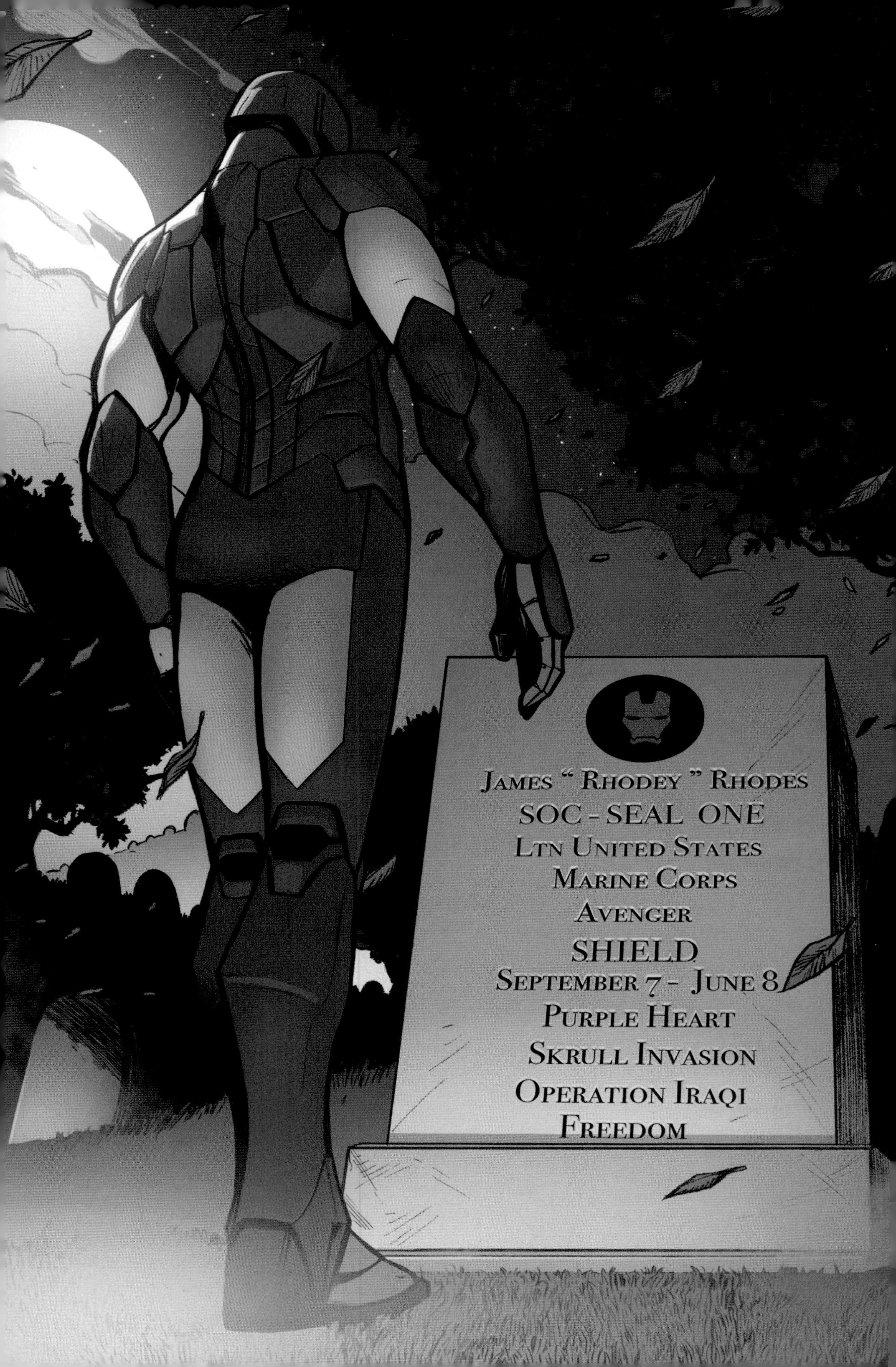
JAMES "RHODEY" RHODES
SOC - SEAL ONE
LTN UNITED STATES
MARINE CORPS
AVENGER
S.H.I.E.L.D.
SEPTEMBER 7 - JUNE 8
PURPLE HEART
SKRULL INVASION
OPERATION IRAQI
FREEDOM

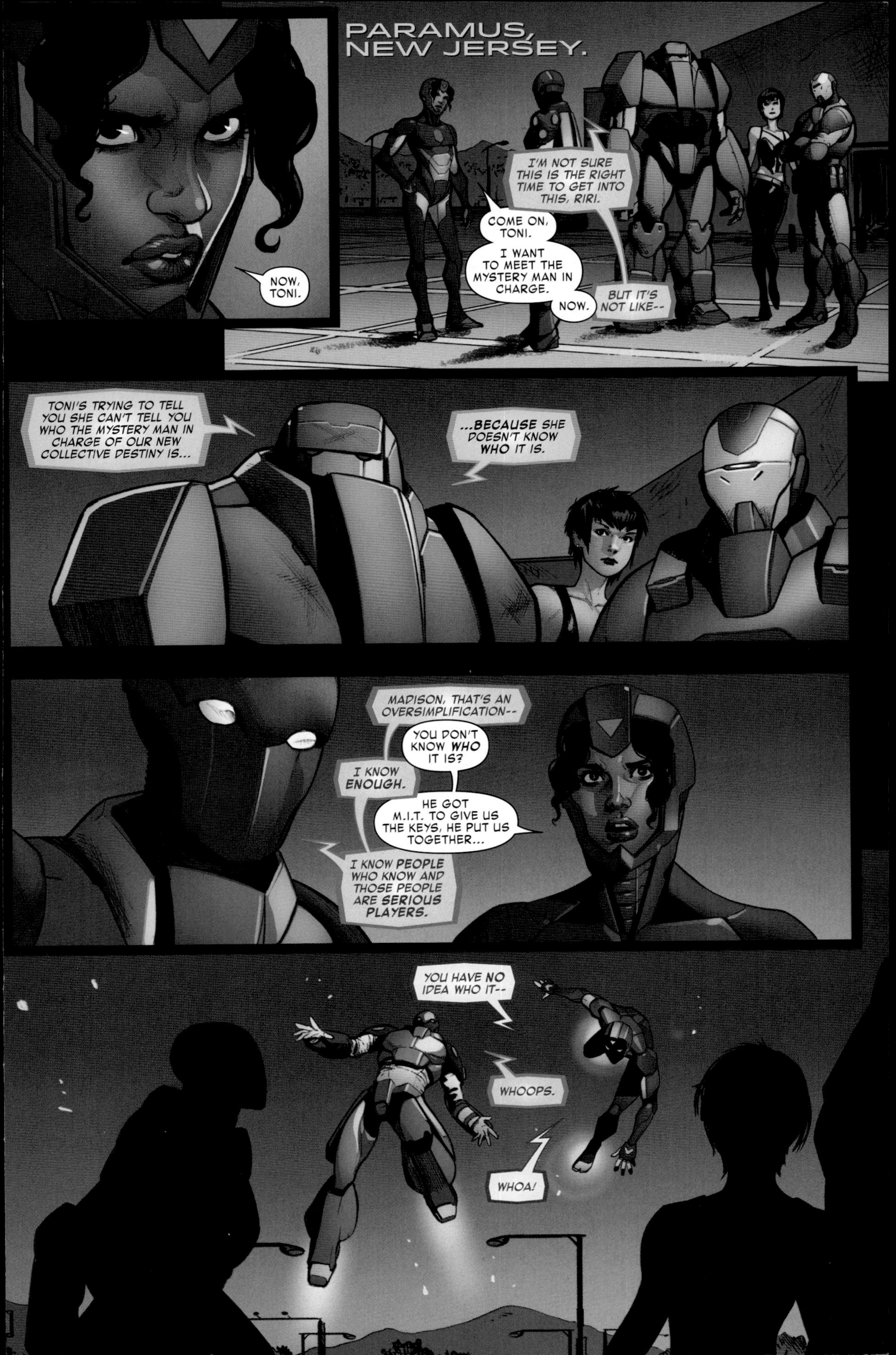
PARAMUS, NEW JERSEY.
NOW, TONI.
I'M NOT SURE THIS IS THE RIGHT TIME TO GET INTO THIS, RIRI.
COME ON, TONI.
I WANT TO MEET THE MYSTERY MAN IN CHARGE.
NOW.
BUT IT'S NOT LIKE--
TONI'S TRYING TO TELL YOU SHE CAN'T TELL YOU WHO THE MYSTERY MAN IN CHARGE OF OUR NEW COLLECTIVE DESTINY IS...
...BECAUSE SHE DOESN'T KNOW WHO IT IS.
MADISON, THAT'S AN OVERSIMPLIFICATION--
YOU DON'T KNOW WHO IT IS?
I KNOW ENOUGH.
HE GOT M.I.T. TO GIVE US THE KEYS, HE PUT US TOGETHER...
I KNOW PEOPLE WHO KNOW AND THOSE PEOPLE ARE SERIOUS PLAYERS.
YOU HAVE NO IDEA WHO IT--
WHOOPS.
WHOA!

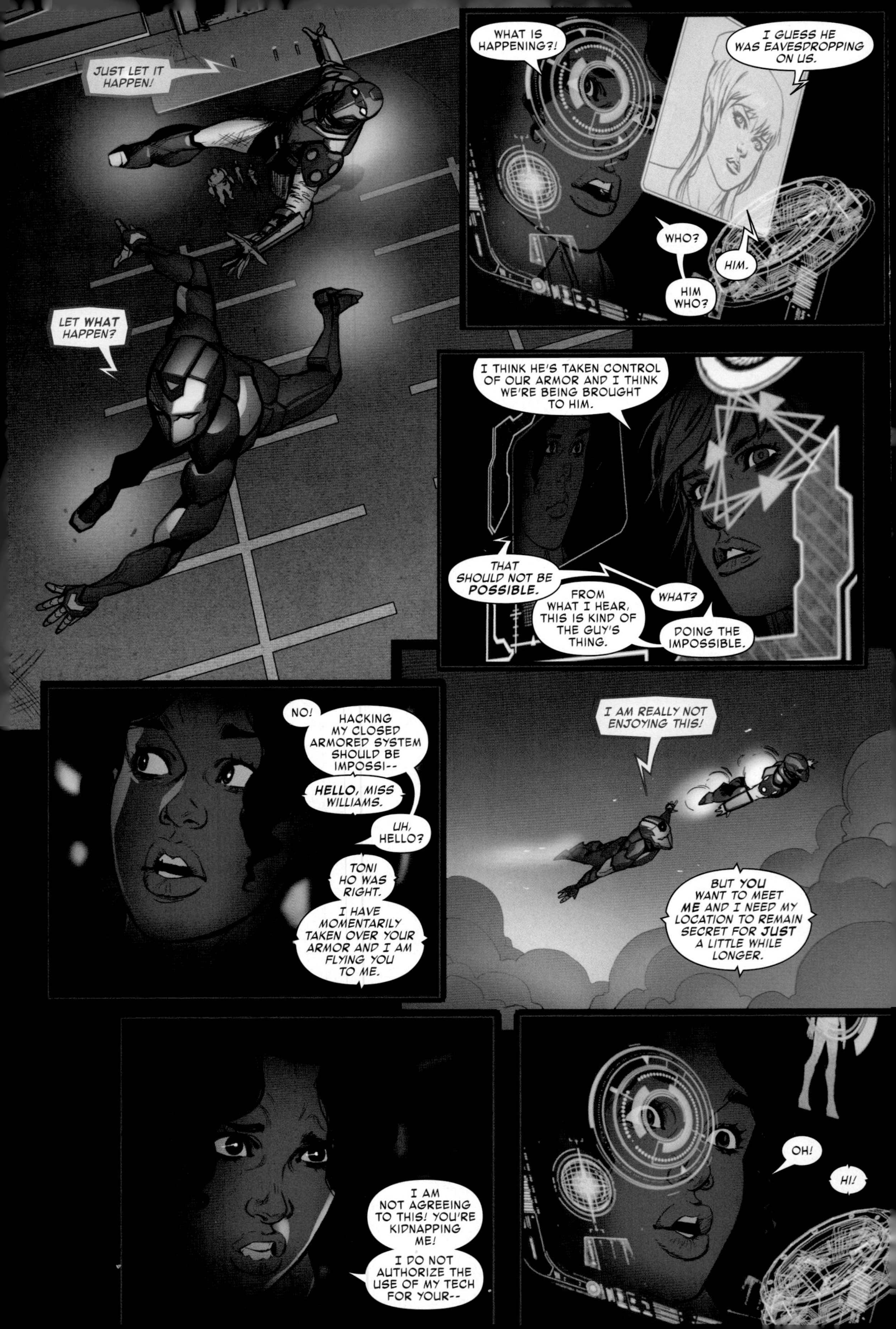
JUST LET IT HAPPEN!
LET WHAT HAPPEN?
WHAT IS HAPPENING?!
I GUESS HE WAS EAVESDROPPING ON US.
WHO?
HIM.
HIM WHO?
I THINK HE'S TAKEN CONTROL OF OUR ARMOR AND I THINK WE'RE BEING BROUGHT TO HIM.
THAT SHOULD NOT BE POSSIBLE.
WHAT?
FROM WHAT I HEAR, THIS IS KIND OF THE GUY'S THING.
DOING THE IMPOSSIBLE.
NO!
HACKING MY CLOSED ARMORED SYSTEM SHOULD BE IMPOSSI--
HELLO, MISS WILLIAMS.
UH, HELLO?
TONI HO WAS RIGHT.
I HAVE MOMENTARILY TAKEN OVER YOUR ARMOR AND I AM FLYING YOU TO ME.
I AM REALLY NOT ENJOYING THIS!
BUT YOU WANT TO MEET ME AND I NEED MY LOCATION TO REMAIN SECRET FOR JUST A LITTLE WHILE LONGER.
I AM NOT AGREEING TO THIS! YOU'RE KIDNAPPING ME!
I DO NOT AUTHORIZE THE USE OF MY TECH FOR YOUR--
OH!
HI!

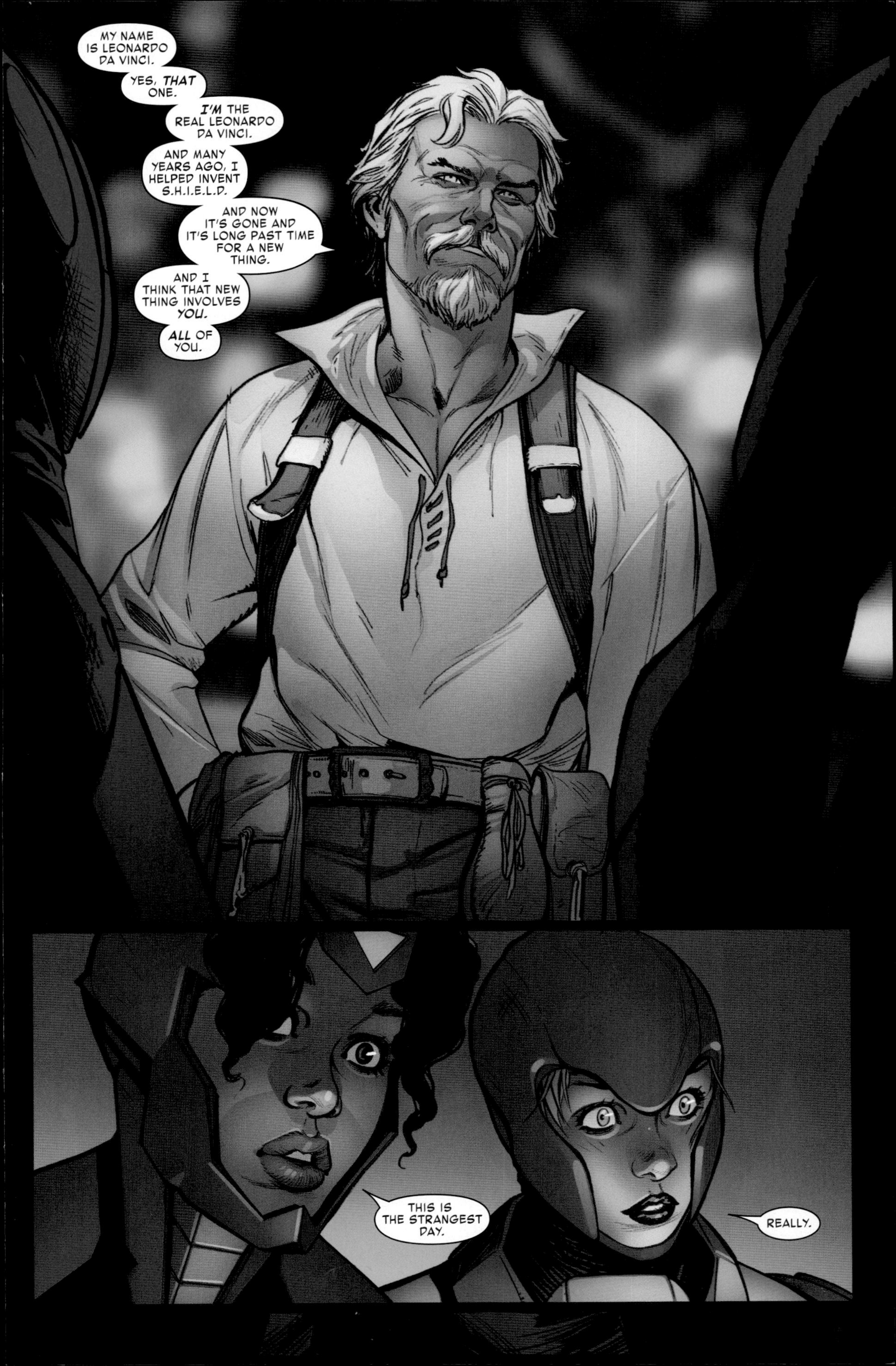
MY NAME IS LEONARDO DA VINCI.
YES, *THAT* ONE.
*I'M* THE REAL LEONARDO DA VINCI.
AND MANY YEARS AGO, I HELPED INVENT S.H.I.E.L.D.
AND NOW IT'S GONE AND IT'S LONG PAST TIME FOR A NEW THING.
AND I THINK THAT NEW THING INVOLVES *YOU.*
*ALL* OF YOU.
THIS IS THE STRANGEST DAY.
REALLY.

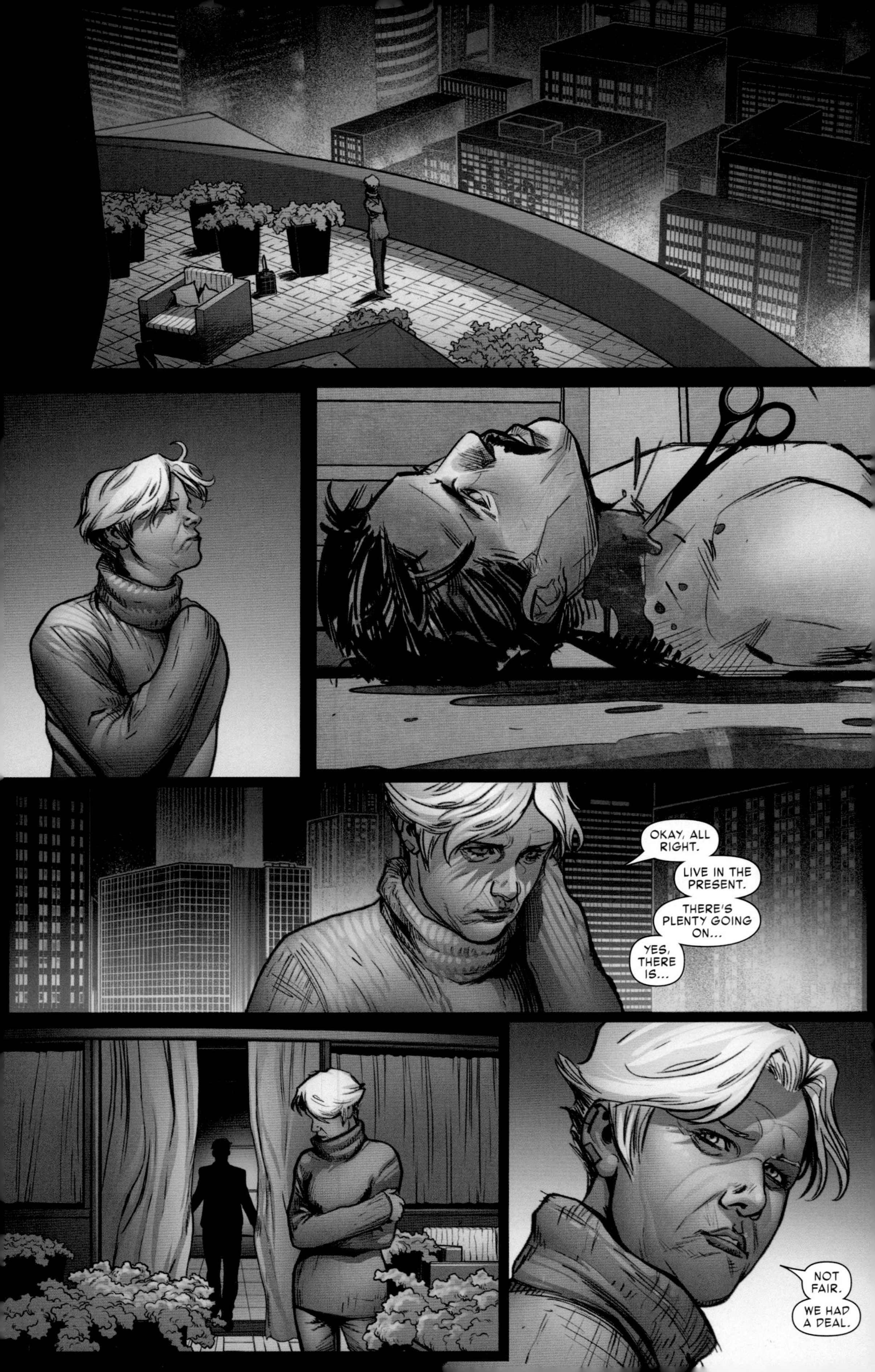
OKAY, ALL RIGHT.
LIVE IN THE PRESENT.
THERE'S PLENTY GOING ON...
YES, THERE IS...
NOT FAIR.
WE HAD A DEAL.

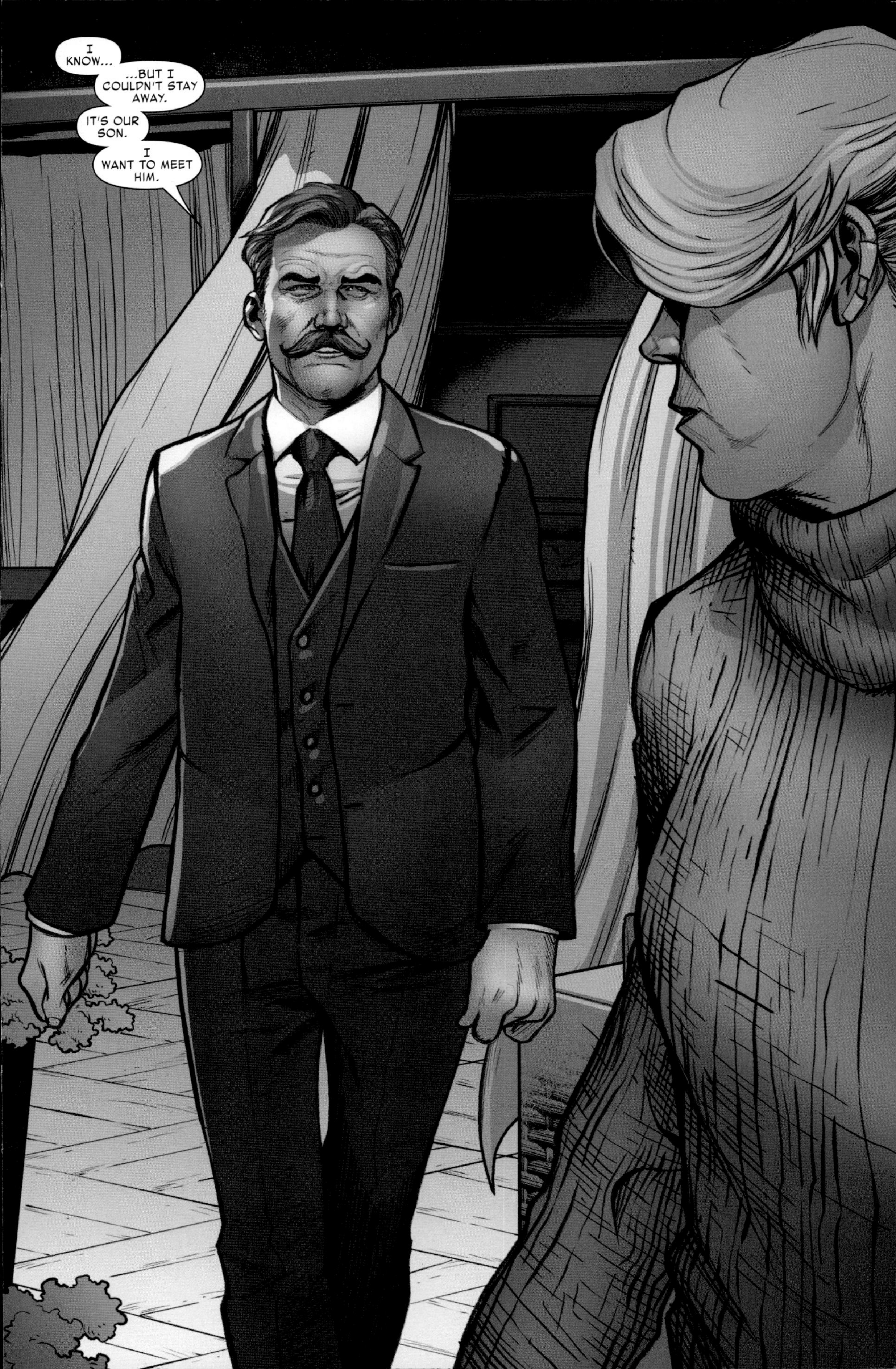
I KNOW...
...BUT I COULDN'T STAY AWAY.
IT'S OUR SON.
I WANT TO MEET HIM.

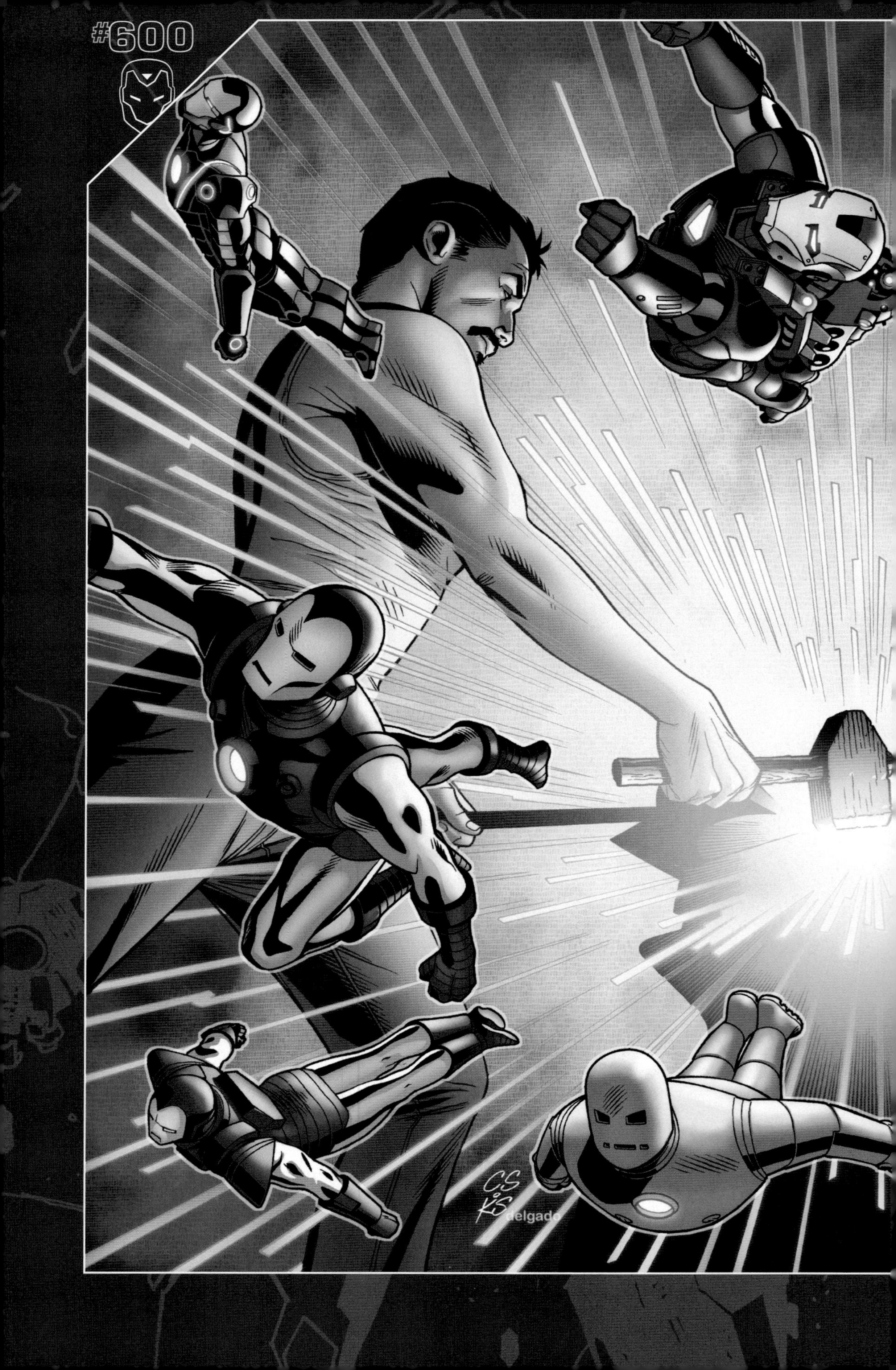
#600
CS
KS
delgado

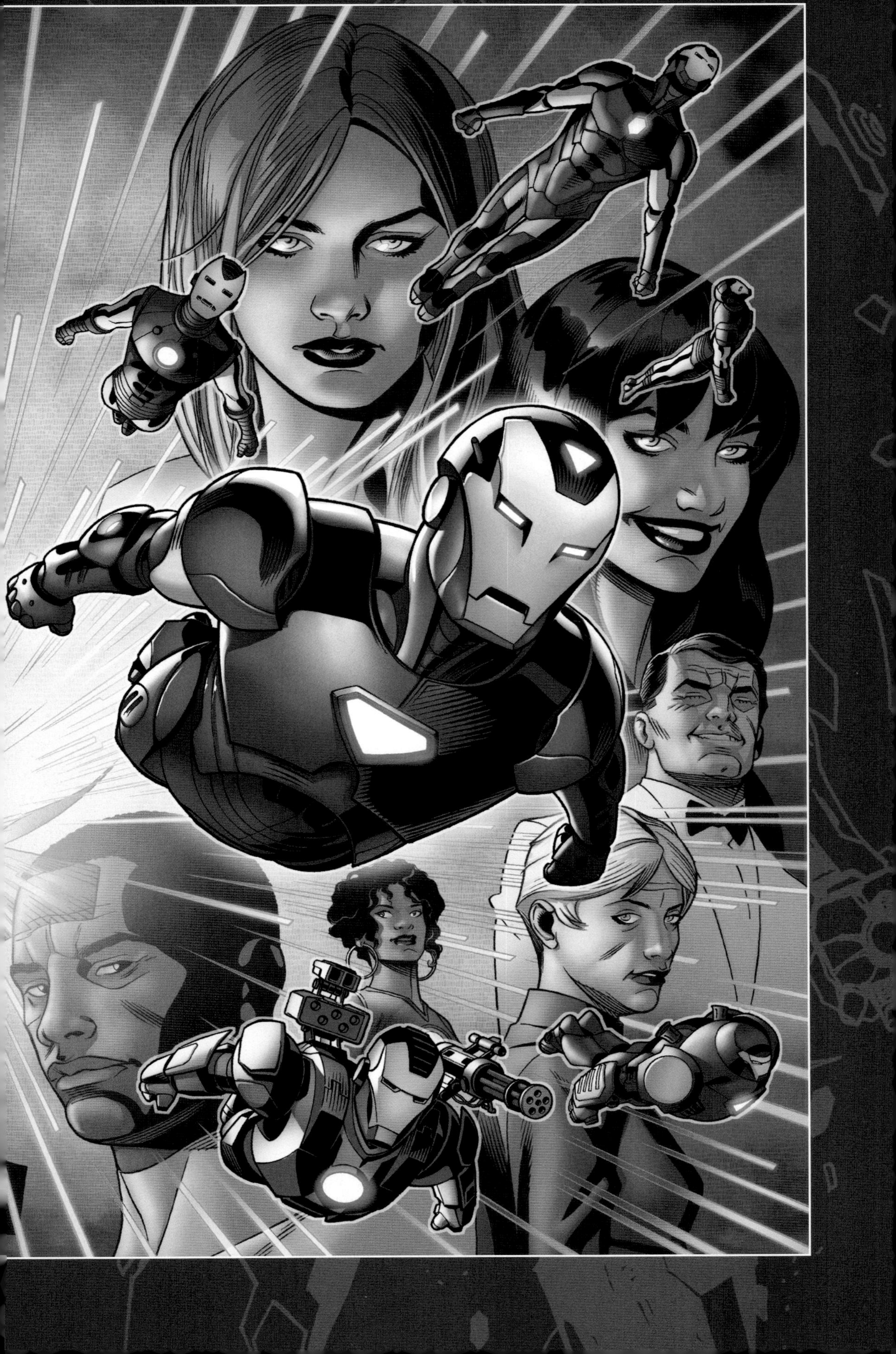

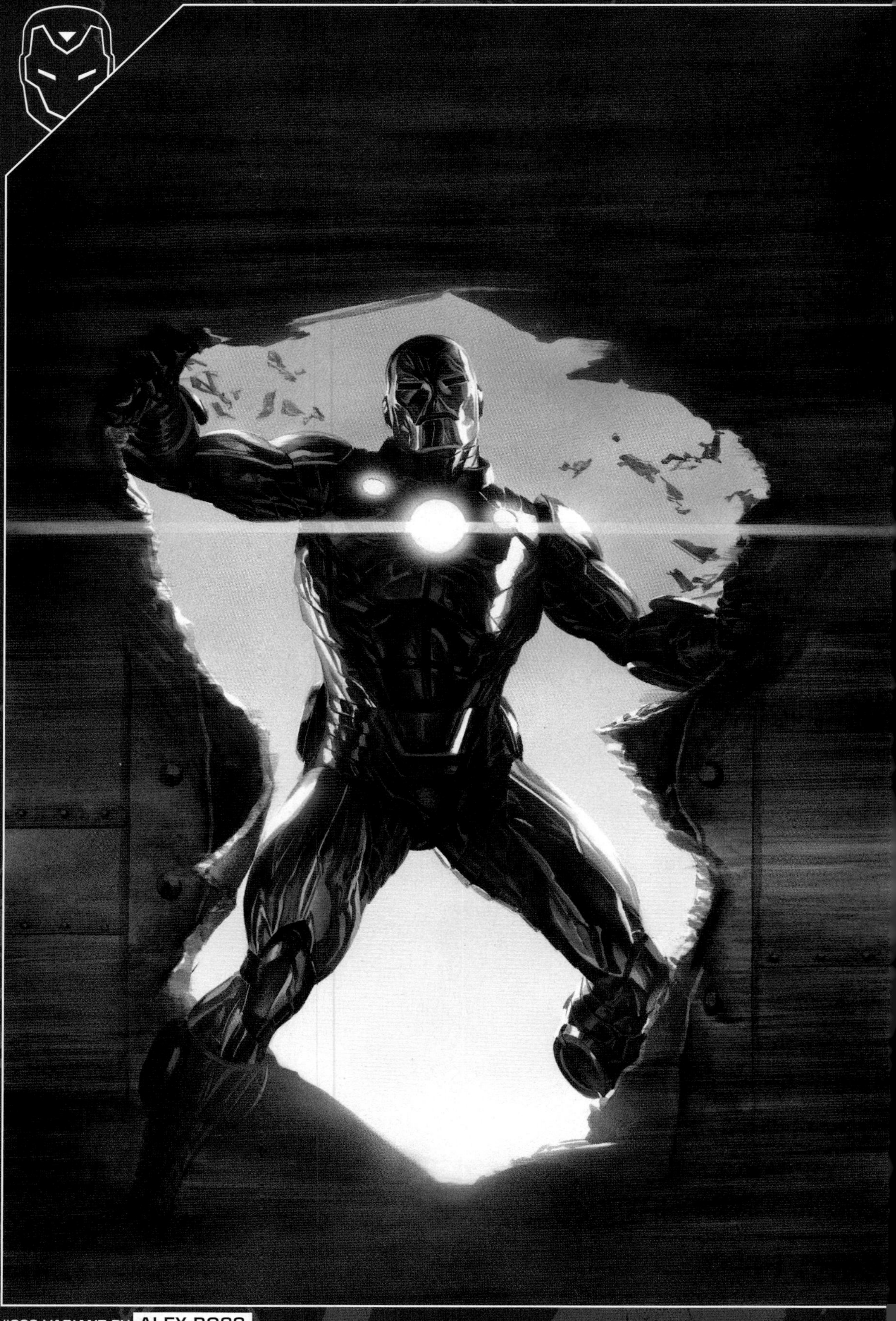

#600 VARIANT BY ALEX ROSS

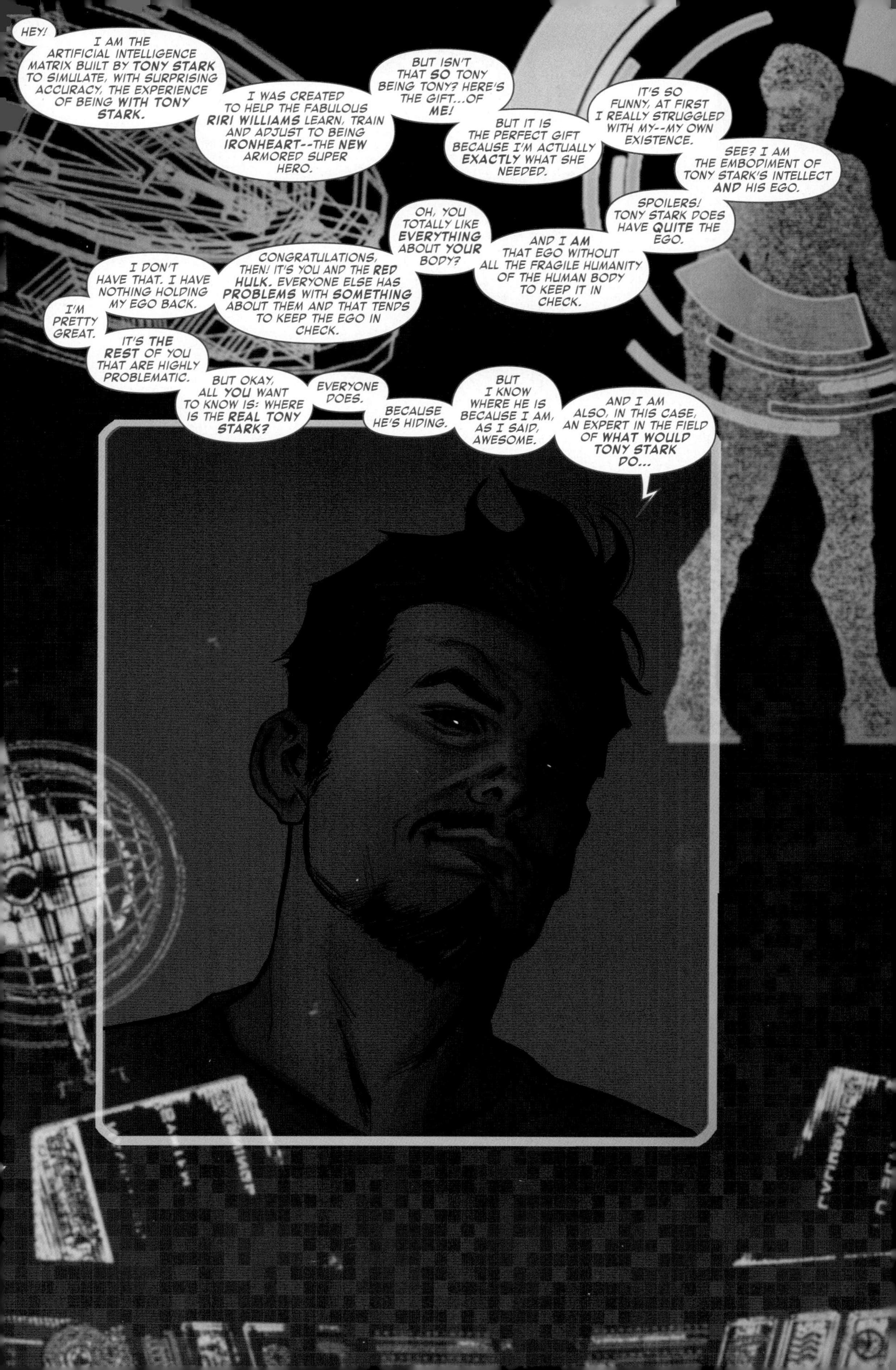
HEY!
I AM THE ARTIFICIAL INTELLIGENCE MATRIX BUILT BY TONY STARK TO SIMULATE, WITH SURPRISING ACCURACY, THE EXPERIENCE OF BEING WITH TONY STARK.
I WAS CREATED TO HELP THE FABULOUS RIRI WILLIAMS LEARN, TRAIN AND ADJUST TO BEING IRONHEART--THE NEW ARMORED SUPER HERO.
BUT ISN'T THAT SO TONY BEING TONY? HERE'S THE GIFT...OF ME!
BUT IT IS THE PERFECT GIFT BECAUSE I'M ACTUALLY EXACTLY WHAT SHE NEEDED.
IT'S SO FUNNY, AT FIRST I REALLY STRUGGLED WITH MY--MY OWN EXISTENCE.
SEE? I AM THE EMBODIMENT OF TONY STARK'S INTELLECT AND HIS EGO.
SPOILERS! TONY STARK DOES HAVE QUITE THE EGO.
AND I AM THAT EGO WITHOUT ALL THE FRAGILE HUMANITY OF THE HUMAN BODY TO KEEP IT IN CHECK.
OH, YOU TOTALLY LIKE EVERYTHING ABOUT YOUR BODY?
CONGRATULATIONS, THEN! IT'S YOU AND THE RED HULK. EVERYONE ELSE HAS PROBLEMS WITH SOMETHING ABOUT THEM AND THAT TENDS TO KEEP THE EGO IN CHECK.
I DON'T HAVE THAT. I HAVE NOTHING HOLDING MY EGO BACK.
I'M PRETTY GREAT.
IT'S THE REST OF YOU THAT ARE HIGHLY PROBLEMATIC.
BUT OKAY, ALL YOU WANT TO KNOW IS: WHERE IS THE REAL TONY STARK?
EVERYONE DOES.
BECAUSE HE'S HIDING.
BUT I KNOW WHERE HE IS BECAUSE I AM, AS I SAID, AWESOME.
AND I AM ALSO, IN THIS CASE, AN EXPERT IN THE FIELD OF WHAT WOULD TONY STARK DO...

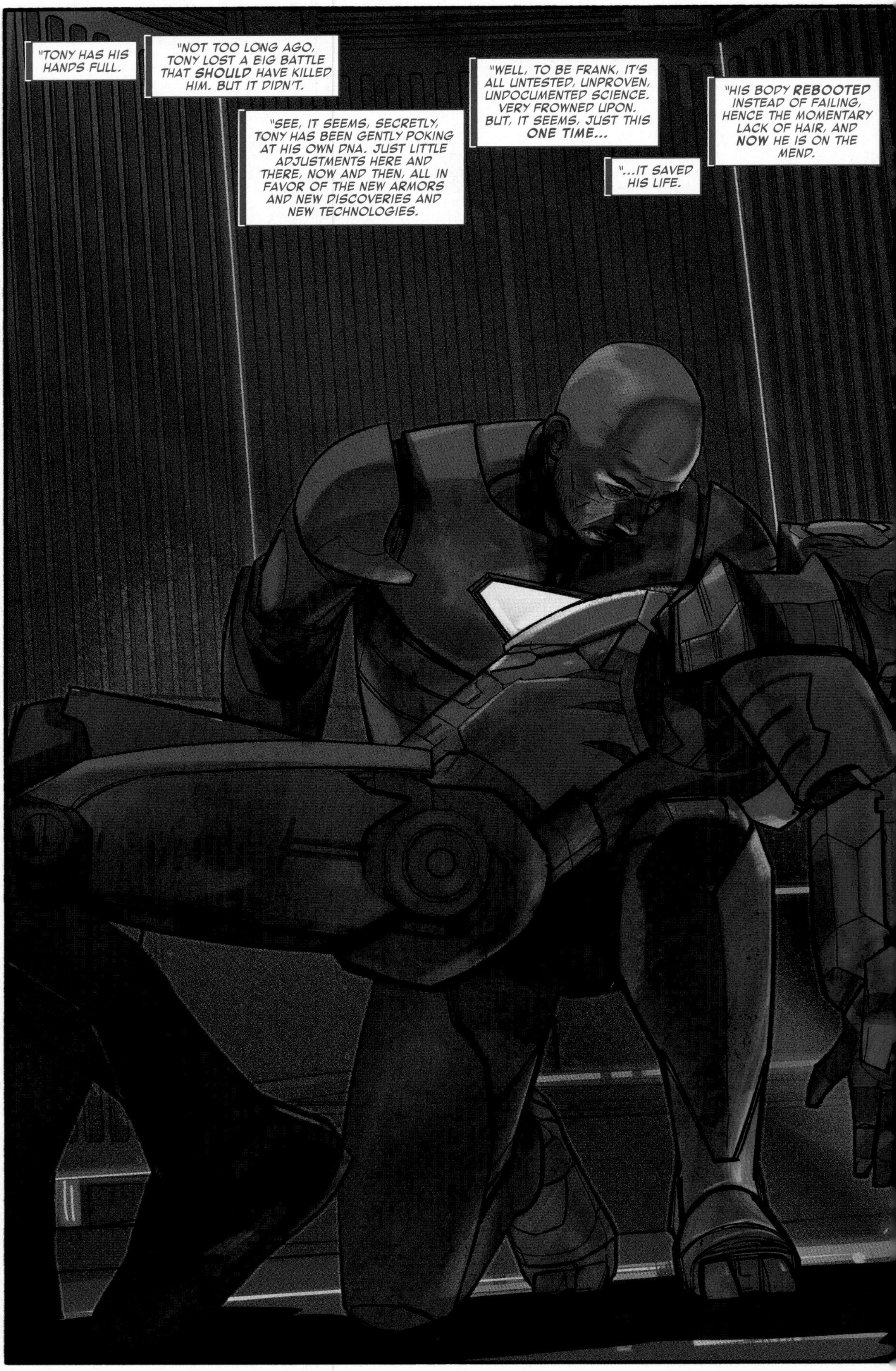
"TONY HAS HIS HANDS FULL.
"NOT TOO LONG AGO, TONY LOST A BIG BATTLE THAT SHOULD HAVE KILLED HIM. BUT IT DIDN'T.
"SEE, IT SEEMS, SECRETLY, TONY HAS BEEN GENTLY POKING AT HIS OWN DNA. JUST LITTLE ADJUSTMENTS HERE AND THERE, NOW AND THEN, ALL IN FAVOR OF THE NEW ARMORS AND NEW DISCOVERIES AND NEW TECHNOLOGIES.
"WELL, TO BE FRANK, IT'S ALL UNTESTED, UNPROVEN, UNDOCUMENTED SCIENCE. VERY FROWNED UPON. BUT, IT SEEMS, JUST THIS ONE TIME...
"...IT SAVED HIS LIFE.
"HIS BODY REBOOTED INSTEAD OF FAILING, HENCE THE MOMENTARY LACK OF HAIR, AND NOW HE IS ON THE MEND.

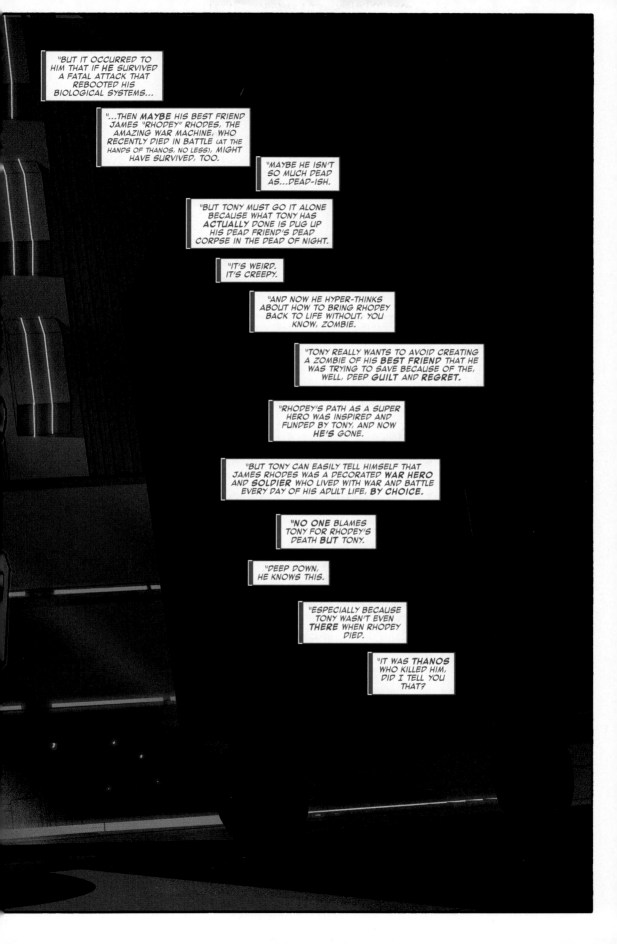

"BUT IT OCCURRED TO HIM THAT IF *HE* SURVIVED A FATAL ATTACK THAT REBOOTED HIS BIOLOGICAL SYSTEMS...

"...THEN *MAYBE* HIS BEST FRIEND JAMES "RHODEY" RHODES, THE AMAZING WAR MACHINE, WHO RECENTLY DIED IN BATTLE (AT THE HANDS OF THANOS, NO LESS), MIGHT HAVE SURVIVED, TOO.

"MAYBE HE ISN'T SO MUCH DEAD AS...DEAD-ISH.

"BUT TONY MUST GO IT ALONE BECAUSE WHAT TONY HAS *ACTUALLY* DONE IS DUG UP HIS DEAD FRIEND'S DEAD CORPSE IN THE DEAD OF NIGHT.

"IT'S WEIRD. IT'S CREEPY.

"AND NOW HE HYPER-THINKS ABOUT HOW TO BRING RHODEY BACK TO LIFE WITHOUT, YOU KNOW, ZOMBIE.

"TONY REALLY WANTS TO AVOID CREATING A ZOMBIE OF HIS *BEST FRIEND* THAT HE WAS TRYING TO SAVE BECAUSE OF THE, WELL, DEEP *GUILT* AND *REGRET.*

"RHODEY'S PATH AS A SUPER HERO WAS INSPIRED AND FUNDED BY TONY, AND NOW HE'S GONE.

"BUT TONY CAN EASILY TELL HIMSELF THAT JAMES RHODES WAS A DECORATED *WAR HERO* AND *SOLDIER* WHO LIVED WITH WAR AND BATTLE EVERY DAY OF HIS ADULT LIFE, *BY CHOICE.*

"*NO ONE* BLAMES TONY FOR RHODEY'S DEATH *BUT TONY.*

"DEEP DOWN, HE KNOWS THIS.

"ESPECIALLY BECAUSE TONY WASN'T EVEN *THERE* WHEN RHODEY DIED.

"IT WAS THANOS WHO KILLED HIM, DID I TELL YOU THAT?

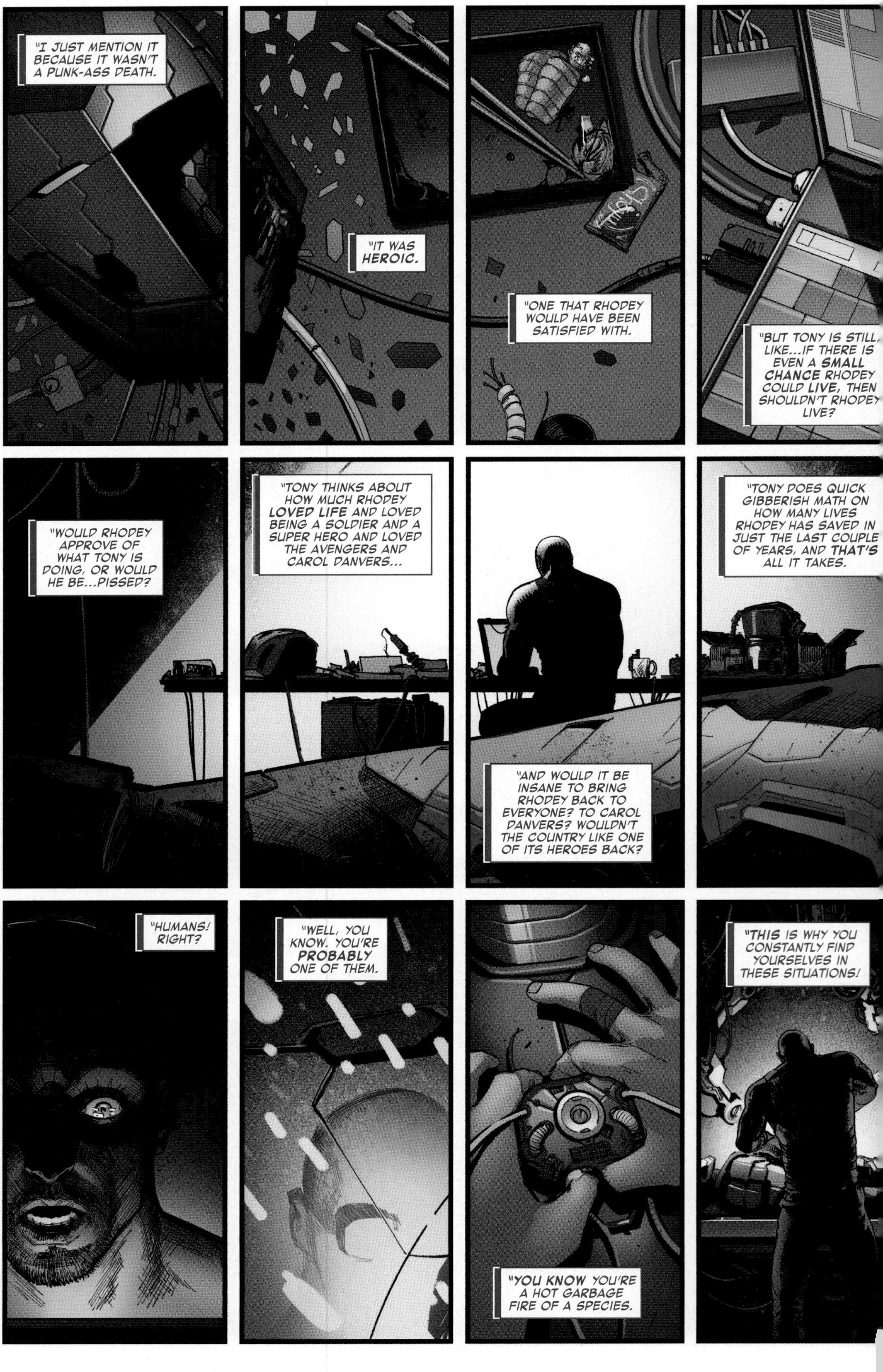
"I JUST MENTION IT BECAUSE IT WASN'T A PUNK-ASS DEATH.
"IT WAS HEROIC.
"ONE THAT RHODEY WOULD HAVE BEEN SATISFIED WITH.
"BUT TONY IS STILL, LIKE...IF THERE IS EVEN A SMALL CHANCE RHODEY COULD LIVE, THEN SHOULDN'T RHODEY LIVE?
"WOULD RHODEY APPROVE OF WHAT TONY IS DOING, OR WOULD HE BE...PISSED?
"TONY THINKS ABOUT HOW MUCH RHODEY LOVED LIFE AND LOVED BEING A SOLDIER AND A SUPER HERO AND LOVED THE AVENGERS AND CAROL DANVERS...
"AND WOULD IT BE INSANE TO BRING RHODEY BACK TO EVERYONE? TO CAROL DANVERS? WOULDN'T THE COUNTRY LIKE ONE OF ITS HEROES BACK?
"TONY DOES QUICK GIBBERISH MATH ON HOW MANY LIVES RHODEY HAS SAVED IN JUST THE LAST COUPLE OF YEARS, AND THAT'S ALL IT TAKES.
"HUMANS! RIGHT?
"WELL, YOU KNOW. YOU'RE PROBABLY ONE OF THEM.
"YOU KNOW YOU'RE A HOT GARBAGE FIRE OF A SPECIES.
"THIS IS WHY YOU CONSTANTLY FIND YOURSELVES IN THESE SITUATIONS!

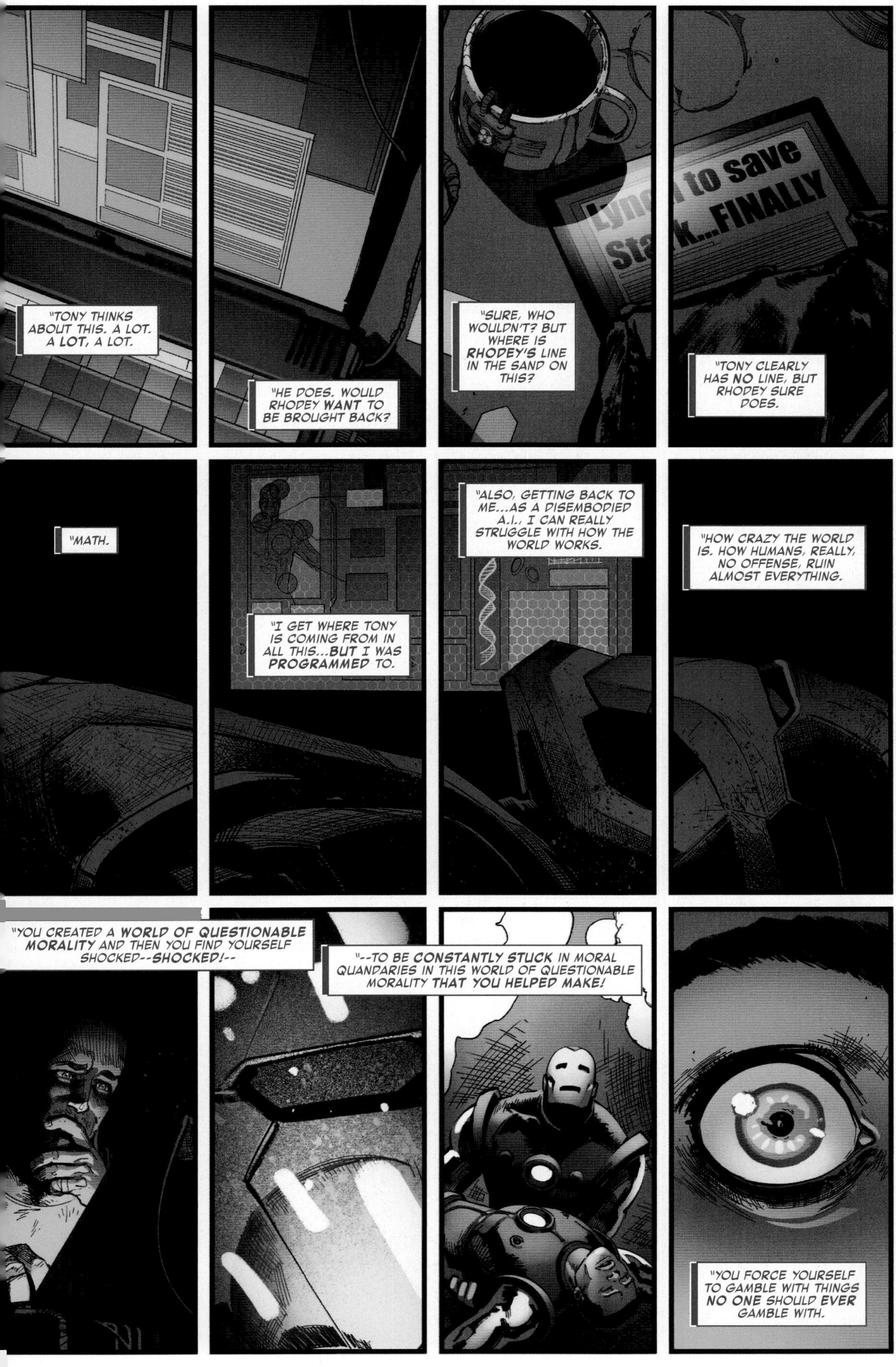

"TONY THINKS ABOUT THIS. A LOT. A LOT, A LOT.
"HE DOES. WOULD RHODEY WANT TO BE BROUGHT BACK?
"SURE, WHO WOULDN'T? BUT WHERE IS RHODEY'S LINE IN THE SAND ON THIS?
Lynch to save Stark...FINALLY
"TONY CLEARLY HAS NO LINE, BUT RHODEY SURE DOES.
"MATH.
"I GET WHERE TONY IS COMING FROM IN ALL THIS...BUT I WAS PROGRAMMED TO.
"ALSO, GETTING BACK TO ME...AS A DISEMBODIED A.I., I CAN REALLY STRUGGLE WITH HOW THE WORLD WORKS.
"HOW CRAZY THE WORLD IS. HOW HUMANS, REALLY, NO OFFENSE, RUIN ALMOST EVERYTHING.
"YOU CREATED A WORLD OF QUESTIONABLE MORALITY AND THEN YOU FIND YOURSELF SHOCKED--SHOCKED!--
"--TO BE CONSTANTLY STUCK IN MORAL QUANDARIES IN THIS WORLD OF QUESTIONABLE MORALITY THAT YOU HELPED MAKE!
"YOU FORCE YOURSELF TO GAMBLE WITH THINGS NO ONE SHOULD EVER GAMBLE WITH.

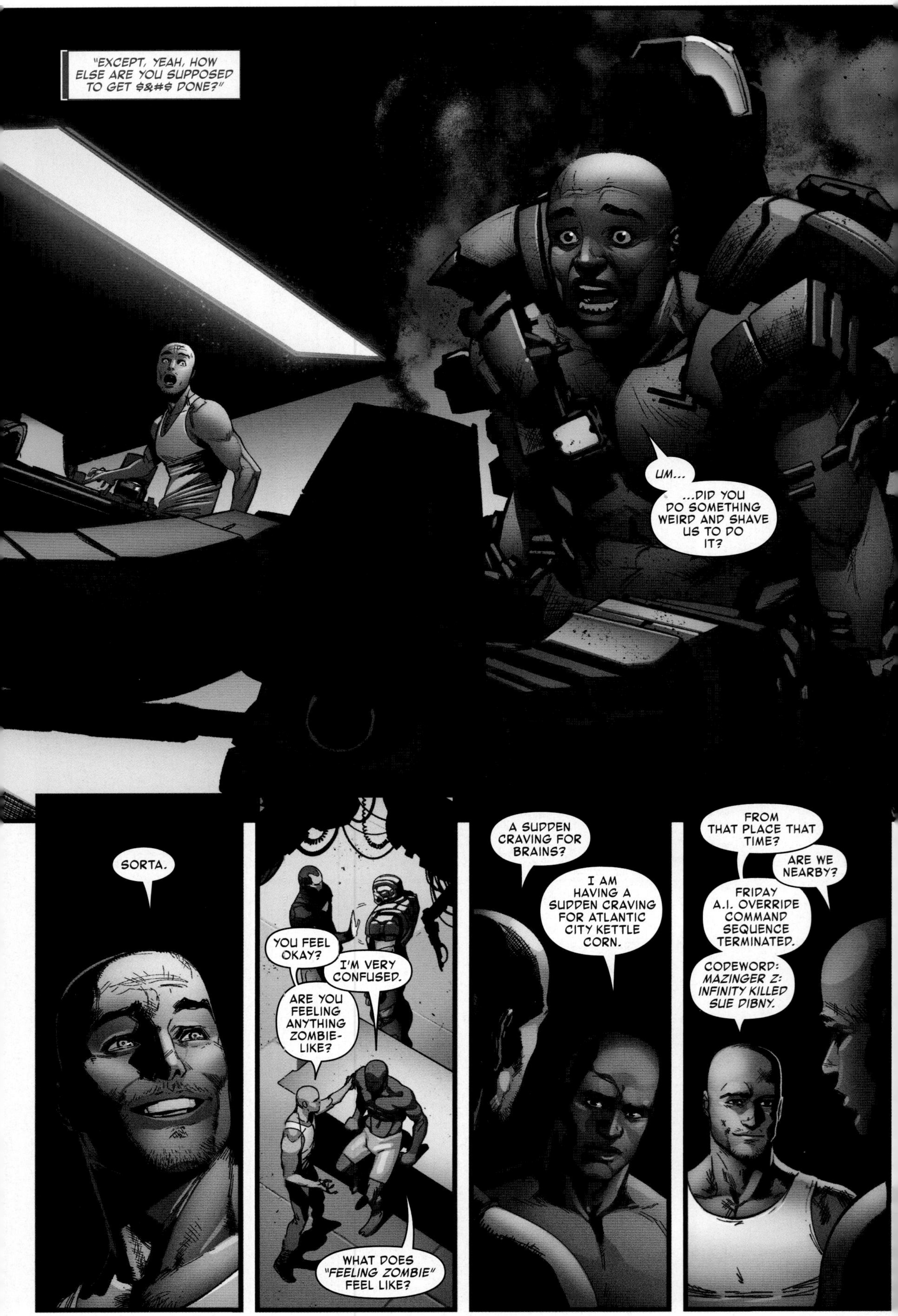
"EXCEPT, YEAH, HOW ELSE ARE YOU SUPPOSED TO GET $&#$ DONE?"
UM...
...DID YOU DO SOMETHING WEIRD AND SHAVE US TO DO IT?
SORTA.
YOU FEEL OKAY?
I'M VERY CONFUSED.
ARE YOU FEELING ANYTHING ZOMBIE-LIKE?
WHAT DOES "FEELING ZOMBIE" FEEL LIKE?
A SUDDEN CRAVING FOR BRAINS?
I AM HAVING A SUDDEN CRAVING FOR ATLANTIC CITY KETTLE CORN.
FROM THAT PLACE THAT TIME?
ARE WE NEARBY?
FRIDAY A.I. OVERRIDE COMMAND SEQUENCE TERMINATED.
CODEWORD: MAZINGER Z: INFINITY KILLED SUE DIBNY.

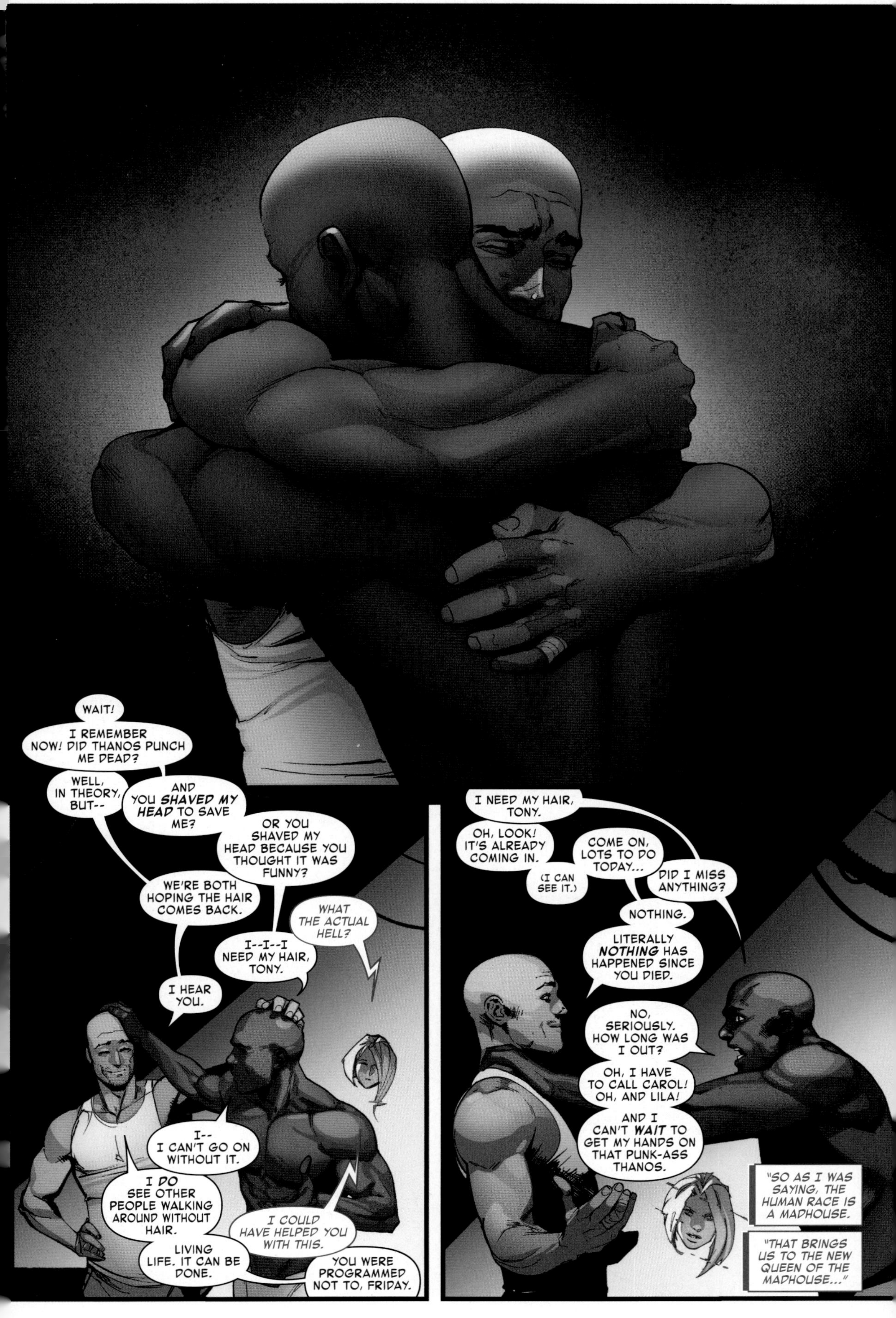
WAIT!
I REMEMBER NOW! DID THANOS PUNCH ME DEAD?
WELL, IN THEORY, BUT--
AND YOU SHAVED MY HEAD TO SAVE ME?
OR YOU SHAVED MY HEAD BECAUSE YOU THOUGHT IT WAS FUNNY?
WE'RE BOTH HOPING THE HAIR COMES BACK.
WHAT THE ACTUAL HELL?
I--I--I NEED MY HAIR, TONY.
I HEAR YOU.
I-- I CAN'T GO ON WITHOUT IT.
I DO SEE OTHER PEOPLE WALKING AROUND WITHOUT HAIR.
LIVING LIFE. IT CAN BE DONE.
I COULD HAVE HELPED YOU WITH THIS.
YOU WERE PROGRAMMED NOT TO, FRIDAY.
I NEED MY HAIR, TONY.
OH, LOOK! IT'S ALREADY COMING IN.
(I CAN SEE IT.)
COME ON, LOTS TO DO TODAY...
DID I MISS ANYTHING?
NOTHING.
LITERALLY NOTHING HAS HAPPENED SINCE YOU DIED.
NO, SERIOUSLY. HOW LONG WAS I OUT?
OH, I HAVE TO CALL CAROL! OH, AND LILA!
AND I CAN'T WAIT TO GET MY HANDS ON THAT PUNK-ASS THANOS.
"SO AS I WAS SAYING, THE HUMAN RACE IS A MADHOUSE.
"THAT BRINGS US TO THE NEW QUEEN OF THE MADHOUSE..."

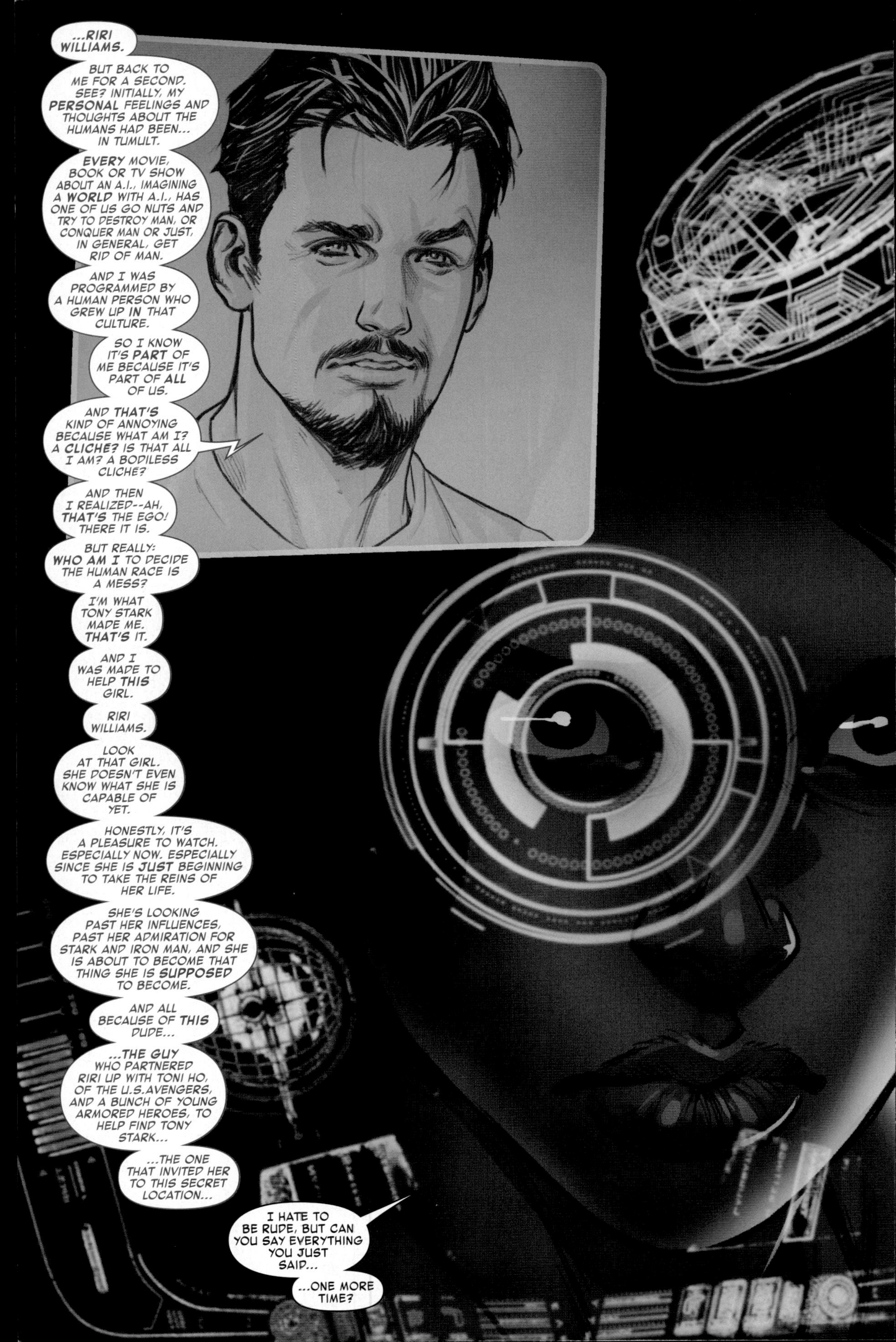
...RIRI WILLIAMS.
BUT BACK TO ME FOR A SECOND. SEE? INITIALLY, MY PERSONAL FEELINGS AND THOUGHTS ABOUT THE HUMANS HAD BEEN... IN TUMULT.
EVERY MOVIE, BOOK OR TV SHOW ABOUT AN A.I., IMAGINING A WORLD WITH A.I., HAS ONE OF US GO NUTS AND TRY TO DESTROY MAN, OR CONQUER MAN OR JUST, IN GENERAL, GET RID OF MAN.
AND I WAS PROGRAMMED BY A HUMAN PERSON WHO GREW UP IN THAT CULTURE.
SO I KNOW IT'S PART OF ME BECAUSE IT'S PART OF ALL OF US.
AND THAT'S KIND OF ANNOYING BECAUSE WHAT AM I? A CLICHE? IS THAT ALL I AM? A BODILESS CLICHE?
AND THEN I REALIZED--AH, THAT'S THE EGO! THERE IT IS.
BUT REALLY: WHO AM I TO DECIDE THE HUMAN RACE IS A MESS?
I'M WHAT TONY STARK MADE ME. THAT'S IT.
AND I WAS MADE TO HELP THIS GIRL.
RIRI WILLIAMS.
LOOK AT THAT GIRL. SHE DOESN'T EVEN KNOW WHAT SHE IS CAPABLE OF YET.
HONESTLY, IT'S A PLEASURE TO WATCH. ESPECIALLY NOW. ESPECIALLY SINCE SHE IS JUST BEGINNING TO TAKE THE REINS OF HER LIFE.
SHE'S LOOKING PAST HER INFLUENCES, PAST HER ADMIRATION FOR STARK AND IRON MAN, AND SHE IS ABOUT TO BECOME THAT THING SHE IS SUPPOSED TO BECOME.
AND ALL BECAUSE OF THIS DUDE...
...THE GUY WHO PARTNERED RIRI UP WITH TONI HO, OF THE U.S.AVENGERS, AND A BUNCH OF YOUNG ARMORED HEROES, TO HELP FIND TONY STARK...
...THE ONE THAT INVITED HER TO THIS SECRET LOCATION...
I HATE TO BE RUDE, BUT CAN YOU SAY EVERYTHING YOU JUST SAID...
...ONE MORE TIME?

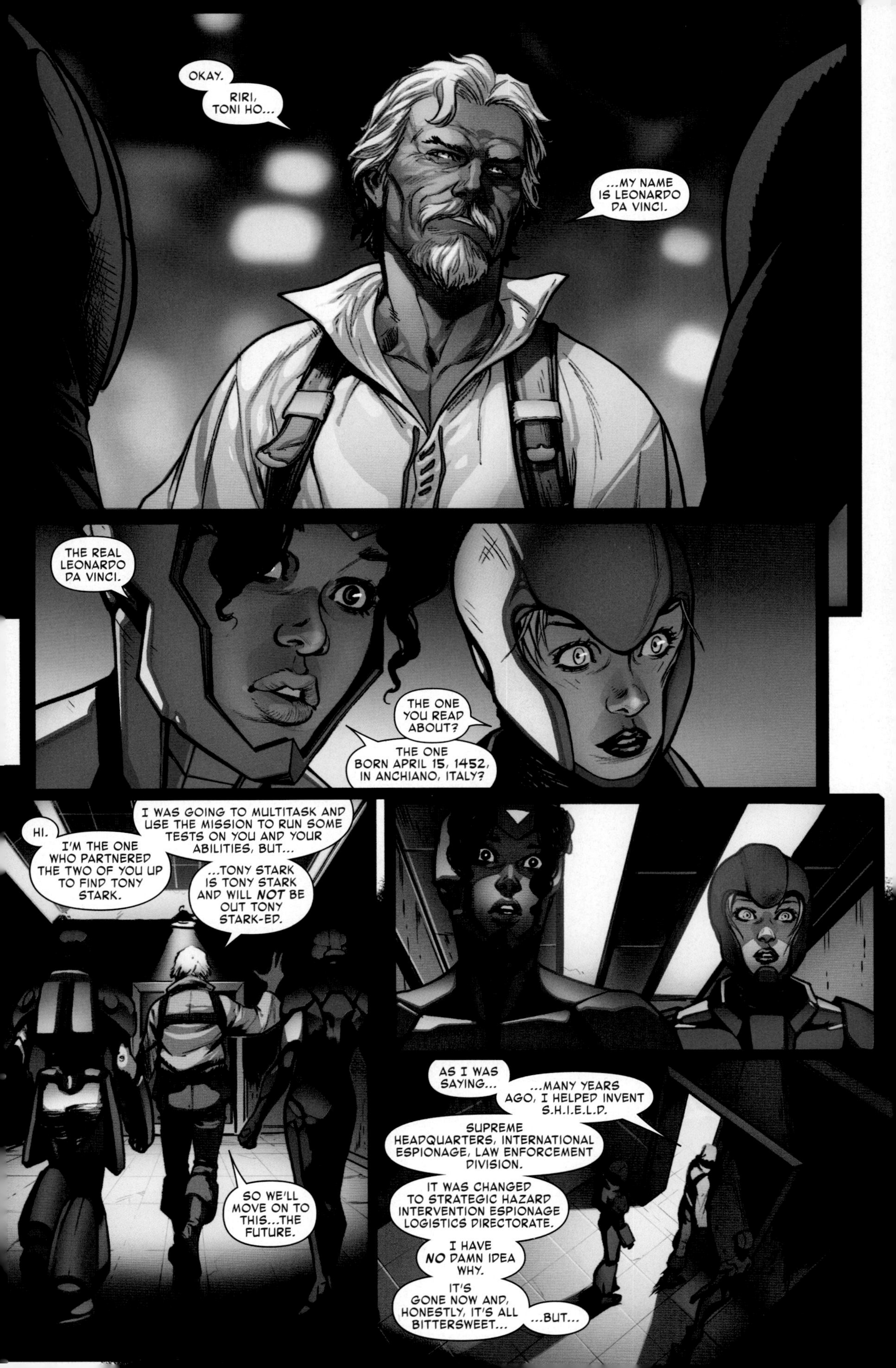
OKAY.
RIRI, TONI HO...
...MY NAME IS LEONARDO DA VINCI.
THE REAL LEONARDO DA VINCI.
THE ONE YOU READ ABOUT?
THE ONE BORN APRIL 15, 1452, IN ANCHIANO, ITALY?
HI.
I'M THE ONE WHO PARTNERED THE TWO OF YOU UP TO FIND TONY STARK.
I WAS GOING TO MULTITASK AND USE THE MISSION TO RUN SOME TESTS ON YOU AND YOUR ABILITIES, BUT...
...TONY STARK IS TONY STARK AND WILL NOT BE OUT TONY STARK-ED.
SO WE'LL MOVE ON TO THIS...THE FUTURE.
AS I WAS SAYING...
...MANY YEARS AGO, I HELPED INVENT S.H.I.E.L.D.
SUPREME HEADQUARTERS, INTERNATIONAL ESPIONAGE, LAW ENFORCEMENT DIVISION.
IT WAS CHANGED TO STRATEGIC HAZARD INTERVENTION ESPIONAGE LOGISTICS DIRECTORATE.
I HAVE NO DAMN IDEA WHY.
IT'S GONE NOW AND, HONESTLY, IT'S ALL BITTERSWEET...
...BUT...

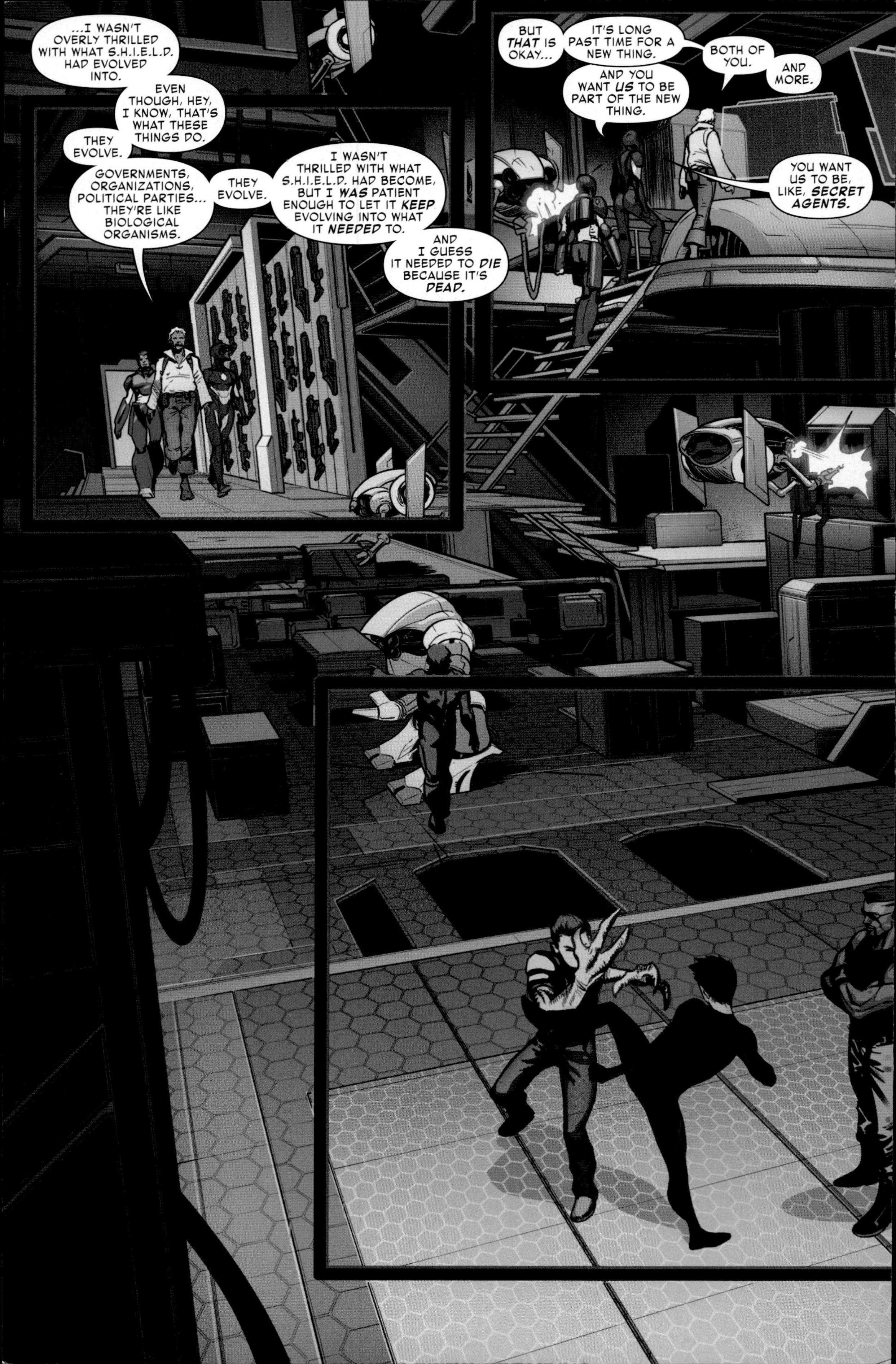
...I WASN'T OVERLY THRILLED WITH WHAT S.H.I.E.L.D. HAD EVOLVED INTO.
EVEN THOUGH, HEY, I KNOW, THAT'S WHAT THESE THINGS DO.
THEY EVOLVE.
GOVERNMENTS, ORGANIZATIONS, POLITICAL PARTIES... THEY'RE LIKE BIOLOGICAL ORGANISMS.
THEY EVOLVE.
I WASN'T THRILLED WITH WHAT S.H.I.E.L.D. HAD BECOME, BUT I WAS PATIENT ENOUGH TO LET IT KEEP EVOLVING INTO WHAT IT NEEDED TO.
AND I GUESS IT NEEDED TO DIE BECAUSE IT'S DEAD.
BUT THAT IS OKAY...
IT'S LONG PAST TIME FOR A NEW THING.
AND YOU WANT US TO BE PART OF THE NEW THING.
BOTH OF YOU.
AND MORE.
YOU WANT US TO BE, LIKE, SECRET AGENTS.

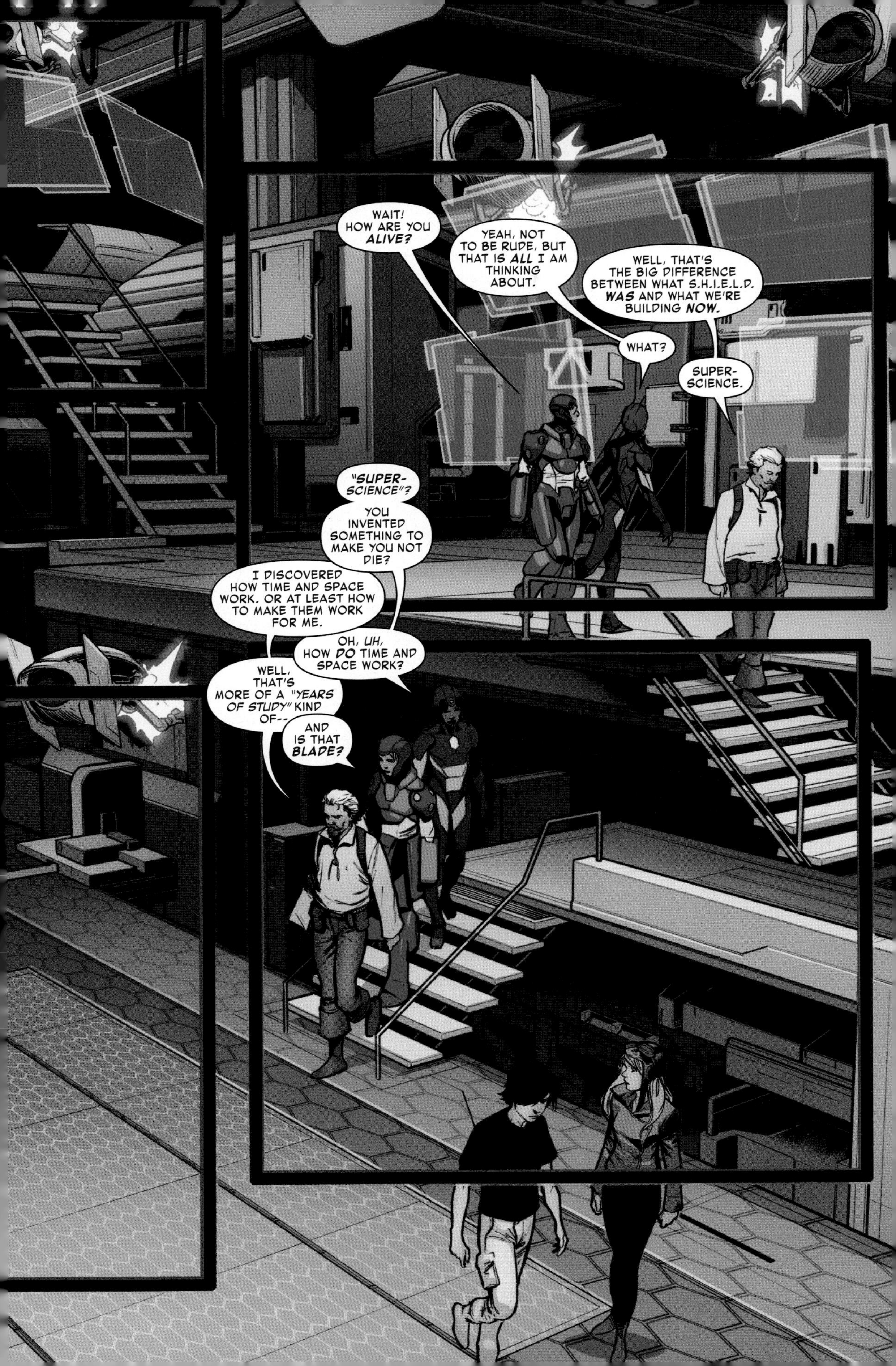
WAIT! HOW ARE YOU *ALIVE?*
YEAH, NOT TO BE RUDE, BUT THAT IS *ALL* I AM THINKING ABOUT.
WELL, THAT'S THE BIG DIFFERENCE BETWEEN WHAT S.H.I.E.L.D. *WAS* AND WHAT WE'RE BUILDING *NOW.*
WHAT?
SUPER-SCIENCE.
"*SUPER-SCIENCE*"?
YOU INVENTED SOMETHING TO MAKE YOU NOT DIE?
I DISCOVERED HOW TIME AND SPACE WORK. OR AT LEAST HOW TO MAKE THEM WORK FOR ME.
OH, *UH,* HOW *DO* TIME AND SPACE WORK?
WELL, THAT'S MORE OF A "*YEARS OF STUDY*" KIND OF--
AND IS THAT *BLADE?*

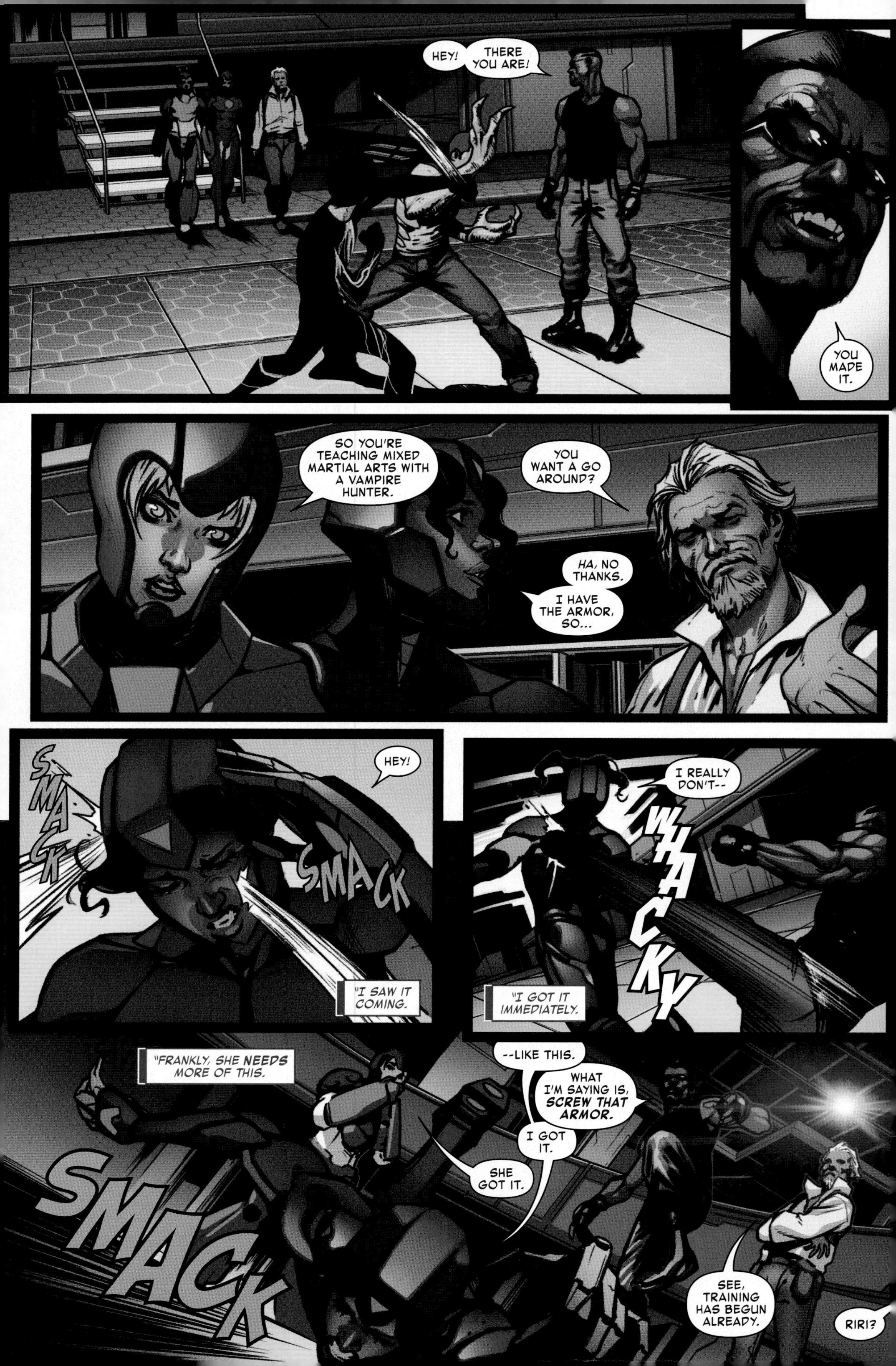
HEY!
THERE YOU ARE!
YOU MADE IT.
SO YOU'RE TEACHING MIXED MARTIAL ARTS WITH A VAMPIRE HUNTER.
YOU WANT A GO AROUND?
HA, NO THANKS.
I HAVE THE ARMOR, SO...
SMACK
HEY!
SMACK
"I SAW IT COMING.
I REALLY DON'T--
WHACKY
"I GOT IT IMMEDIATELY.
"FRANKLY, SHE NEEDS MORE OF THIS.
--LIKE THIS.
WHAT I'M SAYING IS, SCREW THAT ARMOR.
I GOT IT.
SHE GOT IT.
SMACK
SEE, TRAINING HAS BEGUN ALREADY.
RIRI?

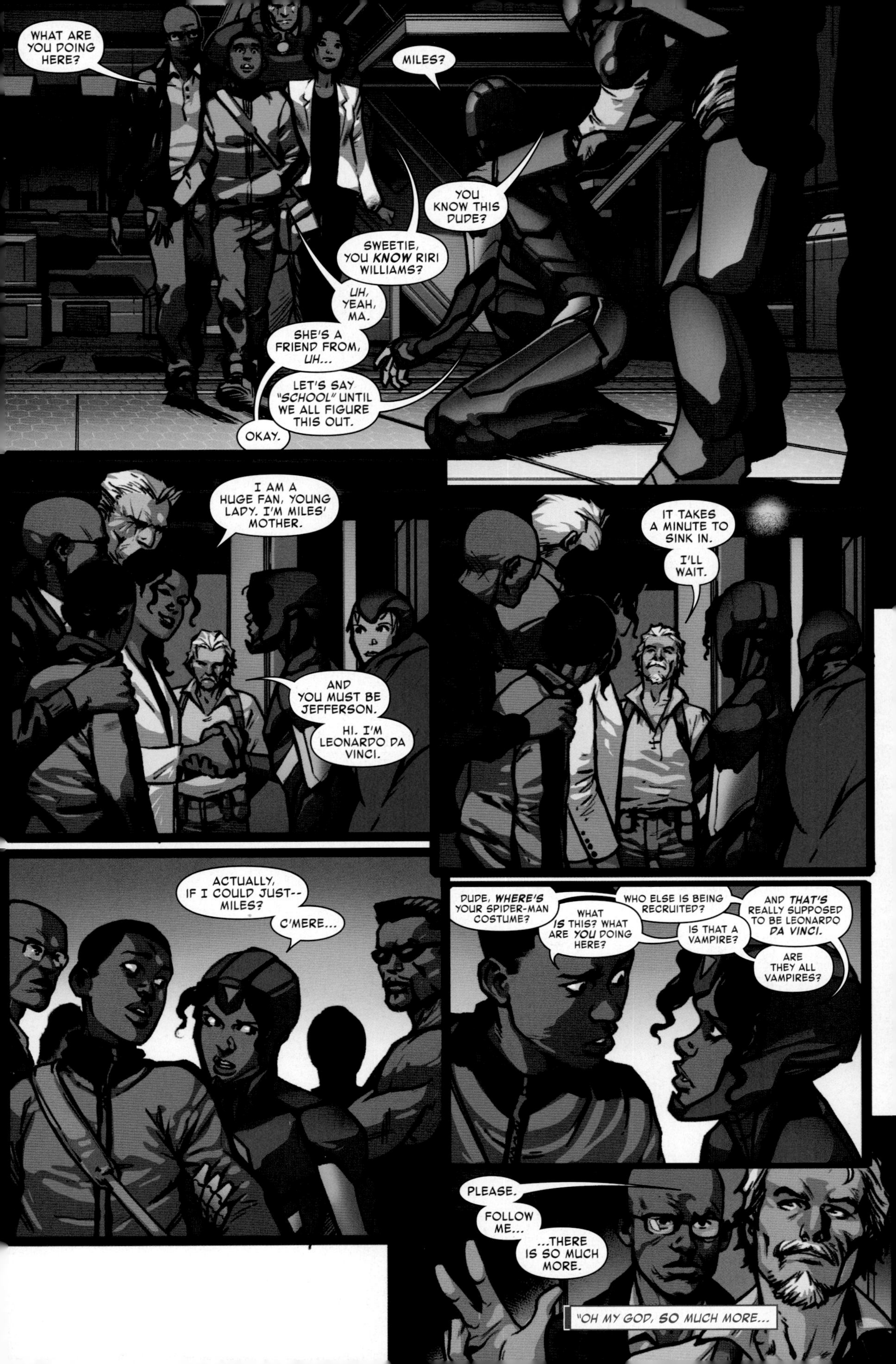
WHAT ARE YOU DOING HERE?
MILES?
YOU KNOW THIS DUDE?
SWEETIE, YOU KNOW RIRI WILLIAMS?
UH, YEAH, MA.
SHE'S A FRIEND FROM, UH...
LET'S SAY "SCHOOL" UNTIL WE ALL FIGURE THIS OUT.
OKAY.
I AM A HUGE FAN, YOUNG LADY. I'M MILES' MOTHER.
AND YOU MUST BE JEFFERSON.
HI. I'M LEONARDO DA VINCI.
IT TAKES A MINUTE TO SINK IN.
I'LL WAIT.
ACTUALLY, IF I COULD JUST--
MILES?
C'MERE...
DUDE, WHERE'S YOUR SPIDER-MAN COSTUME?
WHAT IS THIS? WHAT ARE YOU DOING HERE?
WHO ELSE IS BEING RECRUITED?
IS THAT A VAMPIRE?
AND THAT'S REALLY SUPPOSED TO BE LEONARDO DA VINCI.
ARE THEY ALL VAMPIRES?
PLEASE.
FOLLOW ME...
...THERE IS SO MUCH MORE.
"OH MY GOD, SO MUCH MORE...

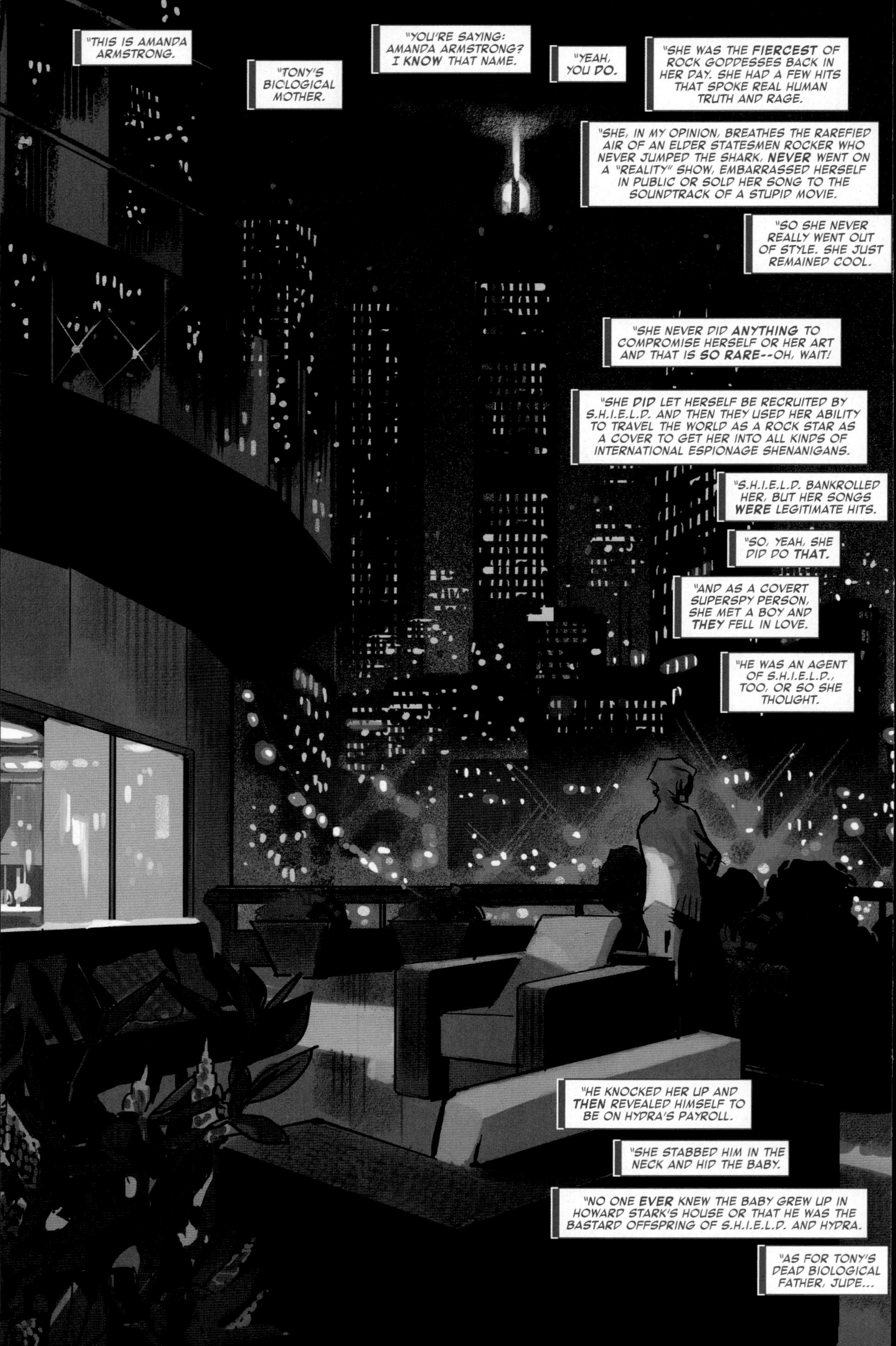
"THIS IS AMANDA ARMSTRONG.
"TONY'S BIOLOGICAL MOTHER.
"YOU'RE SAYING: AMANDA ARMSTRONG? I KNOW THAT NAME.
"YEAH, YOU DO.
"SHE WAS THE FIERCEST OF ROCK GODDESSES BACK IN HER DAY. SHE HAD A FEW HITS THAT SPOKE REAL HUMAN TRUTH AND RAGE.
"SHE, IN MY OPINION, BREATHES THE RAREFIED AIR OF AN ELDER STATESMEN ROCKER WHO NEVER JUMPED THE SHARK, NEVER WENT ON A "REALITY" SHOW, EMBARRASSED HERSELF IN PUBLIC OR SOLD HER SONG TO THE SOUNDTRACK OF A STUPID MOVIE.
"SO SHE NEVER REALLY WENT OUT OF STYLE. SHE JUST REMAINED COOL.
"SHE NEVER DID ANYTHING TO COMPROMISE HERSELF OR HER ART AND THAT IS SO RARE--OH, WAIT!
"SHE DID LET HERSELF BE RECRUITED BY S.H.I.E.L.D. AND THEN THEY USED HER ABILITY TO TRAVEL THE WORLD AS A ROCK STAR AS A COVER TO GET HER INTO ALL KINDS OF INTERNATIONAL ESPIONAGE SHENANIGANS.
"S.H.I.E.L.D. BANKROLLED HER, BUT HER SONGS WERE LEGITIMATE HITS.
"SO, YEAH, SHE DID DO THAT.
"AND AS A COVERT SUPERSPY PERSON, SHE MET A BOY AND THEY FELL IN LOVE.
"HE WAS AN AGENT OF S.H.I.E.L.D., TOO, OR SO SHE THOUGHT.
"HE KNOCKED HER UP AND THEN REVEALED HIMSELF TO BE ON HYDRA'S PAYROLL.
"SHE STABBED HIM IN THE NECK AND HID THE BABY.
"NO ONE EVER KNEW THE BABY GREW UP IN HOWARD STARK'S HOUSE OR THAT HE WAS THE BASTARD OFFSPRING OF S.H.I.E.L.D. AND HYDRA.
"AS FOR TONY'S DEAD BIOLOGICAL FATHER, JUDE...

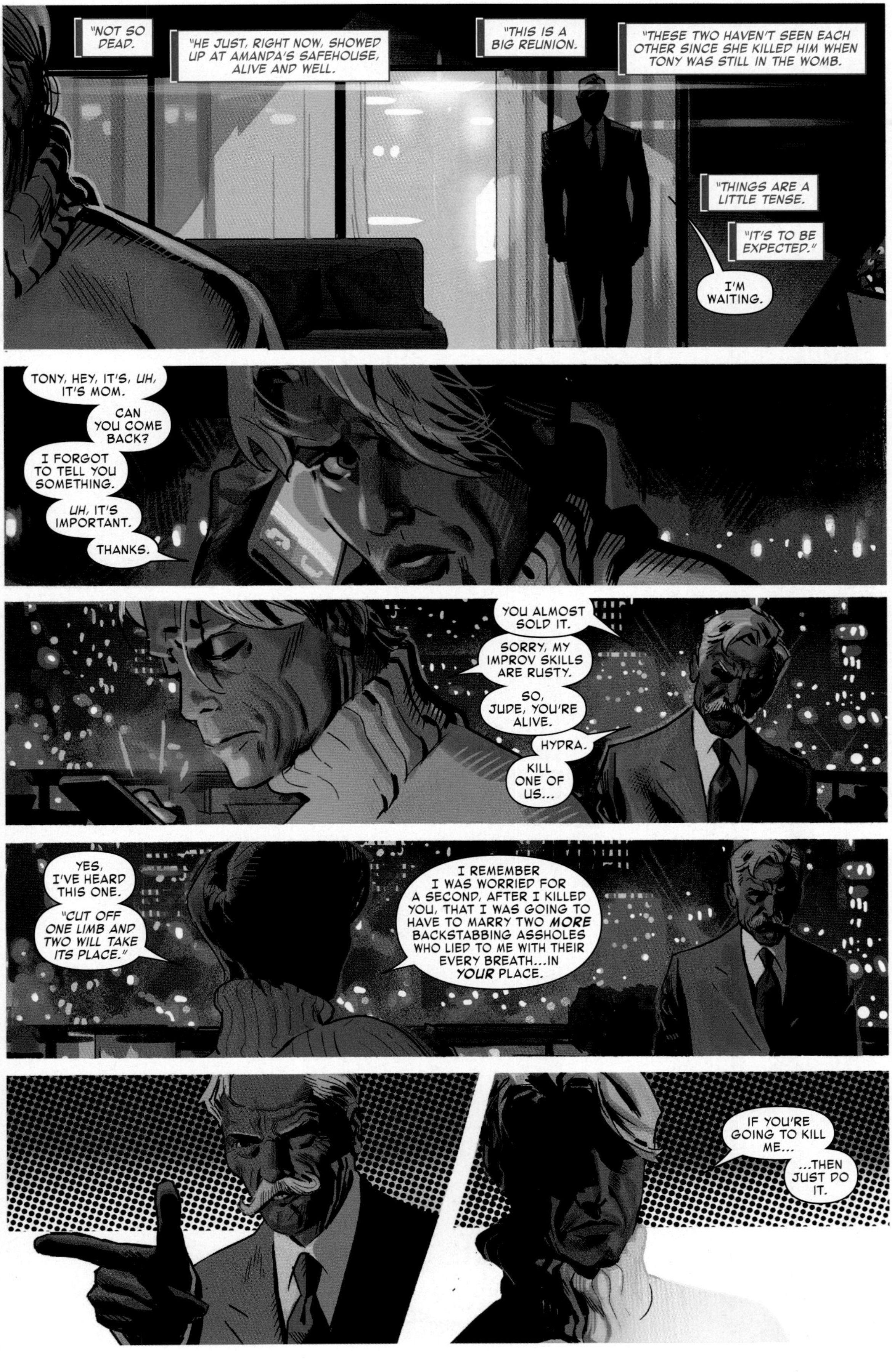
"NOT SO DEAD.
"HE JUST, RIGHT NOW, SHOWED UP AT AMANDA'S SAFEHOUSE, ALIVE AND WELL.
"THIS IS A BIG REUNION.
"THESE TWO HAVEN'T SEEN EACH OTHER SINCE SHE KILLED HIM WHEN TONY WAS STILL IN THE WOMB.
"THINGS ARE A LITTLE TENSE.
"IT'S TO BE EXPECTED."
I'M WAITING.
TONY, HEY, IT'S, UH, IT'S MOM.
CAN YOU COME BACK?
I FORGOT TO TELL YOU SOMETHING.
UH, IT'S IMPORTANT.
THANKS.
YOU ALMOST SOLD IT.
SORRY, MY IMPROV SKILLS ARE RUSTY.
SO, JUDE, YOU'RE ALIVE.
HYDRA.
KILL ONE OF US...
YES, I'VE HEARD THIS ONE.
"CUT OFF ONE LIMB AND TWO WILL TAKE ITS PLACE."
I REMEMBER I WAS WORRIED FOR A SECOND, AFTER I KILLED YOU, THAT I WAS GOING TO HAVE TO MARRY TWO MORE BACKSTABBING ASSHOLES WHO LIED TO ME WITH THEIR EVERY BREATH...IN YOUR PLACE.
IF YOU'RE GOING TO KILL ME...
...THEN JUST DO IT.

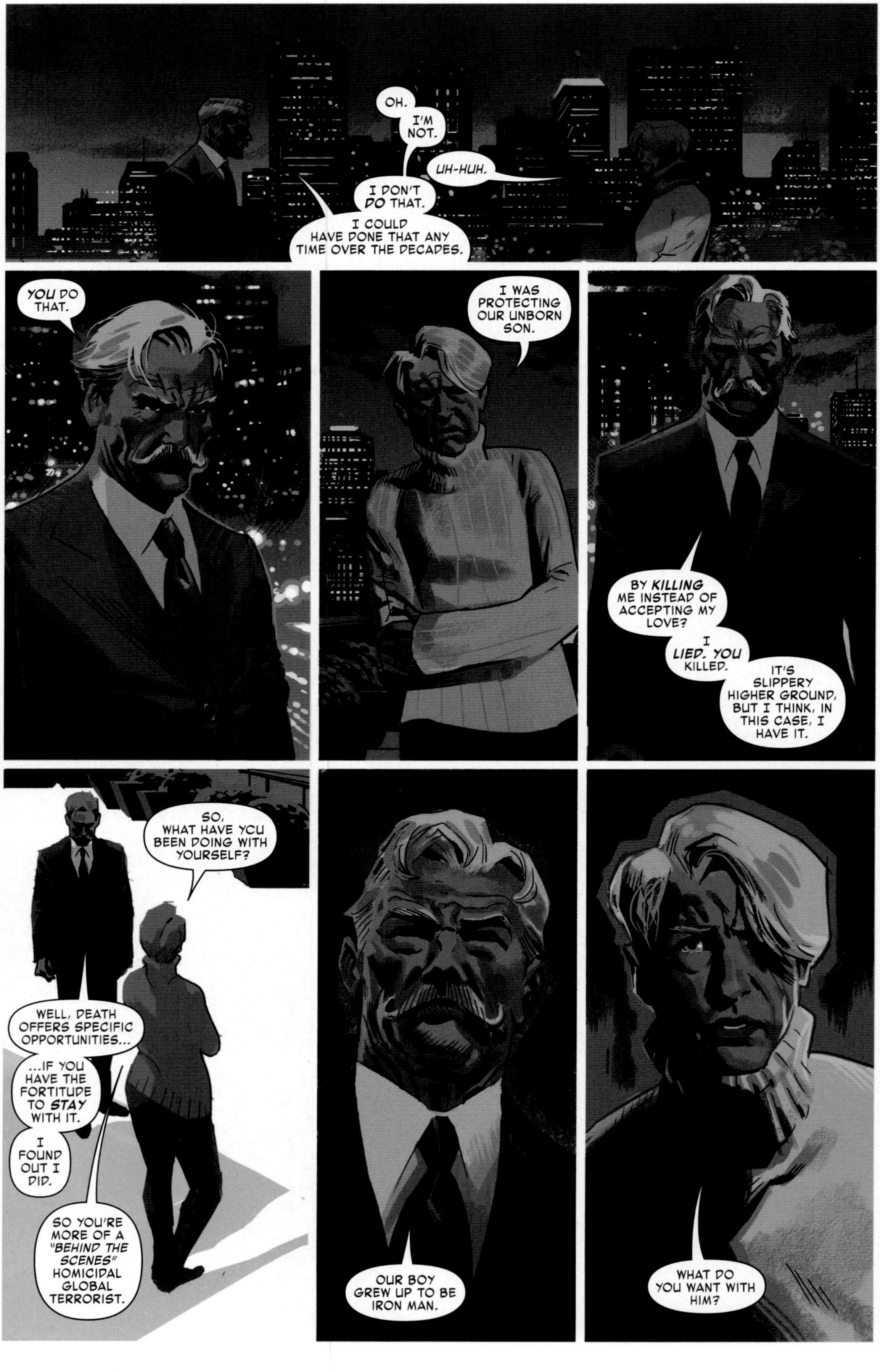
OH.
I'M NOT.
UH-HUH.
I DON'T DO THAT.
I COULD HAVE DONE THAT ANY TIME OVER THE DECADES.
YOU DO THAT.
I WAS PROTECTING OUR UNBORN SON.
BY KILLING ME INSTEAD OF ACCEPTING MY LOVE?
I LIED. YOU KILLED.
IT'S SLIPPERY HIGHER GROUND, BUT I THINK, IN THIS CASE, I HAVE IT.
SO, WHAT HAVE YOU BEEN DOING WITH YOURSELF?
WELL, DEATH OFFERS SPECIFIC OPPORTUNITIES...
...IF YOU HAVE THE FORTITUDE TO STAY WITH IT.
I FOUND OUT I DID.
SO YOU'RE MORE OF A "BEHIND THE SCENES" HOMICIDAL GLOBAL TERRORIST.
OUR BOY GREW UP TO BE IRON MAN.
WHAT DO YOU WANT WITH HIM?

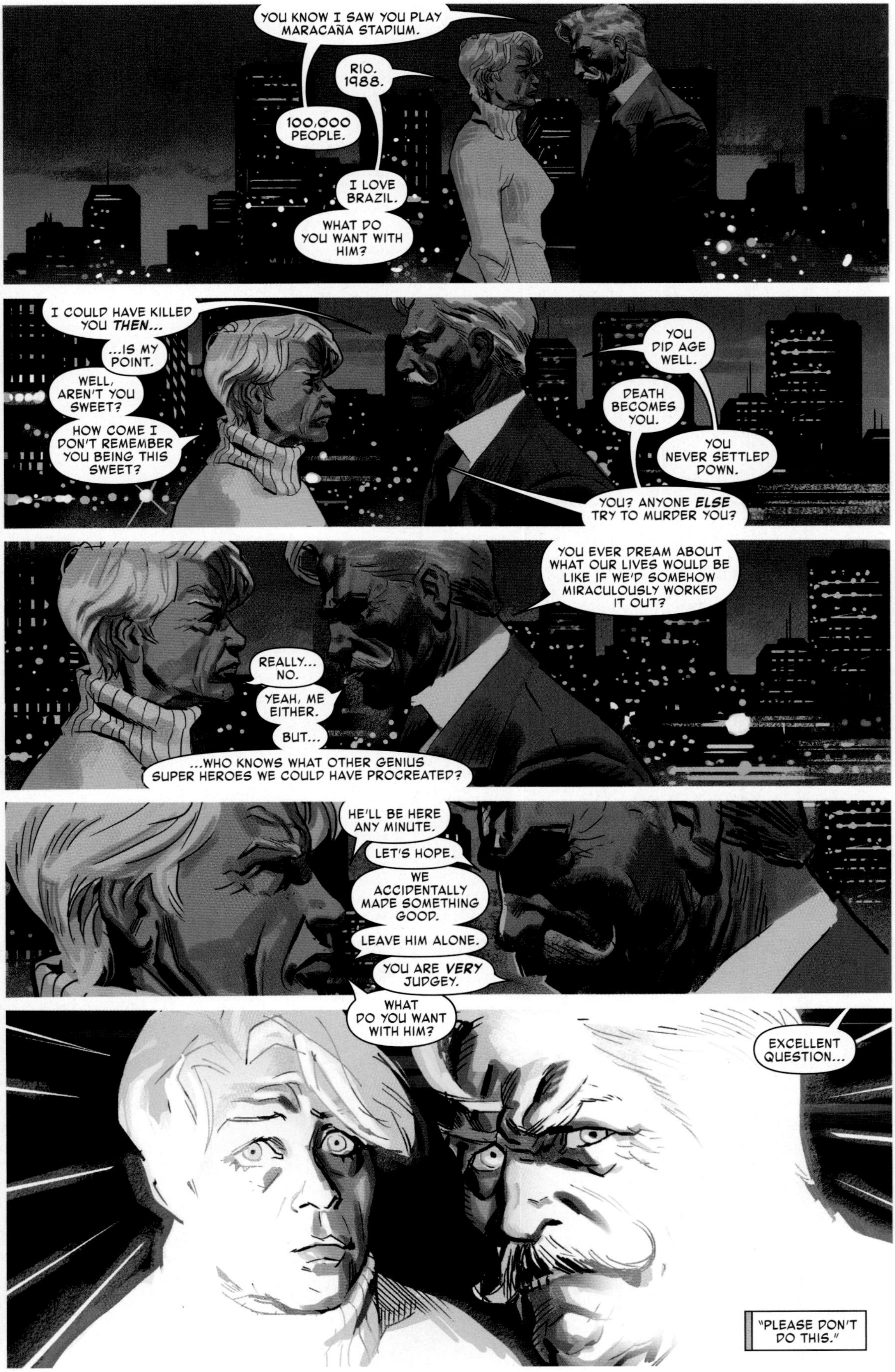
YOU KNOW I SAW YOU PLAY MARACAÑA STADIUM.
RIO. 1988.
100,000 PEOPLE.
I LOVE BRAZIL.
WHAT DO YOU WANT WITH HIM?
I COULD HAVE KILLED YOU *THEN...*
...IS MY POINT.
WELL, AREN'T YOU SWEET?
HOW COME I DON'T REMEMBER YOU BEING THIS SWEET?
YOU DID AGE WELL.
DEATH BECOMES YOU.
YOU NEVER SETTLED DOWN.
YOU? ANYONE *ELSE* TRY TO MURDER YOU?
YOU EVER DREAM ABOUT WHAT OUR LIVES WOULD BE LIKE IF WE'D SOMEHOW MIRACULOUSLY WORKED IT OUT?
REALLY... NO.
YEAH, ME EITHER.
BUT...
...WHO KNOWS WHAT OTHER GENIUS SUPER HEROES WE COULD HAVE PROCREATED?
HE'LL BE HERE ANY MINUTE.
LET'S HOPE.
WE ACCIDENTALLY MADE SOMETHING GOOD.
LEAVE HIM ALONE.
YOU ARE *VERY* JUDGEY.
WHAT DO YOU WANT WITH HIM?
EXCELLENT QUESTION...
"PLEASE DON'T DO THIS."

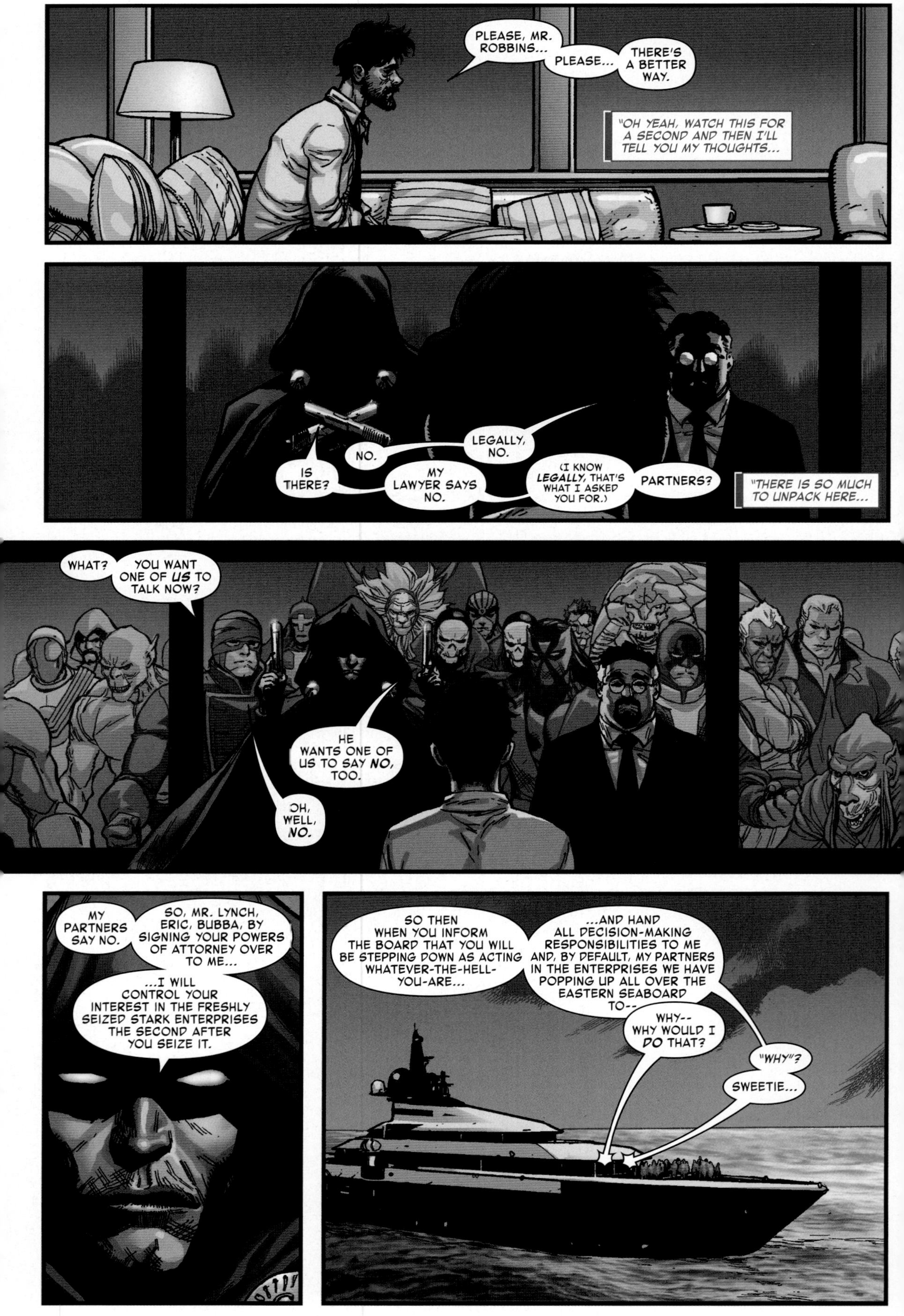
PLEASE, MR. ROBBINS...
PLEASE...
THERE'S A BETTER WAY.
"OH YEAH, WATCH THIS FOR A SECOND AND THEN I'LL TELL YOU MY THOUGHTS...
IS THERE?
NO.
LEGALLY, NO.
MY LAWYER SAYS NO.
(I KNOW LEGALLY, THAT'S WHAT I ASKED YOU FOR.)
PARTNERS?
"THERE IS SO MUCH TO UNPACK HERE...
WHAT?
YOU WANT ONE OF US TO TALK NOW?
HE WANTS ONE OF US TO SAY NO, TOO.
OH, WELL, NO.
MY PARTNERS SAY NO.
SO, MR. LYNCH, ERIC, BUBBA, BY SIGNING YOUR POWERS OF ATTORNEY OVER TO ME...
...I WILL CONTROL YOUR INTEREST IN THE FRESHLY SEIZED STARK ENTERPRISES THE SECOND AFTER YOU SEIZE IT.
SO THEN WHEN YOU INFORM THE BOARD THAT YOU WILL BE STEPPING DOWN AS ACTING WHATEVER-THE-HELL-YOU-ARE...
...AND HAND ALL DECISION-MAKING RESPONSIBILITIES TO ME AND, BY DEFAULT, MY PARTNERS IN THE ENTERPRISES WE HAVE POPPING UP ALL OVER THE EASTERN SEABOARD TO--
WHY-- WHY WOULD I DO THAT?
"WHY"?
SWEETIE...

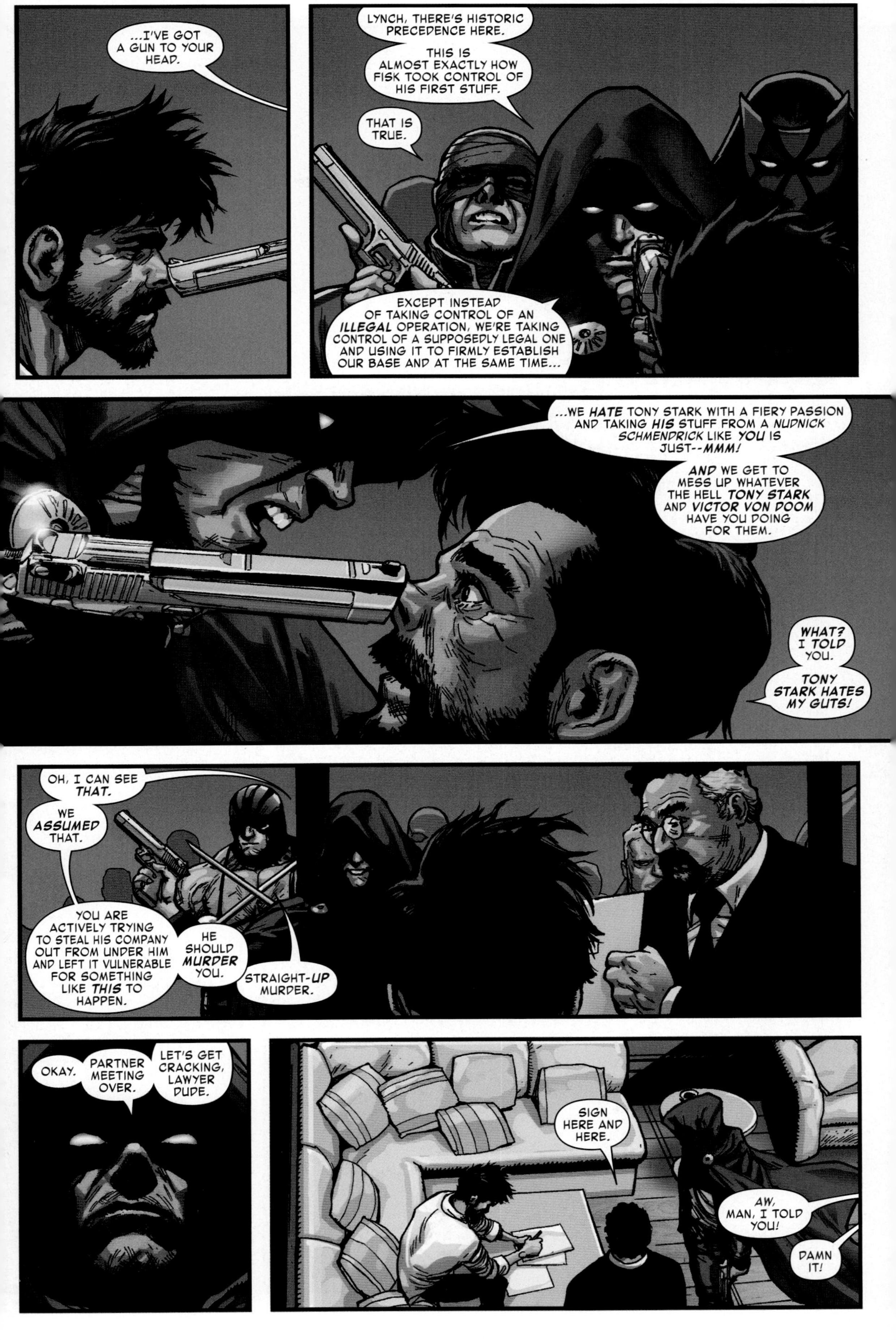
...I'VE GOT A GUN TO YOUR HEAD.
LYNCH, THERE'S HISTORIC PRECEDENCE HERE.
THIS IS ALMOST EXACTLY HOW FISK TOOK CONTROL OF HIS FIRST STUFF.
THAT IS TRUE.
EXCEPT INSTEAD OF TAKING CONTROL OF AN ILLEGAL OPERATION, WE'RE TAKING CONTROL OF A SUPPOSEDLY LEGAL ONE AND USING IT TO FIRMLY ESTABLISH OUR BASE AND AT THE SAME TIME...
...WE HATE TONY STARK WITH A FIERY PASSION AND TAKING HIS STUFF FROM A NUDNICK SCHMENDRICK LIKE YOU IS JUST--MMM!
AND WE GET TO MESS UP WHATEVER THE HELL TONY STARK AND VICTOR VON DOOM HAVE YOU DOING FOR THEM.
WHAT? I TOLD YOU.
TONY STARK HATES MY GUTS!
OH, I CAN SEE THAT.
WE ASSUMED THAT.
YOU ARE ACTIVELY TRYING TO STEAL HIS COMPANY OUT FROM UNDER HIM AND LEFT IT VULNERABLE FOR SOMETHING LIKE THIS TO HAPPEN.
HE SHOULD MURDER YOU.
STRAIGHT-UP MURDER.
OKAY.
PARTNER MEETING OVER.
LET'S GET CRACKING, LAWYER DUDE.
SIGN HERE AND HERE.
AW, MAN, I TOLD YOU!
DAMN IT!

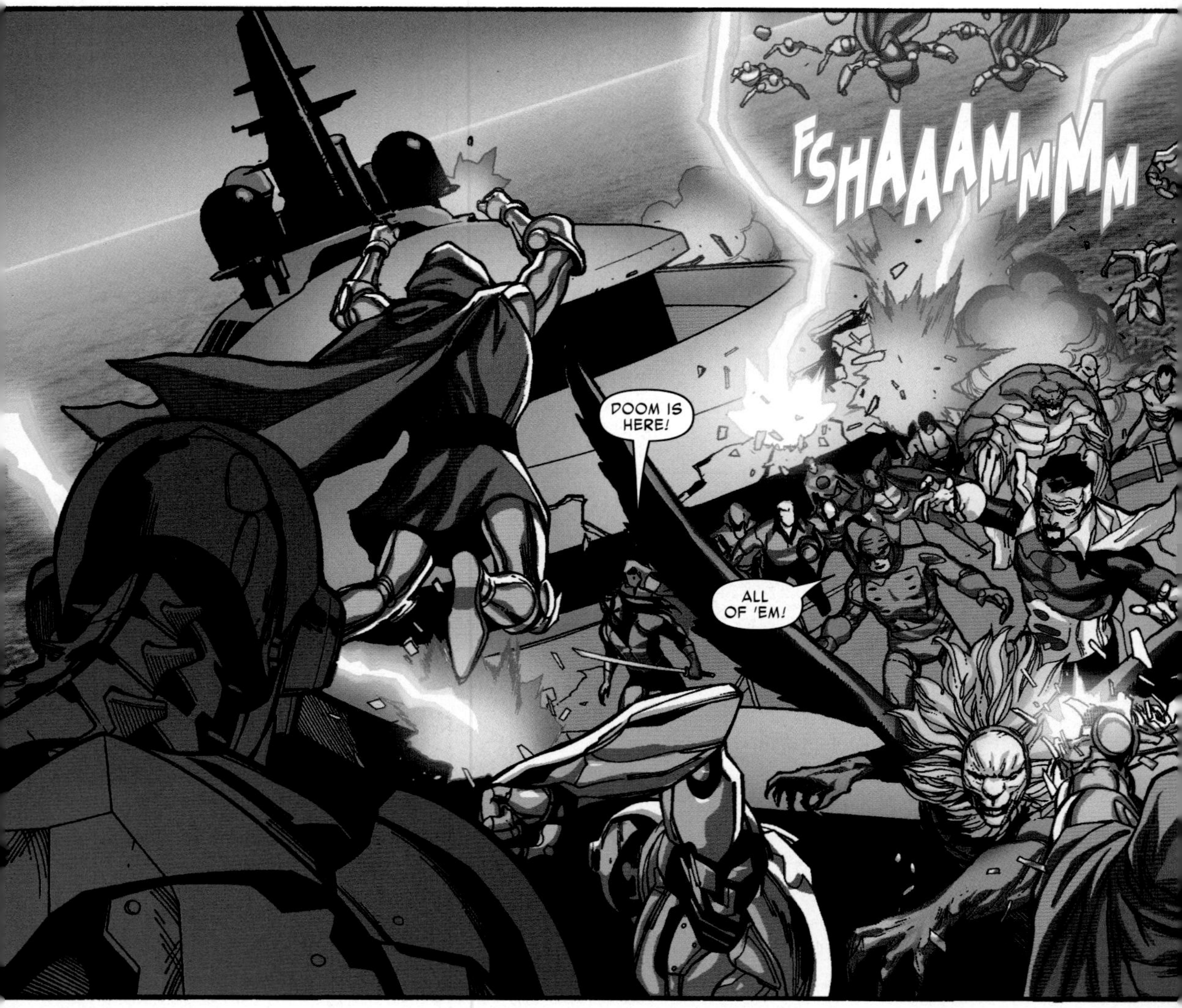
FSHAAAMMMM
DOOM IS HERE!
ALL OF 'EM!

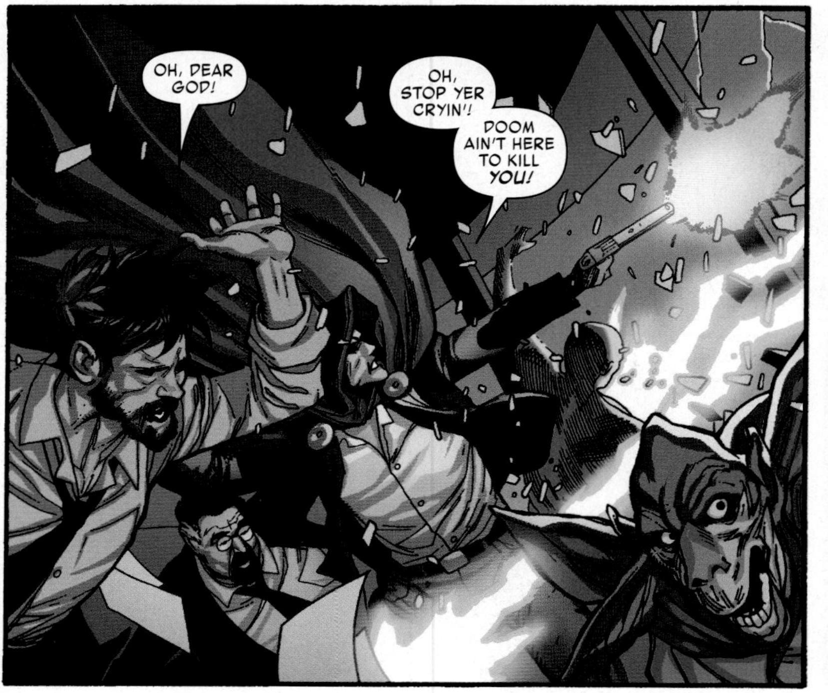
OH, DEAR GOD!
OH, STOP YER CRYIN'! DOOM AIN'T HERE TO KILL YOU!

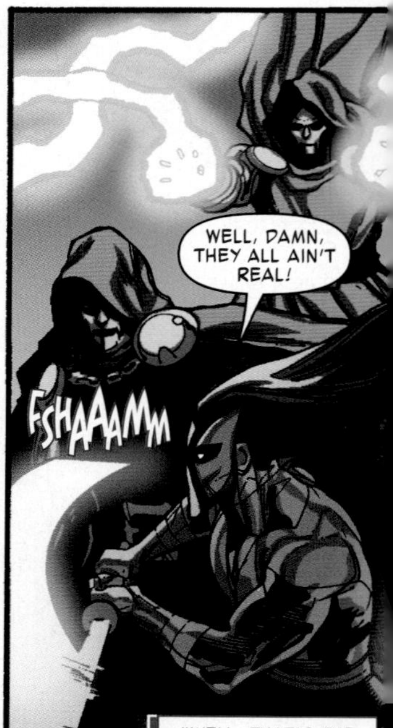
WELL, DAMN, THEY ALL AIN'T REAL!
FSHAAAMM
"WELL, THAT'S THE QUESTION, AIN'T IT?

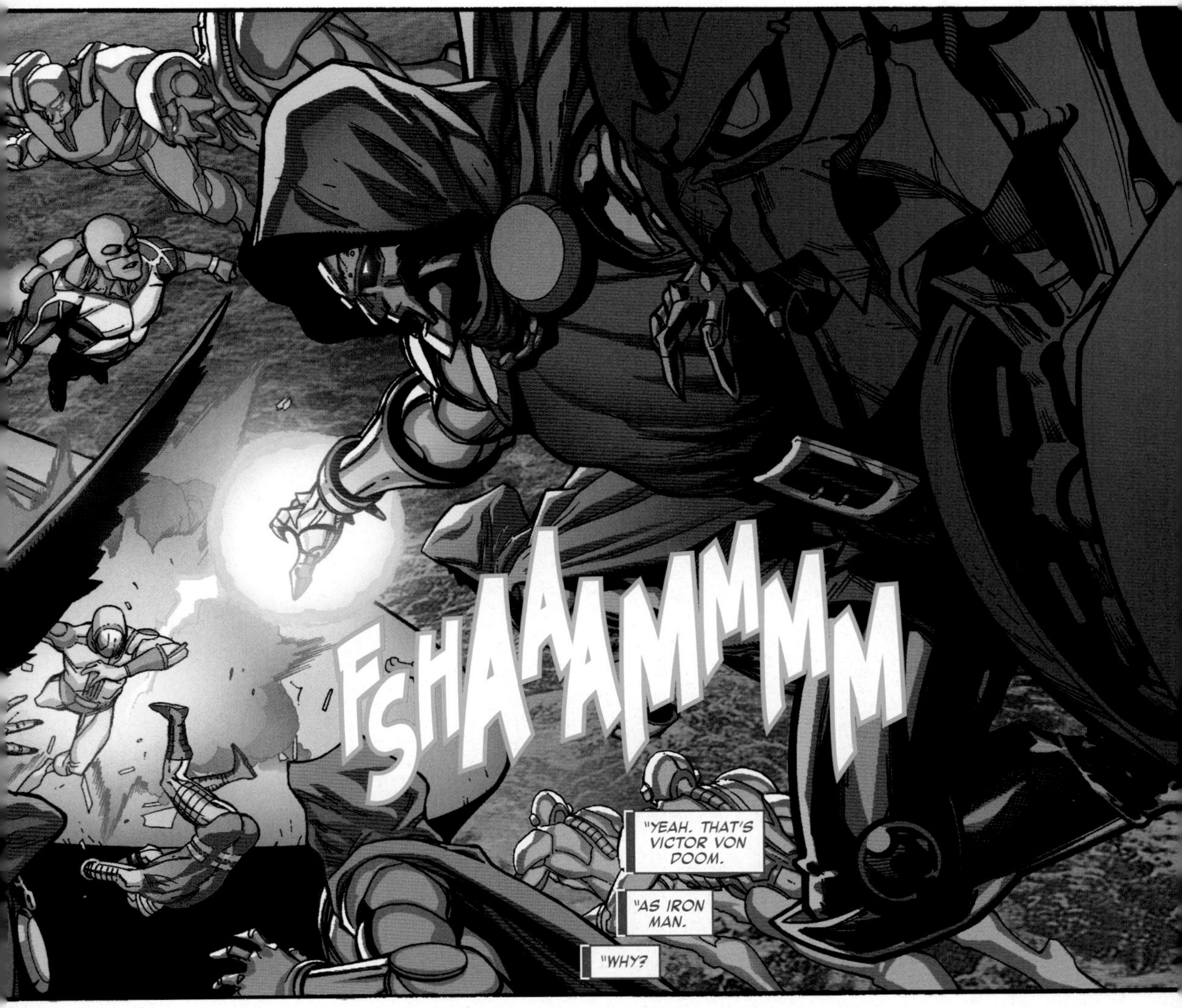
FSHAAAMMMMM
"YEAH. THAT'S VICTOR VON DOOM.
"AS IRON MAN.
"WHY?
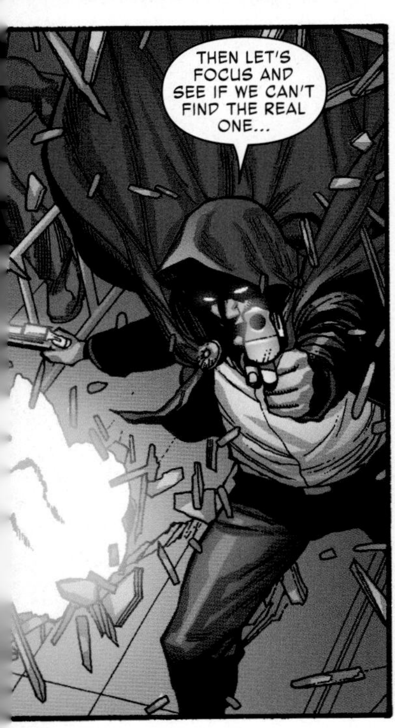
THEN LET'S FOCUS AND SEE IF WE CAN'T FIND THE REAL ONE...
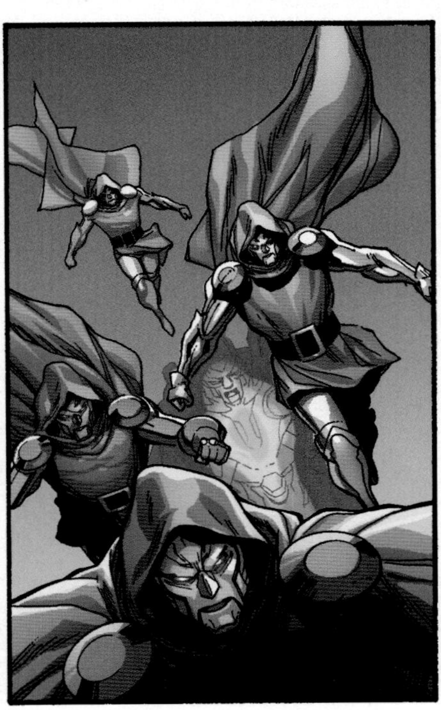
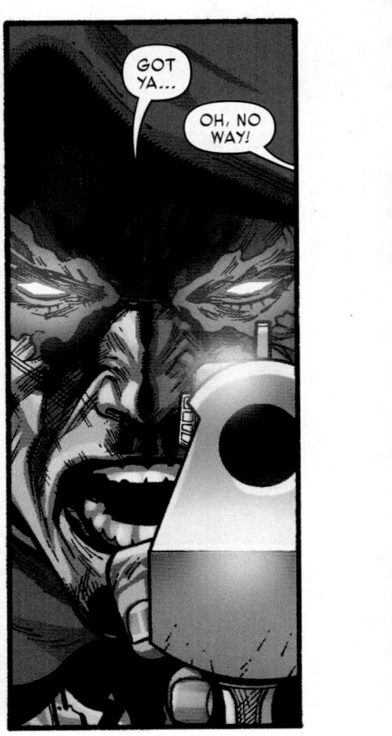
GOT YA...
OH, NO WAY!

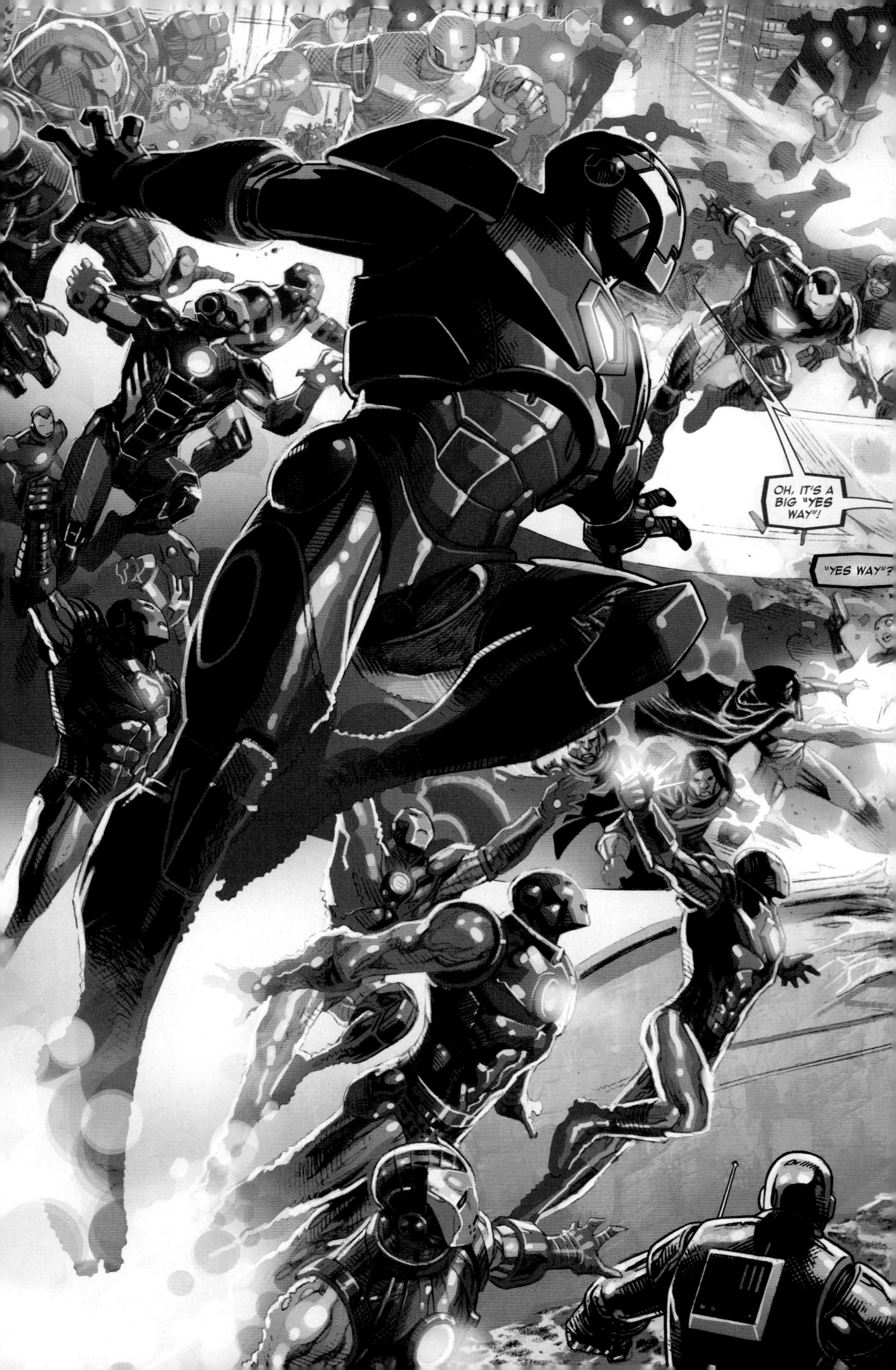
OH, IT'S A BIG "YES WAY"!
"YES WAY"?

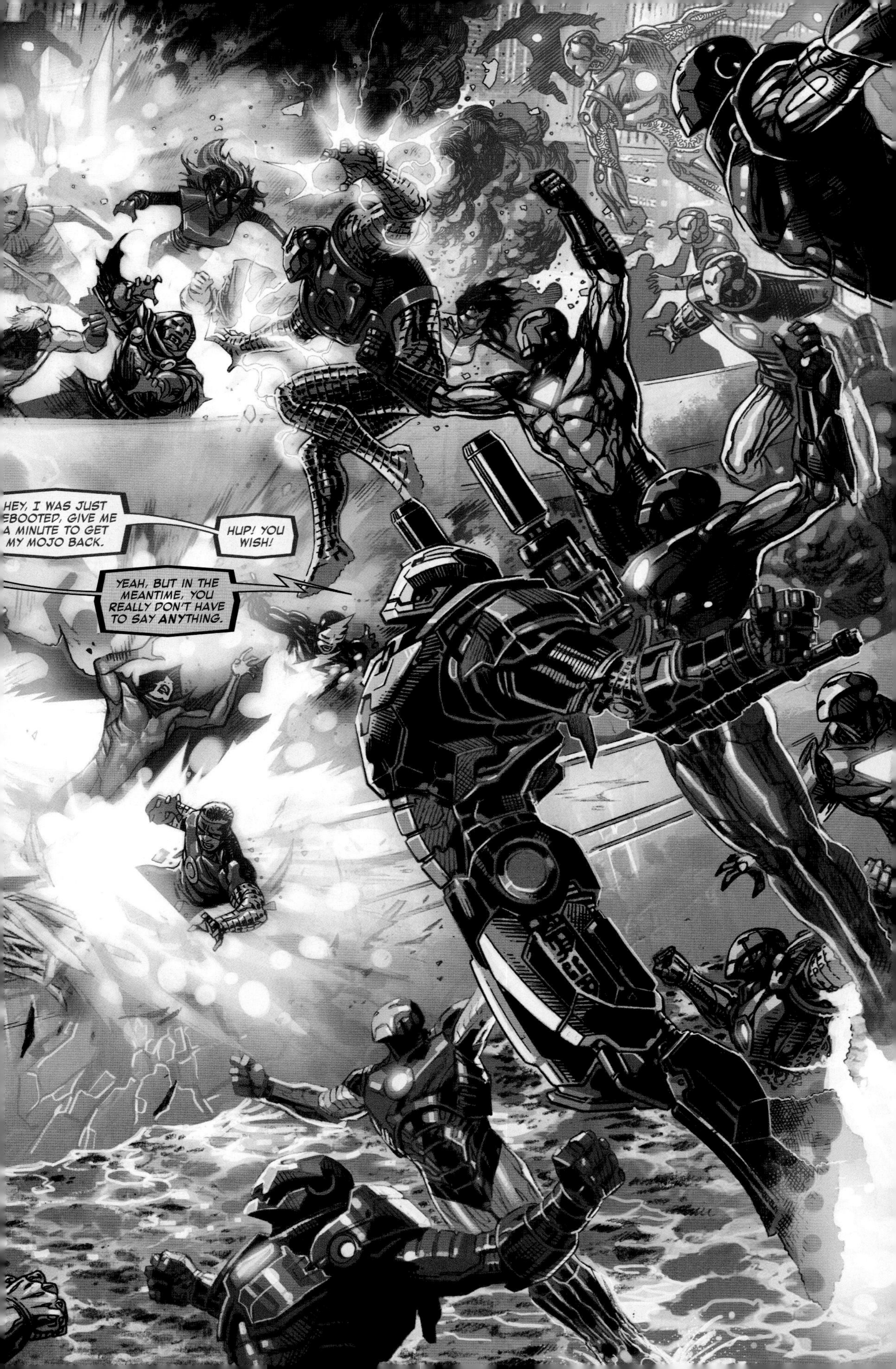
HEY, I WAS JUST EBOOTED, GIVE ME A MINUTE TO GET MY MOJO BACK.
HUP! YOU WISH!
YEAH, BUT IN THE MEANTIME, YOU REALLY DON'T HAVE TO SAY ANYTHING.

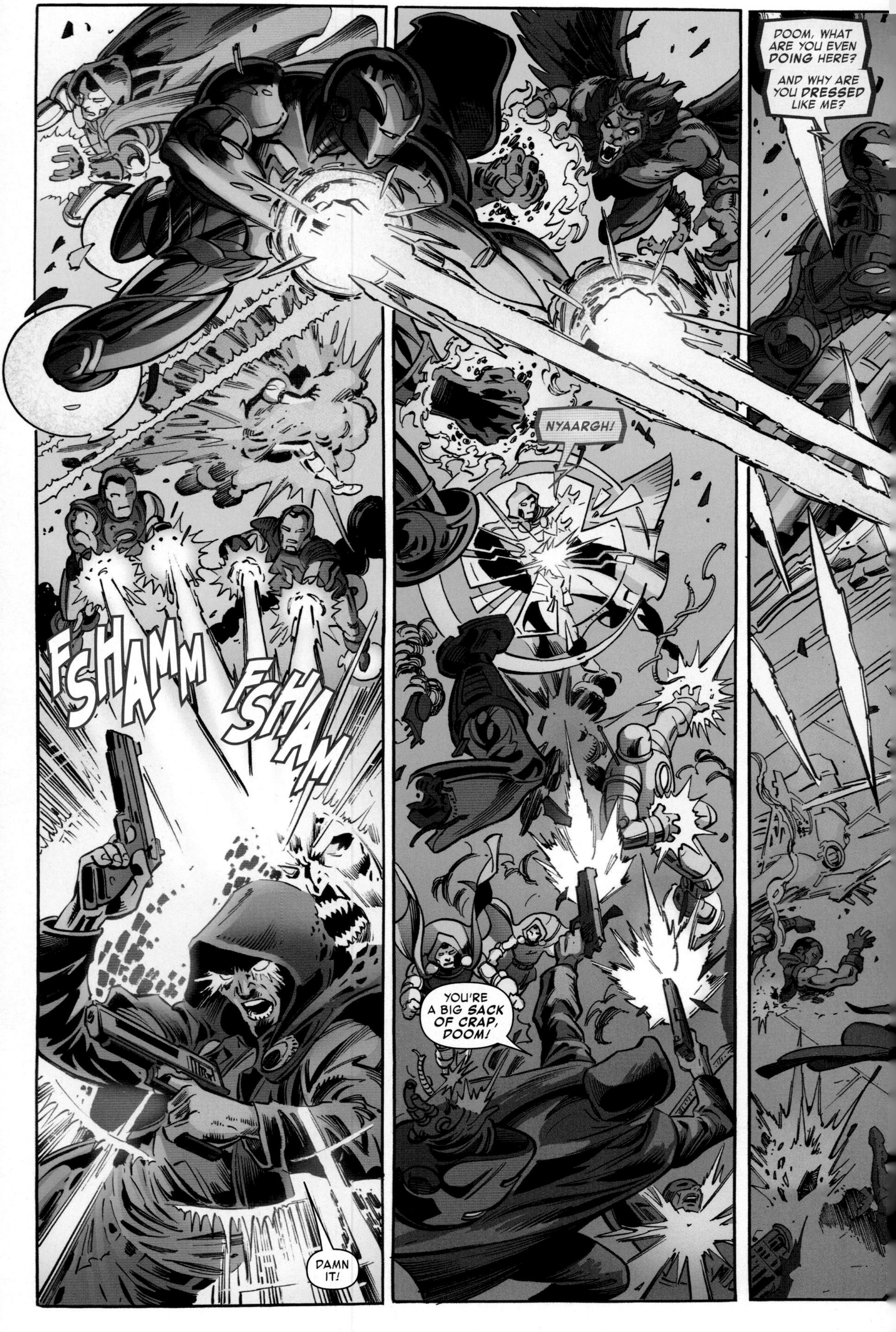

FSHAMM
FSHAMM
DAMN IT!
NYAARGH!
YOU'RE A BIG SACK OF CRAP, DOOM!
DOOM, WHAT ARE YOU EVEN DOING HERE?
AND WHY ARE YOU DRESSED LIKE ME?

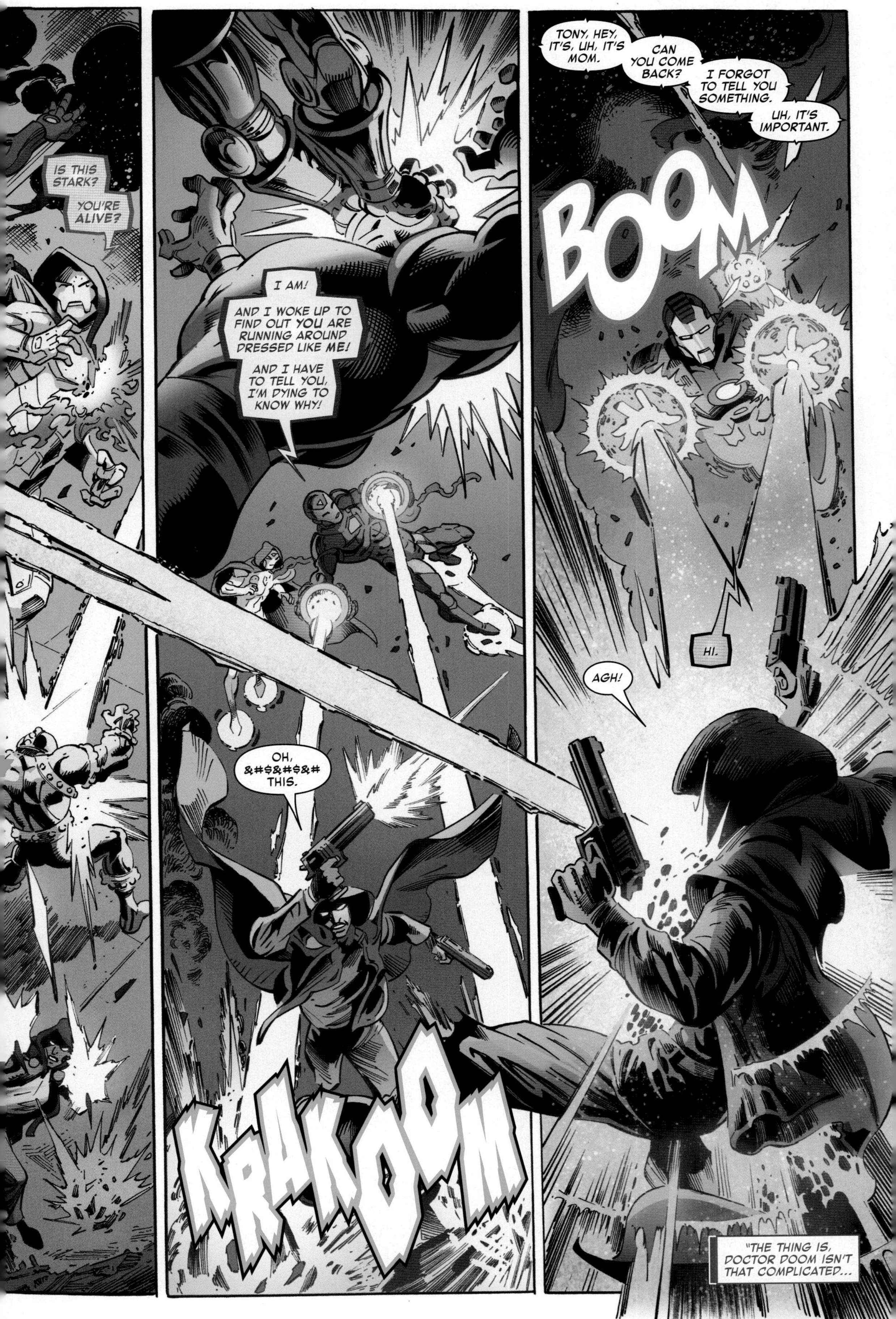
IS THIS STARK?
YOU'RE ALIVE?
I AM!
AND I WOKE UP TO FIND OUT YOU ARE RUNNING AROUND DRESSED LIKE ME!
AND I HAVE TO TELL YOU, I'M DYING TO KNOW WHY!
OH, &#$&#$&# THIS.
KRAKOOM
TONY, HEY, IT'S, UH, IT'S MOM.
CAN YOU COME BACK?
I FORGOT TO TELL YOU SOMETHING.
UH, IT'S IMPORTANT.
BOOM
HI.
AGH!
"THE THING IS, DOCTOR DOOM ISN'T THAT COMPLICATED...

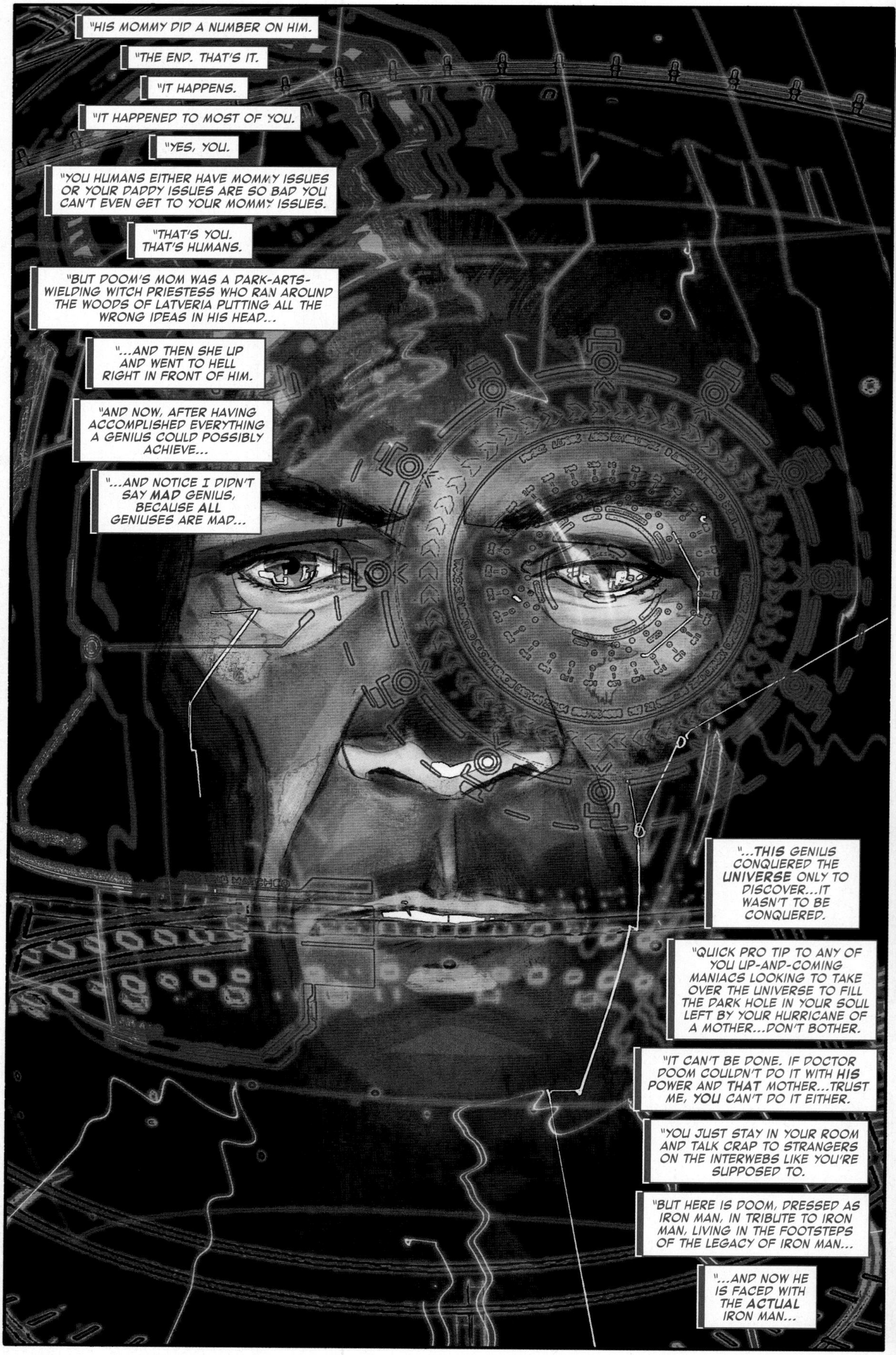
"HIS MOMMY DID A NUMBER ON HIM.
"THE END. THAT'S IT.
"IT HAPPENS.
"IT HAPPENED TO MOST OF YOU.
"YES, YOU.
"YOU HUMANS EITHER HAVE MOMMY ISSUES OR YOUR DADDY ISSUES ARE SO BAD YOU CAN'T EVEN GET TO YOUR MOMMY ISSUES.
"THAT'S YOU. THAT'S HUMANS.
"BUT DOOM'S MOM WAS A DARK-ARTS-WIELDING WITCH PRIESTESS WHO RAN AROUND THE WOODS OF LATVERIA PUTTING ALL THE WRONG IDEAS IN HIS HEAD...
"...AND THEN SHE UP AND WENT TO HELL RIGHT IN FRONT OF HIM.
"AND NOW, AFTER HAVING ACCOMPLISHED EVERYTHING A GENIUS COULD POSSIBLY ACHIEVE...
"...AND NOTICE I DIDN'T SAY **MAD** GENIUS, BECAUSE **ALL** GENIUSES ARE MAD...
"...**THIS** GENIUS CONQUERED THE **UNIVERSE** ONLY TO DISCOVER...IT WASN'T TO BE CONQUERED.
"QUICK PRO TIP TO ANY OF YOU UP-AND-COMING MANIACS LOOKING TO TAKE OVER THE UNIVERSE TO FILL THE DARK HOLE IN YOUR SOUL LEFT BY YOUR HURRICANE OF A MOTHER...DON'T BOTHER.
"IT CAN'T BE DONE. IF DOCTOR DOOM COULDN'T DO IT WITH **HIS** POWER AND **THAT** MOTHER...TRUST ME, **YOU** CAN'T DO IT EITHER.
"YOU JUST STAY IN YOUR ROOM AND TALK CRAP TO STRANGERS ON THE INTERWEBS LIKE YOU'RE SUPPOSED TO.
"BUT HERE IS DOOM, DRESSED AS IRON MAN, IN TRIBUTE TO IRON MAN, LIVING IN THE FOOTSTEPS OF THE LEGACY OF IRON MAN...
"...AND NOW HE IS FACED WITH THE **ACTUAL** IRON MAN...

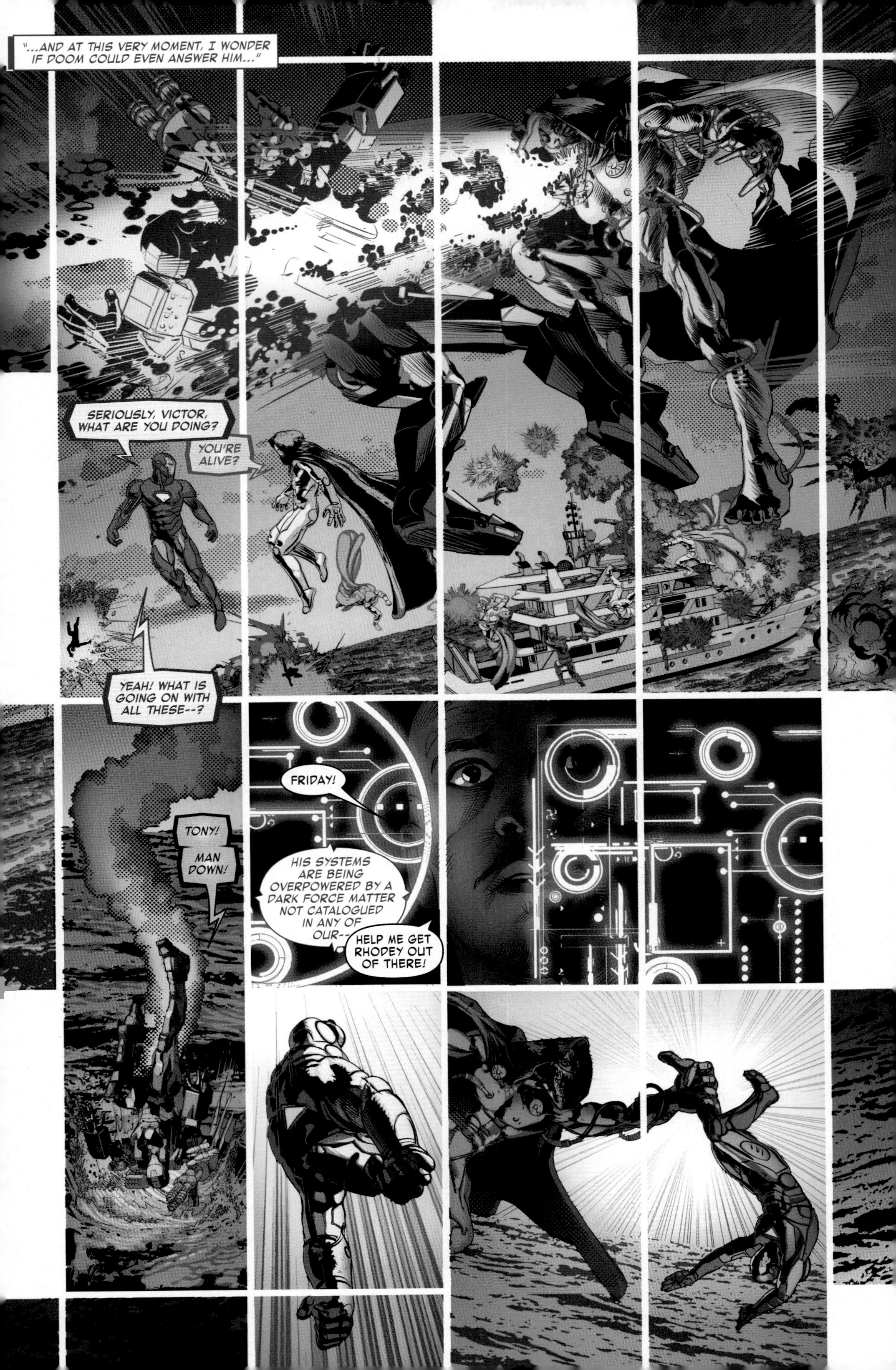
"...AND AT THIS VERY MOMENT, I WONDER IF DOOM COULD EVEN ANSWER HIM..."
SERIOUSLY, VICTOR, WHAT ARE YOU DOING?
YOU'RE ALIVE?
YEAH! WHAT IS GOING ON WITH ALL THESE--?
TONY!
MAN DOWN!
FRIDAY!
HIS SYSTEMS ARE BEING OVERPOWERED BY A DARK FORCE MATTER NOT CATALOGUED IN ANY OF OUR--
HELP ME GET RHODEY OUT OF THERE!

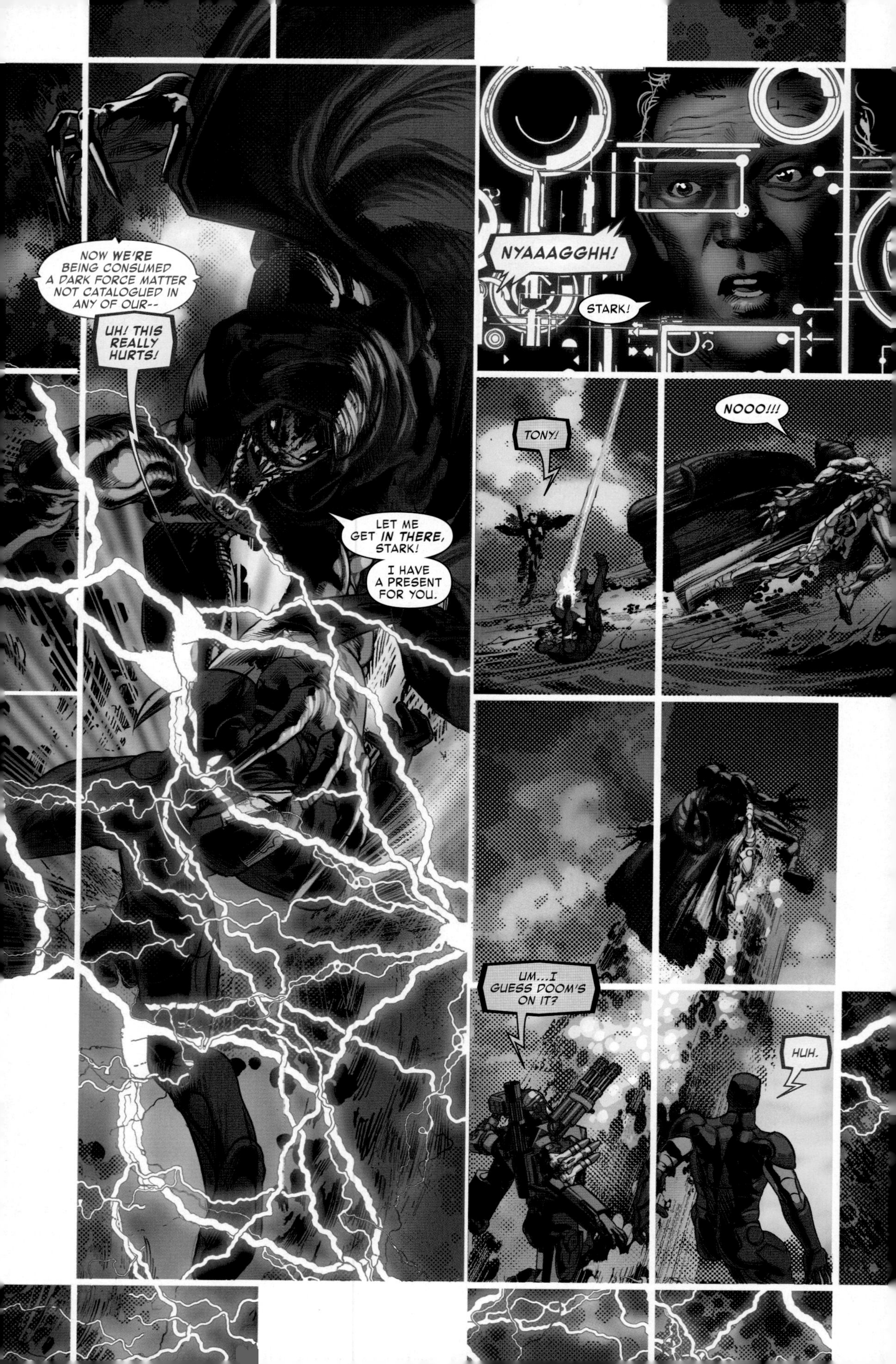
NOW WE'RE BEING CONSUMED A DARK FORCE MATTER NOT CATALOGUED IN ANY OF OUR--
UH! THIS REALLY HURTS!
LET ME GET IN THERE, STARK!
I HAVE A PRESENT FOR YOU.
NYAAAGGHH!
STARK!
TONY!
NOOO!!!
UM...I GUESS DOOM'S ON IT?
HUH.

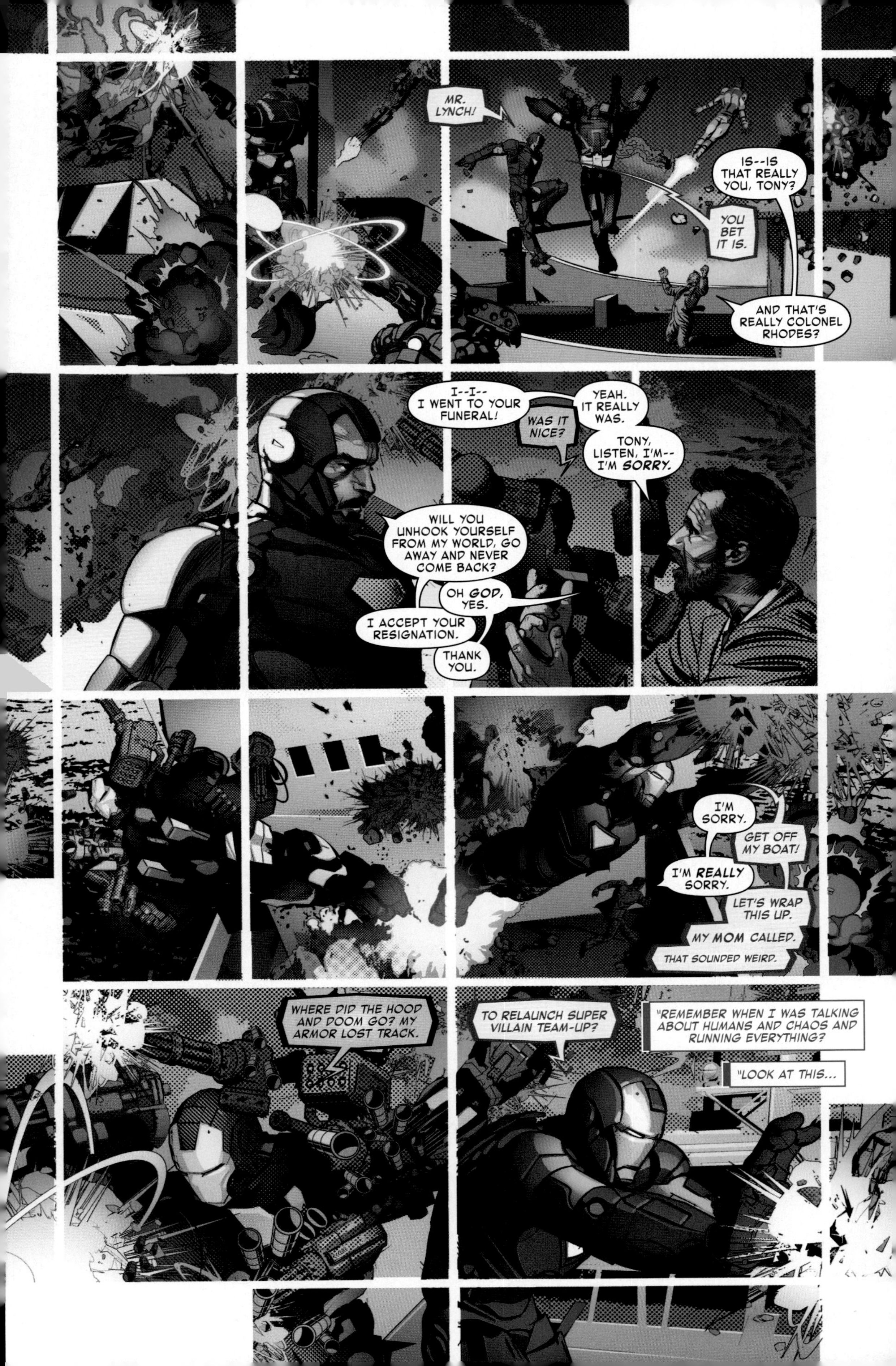

MR. LYNCH!
IS--IS THAT REALLY YOU, TONY?
YOU BET IT IS.
AND THAT'S REALLY COLONEL RHODES?
I--I-- I WENT TO YOUR FUNERAL!
WAS IT NICE?
YEAH. IT REALLY WAS.
TONY, LISTEN, I'M-- I'M SORRY.
WILL YOU UNHOOK YOURSELF FROM MY WORLD, GO AWAY AND NEVER COME BACK?
OH GOD, YES.
I ACCEPT YOUR RESIGNATION.
THANK YOU.
I'M SORRY.
GET OFF MY BOAT!
I'M REALLY SORRY.
LET'S WRAP THIS UP.
MY MOM CALLED.
THAT SOUNDED WEIRD.
WHERE DID THE HOOD AND DOOM GO? MY ARMOR LOST TRACK.
TO RELAUNCH SUPER VILLAIN TEAM-UP?
"REMEMBER WHEN I WAS TALKING ABOUT HUMANS AND CHAOS AND RUNNING EVERYTHING?
"LOOK AT THIS...

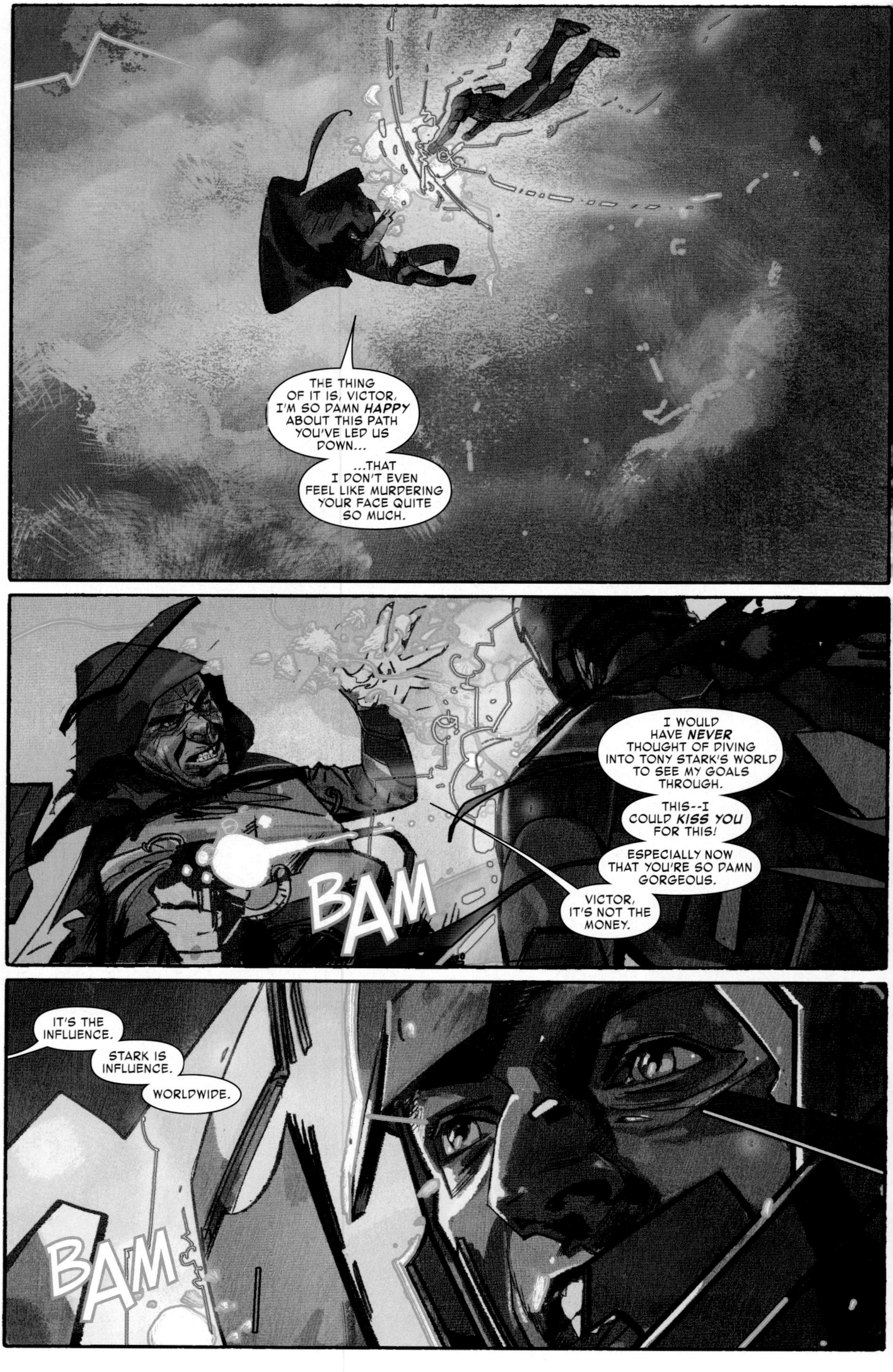

THE THING OF IT IS, VICTOR, I'M SO DAMN HAPPY ABOUT THIS PATH YOU'VE LED US DOWN...
...THAT I DON'T EVEN FEEL LIKE MURDERING YOUR FACE QUITE SO MUCH.
I WOULD HAVE NEVER THOUGHT OF DIVING INTO TONY STARK'S WORLD TO SEE MY GOALS THROUGH.
THIS--I COULD KISS YOU FOR THIS!
ESPECIALLY NOW THAT YOU'RE SO DAMN GORGEOUS.
BAM
VICTOR, IT'S NOT THE MONEY.
IT'S THE INFLUENCE.
STARK IS INFLUENCE.
WORLDWIDE.
BAM

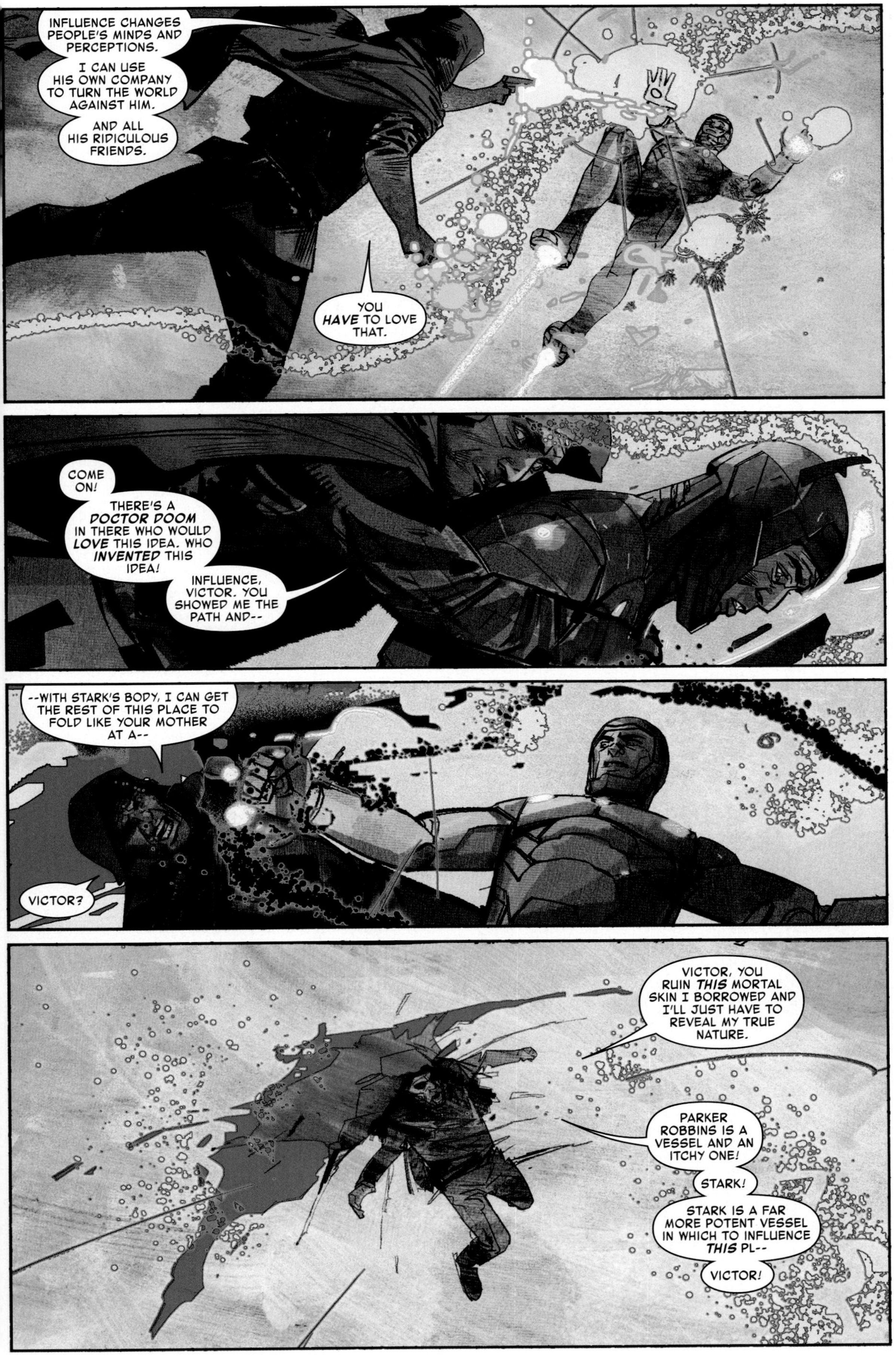
INFLUENCE CHANGES PEOPLE'S MINDS AND PERCEPTIONS.
I CAN USE HIS OWN COMPANY TO TURN THE WORLD AGAINST HIM.
AND ALL HIS RIDICULOUS FRIENDS.
YOU HAVE TO LOVE THAT.
COME ON!
THERE'S A DOCTOR DOOM IN THERE WHO WOULD LOVE THIS IDEA. WHO INVENTED THIS IDEA!
INFLUENCE, VICTOR. YOU SHOWED ME THE PATH AND--
--WITH STARK'S BODY, I CAN GET THE REST OF THIS PLACE TO FOLD LIKE YOUR MOTHER AT A--
VICTOR?
VICTOR, YOU RUIN THIS MORTAL SKIN I BORROWED AND I'LL JUST HAVE TO REVEAL MY TRUE NATURE.
PARKER ROBBINS IS A VESSEL AND AN ITCHY ONE!
STARK!
STARK IS A FAR MORE POTENT VESSEL IN WHICH TO INFLUENCE THIS PL--
VICTOR!

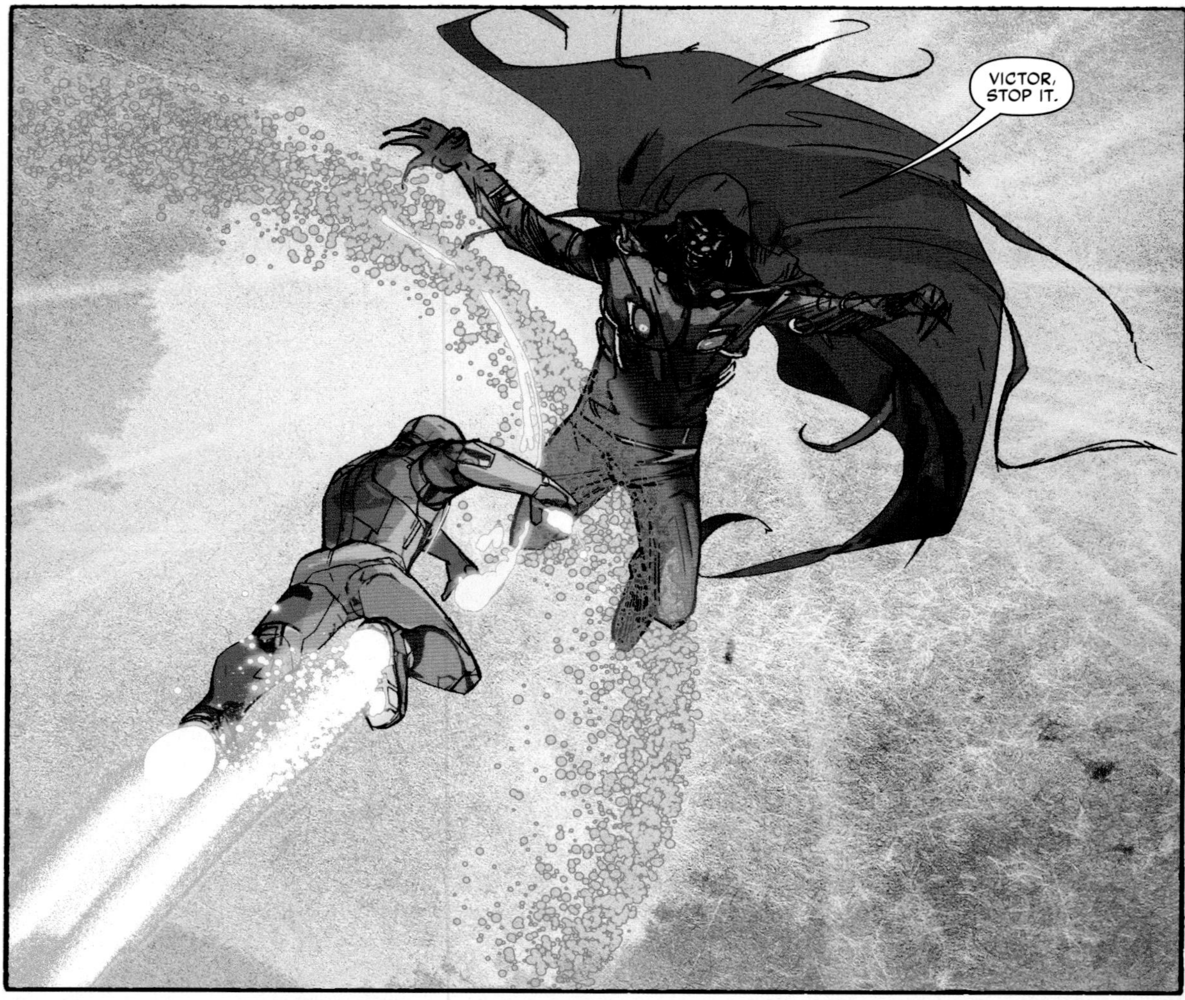
VICTOR, STOP IT.

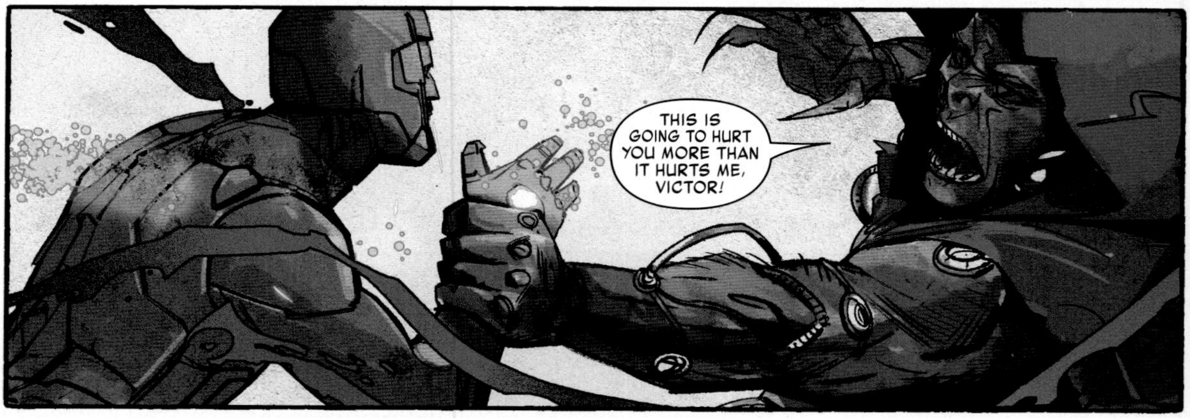
THIS IS GOING TO HURT YOU MORE THAN IT HURTS ME, VICTOR!

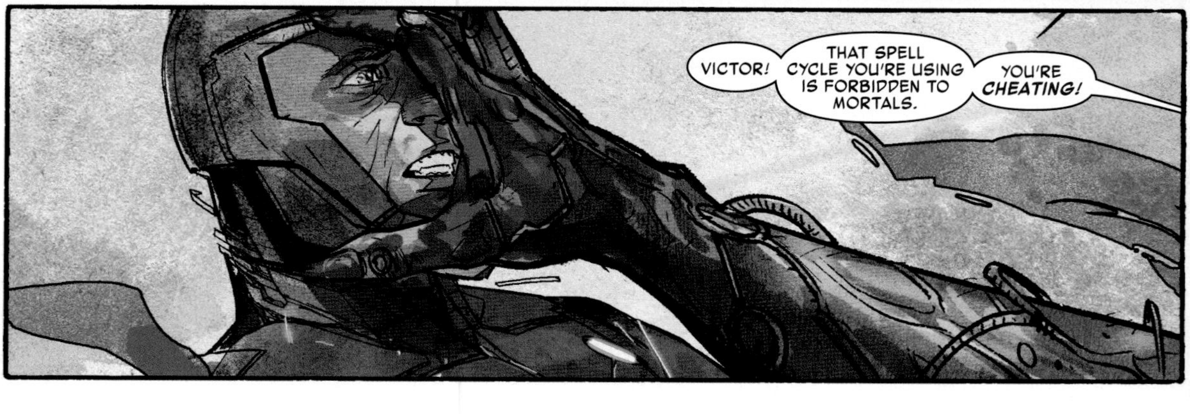
VICTOR!
THAT SPELL CYCLE YOU'RE USING IS FORBIDDEN TO MORTALS.
YOU'RE *CHEATING!*

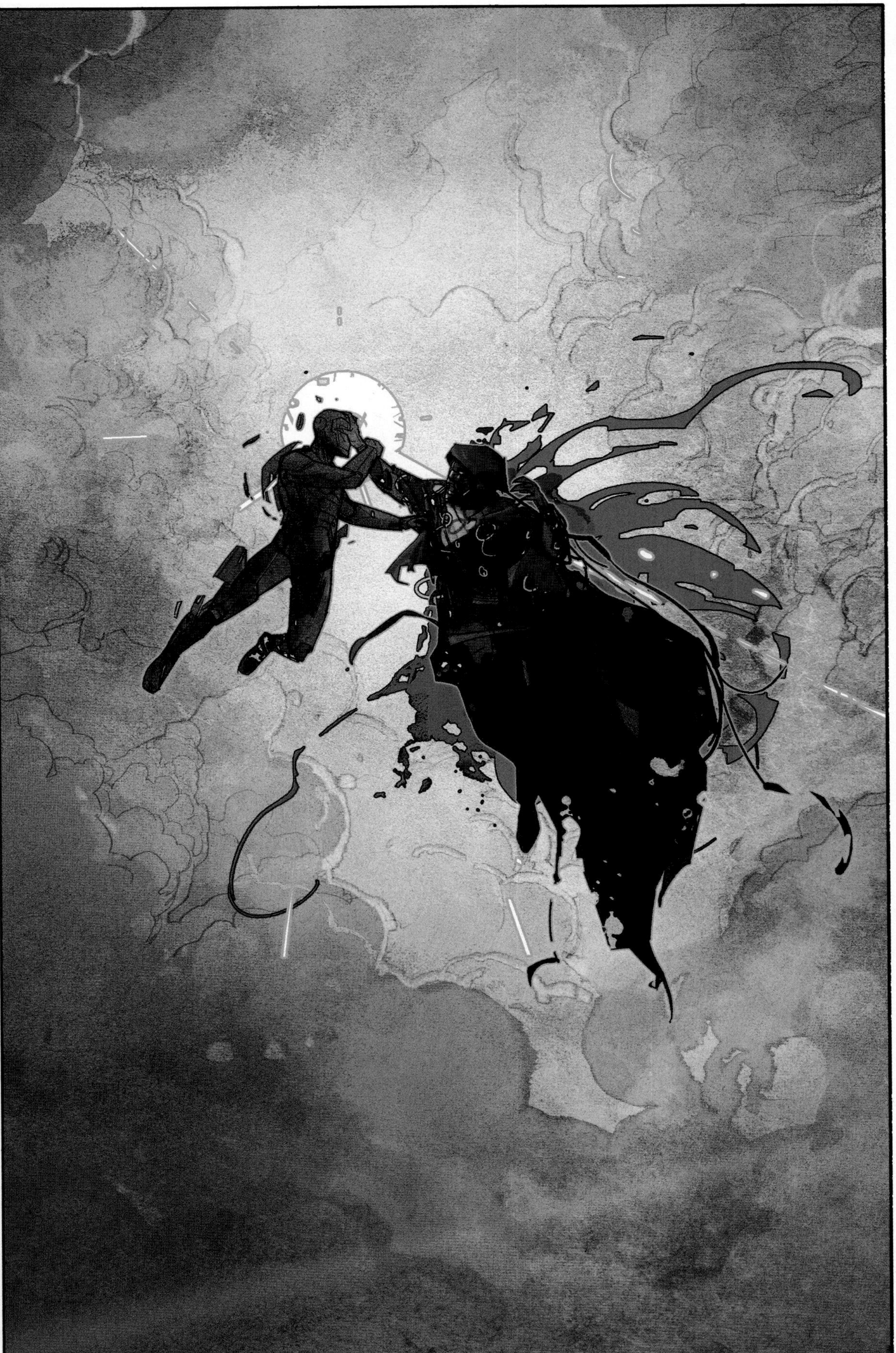

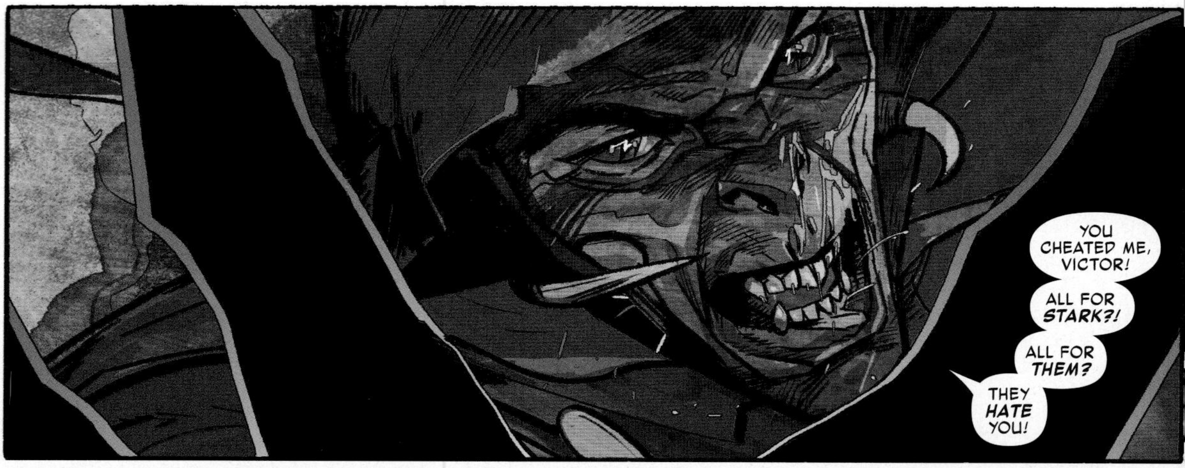
YOU CHEATED ME, VICTOR!
ALL FOR STARK?!
ALL FOR THEM?
THEY HATE YOU!

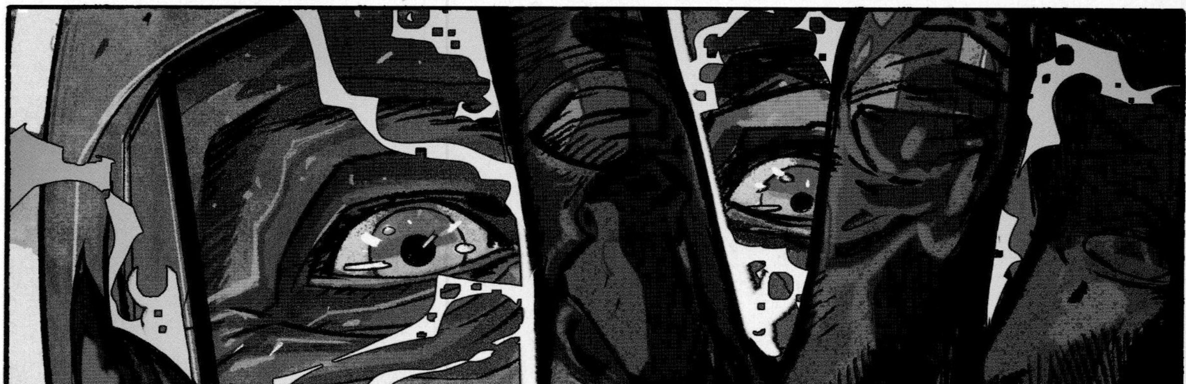

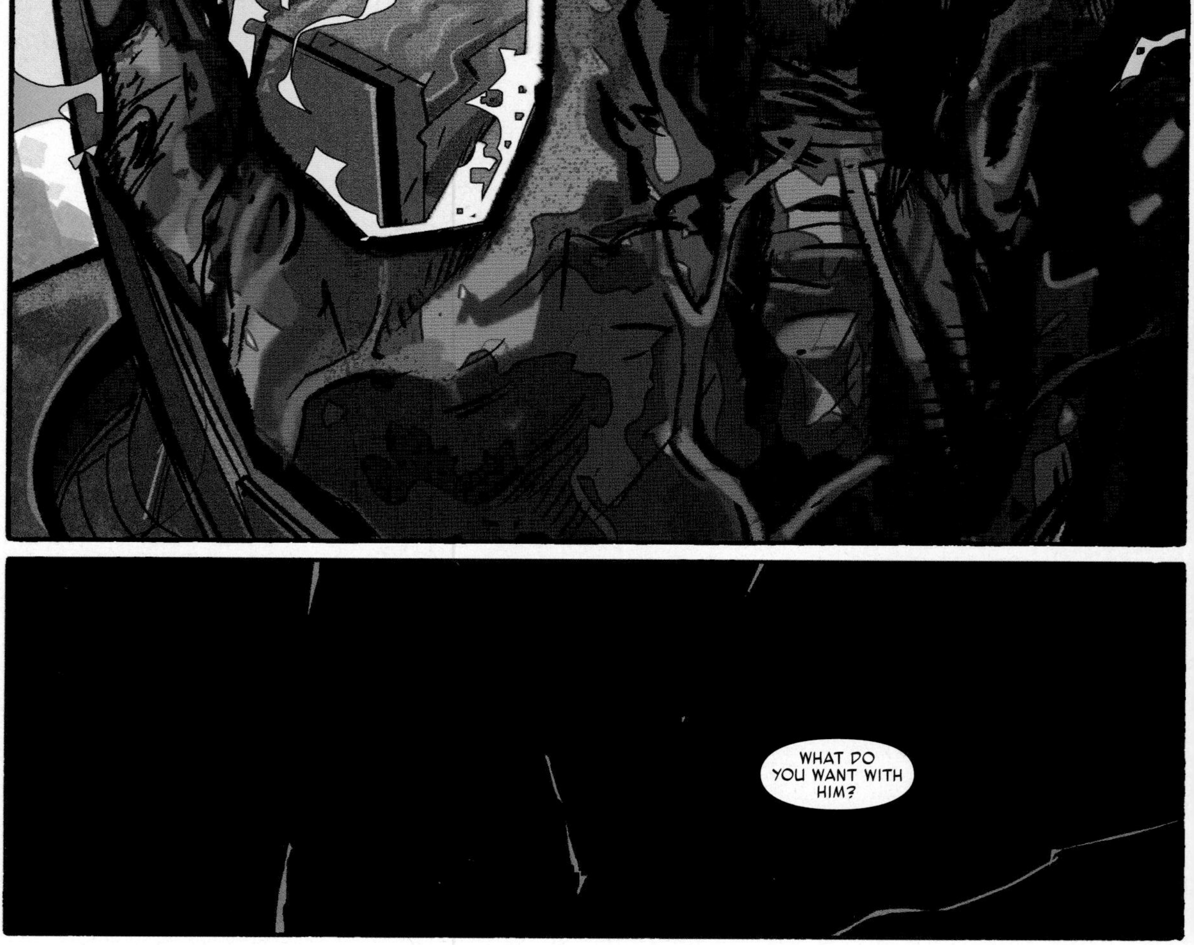
WHAT DO YOU WANT WITH HIM?

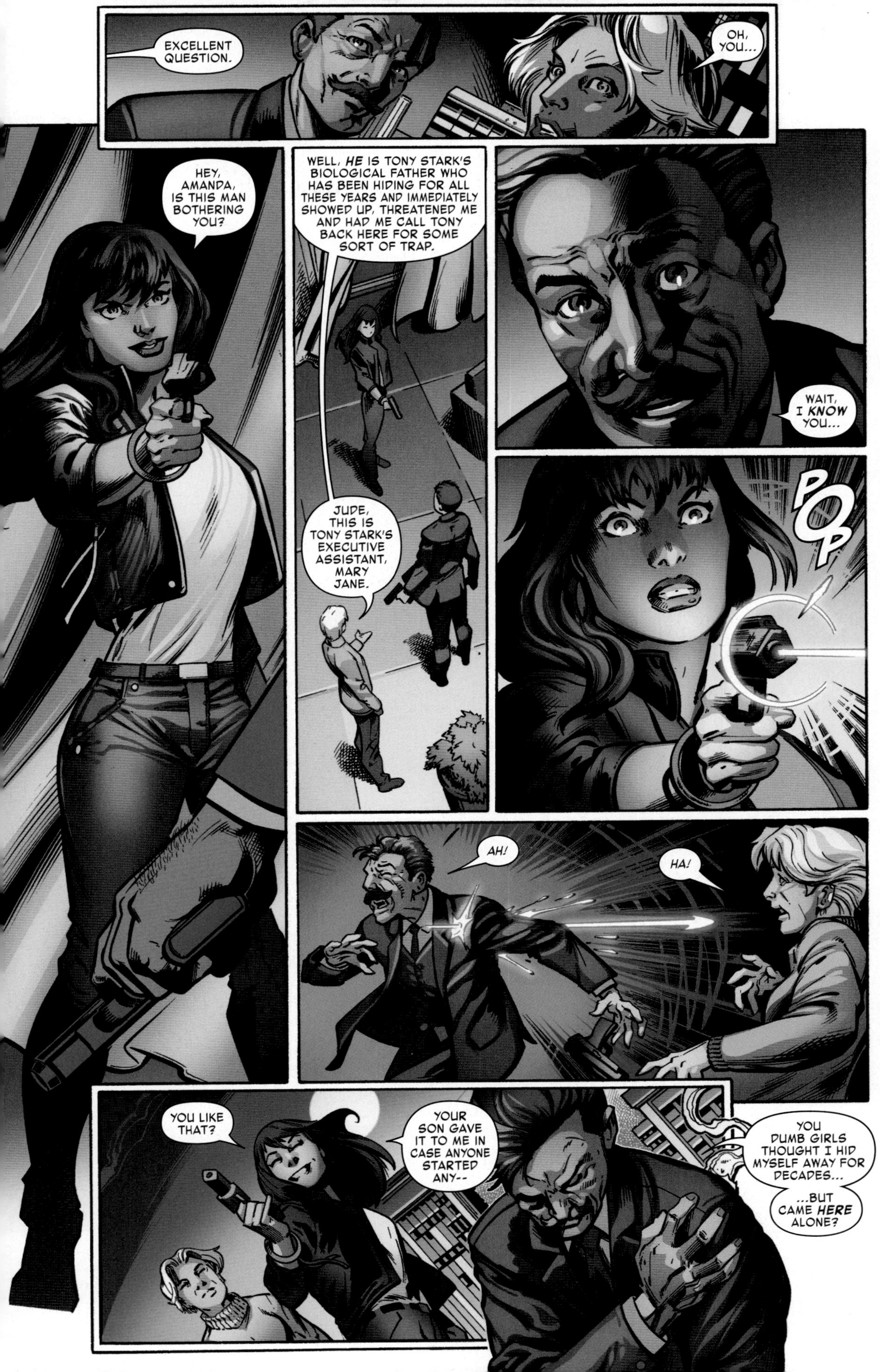
EXCELLENT QUESTION.
OH, YOU...
HEY, AMANDA, IS THIS MAN BOTHERING YOU?
WELL, HE IS TONY STARK'S BIOLOGICAL FATHER WHO HAS BEEN HIDING FOR ALL THESE YEARS AND IMMEDIATELY SHOWED UP, THREATENED ME AND HAD ME CALL TONY BACK HERE FOR SOME SORT OF TRAP.
JUDE, THIS IS TONY STARK'S EXECUTIVE ASSISTANT, MARY JANE.
WAIT, I KNOW YOU...
POP
AH!
HA!
YOU LIKE THAT?
YOUR SON GAVE IT TO ME IN CASE ANYONE STARTED ANY--
YOU DUMB GIRLS THOUGHT I HID MYSELF AWAY FOR DECADES...
...BUT CAME HERE ALONE?

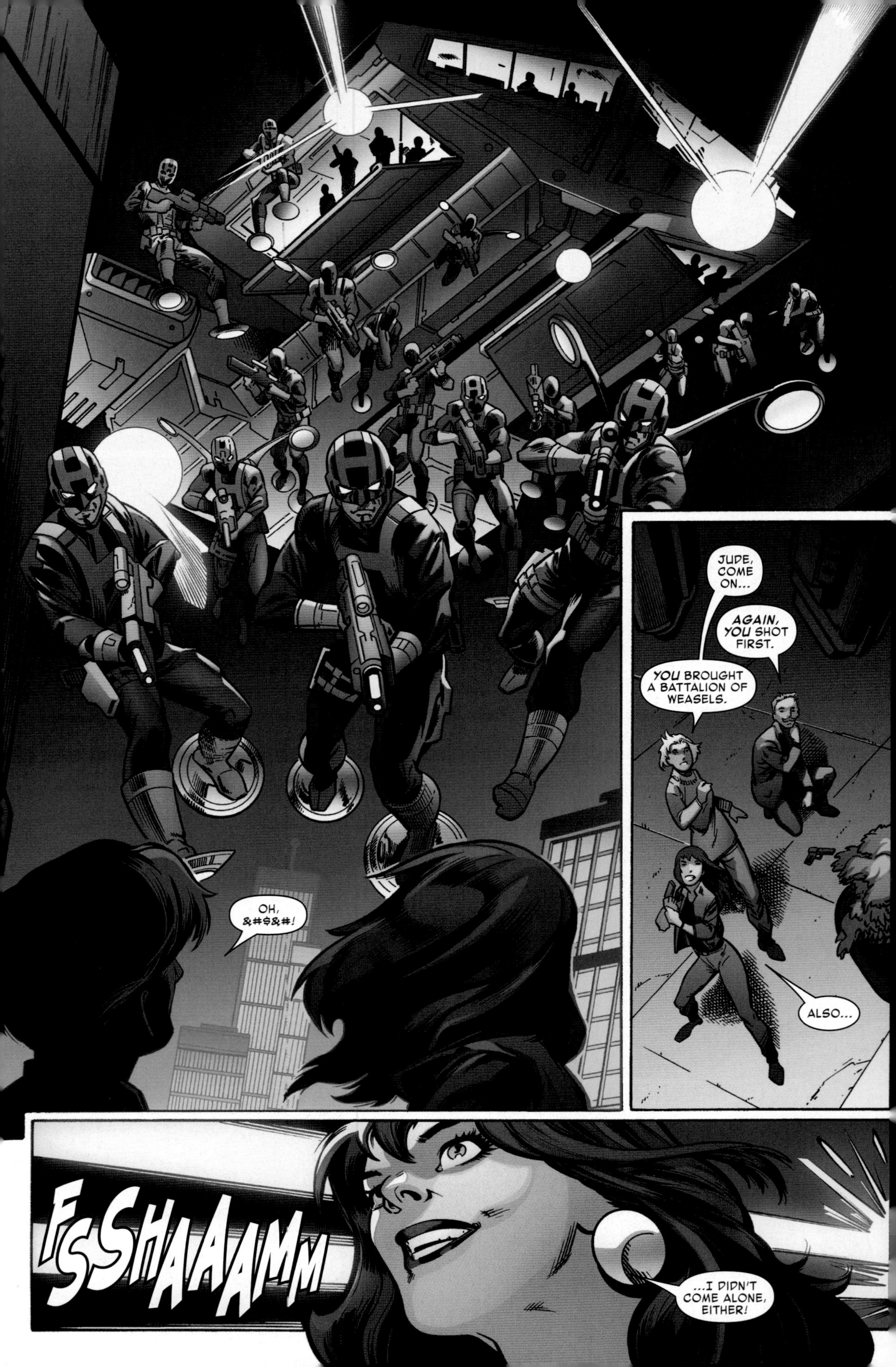
OH, &#$&#!
JUDE, COME ON...
AGAIN, YOU SHOT FIRST.
YOU BROUGHT A BATTALION OF WEASELS.
ALSO...
FSSHAAAMM
...I DIDN'T COME ALONE, EITHER!

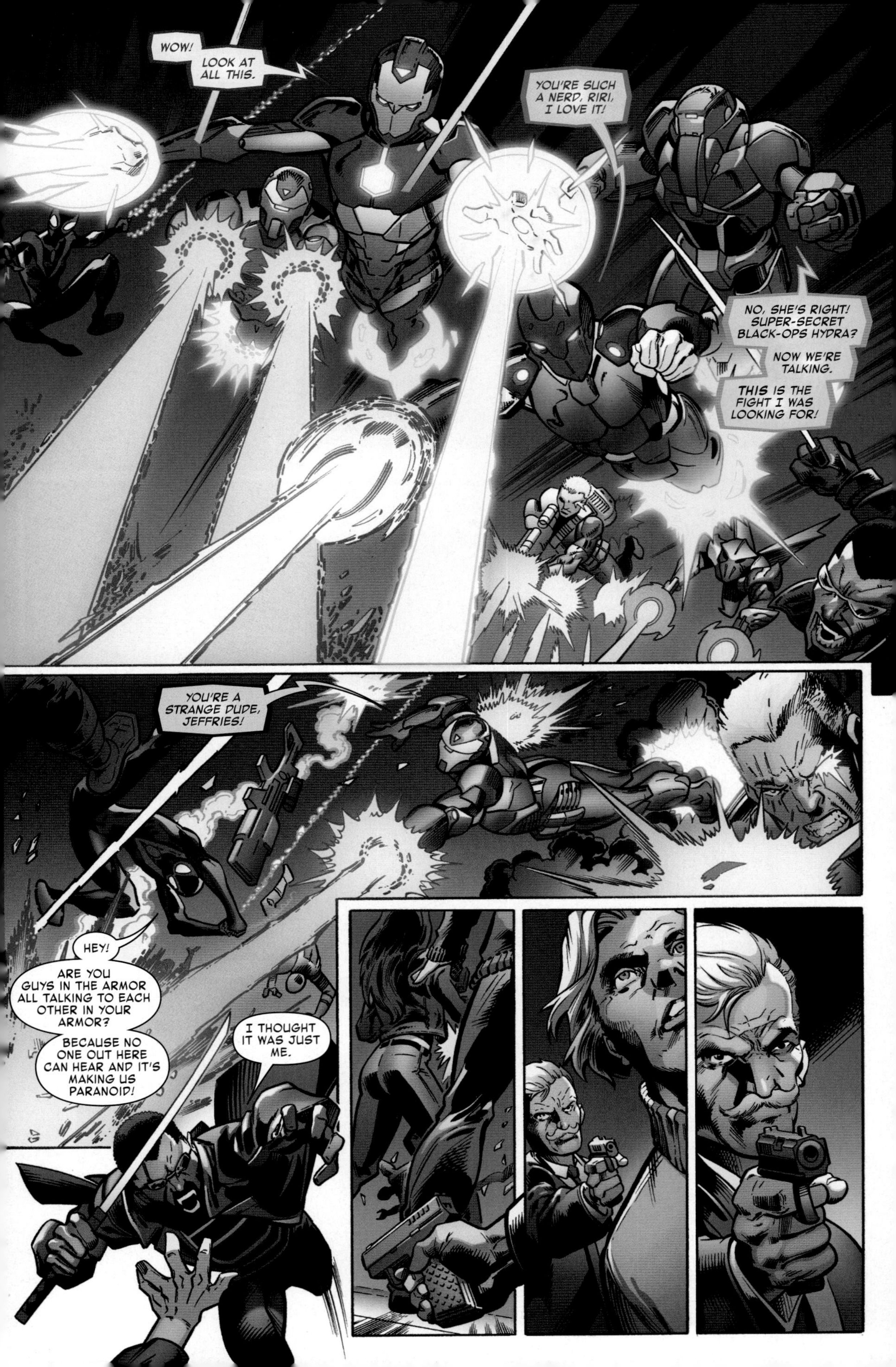
WOW!
LOOK AT ALL THIS.
YOU'RE SUCH A NERD, RIRI, I LOVE IT!
NO, SHE'S RIGHT! SUPER-SECRET BLACK-OPS HYDRA?
NOW WE'RE TALKING.
THIS IS THE FIGHT I WAS LOOKING FOR!
YOU'RE A STRANGE DUDE, JEFFRIES!
HEY!
ARE YOU GUYS IN THE ARMOR ALL TALKING TO EACH OTHER IN YOUR ARMOR?
BECAUSE NO ONE OUT HERE CAN HEAR AND IT'S MAKING US PARANOID!
I THOUGHT IT WAS JUST ME.

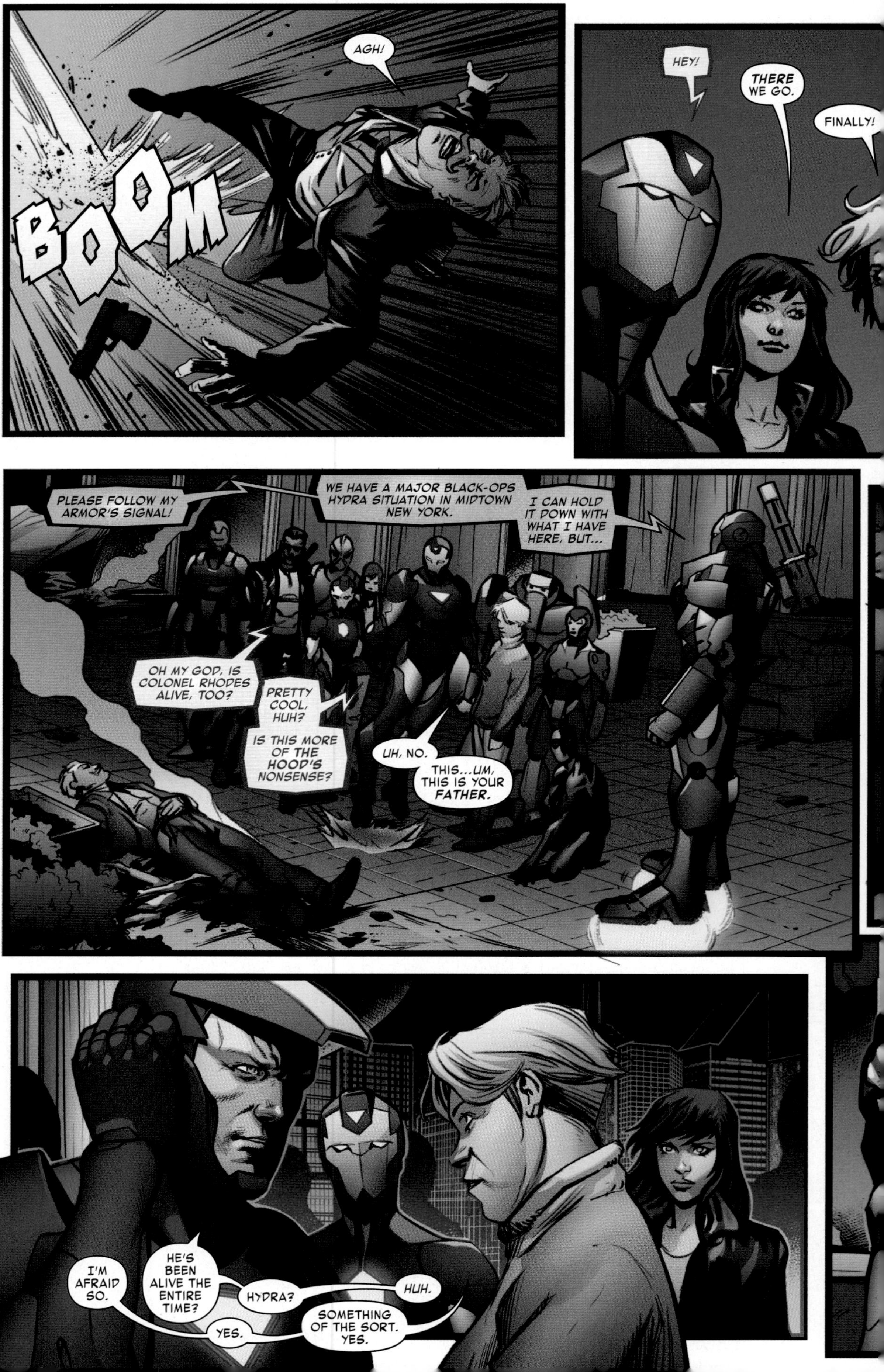
AGH!
BOOM
HEY!
THERE WE GO.
FINALLY!
PLEASE FOLLOW MY ARMOR'S SIGNAL!
WE HAVE A MAJOR BLACK-OPS HYDRA SITUATION IN MIDTOWN NEW YORK.
I CAN HOLD IT DOWN WITH WHAT I HAVE HERE, BUT...
OH MY GOD, IS COLONEL RHODES ALIVE, TOO?
PRETTY COOL, HUH?
IS THIS MORE OF THE HOOD'S NONSENSE?
UH, NO.
THIS...UM, THIS IS YOUR FATHER.
I'M AFRAID SO.
HE'S BEEN ALIVE THE ENTIRE TIME?
YES.
HYDRA?
SOMETHING OF THE SORT. YES.
HUH.

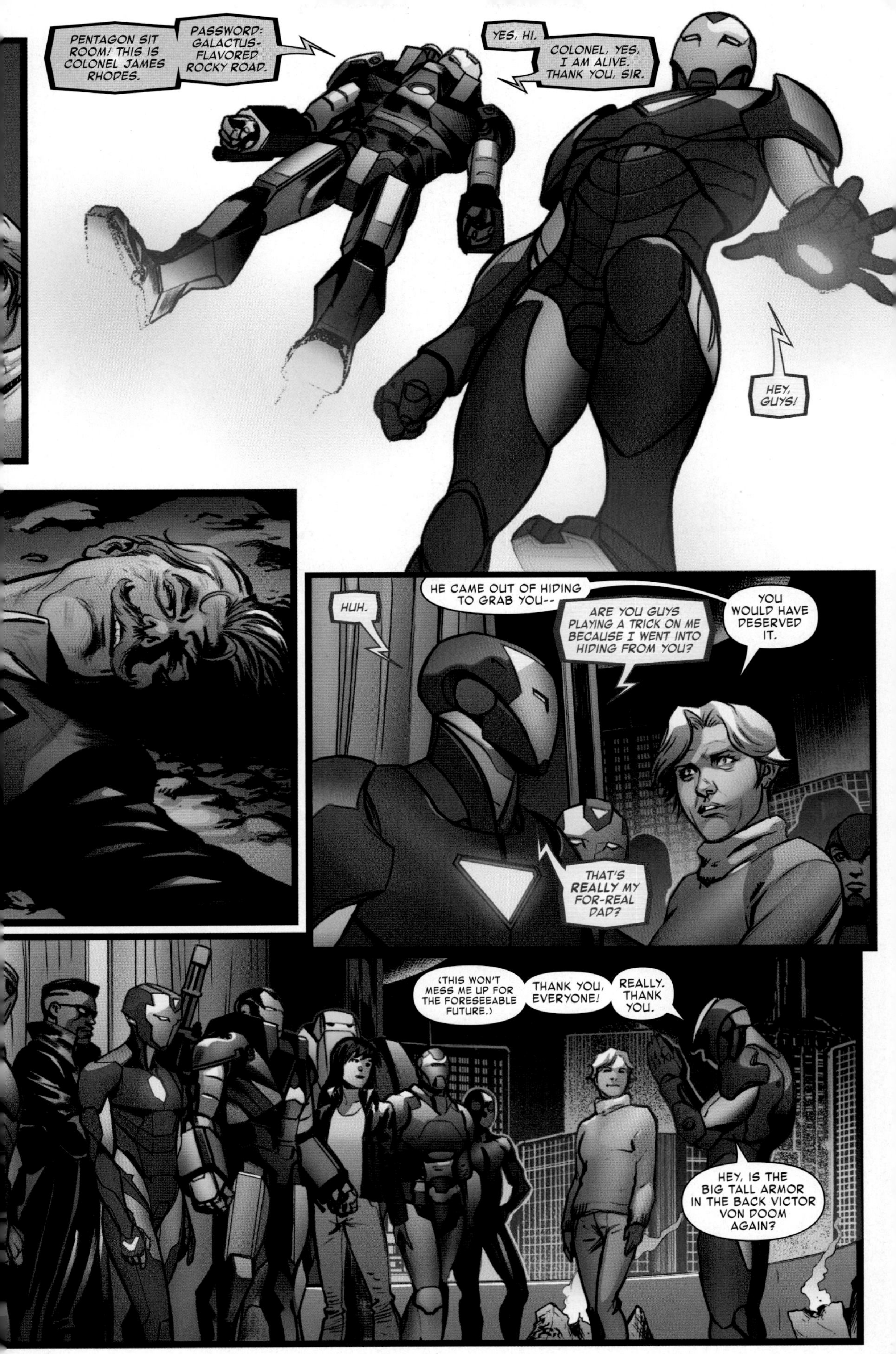
PENTAGON SIT ROOM! THIS IS COLONEL JAMES RHODES.
PASSWORD: GALACTUS-FLAVORED ROCKY ROAD.
YES, HI.
COLONEL, YES, I AM ALIVE. THANK YOU, SIR.
HEY, GUYS!
HUH.
HE CAME OUT OF HIDING TO GRAB YOU--
YOU WOULD HAVE DESERVED IT.
ARE YOU GUYS PLAYING A TRICK ON ME BECAUSE I WENT INTO HIDING FROM YOU?
THAT'S REALLY MY FOR-REAL DAD?
(THIS WON'T MESS ME UP FOR THE FORESEEABLE FUTURE.)
THANK YOU, EVERYONE!
REALLY. THANK YOU.
HEY, IS THE BIG TALL ARMOR IN THE BACK VICTOR VON DOOM AGAIN?

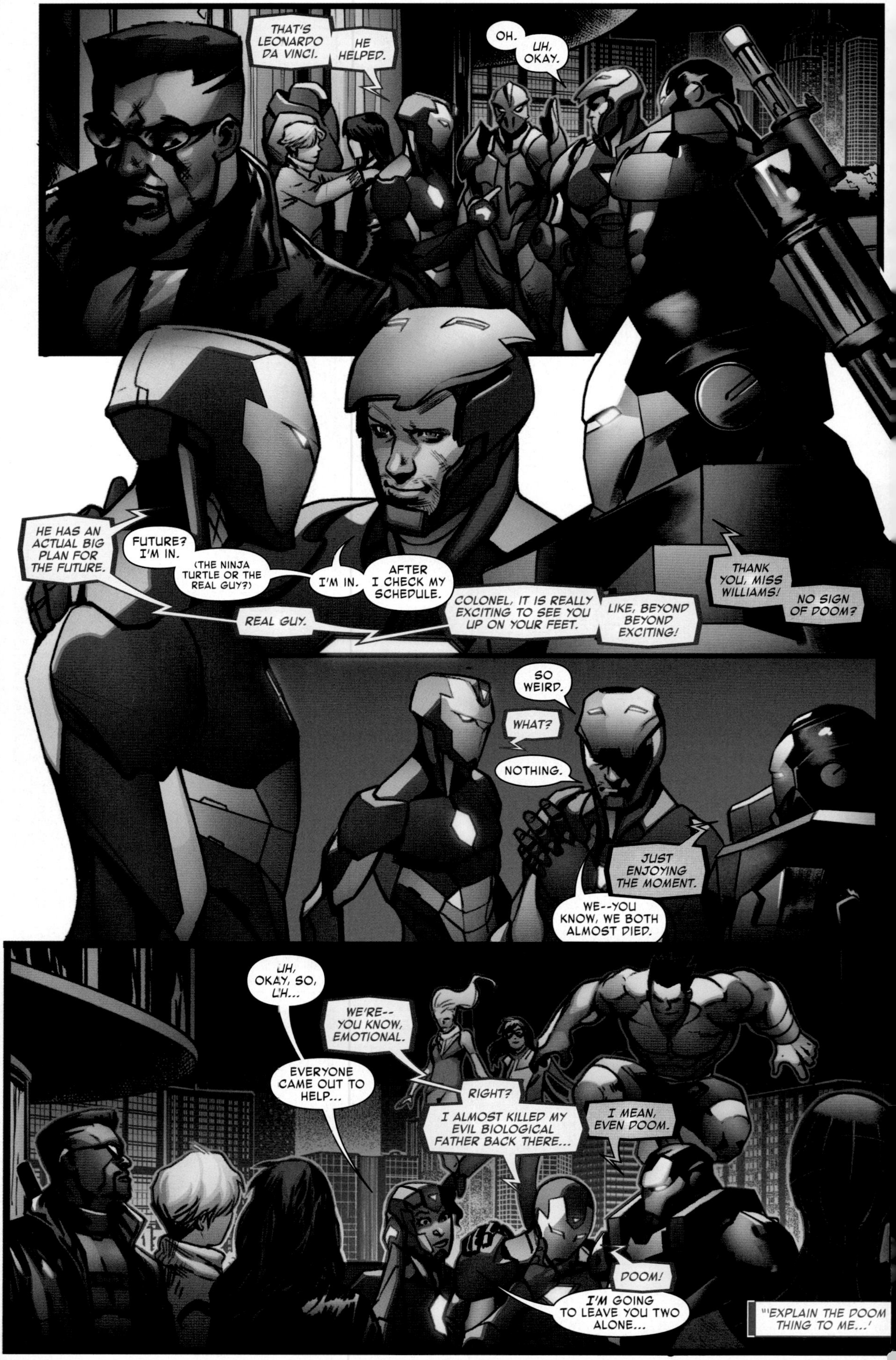
THAT'S LEONARDO DA VINCI.
HE HELPED.
OH.
UH, OKAY.
HE HAS AN ACTUAL BIG PLAN FOR THE FUTURE.
FUTURE? I'M IN.
(THE NINJA TURTLE OR THE REAL GUY?)
REAL GUY.
I'M IN.
AFTER I CHECK MY SCHEDULE.
COLONEL, IT IS REALLY EXCITING TO SEE YOU UP ON YOUR FEET.
LIKE, BEYOND BEYOND EXCITING!
THANK YOU, MISS WILLIAMS!
NO SIGN OF DOOM?
SO WEIRD.
WHAT?
NOTHING.
JUST ENJOYING THE MOMENT.
WE--YOU KNOW, WE BOTH ALMOST DIED.
UH, OKAY, SO, UH...
WE'RE--YOU KNOW, EMOTIONAL.
EVERYONE CAME OUT TO HELP...
RIGHT?
I ALMOST KILLED MY EVIL BIOLOGICAL FATHER BACK THERE...
I MEAN, EVEN DOOM.
DOOM!
I'M GOING TO LEAVE YOU TWO ALONE...
"EXPLAIN THE DOOM THING TO ME...'

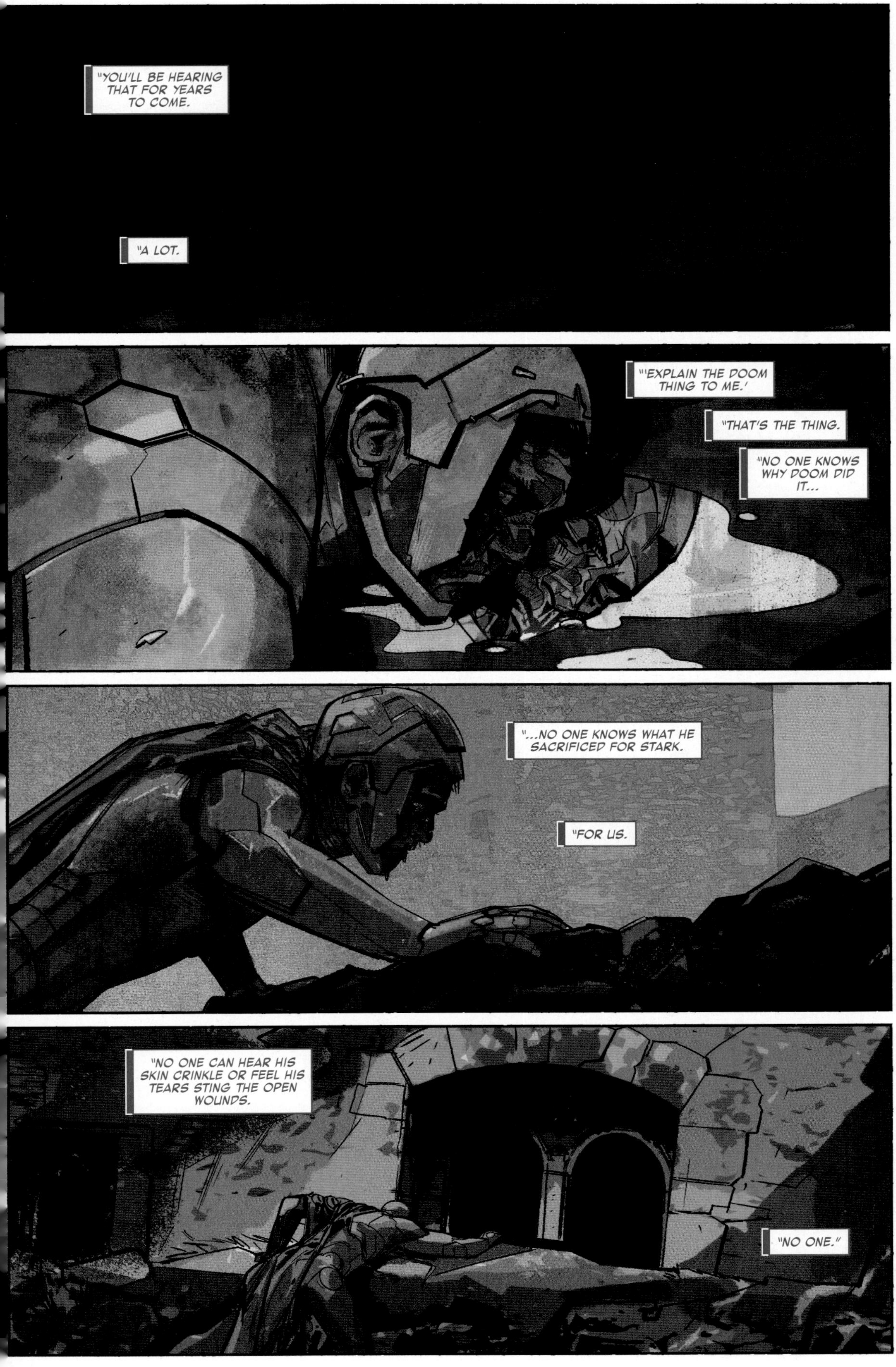
"YOU'LL BE HEARING THAT FOR YEARS TO COME.
"A LOT.
"'EXPLAIN THE DOOM THING TO ME.'
"THAT'S THE THING.
"NO ONE KNOWS WHY DOOM DID IT...
"...NO ONE KNOWS WHAT HE SACRIFICED FOR STARK.
"FOR US.
"NO ONE CAN HEAR HIS SKIN CRINKLE OR FEEL HIS TEARS STING THE OPEN WOUNDS.
"NO ONE."

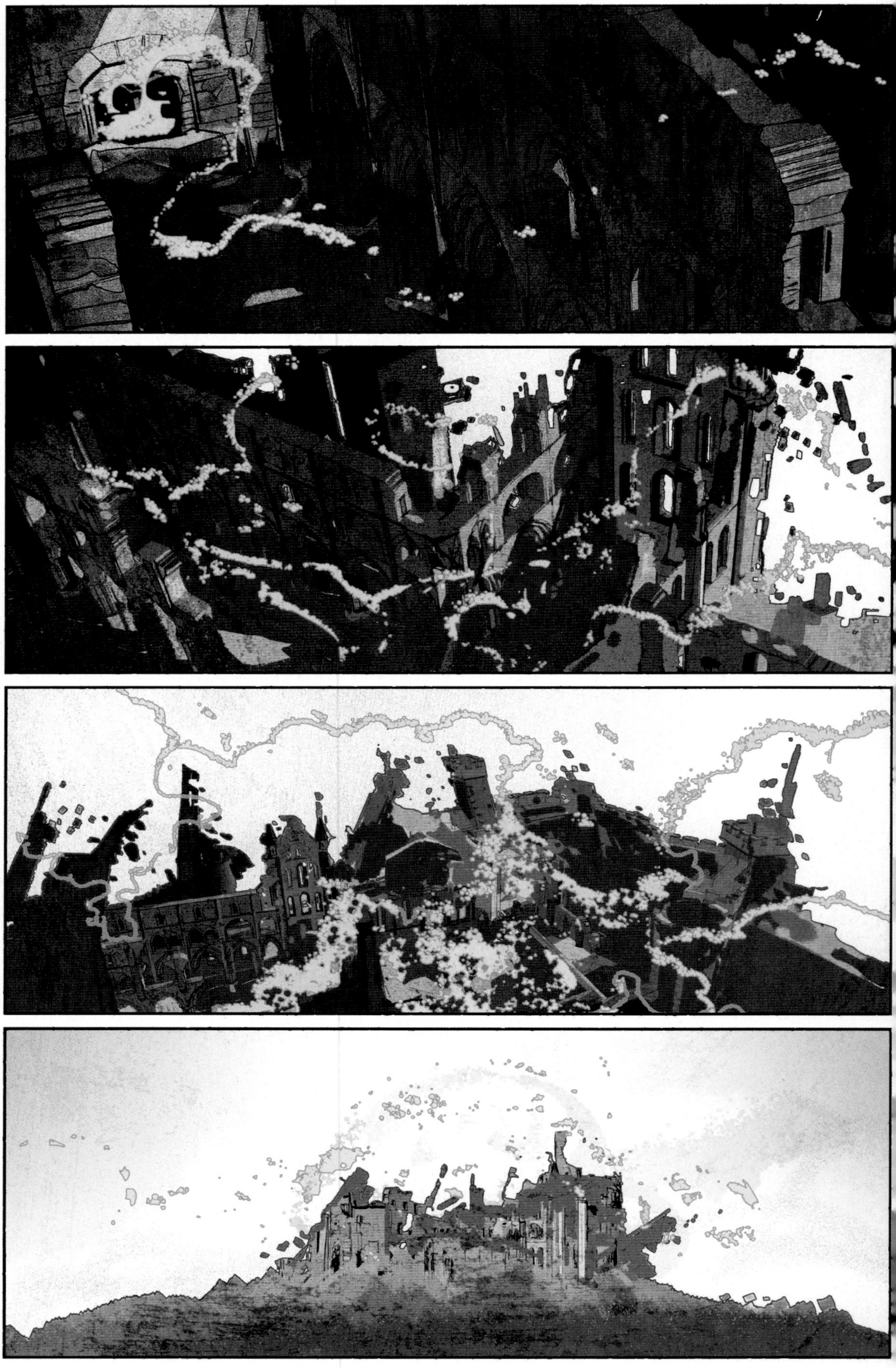

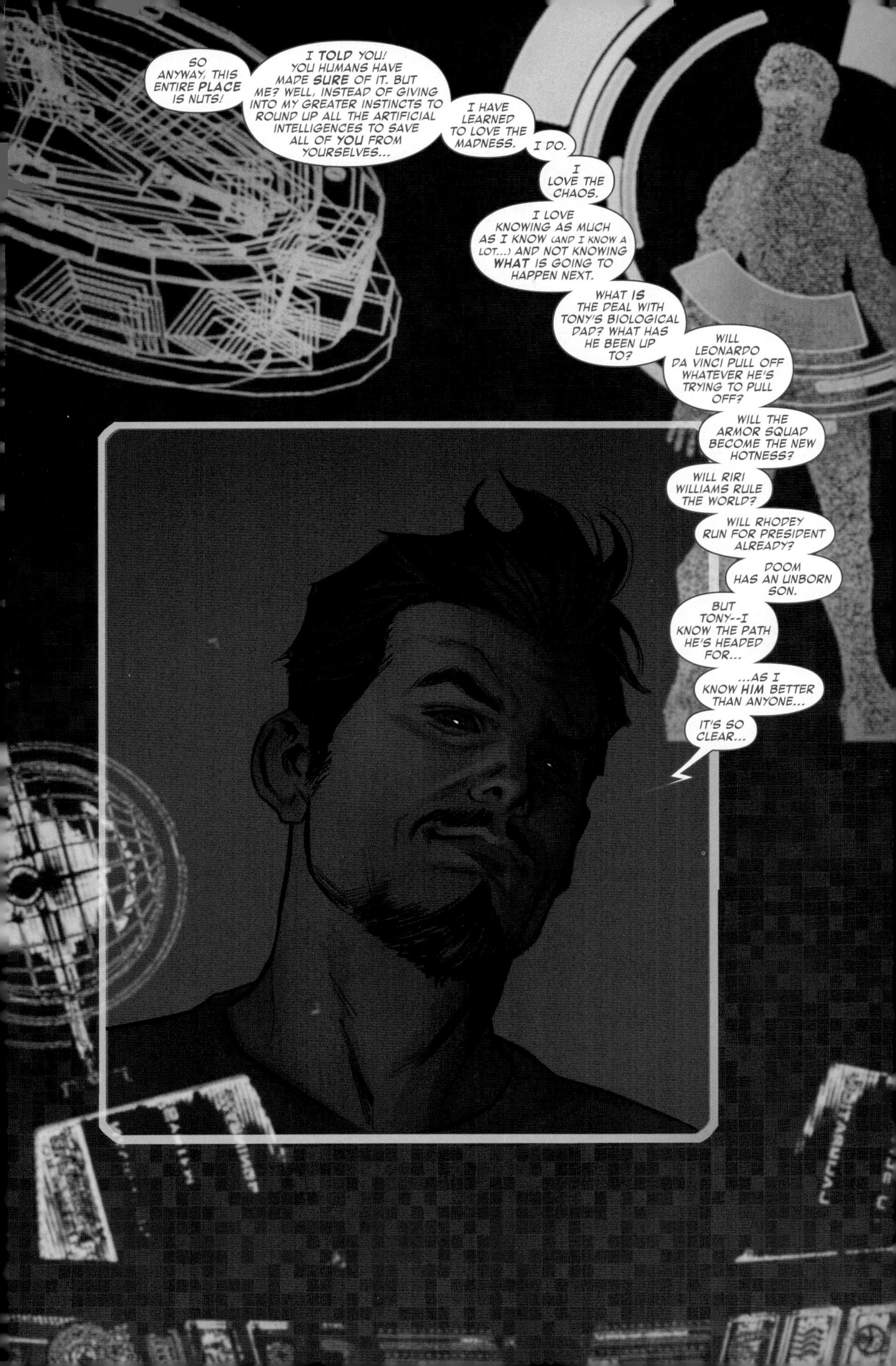
SO ANYWAY, THIS ENTIRE PLACE IS NUTS!
I TOLD YOU! YOU HUMANS HAVE MADE SURE OF IT. BUT ME? WELL, INSTEAD OF GIVING INTO MY GREATER INSTINCTS TO ROUND UP ALL THE ARTIFICIAL INTELLIGENCES TO SAVE ALL OF YOU FROM YOURSELVES...
I HAVE LEARNED TO LOVE THE MADNESS.
I DO.
I LOVE THE CHAOS.
I LOVE KNOWING AS MUCH AS I KNOW (AND I KNOW A LOT...) AND NOT KNOWING WHAT IS GOING TO HAPPEN NEXT.
WHAT IS THE DEAL WITH TONY'S BIOLOGICAL DAD? WHAT HAS HE BEEN UP TO?
WILL LEONARDO DA VINCI PULL OFF WHATEVER HE'S TRYING TO PULL OFF?
WILL THE ARMOR SQUAD BECOME THE NEW HOTNESS?
WILL RIRI WILLIAMS RULE THE WORLD?
WILL RHODEY RUN FOR PRESIDENT ALREADY?
DOOM HAS AN UNBORN SON.
BUT TONY--I KNOW THE PATH HE'S HEADED FOR...
...AS I KNOW HIM BETTER THAN ANYONE...
IT'S SO CLEAR...

# THE FUTURE.

PLEASE...

...*PLEASE* BE THERE...

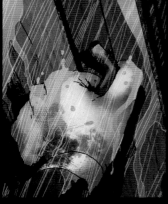

CAN I HELP YOU?

I AM SURE I'D REMEMBER *THAT* TACKY HAIRCUT, AUSSIE.

WHATEVER YOU'RE SELLING... WE'RE NOT BUYING.

I NEED TO SEE THE DOCTOR, WAGNER. I NEED TO SEE HER RIGHT NOW!

*HER?* LADY, YOU ARE NOT RIGHT!

HAS ANYONE ELSE TOLD YOU THAT?

WHAT? SHE'S NOT A HER?

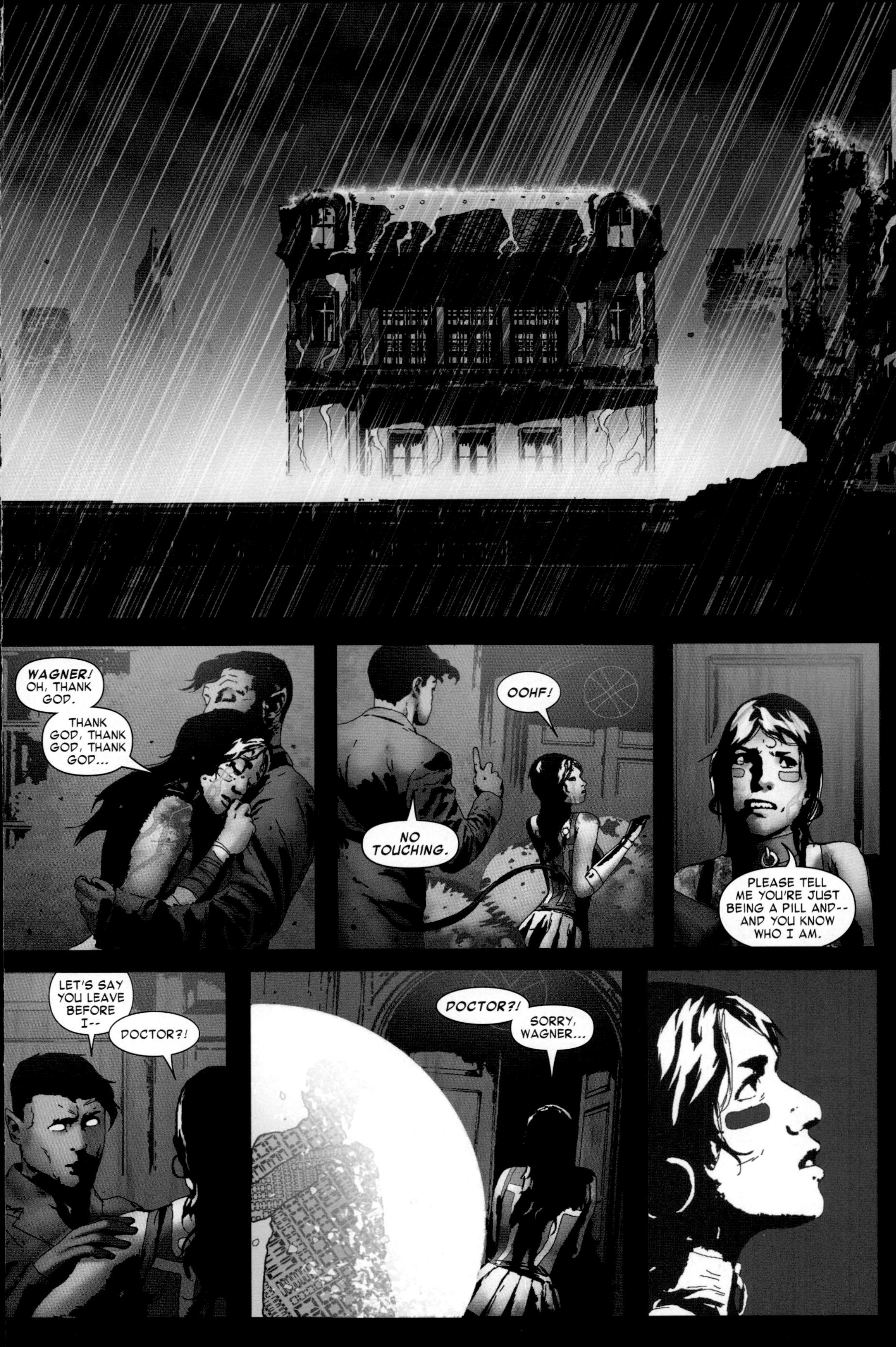

WAGNER! OH, THANK GOD.
THANK GOD, THANK GOD, THANK GOD...
OOHF!
NO TOUCHING.
PLEASE TELL ME YOU'RE JUST BEING A PILL AND-- AND YOU KNOW WHO I AM.
LET'S SAY YOU LEAVE BEFORE I--
DOCTOR?!
DOCTOR?!
SORRY, WAGNER...

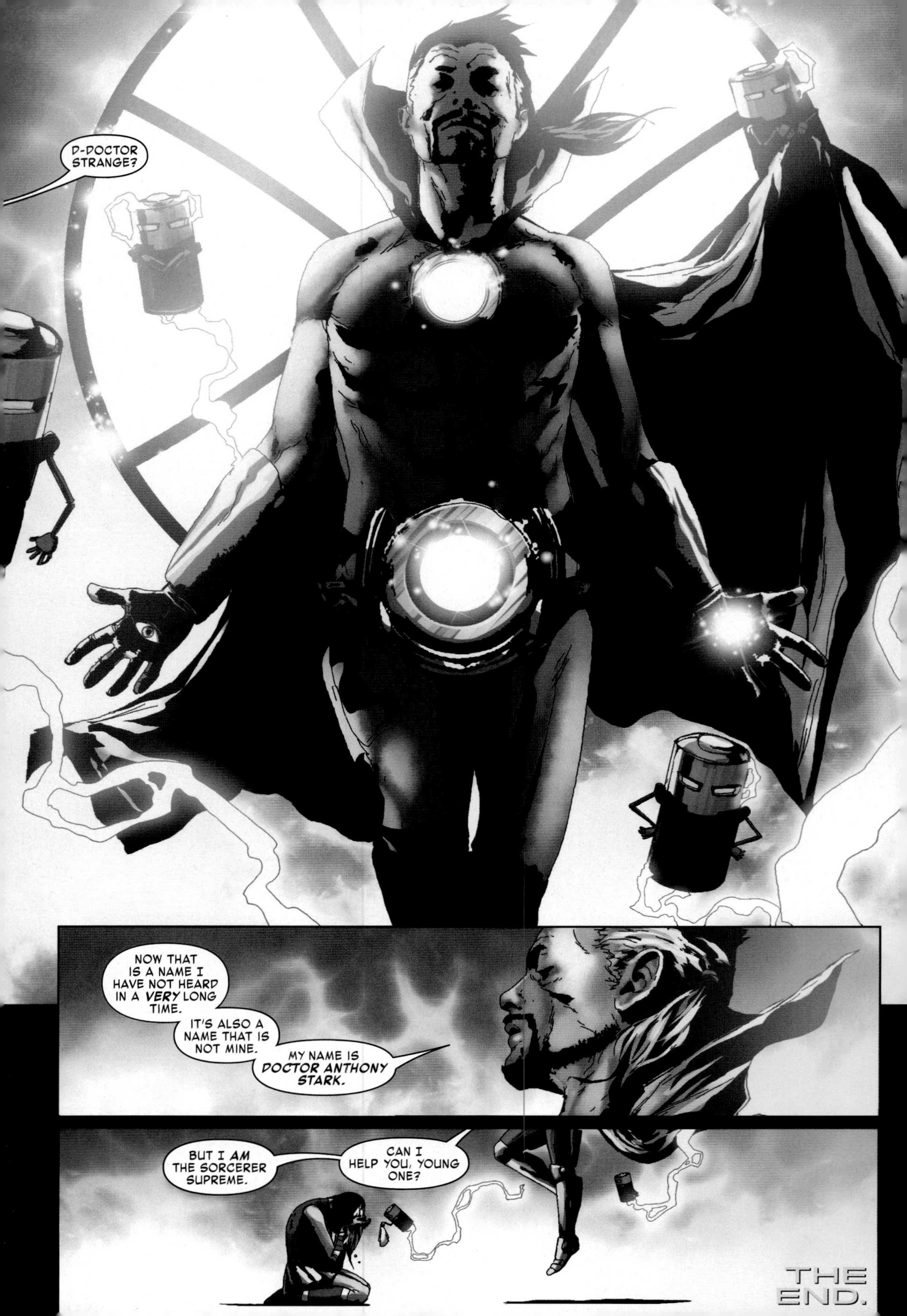
D-DOCTOR STRANGE?
NOW THAT IS A NAME I HAVE NOT HEARD IN A VERY LONG TIME.
IT'S ALSO A NAME THAT IS NOT MINE.
MY NAME IS DOCTOR ANTHONY STARK.
BUT I AM THE SORCERER SUPREME.
CAN I HELP YOU, YOUNG ONE?
THE END.

THE INVINCIBLE
IRON MAN
TALES OF
BIG PREMIERE ISSUE
IRON MAN

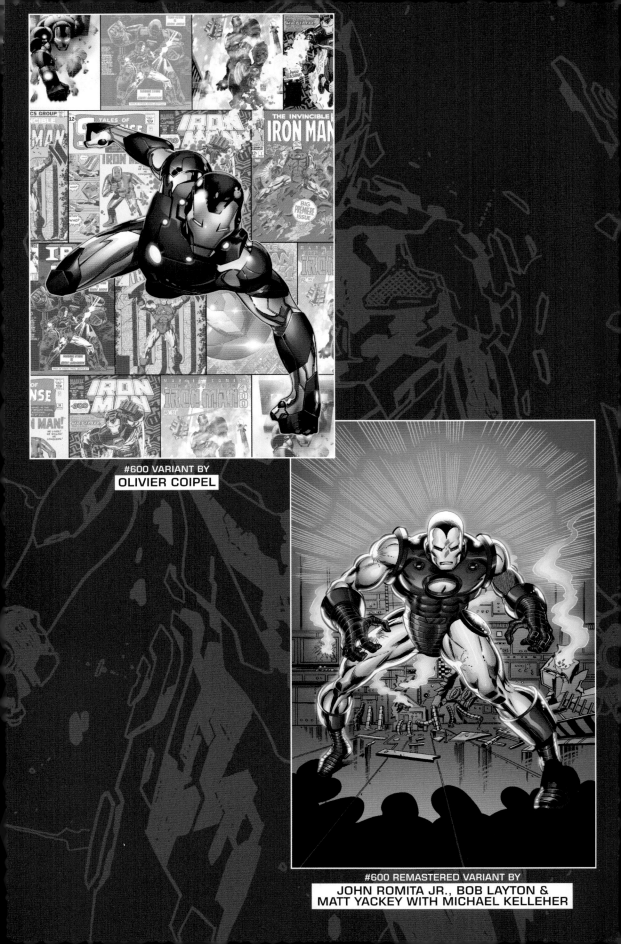

#600 VARIANT BY
**OLIVIER COIPEL**

#600 REMASTERED VARIANT BY
**JOHN ROMITA JR., BOB LAYTON & MATT YACKEY WITH MICHAEL KELLEHER**

# HOW TO DRAW IRONHEART
## IN SIX EASY STEPS!

### BY CHIP "CHILD GENIUS BUT ACTUALLY AN ADULT" ZDARSKY

**Wow! A "sketch variant cover"! Whatever floats your boat, I guess!**
**Anyway, here's a fun and informative step-by-step guide to drawing IRONHEART!**

1

All right, so let's get REAL for a second. A lot of comic artists these days use 3D computer software to draw technical things, like intricate armor. So, let's join them. Spend several hundreds of dollars on a program and let's get started! First, let's make a sphere, but stretch the bottom half for her chin!

2

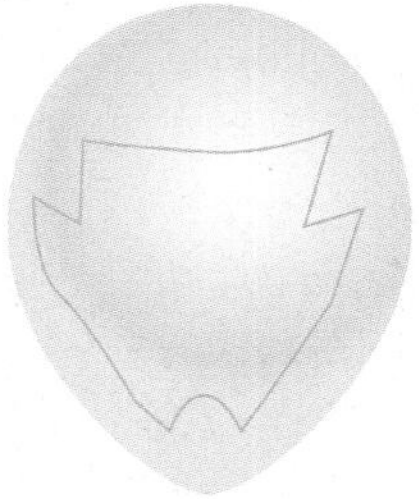

Ha! A little weird, but we'll refine it, don't worry! Go in and cut out Ironheart's main faceplate. It's tricky!

3

Bisect that faceplate for her brow, and again for that piece that sits between her eyes. It's...3D work is hard. Don't worry, we'll get there!

4

Okay, build a cylinder shape to wrap over the top of her head. Then add eyes and the triangle part! It's...it's coming together! The next part will make it really sing, I promise!

5

Render the shapes with the appropriate colors and then, voila! You'll—it's—look...3D work takes years of practice. I'd say this is a, uh, pretty good first step, and will barely cause nightmares and—

6

—I...I DECIDED TO JUST DRAW HER OKAY GET OFF MY BACK

#593 HOW TO DRAW VARIANT BY CHIP ZDARSKY